CHAWTON HOUSE LIBRARY SERIES

MEMOIRS OF WOMEN WRITERS

Contents of the Edition

PART I

PART II

PART III

CHAWTON HOUSE LIBRARY SERIES: WOMEN'S MEMOIRS

Series Editor: Jennie Batchelor

TITLES IN THIS SERIES

Women's Theatrical Memoirs
Women's Court and Society Memoirs
Memoirs of Scandalous Women

www.pickeringchatto.com/chawtonhouse

MEMOIRS OF WOMEN WRITERS

EDITED BY

Gina Luria Walker

NS FACULTY

Volume 7

Mary Hays, *Female Biography; or, Memoirs of Illustrious and Celebrated Women, of All Ages and Countries* (1803)
Volume III

LONDON
PICKERING & CHATTO
2013

Published by Pickering & Chatto (Publishers) Limited
21 Bloomsbury Way, London WC1A 2TH

2252 Ridge Road, Brookfield, Vermont 05036-9704, USA

www.pickeringchatto.com

BRITISH LIBRARY CATALOGUING IN PUBLICATION DATA

Hays, Mary, 1759 or 60–1843.
Memoirs of women writers. Part 2. – (Chawton House library series. Women's
memoirs)
1. Women authors – Biography. 2. Women – Biography.
I. Title II. Series III. Fitzer, Anna M. IV. Walker, Gina Luria, 1942–
828.6'09-dc22

ISBN-13: 9781848930520

Typeset by Pickering & Chatto (Publishers) Limited
Printed and bound in the United Kingdom by Berforts Information Press

CONTENTS

FEMALE BIOGRAPHY;

OR,

MEMOIRS

OF

ILLUSTRIOUS AND CELEBRATED

W O M E N,

OF ALL AGES AND COUNTRIES.

Alphabetically arranged.

———

BY MARY HAYS.

═══════════

IN SIX VOLUMES.

═══════════

VOL. III.

———

LONDON:

PRINTED FOR RICHARD PHILLIPS, 71, ST. PAUL's
CHURCH-YARD.

By Thomas Davison, White-Friars.

———

1803.

MEMOIRS

OF

DISTINGUISHED WOMEN.

CATHERINE II. *(Concluded.)*

BESTUCHEFF, in the failure of his project, lost none of his influence, either with his mistress or her lover, from whom Vorontzoff daily experienced new instances of coldness, till, perceiving his decline certain, he demanded permission, under the pretence of recovering his health, impaired by the fatigues of his office, to travel two years in foreign countries. His request was readily granted: the empress, to whom his presence was irksome, saw him depart with satisfaction, yet with feigned tokens of respect and regret, while she entreated him to hasten his return, and to resume the functions of his office, which, for the happiness of the empire, he had so successfully fulfilled.

Apprehensive lest Catherine should raise to the throne the daring adventurer to whom the unfortunate Peter had in a great degree owed his destruction, the people loudly murmured: various plots were set on foot against the favourite, one of which was on the point of succeeding.

A guard had been placed at the door of Orloff as at that of the empress: a sentinel was, by a bribe, induced to promise to deliver him, while asleep, to three of the conspirators. To a mistake made in the hour, Orloff owed his safety: before the conspirators appeared, the sentinel in their confidence had been already relieved by another, who, astonished at beholding three men apply for admittance to the chamber, summoned by an alarm the guards to his aid. The conspirators had scarcely time to escape under favour of the uniform they wore.

Consternation spread over the palace: the empress was roused and alarmed; while, believing her life not secure, she hastened from Moscow, where this scene was transacted, to take shelter at Petersburg. Demonstrations of joy, full of insult, and approaching to rage, signalised her departure; her cypher was, by the populace, torn

CATHERINE II. 3

down from a triumphal arch on which it had been placed, and dragged through the mire.

Catherine reached Petersburg on the day of the anniversary of her accession to the throne: to dazzle the eyes of the populace, she omitted nothing that might render her entrance impressive and solemn. But this spectacle, however splendid, failed in its effect, or rather tended to increase the public irritation. On every side conspiracies multiplied, in which names the most important in the empire were enrolled. Among the most distinguished of these were count Panin, his brother the general, and the hetman Razumoffsky. A point of union was only wanting to hurl Catherine from the throne. The conspirators differed respecting a successor; while some espoused the cause of the grand-duke, others were for recalling the unhappy Ivan, and restoring to him the rank of his ancestors.

Catherine, apprised in secret of the designs forming against her, hesitated whether to arrest the hetman and Panin: yet, dreading by an ill-timed severity to provoke her fate, and doubtful of the evidence against them, she determined to have recourse to artifice and policy. The princess Dashkoff, whose courage and zeal had been re-

4 ### CATHERINE II.

paid with ingratitude, and who, though recalled to court, had suffered neglect and coldness, appeared to the empress a proper emissary on this emergency. Without doubting her participation in the projects of her friends, or the fortitude and resolution of her spirit, Catherine hoped, through her precipitation and imprudence, to betray her into a disclosure of the secrets with which she was entrusted. For this purpose she addressed to her a long and insidious epistle, abounding in flatteries and promises, equally seductive and alluring. In the name of their friendship, she conjured her to reveal the projects by which she was threatened, assuring her of a full pardon to all whom her information should involve. The princess, incensed that Catherine should presume to use as an instrument of vengeance the woman who had before been made subservient to her elevation, laconically replied to the four pages she had received in four lines—" Madam, I have heard nothing : but, if I had, I should beware of what I spoke. What is it that you require of me ? That I should expire on a scaffold ? I am ready to ascend it."

Surprised at this hauteur, which she was hopeless of conquering, the empress tried to attach to

CATHERINE II. 5

her those whom she dared not punish. Some of the subaltern malecontents, who, having been seized, observed a stubborn silence, were exiled to Siberia : Panin and the hetman were laden with additional favours.

These plots, incessantly renewed, wearied the clemency of the empress, which served but to harden the conspirators in their purpose : severer measures were threatened, without producing the desired effect. The true wisdom of legislation is to prevent rather than to punish crimes. Of this the empress appears not to have been ignorant : in the midst of feuds, which menaced her authority and her life, she occupied herself in institutions for the improvement and prosperity of the nation ; erected hospitals, founded colleges, encouraged commerce, and rewarded genius. New ships of war were also ordered to be placed on the stocks.

Poniatoffsky, about this period, renewed his solicitations for permission to return to Petersburg. The empress refused to listen to his request, yet assured him of her friendship, of which she promised to afford to him convincing proofs : nor was she negligent in the performance of this promise.

Towards the end of this year (1763), Catherine gave to the supreme college of the empire, the

6   CATHERINE II.

directing senàte, instituted by Peter I, a proper form. To facilitate business, it was divided into six departments, four of which were to have their seat in Petersburg, and the remaining two at Moscow. Removing incumbrances, and making new regulations, she diffused through the whole simplicity and order. The active and comprehensive mind of the czarina appeared to embrace all objects; a new spirit was given to the empire. The court also wore a more brilliant form; over its magnificence and splendor taste presided; for the cultivation of the arts and literature foundations sprung up; regulations of convenience and utility multiplied; the temper of the nation assumed a milder form; industry was awakened, diligence quickened, and the comforts of existence more widely diffused.

Augustus III. king of Poland, which had long been under the influence of Russia, declining in his health, was approaching fast towards the grave. The court of Petersburg was the centre of the intrigues of all who had any pretensions to the Polish succession. Catherine, though decided in her choice, encouraged the hopes and fomented the disputes of the contending rivals: she wanted a king on whose devotion she could depend, and with whose weakness she was acquainted. This

CATHERINE II.　　7

rich and unhappy country, which had excited the ambition of the czarina, she long continued to harass, to prepare it the better for a final blow. She began her operations by artfully obtaining from Versailles and Vienna an assurance not to interfere in the affairs of Poland. The promised neutrality of these courts being still insufficient for the purposes of the empress, she was desirous of securing herself on the side of Prussia. Long solicited by Frederic to sign a treaty of defensive alliance, she at length, after various subtle and politic measures, acceded to what was required of her. In this treaty was a secret article, by which the allied powers mutually bound themselves to maintain the republic of Poland in its state of free election, even by force of arms, and that no one therein should, on any pretence, be suffered to make himself absolute, or to render the crown hereditary in his family.

Conscious of her power, Catherine successively dismissed the various candidates for the Polish monarchy, till, to the amazement of Warsaw, her choice, which fell on Poniatoffsky, was made known. Universal discontent ensued ; the Polish nobles enquired of each other, by what services, or by what qualities, this man had rendered himself worthy of so extravagant a reward ? The endowments of the new king, who was handsome, agreeable, accomplished, eloquent, calculated to please, but incapable of command, were better suited to conciliate private affection, than to fit him for a throne. But murmurs and resistance, opposed to the Russian power, were equally vain. Catherine wrote to her minister at Warsaw to employ every engine in favour of her lover. " Remember," says she, "my candidate. I write this to you two hours after midnight : judge if I am indifferent in this affair."

The Russian generals neglected nothing for securing the wishes of their sovereign. The dietines were convoked. Poniatoffsky was, by that of Warsaw, unanimously elected : those of the provinces proved less tractable. Crowds of foreigners had poured into the city, ready to unite at the first signal. In the diet, confusion and tumult prevailed : its marshal, venerable for his age and for his virtues, in vain attempted to reduce it to order: he was answered by drawn sabres and furious outcries. Mokranoffsky, nuncio of Cracow, risked his life under the swords of the Russian soldiers, who tried to pierce him from the galleries of the speakers. Returning into its sheath his sabre, which he had at first drawn, he opposed his breast to their weapons. ' If you must have a victim,'

CATHERINE II. *9*

said he, to the Russians, 'I stand here before you. At least I shall die as I have hitherto lived : *free!*' He had not escaped their rage, but for the generous courage of prince Adam Chartorinsky, who threw his body as a shield between him and his adversaries.

A courtier at Petersburg, sensible of the aversion of Poland to the monarch imposed upon them, had the boldness to hint it to the empress. ' No man,' said he, ' is less proper than Poniatoffsky to fill the throne of Poland : his grand-father having been an intendant of a little estate belonging to the princes Lubominsky.' ' Though he had been intendant himself,' replied Catherine haughtily, ' I *will* have him to be king, and a king he *shall* be.'

Twelve thousand Russians had entered Lithuania, and fresh reinforcements advanced towards Kief : the Russian embassador governed Warsaw, and the armies of Catherine compressed the republic. The spirit of Poland yet struggled : an action took place between the contending parties, in which the Russians were victorious : the sister of a prince of Poland, and his bride whom he had newly espoused, fought with sabres, and mounted on horseback, by the side of a brother and a husband, for the expiring freedom of their country.

10   CATHERINE II.

From measures like those by which Catherine supported him, Poniatoffsky could not fail of his election : on the 7th of September, 1764, he was proclaimed, by the name of Stanislaus Augustus, king of Poland and grand-duke of Lithuania.

The new monarch paraded the streets of the capital, amidst the shouts of the populace, and the same day took possession of the palace of the republic : opposition being no longer availing, the people and the nobles crowded to do him homage : had he been the free choice of the nation, his reign could not have commenced with more apparent tranquillity: the propriety of his conduct did credit to his judgment ; he received with kindness his most zealous opponents, and by his courtesy sought to conciliate the public mind.

Catherine had, previous to this election, signified an intention of making the tour of Livonia, and visiting the theatre of her triumphs; but, while disposing at will of the crowns of other nations, her own trembled on her brow: the power which awed Asia, and made Europe bend, was in itself tottering and unstable ; every breath of discontent, the feeblest engine, and the most obscure agent, appeared to menace its duration.

An event occurred in the course of this summer, interesting in its nature, and deserving of

CATHERINE II.   11

record from the curious and mysterious circumstances by which it was attended. The empress had, in pursuance of her intentions, set out on her journey through Livonia and Courland, accompanied by Orloff, and a small retinue of nobility. The government of Petersburg was, in the mean time, left in the charge of Panin. During this expedition, a disturbance took place in the prison of the dethroned Ivan, which terminated, with his life, the misfortunes of the unhappy captive.

Catherine, soon after the commencement of her reign (as related in her manifesto of August 28th, 1764), had an interview with Ivan, in order, as it is said, to form a judgment of his capacity and talents. The result reported was, that the empress had, to her great surprise, found in the prince a total privation of sense and reason, with an incurable defect in his utterance, that, whatever had been his attainments, would have wholly deprived him of the power of communication. This account, which, however consistent with the probable consequences of his sufferings*, forms a

---

* Ivan had been lodged at Schlusselburg in a casemate of the fortress, of which even the loop-hole had been bricked up. In this subterranean vault a lamp was kept constantly burning ; the prisoner having no time-

striking contrast with the scene already delineated on the visit of the czar to his dungeon, was not received without doubt and hesitation. Ivan, having now attained his twenty-fourth year, appeared fitted, as an instrument, or a pretext, for the purposes of those who wished to raise commotion. His title to the crown, his long sufferings, his youth, his innocence, even the obscurity of his life, excited sympathy, exercised conjecture, and afforded materials for invention.

At the moment the empress was commencing her journey, she received intelligence of fresh conspiracies among the guards : several were seized, but, to avoid irritating the multitude by the frequent exhibition of punishments, they were proceeded against in private, or suffered to pine out their lives in imprisonment. Of those who held in abhorrence the usurpation of Catherine, Ivan was the common object : for the sake of a prince whose person was unknown to them, and whose very existence was doubtful, many persons, urged by a sense of justice, or led by a romantic

---

piece allowed him, therefore distinguished not the night from the day. His interior guard, a captain and a lieutenant, were shut up with him : and, at some periods, not allowed to speak to him, or answer the simplest question.

CATHERINE II.   13

spirit of enterprise, braved the dungeon and the scaffold. It was in vain that the court, in its system of calumny, to which Peter had fallen a victim, represented the royal captive as an ideot, a lunatic, a drunkard, or a ferocious savage : the malignity of party, which finds in falsehood its interest, will, in the minds of the candid, ever provoke distrust. It is not to be doubted but that the situation of Ivan, confined in a loathsome dungeon, and denied the means of instruction, must have produced its effects on his mind. Yet, let it be remembered that, at the earlier periods of his life, he had not been separated from his family, by whom his sympathies had been awakened, his affections exercised, and his faculties roused. From them he had learned the history of his rank, and of his misfortunes; an impressive lesson, calculated to stimulate the dormant powers of reflection. A German officer, it is affirmed, who at one time had him in charge, clandestinely taught him to read. The kindness of Baron Korf, of which he proved, in the presence of the czar, his affecting sense, in calling forth his grateful affection, still farther excited the growth of his sensibility. He had been removed, on various occasions, from prison to prison, at which times he had fallen into different hands, and experienced

CATHERINE II.

new opportunities for observation. Should it be allowed that these sources combined, afforded but a scanty surface for the operations of intellect, yet between ignorance and ideotism there is still an immense void. In an interview with Elizabeth, in 1756, at the house of count Schuvaloff, he touched the passions of all who were present, by the graces of his figure, the accents of his voice, and his affecting complaints; he even drew from the empress a flood of tears. His subsequent conversation with Peter, who had determined on adopting him to the succession, was attested by Baron Korf, a witness of the interview. The attempts made in his favour, and the disquietude of the nation, rendered him formidable to Catherine, and afforded a sufficient motive for the accounts circulated of his pretended imbecility.

A singular occurrence relieved the empress from this inquietude. A company, consisting of about an hundred men, guarded the fortress in which the prince was confined : Vassily Mirovitch, whose grandfather had been implicated in the rebellion of the Kozac Mazeppa, and had fought against Peter the Great under Charles XII., was second lieutenant in this regiment. The estates of his family had been forfeited to the crown : Mirovitch, whose ruling passion was ambition, warmly

CATHERINE II. 15

solicited their restoration; his pretensions had hitherto produced little effect, except flattering promises, upon condition of his proving his activity and loyalty in securing the safety of the empire. Captain Vlassieff and lieutenant Ischekin slept in the cell of Ivan, as his inner guard. By these officers a discretionary order was possessed, signed by the empress, and enjoining them, in case of insurrection, on the presumption that other means were inadequate, to put to death their wretched charge.

Ivan had been removed from his dungeon to a cell in the corridor, under the covered way in the castle; the door of the prison opened under a low arcade, which, together with the cell, formed the thickness of the castle wall within the ramparts. In this arcade, or corridor, eight soldiers usually kept guard: their comrades were stationed in the guard-house, at the gate of the castle. The commander of the detachment was subject to the orders of the governor of the fort. Mirovitch, it has been affirmed, had, in confidence, revealed his project to a friend, who had bound himself by oath to aid the enterprise: but the death of this man, who was drowned in assisting at the launching of a vessel, renders this account doubtful. It is more certain that he spoke of his intentions in

vague terms to one of the valets of the court, and
afterwards to a lieutenant of the artillery, with
whom he talked of the advantages that would
accrue from the deliverance of Ivan, who should
be placed under the protection of the regiments
of the guards.   But while he assumed the importance of a conspirator, without accomplices, he
stated nothing certain either respecting the time
of execution, or the measures to be adopted.   He
had performed the week's duty without any attempt, but, as if condemning his own irresolution,
he requested to be continued on guard another
week.   A petition so extraordinary, which was
immediately granted, did not appear to excite in
the governor any distrust.

On a fine summer's night, about ten o'clock,
on the 14th of July, 1764, after having admitted
into his confidence a man named Jacob Pishkoff,
Mirovitch began his plan of operations, by tam-
pering with the fidelity of three corporals, and
two common soldiers, whom he gained over to
his purpose.   This little band, either from fear or
caution, waited till the night was farther advanced, before they commenced their perilous enterprise.

Between the hours of one and two, having procured as auxiliaries about fifty of the soldiers on

CATHERINE II.   17

guard, they assembled together, and marched under arms towards the prison of Ivan.   On their
way they encountered the governor of the fortress,
who, roused by some noise, had quitted his bed to
enquire into the occasion.   The governor demanded authoritatively of Mirovitch the cause of the
present appearance.   Mirovitch, without reply,
levelled him to the ground with the butt-end of
his firelock, and, with his people, continued his
progress.   Arriving at the corridor, into which
the prison opened, he advanced furiously at the
head of his troop to attack the soldiers on guard.
Being received with spirit by this handful of men,
and driven back, he ordered his soldiers to fire,
which was immediately done.   The fire was returned by the sentinels, and the conspirators compelled to retire : no wound was received on either
side.

The followers of Mirovitch, surprised at this
unexpected resistance, appeared inclined to desist,
but were withheld by their leader, who pretended
to have received an order from Petersburgh, au-
thorising his conduct.   On their request he drew
from his pocket a forged decree of the senate, by
which Catherine was excluded from the throne,
on the pretence of her journey to Livonia to
espouse count Poniatoffsky; and Ivan was, by

the same instrument, recalled to the inheritance of his ancestors. The soldiers, ignorant and credulous, gave implicit belief to this tale, and again put themselves in order of attack. A piece of artillery was now brought from the ramparts, and pointed at the cell, which it was designed to batter. At this instant the door opened, and Mirovitch, with his suite, entered unopposed.

The officers within, alarmed by the confusion, had called to the sentinels to fire. But hearing the formidable preparations, and the orders given by Mirovitch to storm the prison, they took counsel on the measures proper to be pursued. To resist a force so superior, they considered scarcely possible : the consequences to be apprehended were next to be consulted upon. In the enlargement of their prisoner, the public peace and the safety of the empire were involved : neither was their own security to be neglected, nor the punishment and disgrace to which the loss of their charge would subject them. The result of this conference was the dreadful alternative of obeying the order they had received, and sacrificing the captive : on this act, so horrible, and, in their present situation, so replete with danger, they finally concluded. The wretched Ivan, whom the noise of the muskets and the cries of the guards

CATHERINE II.   19

had awakened from his sleep, conjured them to spare his miserable life. Inaccessible to pity, the barbarous ruffians disregarded his agonies : though naked and unarmed, despair gave him strength. His right hand, in his struggles, was pierced through, and his body covered with wounds. Wrenching the sword from one of the assassins, he had broken it in two; but the other stabbed him from behind, and threw him down, while his comrade was struggling to get the piece from his hand. The wretch whose sword had been broken, plunged his bayonet into the body of the victim, and, repeating his blows, the unhappy prince expired under his savage and merciless hand.

The door was then opened, and the bleeding body exposed to the assailants, to whom the order was at the same time given, by which the assassins conceived themselves justified in the action they had committed. Mirovitch, struck with horror at the consequences of his wild scheme, staggered back some paces, and then, throwing himself on the body of Ivan, mournfully exclaimed, ' I have missed my aim—I have nothing to do but to die.' Rising up, he attempted neither vengeance nor escape, but, returning to the governor, whom he had left in the hands of his adherents, he sur-

rendered to him his sword, coldly saying, ' It is
I now that am your prisoner.'

The mangled remains of the unhappy prince,
clothed in the habit of a sailor, were, the next day,
exposed before the church in the castle of Schlusselburg.   Crowds of people from Petersburg,
and the neighbouring towns, flocked to behold
this tragical spectacle : their indignation was
equalled only by their grief.   The misfortunes
and personal endowments of this victim of ambition, called forth the sympathy and touched the
feelings of the populace : tall in stature, with fine
light hair, regular features, and a fair complexion,
the beauty and the youth of the murdered prince
heightened the sensibilities which his unprecedented calamities and relentless fate were so fitted
to excite.   Every heart deplored his destiny, and
breathed curses " deep not loud" against his in-
human persecutors.   The body, wrapped in a
sheep-skin, and placed in a coffin, was afterwards
interred without ceremony.

The assassins, to avoid the popular fury, escaped on board a vessel bound for Denmark, where,
on their arrival, they were protected by the Russian minister.   Shortly after they returned to
Russia, and were advanced in the service.

The governor of Schlusselburg dispatched to Petersburg a narrative of the transaction, which he accompanied with the manifesto found in the pocket of Mirovitch, and fabricated for his purpose. In this paper, which contained scurrilous invectives and imprecations against Catherine, Ivan was represented as the sole legitimate emperor. Its publication was to have taken place at the moment of the liberation of the prince, and of his entry into Petersburg. Panin dispatched a courier to the empress, with an account of what had passed.

Catherine, then at Riga, was observed to suffer under a visible disquietude of mind, for which the state of the empire and the multiplicity of plots were sufficient to account. She would frequently arise in the night, to enquire if any courier had arrived with intelligence from Petersburg. The dispatches of Panin were at length brought to her hand.

The trial of the conspirators was remitted by her to the senate. Mirovitch was condemned to death, and publicly executed in pursuance of his sentence. The inferior actors escaped death for punishments perhaps not less severe. The assassins of the prince were rewarded for their loyalty and fidelity to their trust. A manifesto filled with expressions of piety and humanity, the office-style of the court, and published by authority, narrated the whole proceeding.

The public opinion respecting the transaction appeared to be divided. That a private individual should hazard an enterprise so rash and so romantic, so prosperous in its commencement, and so tragical in its catastrophe, that no one should suffer injury in the contest, that the death of its object should produce so immediate a calm, and that no enquiry should be set on foot for accomplices, seemed to many singularly wonderful. The destruction of the victim appeared to be the sole *end* towards which the whole machinery tended. During the absence of the empress, assuredly none of her party would, without her knowledge and consent, have undertaken this service.

But, on the contrary, the manifesto found upon Mirovitch, in which Catherine was calumniated, had been actually produced, perused, and sent to Riga; while the author had publicly suffered the punishment of his temerity, if some unknown malefactor had not, indeed, been substituted in his place.

The decision, it must be confessed, abounds with difficulties; the reader must therefore on this subject be left to form his own conclusions : to those who have studied the human mind, the powers of the imagination, and the progress of the passions, it is probable there will appear nothing very incredible in the enterprise of Mirovitch. The unsettled state of the empire, the ferment in the public mind, the peculiar situation of his own family and affairs, his vicinity and office near the prince, the apparent facility of his project, in a fortress which seems to have been but slenderly guarded, his ardent temper, and his fancy heated by incessant contemplation on the subject, afford a combination of motives not inadequate to the circumstances produced. In this case, to suspect the empress of a plan so unnecessarily complicated and refined, appears to be substituting, for a simple solution, an hypothesis perplexed with entanglement, and replete with contradiction.

The popular emotions of compassion and displeasure, which this disastrous catastrophe excited, were variously, but uniformly, testified. The multitudes that continued to flock to the castle and demand a sight of the corpse, gave alarm to the government: the body was ordered to be secretly removed in the silence of the night, from the church of the castle, and conveyed to the monastery of Tichfina, two hundred versts from Petersburg. Violent commotions arose

among the regiments of the guards, who, like the
Roman prætorians, conceived the right of depos-
ing and murdering emperors to be exclusively
vested in themselves.   In the night of the 24th
of July, when the ferment reached its crisis, the
prudent measures of the prince Galitzin diverted
the bursting storm.   Tranquillity was at length
happily restored, and the commotions gradually
subsided.   But on the return of the assassins of
Ivan to court, every eye beheld them with scorn,
every tongue muttered curses against them.

   The throne of Catherine thus firmly established,
she extended her clemency towards the surviving
members of the persecuted family of the murdered prince, who were liberated from their captivity,
and sent to Denmark, in consequence of a negociation with the Danish court. Catherine presented
to them, on their departure for the place of their
destination, two hundred thousand rubles, for the
purpose of providing them with clothes and equi-
page suited to their station and rank.   This was
accompanied by a present of rich furs and jewels
from the imperial cabinet, while persons of distinction were appointed to attend them on their
voyage.   The city of Horsens in Yutland was
selected by the court of Copenhagen as their
place of residence.   A deed of renunciation of

CATHERINE II. 25

all pretensions, either of themselves or of their posterity, to the Russian succession, it is probable was required of the illustrious exiles; pretensions which had cost them too dear to be resigned with regret. Towards their establishment in Denmark, the empress presented to them twenty thousand rubles; while thirty thousand were allowed annually for the maintenance of their dignity.

Catherine, soon after the tragedy at Schlusselburg, returned to her dominions through the conquered provinces. On her entry into Petersburg, the people crowded round her, to discover in her countenance what passed in her heart. Ever mistress of herself, her face beamed with smiles, her aspect was serene, and her step firm : her deportment announced no symptom of disquietude or internal reproach.

Mirovitch and his accomplices, having been privately examined by lieutenant-general Veymar, had been brought to Petersburg, and tried before a commission, composed of five prelates, an equal number of senators, and several general officers. Mirovitch maintained before his judges a composed and tranquil demeanor; he even replied to their interrogatories with a frivolous and insolent air. The judges, it is said, appeared by their questions fearful of investigating the mysterious business. One alone, having declared against their procedure, was checked for his indiscreet zeal, and threatened with degradation. The prisoner was condemned to lose his head, not as guilty of high treason, but as a disturber of the public peace. He appeared unmoved at his sentence, and advanced to the scaffold with a fearless. air, as if, at the last moment, assured of a reprieve. If this hope was well founded, he was assuredly most cruelly deceived : the time of his execution was accelerated; he became the victim of a policy of which he was supposed to have been the instrument.

On the supposition of the concurrence of the empress in the plot to which Ivan owed his death, a conjecture which certainly admits of doubt, it would have been difficult, without implicating herself, to screen him from punishment. Questions like these can perhaps scarcely be determined by individuals, who, happily removed by the obscurity of their station from a perfidious state policy, are incompetent to judge of its motives or its crimes : crimes, in the comparison of which, private passions and private offences appear but as venial errors. By Omniscience only can the thoughts be scrutinised, and the heart made manifest. If different systems of morals seem necessarily to belong to sovereigns and to their people ; if power, in its

CATHERINE II.   27

natural operation, and in proportion to its extent, tends to stifle humanity, and to confound truth and justice'; let us, in scanning the conduct and characters of princes, exercise candor : and, in contemplating the dazzling advantages which appear to surround them, contrast with them their perils, their disquietudes, and their temptations, and learn to rejoice in a humbler destiny.

The beneficial consequences of the regulations and establishments of Catherine became daily more apparent through all parts of the empire. The government, more simply organised and animated with a new energy, displayed a spirit of independence worthy a great nation. "The volumes of modern history," says an historian*, "can produce no reign like this : for no monarch has ever yet succeeded in the attainment of such a dictature in the grand republic of Europe as Catherine II. now holds ; and none of all the kings, who have heretofore given cause to dread the erection of an universal monarchy, seem to have had any knowledge of her art ; to present herself with the pride of a conqueror in the most perilous

---

* M. Spittler. " Sketch of the History of the Governments of Europe."

situations, and with an unusual, a totally new dignity, in the most common transactions. And it is manifestly not only the supreme authority which here gives law, but the judgment which knows when to shew that authority, and when to employ it."

Catherine knew how to assign limits to the encroachments of those whom she favoured with her esteem and friendship; to punish those who offended her; and to issue her commands with mildness and firmness. Mistress of her passions, however moved, she controlled their emotions, and appeared tranquil till the moment when the maturity of her plans ensured success. Judicious in her bounty, she bestowed, by her manner of conferring them, a double value on her favours. While she gave laws to Poland, amused Austria, conciliated Prussia, and treated with England, she extorted the respect of every court in Europe. She afforded to the commerce of Russia a new spirit, augmented its navy, softened the manners of the people, and advanced the progress of civilisation.

In the midst of these occupations, the turbulence of internal division continued to interrupt and harass her: every day teemed with plots and conspiracies, from which her prudence and her fortune combined to deliver her: the favours she

CATHERINE II. 29

showered on those whom it was important to conciliate, but stimulated their rapacity; her punishments, though secret and terrible, proved unavailing to preserve her from new outrages.

A contention between the favourite and the minister proved yet more perplexing; the courage and activity of the former, and the abilities of the latter, being equally essential to her safety. The defects and imperfections of Panin were balanced by his capacity for business; but the influence of Orloff, which he continually abused, rested on a different basis: his favour with the empress, which he took no pains to secure, was gradually declining; negligent, insolent, absorbed in the amusements of the chace, and careless of his influence at court, from which he perpetually absented himself, the attachment of Catherine became gradually alienated, while disgust and indifference succeeded to its place.

This change escaped not the sagacity of Panin, who watched for an occasion of triumphing over his adversary. The empress had appeared to behold with complacency Vissensky, a young officer, who, tutored by the minister, improved and flattered her predilection. The hour of the dismissal of Orloff appeared at no great distance.

But at this crisis the favourite perceived his

danger, and altered his conduct; his influence was regained, the hopes of the minister blasted, and Vissensky, with brilliant presents, dismissed to an employment that fixed him remote from Petersburg.

The honours and interest enjoyed by Panin were yet insufficient for the cravings of his ambition: the return of the chancellor Vorontzoff, whose functions he had performed during his absence, gave him new inquietude; to secure his advantages and to supplant his rival, he humbled himself before the man whose ruin he had projected, and was enabled, through the influence of Orloff, to supersede the chancellor and to maintain his post. It was intimated to Vorontzoff that he would do well to retire from court, while a gratuity of fifty thousand rubles, and a pension of seven thousand, rewarded his acquiescence.

Among the various means employed by Catherine for detecting the designs of her enemies, was the interception of the letters of the foreign ministers; in those of the agent of France she thought she perceived a cognisance of the projects formed against her. Hurt at this discovery, the coldness of her manner intimated to the minister the propriety of a retreat. His place was supplied by a man of little capacity, and ill calculated

CATHERINE II. 31

to repair the errors of his predecessor. The empress maintained a correspondence with Voltaire and d'Alembert. To the latter she offered, with the place of governor to the grand-duke, a salary of twenty-four thousand livres, and accommodations for finishing at Petersburg the Encyclopædia: advantages which the philosopher thought proper to refuse. Having received information that Diderot, in straitened circumstances, was desirous of selling his books for a portion to his daughter, Catherine, with royal munificence, purchased the library, and, leaving it in the possession of the original owner, appointed him librarian, with a liberal endowment. To Morard, a celebrated surgeon, she sent, as a testimony of her respect for his talents and skill, a collection of the medals, in gold and silver, which had been struck in Russia. Among the men of letters and artists in Paris, distinguished for their talents, there were few who received not marks of her bounty.

The purposes for which Poniatoffsky had been raised by the empress to the crown of Poland, gradually began to unfold themselves. Conceiving herself secure in the submission of the monarch she had made, she threw off all constraint and openly avowed her pretensions; while, at the moment of this declaration, her troops were in readiness to give it validity and support. Having traced on a map a line of demarcation, by which a great part of the Polish territory was assigned to Russia, she insisted, in a tone of command from which there seemed no appeal, on the recognition of these limits, and the propriety of her claim. It was also farther exacted, that the king and republic should conclude with Russia a treaty of alliance, offensive and defensive; likewise, that dissidents and catholics should, without exceptions, enjoy equal rights.

This last, and most equitable of her demands, excited the loudest murmurs from the indignant nobles. Complaints were heard on every side; recourse to arms was loudly threatened; even the king, whether from fear or shame, refused the sacrifices exacted of him. Palliatives were attempted without success; an intolerant and despotic nobility would listen to no accommodation: having ventured to recommend more moderate sentiments, the monarch was grossly insulted. In a public assembly, the bishop of Kief had the temerity to say: ‘That were his advice taken, they would have the king hanged, if there were still to be found among the Poles men sufficiently charitable to do the state that service.’ He had afterwards the insolence, in the presence of the

CATHERINE II. 39

court, to tell the king to his face:—' I used formerly to pray to God for your prosperity; my prayer to him at present is, that he would send you to the devil.' Such in Poland was the spirit of the ministers of a meek and holy religion. From religious to political feuds the progress is easy: Poland was split into parties and factions; a civil war, with all its horrors, ravaged this unhappy and devoted kingdom.

The Russian army, which had been gradually advancing, at length surrounded and invested the capital; the prelates and nobles, who had most furiously opposed the emancipation of the dissidents, were seized by a detachment of Russian troops, carried off to Siberia, and retained in exile six years The deliberations of the diets were governed by force; the dissidents obtained their privileges; an act of justice unjustly extorted. The only real affliction to the true friends of the liberty of Poland was the regulations admitted, by the orders of Catherine, the tendency of which was to exasperate the troubles of the country, and to leave it defenceless against her future usurpations.

A servile obedience succeeded in Warsaw to the excesses of a turbulent resistance: but this forced sentiment was of no long duration; murmurs, complaints, and clamours, ensued. Confederacies were formed for the defence of the Romish faith; crosses were embroidered on the garments of the confederates, as in the times of the crusades, while Jesus and the Virgin were painted on their standards. These zealous Christians, armed against their brethren, placed themselves, with a curious consistency, under the protection of the Turks: the banner of Mohammed was preparing to wave with the standard of Christ.

The unfortunate Poniatoffski, despised by his subjects and contemned by Russia, the friendship of which he had forfeited, lived in his capital, accused by all parties, as a prisoner of state rather than as a king. The influence of Orloff kept alive in the mind of Catherine the sense of his defection; while prince Repnin, who commanded as a despot in Warsaw, lost no opportunity of making his court to the favourite, by adding to the humiliation of the feeble and fallen king. Europe beheld with surprise the conduct of the empress; a persecutor of the man, who had owed to her his elevation: but the faint remembrance of an extinguished passion opposed but a slight barrier to the ambition of a princess who, by imposing shackles on Poland, aimed to render herself arbitress of the north. Aware of the desire of Prussia to share her spoils, she had nothing to fear from

CATHERINE II. 35

Frederic ; Sweden and Denmark she managed at pleasure ; while a treaty of alliance and commerce secured her with England. Every event combined to favour her views.

The duke de Choiseul was the first to penetrate the designs of Catherine : he saw in the augmentation of her power the diminution of the influence of the court of Versailles ; to attack the evil in its source, he resolved to involve Russia in a war with the Ottoman porte. Tutored for the occasion, Vergennes, the embassador from France to Constantinople, whose long residence in Turkey afforded him the means of negociating with success, represented to the porte the injustice of Russia in its conduct towards Poland, the consequences attending its increase of power, and the necessity for opposing its usurpations. The Ottomans, whom the confederates had already petitioned for aid, took the alarm, and complied with the counsels of the crafty Vergennes. An intimation of its favourable intentions was sent by the porte to Poniatoffsky, who, fearful of giving umbrage to Catherine, and solicitous to regain her friendship, disavowed the necessity for any interference. The divan, having received this assurance, relapsed into its usual indifference.

Between the courts of Petersburg and London

a treaty of alliance and commerce advantageous to the latter was concluded. To her inclination for England, Catherine added the desire of securing additional succours in the war which she already meditated against the Turks.

Whatever might be the irregularities of her own conduct, the empress strictly discountenanced violations of decorum, thereby paying a tacit homage to virtue. Her partiality for the British nation failed of pleading an excuse for the improper conduct of its minister, an affair of gallantry between whom and one of the ladies of honour becoming public, the lady was dismissed from her post, and the lover, for some time, prohibited from appearing at court. Two ladies also, who at a masquerade entertained themselves with talking too loudly of their respective admirers, received from Catherine a severe reprimand. With a stern countenance she ordered them to leave the ball-room, since they paid no more respect to modesty.

Princess Dashkoff, whose enterprising spirit delighted in braving dangers, and who had, to avenge herself on the ingratitude of the empress, fomented the discontents against her, revealed the crimes of the conspiracy against the czar, in which she had herself been a principal actor. By this

CATHERINE II.   87

conduct she obliged Catherine, a second time, to banish her to Moscow. Without esteeming the princess, many persons partook in her resentments : the seeds of sedition which she had artfully sown, continued to ferment on every side.

Informed of the discontents at Moscow, Catherine, while affecting to contemn her danger, resolved to suppress them by her presence. But the severity of the season having protracted her purpose, she sought, in the mean time, by a tumult of pleasures, to amuse the disaffected courtiers. The spectacles of chivalry were revived, and the prowess of the Russians exercised in tournaments, in which strength and magnificence, rather than gallantry and skill, were ostentatiously displayed. The nation murmured at exhibitions, which were considered by the severe as frivolous and expensive. The manners and costume of different countries, Sclavonians, Indians, Turks, and Romans, were, in these games, exhibited by the combatants. A profusion of gold and jewels adorned the champions, who, with their ladies, were divided into four troops. The band of Romans, led off by Orloff, appeared in the lists with peculiar splendor. Tilting at the ring, and beheading the infidels, artificially represented ; tossing the heads and catching them on the point

of a sabre; firing at a shield, with similar achievements, performed at full gallop, and in musical
time, formed the principal parts of the spectacle,
which continued, with variations, for several days.
The festival concluded with the distribution of
prizes, and a speech from the venerable marshal,
count Munich, grand judge of the field.   The
ladies of the court, like the heroines of old, just-
ed at these tournaments; on which occasion the
highest prize, valued at five thousand rubles, was
adjudged to the countess Bourthurlin, the sister of
princess Dashkoff.   A splendid repast crowned
the ceremonies, in the dessert of which was an
admirable representation of the circus wherein
the sports had been performed.   The imperial
summer gardens were grandly illuminated with
arches of lamps burning with naphtha, radiant
temples, resplendent fountains, and magnificent
fireworks, terminating with a masquerade, which
continued till the dawn.

Nor was Catherine, for the establishment of
her authority, negligent of worthier means; useful institutions were erected and reforms made;
the tribunals were corrected, schools founded, hospitals built, and colonies planted.   She sought to
inspire the nation with a respect for the laws, and,
by instruction, to soften their manners.   Rapa-

CATHERINE II. 39

cious of power and jealous of glory, she aimed at once to be a legislatrix and a conqueror. Amidst internal dissensions, and preparations for war, amidst public pleasures and private indulgences, she omitted nothing that might attract the admiration of her contemporaries, and consign her name with renown to posterity.

The perplexed and uncertain jurisprudence of Russia more peculiarly engaged her attention, to the disorders of which she determined to apply a remedy. For this purpose she simplified and divided the departments of legislation, and augmented the emoluments of the judges, to deprive them of a pretext for rapacity and negligence. In the ukause published on this occasion, " Indigence," says she, " may, perhaps, hitherto have led you to self-interest; the country itself shall reward your labours, and render henceforth criminal what might have been venial." Beside the augmentation of their salaries, the judges had an appointment of half-pay secured to them for the season of age and infirmities.

The primary business being arranged, the empress proceeded in the composition of a new code of laws. The provinces of the empire, without excepting any, however barbarous or remote, had orders to present, by deputies to Moscow, their

ideas on the regulations fitted to their peculiar
exigencies. Catherine having herself repaired to
the ancient capital, the opening of the states was
held with solemn pomp.

To behold the deputies of a numerous people,
various in manners, dress, and language, ignorant
of law, and accustomed to the arbitrary will of a
master, assembled for the purpose of a legislative
discussion, afforded a novel and affecting spectacle. To leave to the assembly an unconstrained
appearance, a gallery had been constructed in the
hall, where the empress, without being perceived,
witnessed all that passed. The business commenced by reading, translated into the Russian
language, those Instructions, the original of which,
written in French, almost wholly in the hand of
Catherine, has been since, enclosed in a case of
silver gilt, deposited in an apartment of the imperial academy of sciences at Petersburg.

Peter the Great, so worthy of admiration, and
so justly celebrated, had framed no permanent
laws ; to Catherine II. the work of legislation was
left; it was she only who, having conceived this
grand idea, had the courage and magnanimity to
put it in execution. A code of laws *, founded

---

* This work, though principally taken from Montes-
quieu and the French writers, must ever redound to the

CATHERINE II.   41

in truth and justice, was, by a *woman*, presented to the Russian empire.

Bursts of applause interrupted the reading of the Instructions, while the sagacity, the wisdom, the humanity of the czarina were loudly extolled. In these acclamations, doubtless, fear and adulation had their share. One only, the deputy of the Samoyedes, had the courage to speak with freedom in the name of his brethren : 'We are a simple and honest people,' said he ; ' we quietly tend our rein-deer. We want no new code : but make laws for the Russians, our neighbours, that may put a *stop to their depredations.'*

The succeeding sittings passed less quietly. Liberty to the boors had been proposed: thousands of this oppressed class prepared to support by force what they expected from equity. An insurrection was dreaded by the nobles, who feared still more a defalcation of their revenue. Among them were some who rashly asserted, that the first man who should move for the affranchisement of the vassals, should fall by their poniards. In despite of these menaces, count Scheremetoff, the richest individual in Russia,

---

glory of Catherine, whose liberality of mind led her to draw from such sources.

to whom an hundred and fifty thousand peasants appertained, rising up, declared, that for his part, he would cheerfully accede to the affranchisement. The debate grew warm, fatal consequences were apprehended, and the deputies were dismissed to their respective provinces.

Previous to the dissolution of the assembly, it was required of the members to signalise their meeting by a memorial of gratitude to the empress. The titles of *great,* wise, prudent, and mother of her country, were by unanimous acclamation conferred upon Catherine. When informed of this decree, she replied, with apparent modesty, ' That if she had rendered herself worthy of the first title, it was for posterity to confer it on her. That wisdom and prudence were the gifts of Heaven, to which she daily gave thanks, without presuming to arrogate merit to herself. But that *the mother of her country* was the title to her the most dear, the only title she could accept, and which she regarded as the benign and glorious recompence for her solicitudes and labours in behalf of a people whom she loved.'

Proud of the work which had obtained her this flattering homage, copies of the Instructions were dispatched to those sovereigns whose esteem she

CATHERINE II. 43

courted. Having complimented her on her labours, they hesitated not to pronounce that they would afford to her honour an eternal monument. The king of Prussia, among other flattering observations, thus expressed himself: " Semiramis commanded armies, Elizabeth of England was accounted a politician, but no woman has hitherto been a legislatrix; a glory reserved for the empress of Russia, who so well deserves it."

This letter was received at Kasan by Catherine, who had long desired to visit her provinces in Asia, and the shores of the Volga. Her Instructions, founded on the principles of an enlightened humanity, recognise no legitimate authority which does not originate in justice. Though an absolute monarch, her laws tended to enfeeble despotism, and to render equity respectable; their purpose was to form a solid, rather than an arbitrary legislation; to restrain caprice and tyranny, and to subject those to whom their administration was confided to a just and invariable conduct. It is to be lamented, that the accomplishment of this great design was impeded by difficulties probably unforeseen: in an assembly, composed of tribes so adverse and customs so various, a common conclusion could scarcely be expected; the whole apparatus was suffered to fall, after appearing as a machine, directed to a vast but inadequate end.

The spirit of the Instructions, respecting the proportion to be observed between punishments and crimes, the rare occasions on which death ought to be inflicted, the rules to be observed in forfeitures and confiscations, which could not extend beyond acquired property, with many other just and mild regulations, bespoke profound meditation, rectitude of judgment, and benevolence of heart. The publication and dispersion of this work throughout the empire, could not fail, by diffusing just principles, of producing beneficial effects. The legislation of Russia had been, like that of most countries, complicated, perplexed, and contradictory; drawn out to a voluminous length, loaded with precedents, cases, and opinions, calculated rather for eternal altercation than for the administration of equity. Catherine determined to reduce this chaos to order; if her endeavours failed of their complete accomplishment, the very attempt was glorious, and the way was cleared for future amelioration and success. "If," says she, in these Instructions, "it be not, for political reasons, practicable to free the boors throughout the empire from their vassalage, yet means should be thought of to en-

CATHERINE II. 45

able them to acquire property. In pursuance of this idea, should not a method be devised for gradually improving the condition of this lower order of the people ?" The whole performance is a compendium of just maxims and generous sentiments, illustrated by passages from the most celebrated of the philosophers of Greece and Rome, with examples from ancient and modern history, and from the manners of cultivated and savage nations.

Catherine, proceeding on the same enlarged and liberal principles which dictated the Instructions, continued to cultivate the sciences and arts, to make her kingdom the asylum of learning and genius, to reform the manners and instruct the minds of the people.

The transit of Venus over the sun, which was expected to take place in the summer of 1769, afforded to the empress a new opportunity of displaying her munificence and liberal curiosity. In a letter, written by her own hand from Moscow, to the director of the academy of sciences at Petersburg, she desired to be informed of the most proper situation for making observations on this occasion, and offers every requisite assistance to the undertaking.

While thus seeking to build her fame on a solid

foundation, the czarina was not free from the weaknesses of humanity; she discovered an extraordinary anxiety to obtain from the powers of Europe an acknowledgment of the title of *Imperial majesty,* which some had persisted in refusing to her. This style was pertinaciously resisted by Lewis XV. a resistance which, combined with other sources of dissatisfaction, irritated the empress against France. The vexations arising from foreign powers, the dangers of war, and the cares of empire, by dividing the attention of Catherine, enabled her to elude reflections that more bitterly pressed upon her mind: one adverse moment, she felt, might despoil her of the fruits of her toils; and even that moment, many among the people for whose welfare she laboured were but too eager to accelerate. The name of Peter III. was become dear to the Russians; in the recollection of his good qualities, and in compassion for his fate, his vices and weakness were remembered no more. In the multitude of malecontents, dispersed through the nation, an avenger of the czar might yet be found.

Tschoglokoff, a young officer, believing himself inspired by Heaven, resolved to appear in this character: having reflected on the execution of his sanguinary project, he lurked, for several suc-

CATHERINE II. 47

ceeding days, in the dark passages of the palace, leading to its retired and interior apartments. Catherine, on this occasion, owed her preservation to an accidental circumstance, which procrastinated the time of her passing through the avenues, where the assassin laid in wait to receive her. Tschoglokoff, impatient of this delay, and eager to strike a blow in his heated fancy so propitious to his country, boasted of his purpose to a brother officer, whom he believed to be his friend. By this imprudence he was betrayed. Orloff, informed of his measures and designs, had him seized in the ambuscade, where he awaited the empress: a long poniard was found upon him, when he confessed, without hesitation, the use for which it was designed.

Catherine, mistress of her indignation and of her fears, affected to forgive the attempt of a youth whom political fanaticism had deluded from his duty: she even desired to see him, and spoke to him with mildness. By this apparent generosity she sought to suppress the transaction, lest imitators should be found of an example so pernicious. But, hopeless of converting a man whom humanity had made an assassin, she caused him secretly to be imprisoned, and afterwards exiled to the heart of Siberia.

48   CATHERINE II.

In the middle of the year 1767, the empress conceived the idea of deputing men of learning to travel into the interior of her immense territories, for the purpose of determining the geographical position of the principal places; also to mark their temperature, to examine their soil, their productions and wealth, and to ascertain the manners and character of the people. For the prosecution of these useful investigations, orders were given to the academy of sciences, to whom the office was left of selecting proper persons.

Among the ingenious men who, at the invitation of Catherine, had sought an asylum at Petersburg, was the celebrated professor Euler, from Berlin, on whom the empress, with other marks of favour and protection, settled a large annual stipend. Aware that in the precedence of knowledge and the useful arts consists the real happiness and distinction of a nation, Catherine encouraged artists and scholars of all denominations. New privileges were granted to the academy of sciences, and its members exhorted to add to the names which had conferred a lustre on their society, those of distinguished foreigners. Nor was the empress less attentive to the academy of arts; the number of its pupils was augmented, scholars were not to be admitted after the

CATHERINE II. 49

age of six years, lest by the previous defects of a bad education, their manners should have been corrupted or their tempers spoiled. After having been three years in the care of women, they were devoted to the art for which they displayed a pre-dilection. During their residence in the academy, they were to receive nothing from their parents; they were clothed, lodged, and boarded, at the public expence. At the end of fifteen years they were to leave the institution, and to receive patents of nobility, should it then be found that their conduct corresponded with the education that had been bestowed on them. To those of the pupils who gained by their talents the highest prizes, pensions were allotted for travelling three years over Europe. As a still farther encouragement to knowledge, an annual sum of five thousand rubles was assigned by Catherine for the translation of foreign literature into the Russian language.

The small-pox, about this period, was rife in Petersburg, where it committed dreadful devastations. To avoid infection, the empress and her son remained at Tzar-sko-selo. The danger to which they were exposed, and the welfare of the nation, gave rise, on this occasion, to the introduction of inoculation. It was determined by

the first personages in the empire, to submit to
the operation as an example to the people; for
which purpose a physician was invited from England.

In the beginning of July, 1768, Dr. Thomas
Dimsdale received, at Hertford, a letter from the
Russian minister at the court of London, con-
taining information of the wishes of the empress,
Domestic considerations produced in the doctor a
transient hesitation, when a second courier from
Petersburg determined his departure.

The doctor was received at court by count
Panin; but the empress came to town on hearing
of his arrival. Catherine discovered great sagacity in the questions she put to him relative to the
practice and success of the inoculated small-pox:
on retiring, he received from her an invitation to
dinner. The doctor, in describing this repast,
thus speaks of the empress: " But what most
enlivened the entertainment was the unaffected
ease and affability of the czarina. Each of her
guests had a share of her attention and politeness;
the conversation was kept up with a freedom and
cheerfulness rather to be expected from persons
of the same rank, than from subjects admitted to
the company of their sovereign."

On the following day a second conference took

CATHERINE II. 51

place, in which Dr. Dimsdale required the assistance of the court physician, to whom he proposed to communicate the methods he meant to pursue. Catherine, with great good sense, objected to a measure which could tend but to his embarrassment, and which would seem to imply her want of confidence in his skill:—' My life is my own,' said she, ' and I shall with cheerfulness confide it to your care. With regard to my constitution, you shall receive from myself every necessary information. I have also to acquaint you, that it is my determination to submit to the operation before the grand-duke, and as soon as you judge it convenient. This, for the present, must remain a secret: the preparations for the duke will countenance your visits to the palace,' &c. The physician engaged obedience to all her commands; but was desirous that some experiments might be first made on persons of her own sex, age, and, as nearly as possible, constitution. ' If the practice had been novel,' replied the empress, ' or any doubt of its general success had remained, such precautions might be necessary; but, satisfied in these particulars, why should there be any delays ?'

Having been privately inoculated on the 12th of October, Catherine returned the next morning

to Tzar-sko-selo, a palace four-and-twenty versts
from Petersburg. She was at first accompanied
only by her attendants; but several of the nobility
following, and, among the rest, some who had not
had this distemper, the empress charged Dr.
Dimsdale to advertise her when it would be
possible for her to communicate the disease.
' Though I wish to keep my inoculation secret,'
said she, ' I would be far from concealing it a
moment, when it might become hazardous to
others.' During this interval, she took part in
every amusement with her usual affability and
unconcern, constantly dined with the nobility, and
enlivened the court with the peculiar graces and
vivacity of her conversation.

The grand-duke, shortly after, submitted to the
operation. On his recovery, Catherine rewarded
the operator by creating him a baron of the Russian empire, appointing him actual counsellor of
state, and physician to her imperial majesty, with
a pension of five hundred a-year to be paid to him
in England : he also immediately received a present of ten thousand pounds sterling, with a miniature picture of the empress, and another of the
grand-duke, as a memorial of his services. On
his son, by whom he had been accompanied,
Catherine conferred the same title; and ordered

CATHERINE II. 53

a superb golden snuff-box to be given to him, richly set with diamonds.

The principal families of Petersburg and Moscow were impatient to follow the imperial example. This business being happily accomplished, baron Dimsdale, laden with wealth, was preparing to return to his native land, when he was informed by a nobleman that the empress desired to see him. The baron found her, to his concern, with every symptom of a pleuritic fever, and, at her desire, he delayed his departure. After losing some blood, she experienced relief, and in a short time began to recover.

At the end of three weeks, the baron again prepared for his voyage to England; and on his audience of leave, experienced farther proofs of the munificence of the empress.

On the third of December, 1768, the recovery of the czarina, and of the grand-duke, from the small-pox, was celebrated with solemn pomp, by a thanksgiving service, in the chapel of the palace; and an annual festival in commemoration of the event was decreed by the senate.

Catherine, not yet prepared for hostilities, had, on the first menace of the Turkish war, suspended the settlement of the Polish limits; but her purpose, though deferred, was not relinquished : the

54   **CATHERINE II.**

Russian troops continued to harass Poland, which had become the theatre of a complicated and cruel war. Encouraged by France and Austria, and impatient of a foreign yoke, a confederacy against their oppressors had been formed among the Poles. Provoked by this resistance, Russia poured in fresh reinforcements, who, under the command of lieutenant-general Soltikoff, ravaged and divided the country. Thus pressed, a second application, supported by the minister of France, was made by the confederates to the Ottoman empire, and favourably received by the divan. The Russian embassador was, previous to a declaration of war, shut up in the prison of the seven towers, and hostilities were commenced in form.

The Porte having complained of the ambition and rapacity of Catherine, of the violation of their territory, and the infringement of treaties, proposed to open the campaign with an army of 500,000 men. This event, foreseen, if not desired, by the Russian court, was regarded by the empress with little dismay: the army, the magazines, and the stores, had been for some time in a state of preparation. Catherine loudly justified the conduct of her minister, and expected the enemy with firmness. The measures of the Porte on this occasion were not less politic than just:

CATHERINE II. 55

those of Russia exhibit a picture of despotism, oppression, and cruelty; at the contemplation of which humanity sickens. A dark and sanguinary cloud obscured at this period the reign of Catherine, and threw into shade the lustre of her magnanimous qualities.

The empress and the king of Prussia, long solicitous for a conference respecting the partition of Poland, had hitherto forborne to indulge this desire, fearful of giving umbrage to the potentates of Europe. The better to conceal their purposes, it was determined that prince Henry, the brother of Frederic, under the pretence of a visit to his sister, the queen of Sweden, should be charged with the negociation of the Polish affairs. When arrived at Stockholm, the prince talked of returning to Prussia through Denmark, but was induced without difficulty to change his design, by the complaisance of Catherine; from whom he received an invitation, while so near her dominions, to visit Petersburg. The premeditated purpose of his journey was thus veiled under the appearance of accident.

The prince was received at Petersburg with sovereign honours; after the first ceremonials, he conversed with the empress without restraint; while every day was marked by new scenes of

CATHERINE II.

festivity. The entertainment given in honour of
the prince, at Tzar-sko-selo, the seat of the czars,
and the summer residence of Catherine, was distinguished by peculiar magnificence, and is deserving of commemoration. In this superb mansion,
which owed its origin to Catherine I., was embellished by Elizabeth, and indebted for its elegant completion to Catherine II., a little temple
of simple architecture was by the latter devoted
to reflection and retirement. In this retreat, surrounded by books, and the scenery of beautiful
nature, she descended from her rank, contracted
her sphere of action, remembered that she was
human, and delivered herself up to quiet meditation. It was at this seat, celebrated for its
grandeur, magnificence, and taste, that the empress determined to entertain her guests with a
truly regal munificence.

On the appointed evening, Catherine, the grand-
duke, the prince of Prussia, with several of the
nobility, amounting in the whole to sixteen persons, seated themselves on a sledge, drawn by
sixteen horses, covered and enclosed by double
glasses, which from within and without reflected
numberless images. More than two thousand
sledges followed that which conveyed the imperial
family; every person masked and dressed in fancy

CATHERINE II. 57

habits. At the distance of two versts from Petersburg, the train of sledges passed under a triumphal arch, illuminated with various coloured lamps, and adorned with transparent emblems. A pyramid of lamps, a superb structure, a magnificent temple, a display of fireworks or illuminated colonnades, was exhibited at every succeeding verst; opposite to each was erected a house of public entertainment, where rustics of both sexes, dressed as shepherds and shepherdesses, mingled in the dance, or amused themselves by sports, as at a country wake. Each of these houses was, by the costume of the people, the music, the dances, and the sports, made to represent a different nation. Vaulting, tumbling, interludes, &c. were performed at intervals. On the approach to Tzar-sko-selo, within the distance of two versts, a high mountain appeared, which, seen through an avenue cut in the wood, represented Vesuvius throwing out torrents of flame, which illuminated the surrounding atmosphere. This artificial eruption continued during the time the sledges were passing in sight of the mountain, and till they entered, through a lofty portal in a rock, into a Chinese village, which led to Tzar-sko-selo. In the several apartments of the interior of the palace, lighted by innumerable wax tapers, the

company amused themselves for two hours with
dancing. Suddenly a grand discharge of cannon
was heard, the ball ceased, the tapers were extinguished, while the company ran to the windows,
through which were beheld magnificent fire-works,
extending the length of the palace. A thunder-
ing discharge of artillery concluded the exhibition; when the tapers were re-illumined as by
enchantment, and a splendid supper appeared already served up. The repast being concluded,
the dancing was resumed, and continued till a late
hour in the morning. During the whole of her
reign, Catherine was accustomed to entertain the
public with magnificent spectacles, not exceeded
by any court in Europe.

Prince Henry passed every evening in company
with the empress, in her favourite suite of apartments, which she had named her hermitage. This
sumptuous edifice, to which its modest appellation
but little suited, was contiguous to the imperial
palace, with which it communicated by a covered
passage erected over an arch. It was in these
apartments, which every luxury combined to em-
bellish, that Catherine enjoyed with her friends
the pleasures of familiar and social intercourse.
Here was her private library, here the picture
gallery, with cabinets of medals, of coins, col-

CATHERINE II. 59

lections of prints, of natural history, of mine-
ralogy, of curious pieces of art, of mechanical inventions, of antique and modern gems, &c. &c.
Here were placed the busts of great and eminent
men. In one of the apartments was to be seen that
of the English patriot, Mr. Charles James Fox,
placed between two others in the middle of a
marble chimney-piece. One room was allotted to
musical entertainments, another to billiards, and
others to various games and amusements. From
one of the apartments you enter a pleasure-garden,
supported by arches with furnaces beneath, which
produce amidst the rigours of winter an artificial
summer, in which the peach, the anana, the rose,
and the hyacinth, bloom and ripen. A fine brass-
wire covers this northern Eden, in which beautiful
and rare birds, from every country and from every
clime, fly among the trees, sport in the blossoms,
and hop in the walks. These little animals, tamed
by their situation, would take food from the hand
of their royal mistress. Here Catherine, in the
depths of winter, wanders with her friends and
favourites in a paradise of her own creation, on
downy lawns, and beneath verdant trees, amidst
a profusion of nature's bounties artificially produced.

Above this garden, on a terrace, is a second,

CATHERINE II.

in the Asiatic taste, uncovered, and appropriated to more genial seasons. From this palace of Armida, a covered gallery leads to the court-theatre, to which a select company only is admitted. The remaining apartments of the hermitage are composed of two spacious and elegantly-ornamented halls, and a dining-room, in which dinner is served up by a mechanical apparatus, without the visible aid of servants, the dishes rising on small tables through doors in the floor. The company being seated, each, on wishing his plate exchanged, has only to strike it in the centre, when, having fallen through the table and floor, it starts up again, furnished with whatever was written on a small piece of paper, that had descended with it. At a certain signal the whole course descends, and is succeeded by another.

The prince of Prussia expressing a desire to see Moscow, the sledges were immediately prepared, which transported him with celerity to the ancient capital. Three weeks afterward he was already returned to Petersburg. Among the various presents which he received from the empress was the star of the order of St. Andrew, full of large brilliants, together with a single diamond valued at forty thousand rubles. The portrait of Catherine was enclosed in the ring.

CATHERINE II. 61

Amidst these festivities and pleasures, the dismemberment of Poland was, in private conferences between the empress and the prince, finally resolved upon. This measure was by Catherine and Frederic equally desired, but a third ally was wanting, which Joseph II. promised to supply. Turkey, France, and England, guarantees of the treaty, appeared indifferent to the fate of this unhappy country, or unable to give it aid. ' I,' said Catherine to the prince of Prussia, ' will frighten the Ottomans, and flatter England; do you buy over Austria that she may amuse France.'

The conditions to be served in the dismemberment of Poland were thus settled; and the extent of country to be allotted to each of the powers finally fixed. This treaty, however, was not signed till two years afterwards, in February, 1772.

The war continued to rage on the frontiers of Turkey with alternate success: after ten months, at the end of the campaign, the advantage appeared manifestly on the side of the Russians. By the artifices of Catherine, and the devotedness of its king, Poland was induced to join its oppressors, and to declare war against the Porte. But from a country drained of its resources, plunged in anarchy, and without an army, no essential service could on either side be expected. While the troops of Russia were thus engaged, a project worthy her daring genius was conceived by Catherine, who resolved to attack her enemies in the isles of Greece. For the execution of this plan, notwithstanding the opposition of her ministry, preparations were immediately commenced.

In September, 1769, two squadrons of Russian men-of-war were prepared for the occasion with inconceivable celerity: sailing from Revel and Archangel, they steered for the Mediterranean, a course hitherto unexampled. This fleet, accompanied by numerous small vessels conveying troops, having crossed the north seas, passed the straits of Gibraltar, been dispersed by a tempest, and again collected, displayed at length in the Archipelago its victorious flag. Europe beheld with astonishment a nation scarcely known till the present century, braving its coasts and entering its harbours. In the islands, on Paros and Melos, and on the continent of ancient Greece, Russians appeared: the Pylas of Nestor, the famous Sparta, was conquered by barbarians, who laid siege to Corinth, and captured Lemnos, with Mytelene. In Syria and in Egypt the Russian armies were beheld supporting the enterprising Ali-bey for three years.

CATHERINE II. 63

On the war against the Turks depended the fate of Poland: aware of this, Catherine omitted no effort to ensure its success. New squadrons were built, and numerous recruits joined her camps. The campaign was opened by the siege of Bender, celebrated for the sojourn of Charles XII. and at length decided by two signal and more important actions, in which victory remained with the imperial army. Great and repeated successes augmented the pride and the security of Catherine: the restless spirits were employed, murmurs were no longer heard; every conspiracy was crushed, and every discontent overpowered in the splendor of victory. Distant provinces, sending deputies to Petersburg, did homage to a victorious and triumphant princess, who received them with magnificence, and loaded them with benefits. Foreign officers from England, from Denmark, and from Holland, of tried valour and experience, offered their services to the empress, and were incorporated in the Russian navy.

When but recently elevated to the throne, Catherine had, from the conversations of Munich, conceived the idea of wresting Constantinople from the Turks, and driving them out of Europe; the ancient veteran had, at the time, offered to conduct the enterprise, which too many obstacles then opposed. The propitious moment seemed now arrived. The empress, though hopeless of retaining the Grecian islands, determined to rend them from the Ottoman Porte, to be the patroness of liberty in Greece, and the foundress of a new republic. The people were disposed, by secret agents, to rise up in arms, and to hail the Russians as their deliverers. At the instant the squadron reached the height of cape Matapan, the whole Archipelago believed itself free. The Mainots, descendants of the ancient Lacedæmonians, were the first to take arms; their neighbours followed the example, and a massacre of the Turks ensued. This insurrection was cruelly avenged: thousands of the debased and miserable Greeks fell, in their turn, under the sabre of the Janissaries.

Between the Russians and the Turks a terrible conflict ensued, that terminated in the destruction of the Turkish fleet; which, linked together, and blocked up in a narrow and slimy bay, became a prey to devouring flames. Three Englishmen, Elphinston, Greig, and Dugdale, more particularly distinguished themselves on this occasion. *Dugdale, observing the position of the enemy,* advanced with his fire-ships, and, in the face of a vigorous fire, encouraging by his example the Rus-

CATHERINE II. 6*

sians, himself fastened the grapplings of a fire-ship to a Turkish vessel. Having effected his daring purpose, he threw himself into the sea, his hair, face, and hands scorched, and, in this condition, swam back to the Russian squadron. The rising sun no longer discovered the Turkish flag. Catherine thought fit to deprive the Englishman of his severely earned laurels, by ascribing the idea to Alexius Orloff: she expressed this to Voltaire, and repeated it again to the embassador of France.

The Russians, after the destruction of the enemy's fleet, anchored at Paros, whence they commanded the Grecian seas, and extorted homage from every vessel that appeared. A rebellion which had broken out in Turkey, rendered the vicinity of such an adversary still more formidable. The incapacity of her generals only opposed this career of fortune, and prevented Catherine from wresting Syria and Egypt from the Ottoman empire.

The empress was the first person in Petersburg who learned from a courier, dispatched for the purpose, the catastrophe of the Turkish fleet. The minister of the marine department had, by a quarrel with the college of admiralty, occasioned some embarrassment in an affair of little moment.

66　　　　　CATHERINE II.

When sent for by Catherine, on the intelligence from the navy, he expected a reproof, and, eager to exculpate himself, exclaimed on entering, ' It was not my fault, I do assure you, madam.' ' Oh! I know that well,' replied the empress; ' nevertheless it is true.' ' Alas! yes, madam, and I am very sorry for it.' ' What, are you sorry that the Turks have no longer a fleet?' Having thus said, she, smiling, communicated to him the dispatches. This event was celebrated at Petersburg by magnificent festivals: a palace was afterward built, and the foundations of a town laid, to consecrate to posterity a victory so decisive.

Count Alexius Orloff, who had the command of the expedition, returned to Petersburg (March 15th, 1771) to enjoy his triumphs, and to solicit the means of extending his conquests. His appearance renewed the public rejoicings, while he received from his sovereign the grand riband of St. George.

Having laid before the council a plan by which he proposed to render himself master of Greece, and to rescue Egypt from the power of the Turks, he demanded for its execution ten millions of rubles. ' I grant you twenty,' replied Catherine, with quickness; ' I am resolved you shall want for nothing.' Orders were immediately issued for the equipment of a new squadron, to reinforce the Archipelago fleet.

The Turkish empire, reduced to extremities, was convulsed in all its parts : insurrection, massacre, and pestilence, combined to ravage the country, and to fill it with desolation.

Alexius Orloff, intoxicated with fortune, and elate with the favour of his sovereign, departed from Petersburg on his return to the Archipelago. At Vienna, where he made some stay, he distinguished himself by a boundless luxury, and by indiscretions that reflected discredit on the court by which he was employed. One evening, at a supper with the Russian embassador and a numerous company, he spoke of the revolution and the fate of the czar. No one presumed to question him on the circumstances of this event, which he voluntarily narrated with all its horror and atrocity. Perceiving the company shudder, he endeavoured to extenuate, in some degree, the crime, in which the instant before he appeared to glory. ' It was a lamentable thing,' he observed, ' for a man of his humanity to be compelled to such an action.' But the impression produced by his character was already indelible, and not to be effaced. On leaving Vienna, he rejoined the squadron, which lay expecting him at Leghorn, and with which, though in a shattered condition, he continued to complete the ruin of the marine and commerce of the Turks.

He had been commissioned by the empress to cause four pictures to be painted in Italy, representing the engagements of the fleets, and the conflagration of the Ottoman ships. Orloff, in compliance with this command, applied to a painter named Hackert. The artist having informed him that he had never witnessed the blowing up of a ship, the Russian scrupled not, at the hazard of firing all the vessels in the road of Leghorn, to satisfy his curiosity, by affording him an opportunity of exhibiting with greater truth the subject proposed for his pencil*.

But this conduct, however extravagant, excites a transient indignation, when compared with the perfidy practised by this wretch, in ensnaring into his power a young and innocent victim, the daughter of the empress Elizabeth, by a clandestine marriage, whose birth rendered her obnoxious to Catherine. This young person, betrayed by the basest artifices, dishonoured by a fictitious marriage, and delivered over to a powerful and vin-

---

* The four pictures hang in the hall of audience at Peterhoff.

CATHERINE II. 69

dictive rival, to languish out her days in the gloom
of a dungeon, or fall beneath a secret execution,
afforded a new instance of the barbarity of a man
whose career of ambition neither guilt nor remorse
was able to impede.

The Ottoman armies, though repeatedly vanquished, still resisted the efforts of their enemies;
the war continued with alternate successes; but
victory predominated on the side of Russia. With
the scourge of war pestilence combined, to sweep
away those whom the sword had spared.

This dreadful disease, having for some time ravaged the interior of Russia, appeared at length at
Moscow, where the ignorance of the physicians,
and the superstition of the people, united to augment its force. It had been for some time mistaken by the medical men for an epidemic fever;
when the populace, perceiving every remedy fail,
with blind rage attacked the physicians, pursued
them on every side, and forced them into con-
cealment. This disorder had been brought from
Turkey by the victorious Russians, of whom the
enemy was thus avenged. The folly of the generals, who expected to subject nature to military
command, increased the malady. In the winter
of the preceding year, its name was, by peremp-
tory orders, forbidden to be pronounced: the

70   CATHERINE II.

physicians and surgeons were even compelled to
draw up a declaration that it was only a spotted
fever. One alone refused to sign it. Prevention
was by these means neglected, and the people
were mowed down as with a scythe. The camp
was depopulated: the general fell a victim to his
incredulity and obstinacy. The baggages, on being opened, spread the contagion; the people employed in unpacking them were instantly seized
with morbid ulcers. The free intercourse in the
markets and churches aggravated the evil, which
the plunder of the effects of the deceased served
to extend. The cleansing and ventilating the
houses were neglected by the governor, whom
avarice impelled to stow under the vaults of his
palace goods and chests of linen brought from infected houses. He was even induced by his ignorance to authorise a ridiculous and pernicious superstition, by which a Turkish prisoner, imposing on his credulity, purchased his freedom. A
ticket was written by this man, containing the following adjuration: " Oh, Mohammed ! for this
once have pity on the Christians, and free them,
for the sake of our deliverance from captivity,
from the pestilence." This writing, or charm,
was, by order of the governor, stuck on poles
against the belfries of the churches. The people,

CATHERINE II.

trusting to the remedy, became still more careless : the ravages of the pestilence spread far and wide ; within a few months of the year 1770, upwards of six thousand persons perished in one quarter of the town.

The distemper, owing to this wretched negligence, had by Christmas reached Moscow. Here also, at its commencement, the people were assured by an ukause that a false alarm had been raised by wicked incendiaries, and that no pestilence existed. Several surgeons and physicians joined in this assurance. Catherine was no sooner informed of the dreadful truth, than she dispatched assistance with all speed to the city, where the calamity had already risen to its height. The contagion spread rapidly through the neighbouring towns and villages, where thirty thousand persons became its victims. At Moscow it was computed that a fourth part of the inhabitants only were left alive. In December, 1771, it was found, on its ceasing, that upwards of sixty thousand had died within the city of Moscow in less than a year. The dead lay without interment in the streets, where they had fallen or been thrown from the houses : the police possessed neither carts nor people sufficient to remove the bodies.

Every exertion in his power had been made by

general Yerapkin, when the empress, in September, suffering private feelings *to* yield to her solicitude for the welfare of her subjects, commissioned her favourite Gregory Orloff, with full and extraordinary powers, to check the incursion of the malady, and put a stop, if practicable, to its devastation. The sum of 100,000 rubles was issued from the treasury on this occasion.

The exertions of the favourite were in a great degree successful: a commission of health was appointed: in addition to the pest-houses, monasteries and palaces were converted into lazarets: a building was appropriated for the orphan children of infected houses; the public offices were converted into places of quarantine; and other measures, equally wise and salutary, were adopted. The physicians and surgeons were rewarded according to their diligence and zeal, and the assistants at the various establishments put immediately upon stipends. By these precautions the contagion was checked and confined, but it was the severe winter only by which it was terminated. To increase the calamity, during the night of the 30th of December, in the midst of a storm of wind, a fire broke out in the imperial palace, inhabited by prince Volkonsky, the newly appointed governor. The whole structure, chiefly built of

CATHERINE II. 73

timber, was, together with the church, consumed in the flames. In the disastrous history of this devoted city, another incident yet remains to be told.

The populace, sunk in a deplorable ignorance, contemned alike the regulations of the government, and the medical prescriptions: the physicians, as they passed through the streets, more especially if foreigners, were in danger of their lives, from a brutal and misguided fanaticism. Prayers to the pictures of the saints were, by these miserable wretches, believed the only method of cure: by a natural gradation their folly speedily grew into a crime. A fortnight before the arrival of Orloff, an enthusiast of the lower class of people, summoned a crowd, to whom he declared, that a picture of the mother of God, near the Varvaskoï gate*, appearing to him, had complained of the people's neglect in worshipping her image; and promised, in case of a reformation, to quell, by a miracle, the pestilence. Standing at the gate, he continued to repeat to the priests and passengers the same story. The tale spread, and the populace are seldom given to infidel doubts. The faithful flocked to St. Barbara's gate from all

---

* The bridge-gate of St. Barbara leading to a chapel.

parts of the town; the picture was addressed by cries and exclamations; ornaments were hung about it, and presents made to it of gold and jewels. Processions marched in endless succession. The sick and the healthy, pressing forward, mingled together. In the dæmon of superstition, the dæmon of pestilence found a friend and ally. The primate of Moscow, a virtuous and enlightened man, applied to the general for the means to put a stop to this tragic farce. Five soldiers were sent to him, whom he commissioned silently to remove the picture, the cause of the tumult, in the dead of the night. But neither the night nor the day deprived the mother of God of her zealous votaries. The soldiers were driven back, and invectives were poured forth on the author of the profanation, who was by one and all accused of heresy. The bells were rung, the populace were roused, and brought together to be informed of the purposed outrage. A common cause was made with the insurgents, while the prelate, justly alarmed for the consequences of his temerity, fled without the city, and took refuge in the monastery of Donskoï. His retreat becoming known the ensuing morning, the multitude flocked to his asylum, where they found him engaged in the celebration of worship. His

CATHERINE II. 75

venerable age, his habit, his occupation, his office, the place, pleaded in vain for mercy: the fanatic barbarians falling upon him, threw him to the ground with savage fury, beat him on the head, and with their knives completed the tragedy. The body of this friend of mankind, this martyr to humanity and an enlightened mind, remained till the following day exposed before the gate of the monastery.

The crowd, after effecting their atrocious purpose, ran back to the city: a party of them attacked a monastery which had been converted into a lazaret, brought out the diseased, and ill treated the surgeons. The same conduct was repeated at the house of quarantine. The archiepiscopal residence being plundered, and the most valuable of the goods taken away, the rest were destroyed: the store-cellars beneath it, hired by a merchant for wine and liquors, were presently emptied. Those among the officers who attempted to restrain these excesses, were turned back with bleeding heads.

The madness augmenting every moment, the rage was now directed against medical practitioners, to whom the pestilence was attributed. An Italian dancing-master unfortunately passing, was mistaken for a physician, his legs and arms broken, and left in that condition to perish in the streets. Having attacked and plundered the house of a physician, they proceeded in triumph to the principal hospital, from which the director and attendants, even the soldiers, amounting to an hundred armed men, fled away. Towards evening general Yerapkin, at the head of one hundred and fifty soldiers, carabineers and hussars, with two field-pieces, marched against the maniacs: the contest was obstinate, and lasted till midnight: two hundred and fifty of these misguided wretches were laid dead in the streets; three hundred taken prisoners; and of the dispersed, many dropped wounded and dying by the way. Early in the morning, the general, at the head of his men, rode with drawn sabres through the streets of Moscow, and fixed piquets in proper places. A regiment of infantry from the villages the next day entered the town, whence those whose duty it was to guard it had prudently retired. Catherine rewarded the brave Yerapkin with imperial magnificence. This aggravation of the distress of a city devoured by pestilence, affords to the imagination an afflicting picture: by the promiscous mixture of the people the malady must of course have been incalculably increased.

At the re-appearance of spring its return being

CATHERINE II. 77

apprehended, the cares and precautions of the police were redoubled. It was proclaimed through the city, with a wise and magnanimous policy, that a reward should be given to those who would produce infected goods, even though they had been stolen; and that effects in possession of infected persons, should, on being delivered to the flames, be paid for to their full value. Measures like these could not fail of producing a salutary effect. By such and similar means, at the close of January, 1772, the plague had entirely disappeared. By some statements it was calculated, that the pestilence, during its continuance, from December, 1771, to December, 1772, had cost the Russian empire 133,299 persons.

Praise was due to Orloff for his courage and services on this occasion. The presence of a person in authority was necessary to awe the populace, and to enforce the regulations. The favourite braved both the pestilence, and a superstition but little less formidable. Having prohibited all assemblies, he himself visited the sick, procured them assistance, and in person witnessed the burning of the infected clothes.

On his return to Petersburg he found in Catherine a grateful mistress: by her order a column was erected, and a medal struck, as memorials to posterity of this important service.

The contending armies of Ottomans and Russians had not escaped the pestilence on the banks of the Danube ; whence, spreading into Poland, it served the king of Prussia as a pretence for his meditated invasion.

The yoke of Catherine on this unhappy country became daily heavier and more oppressive : the confederates were on all sides pursued and pillaged by her troops ; nor did the empress disdain to partake of the spoil. The celebrated library of prince Radzivil, containing an invaluable collection of Lithuanian history, was transported to Petersburg, whence it never returned. Catherine, amidst these depredations, spoke only, in her declarations to Warsaw, of equity, beneficence, and her desire of peace.

The Poles, justly irritated by this union of tyranny and mockery, struggled to free themselves : their king became suspected as conspiring against their liberties in concert with Russia. A conspiracy among the confederates to seize his person was the natural consequence of these jealousies : their general Pulaufsky, whose intrepidity only equalled his passion for freedom, hesitated at no

C\THERINE II. 79

means, however criminal, for the acquirement of
his end. An ambuscade was formed, the king
seized, wounded, forced from his carriage, and
dragged through the streets between the horses of
the assassins. After fatigues and terrors almost
insupportable, he at length escaped with life, and
found shelter in a mill, whence a countryman
was dispatched to the colonel of his guards. His
hat had been found covered with blood. Warsaw
was in consternation when intelligence arrived of
his safety. The inhabitants received him with
transports of joy : several of the conspirators perished on the scaffold ; while their chief, by a
manifesto to which no one gave credit, exonerated
himself from all share in the transaction.

The danger incurred by Stanislaus in this enterprise, afforded to Russia a new pretext for pursuing the confederates, and preparing the dismemberment of the kingdom. The Russians and the
Ottomans, exhausted by war and pestilence, and
wearied with the conflict, submitted to a negociation by the intervention of the ministers of Austria and Prussia. An armistice was agreed on,
and a congress appointed to meet at Fokshiani.

The present appeared a crisis favourable to the
ambition of Orloff, who had long aspired to share
with Catherine the throne. He sought and ob-

tained the honour of treating with the plenipotentiaries of the divan. By obtaining a peace, he flattered himself with acquiring the gratitude of the
empire, and surmounting the difficulties which
had hitherto opposed themselves to his views. The
empress had been, and was still, personally attached to him : gratitude and ambition were the
only sentiments which bound him to her ; proud
of the favour of his sovereign, he had been zealous to deserve it ; but, when once secured, his
ardour had cooled, and his behaviour become distant and reserved. In proportion as Catherine
sought to revive in him his former sentiments, he
retreated and carried his devoirs to other shrines.
However piqued by his insensibility, and offended
at his ingratitude, the fondness of Catharine for
the child which had been the fruit of this connection, enabled her for some time to subdue her resentments, and bear with the caprices of the father. The boy had been privately reared in one
of the suburbs of the city, where the empress, disguised and under a borrowed character, frequently
visited him. It is said, that a proposal was made
to Orloff by his mistress of a clandestine marriage, which he rejected disdainfully, conceiving himself authorised to aspire to share with
her a throne, for which she had been in a

CATHERINE II. 81

great measure indebted to his exertions. Catherine dissembled her surprise and disappointment, while she secretly resolved to subdue an attachment, become dangerous to her peace and humiliating to her character.

Panin, though not daring to attack him openly, had long regarded the favourite with jealousy and aversion. Orloff, bold and open in his conduct, hated no one, yet by his arrogance provoked numerous enemies. Every one saw him retire from court with satisfaction; while the empress hoped, in his absence, to root out from her heart the lingering remains of her former partiality. His adversaries seized the opportunity of undermining his interest: he was represented to Catherine as a man whose ambition and unbounded presumption risqued the safety of the empire. Panin, who attentively watched the inclinations of his mistress, perceived that she beheld with complacency a young man, named Vassiltschikoff, a sub-lieutenant of the guards. Every art was used to flatter this rifing preference; and as the lieutenant became daily more acceptable to Catherine, the influence of Orloff declined in proportion. Youth and a good figure were the sole attractions of Vassiltschikoff; he was indebted for his fortune rather to the arts of his supporters than to his personal merit : appointed chamberlain to the empress, and distinguished by magnificent presents, his preferment became soon apparent to the courtiers.

Orloff had expected, that his refusal to agree to the secret nuptials would have irritated the desire of the empress, and prepared his way to the throne ; accustomed to receive testimonies of her affection, he thought not of the possibility of forfeiting her favour. On receiving an intimation of what was passing in his absence, rage and surprise were his first emotions : pride at length coming to his relief, he doubted not of being able to revive by his presence the expiring flame of his mistress. Possessed with this idea, the peace, the negociations, the concerns of the state, were all forgotten : without asking permission, he left Fokshiani, and arrived at the gates of Petersburg.

Two days previous to his coming, news had been received of his retreat from Fokshiani : the empress, aware of his temper, and apprehensive that he would force his way to her presence, gave orders to double the guards of the palace, and to place sentinels at the gate of the new favourite. To increase her security, she caused the locks to be changed of those apartments to which Orloff had keys. Her precautions were useless ; the discarded favourite was no longer to be feared; not a partisan appeared in his favour, while his enemies pressed forward from all parts. Orloff beheld his danger without being dismayed: when, in the name of the empress, his employments were required of him, he haughtily refused to comply. `

Catherine chose to treat with lenity, rather than to punish, a man to whom she owed obligations, and whom she had long been accustomed to regard. A compromise was accordingly proposed. Orloff, subdued by her bounty, consented to travel through Europe, and, as a recompence for his submission, received 100,000 rubles, the brevet of a pension of 150,000, a magnificent service of plate, and an estate with six thousand peasants. He had already obtained a patent of prince of the Roman empire : Catherine chose that a man who had been her favourite should appear in foreign nations with dignity and splendor. This conduct was not impolitic; the empress was desirous of proving that her gratitude survived her affection.

The congress at Fokshiani afforded at its opening the prospect of peace : the Russians received from the Turks presents of excellent arms, fine stuffs, and superb carpets. It was declared by Osman Effendi, who first broke silence, ' That

the grand-seignior, his master, had recommended
him to serve God, and to love peace.' The Russians, in return, presented to Osman diamonds
and precious stones, trinkets of gold and rich
furs; on the delivery of which they also professed themselves lovers of peace and justice. Notwithstanding these appearances, the sacrifices demanded by Russia were of such extent as to
disgust the Ottomans : after a fruitless altercation
the congress broke up, and the plenipotentiaries
separated.

During these negociations, preparations were
making for new hostilities. But the mind of Catherine was then occupied by more important objects : she at length beheld herself on the point of
reaping the fruits of those divisions she had been
so long sowing among the Poles. To Prussia had
been left the care of securing the consent of Vienna to the dismemberment of Poland. The minister of France was not endowed with much
foresight. England was by its commerce bound
to Russia. The states bordering on the Baltic,
however jealous of these encroachments, wanted
power to oppose them. Nor were the Ottomans,
whom pestilence and war had exhausted, in a condition more formidable.

The plague, which had ravaged the frontiers of

CATHERINE II. 85

Poland, afforded a pretence to Frederic for advancing his troops into Polish Prussia: the emperor also, on the same pretext, sent troops into such of the provinces as lay contiguous to his dominions. The confederates, pressed by the foreign armies, which spread through the country, were compelled to separate : a part returned to their homes, while the majority, dispersed in foreign nations, published their misfortunes and their complaints. Europe had its attention fixed on Poland : it appeared a moral phenomenon that three powers should, during a time of peace, seize on a country, the independence of which had been guaranteed by solemn treaties. The first who gave notice to the king and senate of Poland of the treaty of Petersburg, was the minister of Vienna. The embassador of Russia, and the Prussian envoy, immediately followed in support of the declaration. The conduct of the partitioning powers had gradually unfolded their rapacious designs; the arrangements now concluded, had been silently progressive ; they had by degrees familiarised themselves with their own designs, and prepared Europe for the atrocious novelty. The king of Prussia, less solicitous of appearances, had made no secret of his intentions : he gave to his acquisitions, as to countries lately discovered, the title of *New Prussia.* A manifesto was delivered at Warsaw, September 18th, 1772, by the ministers of the respective powers, in which their purpose was openly avowed. This declaration was followed by a specification of the countries to be appropriated.

The indignant Poles protested in vain against this injustice, and appealed to the treaty of Oliva, that had assured to them their territory, and had long been regarded as the grand charter of the north. The confederated despots, not content with despoiling them of their country, insisted that the cession should be a solemn act of the nation. In a diet convoked with reluctance, every thing was over-ruled by corruption and force: the courage of individuals, who protested against the proceedings, was of little avail against armed troops. The uniform opposition of the king to the partition, procured him no credit with a people prepossessed with his devotion to Russia. Poland by its dismemberment, lost nearly 5,000,000 of inhabitants. The country allotted to Russia contained 1,500,000. That to Austria, on a territory less extensive, 2,500,000. Prussia acquired only 860,000 people, but received, in compensation, other advantages. The government of Poland was, for the security of the usurpers, rendered

CATHERINE II. 87

yet more corrupt : under the specious pretence of correcting its defects, they were aggravated by the confederated powers, and rendered altogether incurable. The Prussian troops ravaged the country by new modes of rapine, oppression, and tyranny : no forms were observed, no measures kept, even the appearance of justice was insulted and violated. Crushed beneath a yoke the most insupportable and oppressive, the nobles fled from their estates, the monks from their monasteries, the priests from their cures : while those whom infirmity or age yet retained, were bound hand and foot, and carried away as criminals. The young men and maidens were torn from their parents : the former were destined to supply the Prussian armies ; the latter, with dowries with which their friends were compelled to furnish them, sent to increase the population of the country of their merciless tyrants. These oppressions continued from the latter part of the year 1770, to the same period in the year 1772, when the partition of Poland was formally declared.

An estimate of the wealth of Russia, and the magnificence of the czarina, may be made, when we are informed, that in the expences of a long and extended war, in rewards to the officers and generals, in presents to men of learning, in the encouragement of arts, in the purchase of libraries, statues, antiques, pictures, jewels, the sums expended by Russia greatly exceeded those of any European prince or potentate, if Lewis XIV. of France be excepted. During this year, Catherine purchased a diamond of an extraordinary size, weighing 779 carats, brought by a Greek from Ispahan to Holland, for which she paid upwards of 100,000 *l.* sterling, beside settling a pension of 4000 rubles upon the person of whom it was bought.

While the provinces of Poland were acquired -by negociation, the Russian armies continued, with various success, to ravage the frontiers of Turkey : a ruinous and sanguinary war, in which blood was spilt without effect, and courage displayed to no purpose. Dissatisfied with this waste of men and treasure, the empress in her dispatches to marshal Romantzoff, enquired why he forbore to risk a battle ? ' Because,' replied the general, ' the grand-vizier, whose people exceed threefold the number of ours, would find his advantage in such an event.' Catherine answered—' The Romans enquired only where their enemies were, and not after their numbers, in order to engage them.'

The Russian operations in the Levant, notwith-

CATHERINE II. 89

standing the destruction of the Turkish fleet, were attended with little advantage : an unsuccessful attempt, in which great loss was suffered, was made on the island of Negropont : in those descents, which were made with better fortune, plunder was the only advantage obtained : four sacks filled with Russian heads were sent from the isle of Stanchio as a present to Constantinople.

In the year 1773, Catherine, who meditated an alliance for the grand-duke, found herself embarrassed in the choice of a consort. She dreaded a rival, and wished to find a princess whom neither talents nor ambition could render in any degree formidable. The daughters of the landgrave of Hesse Darmstadt fixed her attention. These princesses, three sisters, were, with their mother, invited to the court of Petersburg. The invitation was unhesitatingly accepted by the landgravine, whom ambition rendered desirous of securing for one of her daughters the imperial throne. She was received by Catherine with magnificence, and laden with presents. The empress, having thus taken time to form a judgment of the characters of the princesses, selected the eldest as a spouse for the grand-duke. The young lady, as a preliminary, embraced the faith of the Greek church, and was united in form to the heir of the czars.

It was expected by the party of Orloff, that the marriage of Paul Petrovitch would be followed by the fall of Panin; who, on this event, received orders to leave the apartments which, as governor to the grand-duke, he had occupied in the palace. The courtiers began to shun him, and his friends took the alarm, when the generosity of his pupil averted the gathering storm. By his representations the empress was induced to change her designs; Panin, instead of a mandate to retire, received from Catherine a friendly letter, thanking him for the cares bestowed on the education of her son, and confirming him in his appointment of minister for foreign affairs. A few days previous to the nuptials, and on the anniversary of her coronation, she loaded him with emoluments and honours: he received in perpetuity an estate valued at 7000 *l.* a-year; a pension for life to an equal amount; and an appointment of half the sum for the conduct of his department; with the choice of any house in Petersburg to be purchased as his residence; also an allowance of 35,000 *l.* for plate and furniture. A proportional munificence was displayed to every officer of the duke's late household.

Among the men of letters with whom Catherine regularly corresponded, Voltaire and Diderot

CATHERINE II.   91

were the most distinguished: pressed by her to visit Petersburg, the former, experienced in courts, declined the dangerous honour. Diderot was more complaisant, and received during his stay in Russia liberal proofs of the bounty of the empress; she discoursed with him daily, at the conclusion of dinner, on subjects of policy, philosophy, and legislation. While, with eloquence and enthusiasm, he unfolded his principles on the rights and liberties of nations, the empress sat beside him, and listened with apparent pleasure. The rectitude of her understanding rendered her sensible to the charms of a theory, from the practice of which she was withheld by stronger motives. ' Monsieur Diderot,' said she, ' is in some respects an hundred years old, but in others no more than ten:' a fine compliment, which implied a combination of the wisdom of a sage, with the innocence and simplicity of a child.

Of Voltaire, perhaps as the dispenser of fame, she ever spoke with singular respect and deference. In her letters to this celebrated writer, she artfully courted those eulogiums which he so lavishly bestowed. In a letter, dated the 2d of August, 1771, she thus expresses herself: "Now we are speaking of haughtiness, I have a mind to confess to you. I have had great successes during

this war, of which I am glad, as you will conclude. I have said Russia will be known by this
war.—It will be seen that we possess men of
merit—that we are not deficient in resources, &c.
Full of these ideas, I have not once thought on
Catherine, who, at the age of forty-two, can improve neither in body nor mind, but in the order
of things must remain as she is. Do her affairs
prosper ? so much the better. Did they prosper
less, she would exert all her faculties to put them
in better train. This is my ambition. I have no
other. I wish for the sparing of human blood. I
sincerely wish for peace. The Turks desire it
from different motives, but know not how to set
about it. I desire equally the pacification of the
unreasonable contentions of Poland. But I have
to do with brainless heads, who by caprice and
levity throw impediments in the way. My embassador has, by a declaration, tried to open their
eyes. But rather than adopt a consistent line of
conduct, they choose to expose themselves to the
last extremity. The vortices of Descartes exist
only in Poland, &c.—Do not scold your rustics
for having sent me a surplus of watches: the expence will not ruin me. Judge not of our finances
by those of the ruined potentates of Europe.
Though we have for three years been engaged in

CATHERINE II. 93

a war, we proceed in our buildings, and every thing goes on as in a time of profound peace.—I am satisfied when I meet with your approbation. I have been reading again my instructions, to which much yet remains to be done, before they are brought to the perfection at which I aim, &c.— The khan of the Crimea will perhaps in a little time be brought to me in person.—Should he come, we will endeavour to polish him.—To take my revenge on him, I will make him dance, and go to the French comedy. When about to fold up this letter, I received yours of the 10th of July, in which you inform me of the adventure that happened to my Instructions in France. I knew the anecdote, and even its appendix, in consequence of the order of the duke de Choiseul. I confess that I laughed on reading it in the newspaper, and found that I was amply revenged."

The successes of the Turkish war excited in the minds of the people, who rejoiced at the humiliation of the oriental pride, a lively attachment to their sovereign. To perpetuate the memory of their victories, Catherine caused medals to be struck and columns to be erected. The advantages gained by the Russians in a new campaign, determined the Porte to sue for peace. The plenipotentiaries having met, Russia persisted

in its former demands, to which the Turks at
length agreeing, the preliminaries of the treaty
were mutually signed. Russia obtained the free
navigation of the Ottoman seas, and the passage
of the Dardanelles, with the independence of the
Krimea, a clause most severely felt by the Turks;
also a tract of land between the Bohg and the
Dniepr; a sum of money to defray the expences
of the war; and the title for Catherine, hitherto
refused to her, of Padishah or empress.

The czarina, by these stipulations, weakened
the enemy while she increased her power: the
commerce of the Euxine and the mart of the Levant opened to her an immense source of riches:
the protection granted to the Tartars furnished the
means of dividing them, and of conquering their
country: while the acquisition of the Ukraine afforded her the means of overawing the Ottoman
empire, and completing the ruin of Poland. In
a word, she beheld her influence and reputation
extending throughout Europe.

On the confirmation of a peace so advantageous, joy and festivity prevailed at Petersburg: eight days were by the order of Catherine
devoted to public rejoicing: rewards were distributed in the spirit of her usual magnificence, while
the prison-doors were set open to all not attainted

CATHERINE II. 95

of high-treason, that the wretched might share in the general joy. Even the miserable exiles languishing in Siberia were in this season of prosperity not forgotten: an order was issued from the sovereign for the liberation of all such as had been condemned since the year 1746.

Amidst all these external appearances, a gangrene corroded the heart of the empire: the finances were in a state of dilapidation: the succours received from England were at the expence of immense advantages granted to their commerce: the pestilence had ravaged the nation, devoured the armies, and penetrated to the fleets: the provinces were a prey to revolt, which even threatened Moscow; while an extraordinary emigration had changed into a desert once flourishing and commercial countries.

The court of Petersburg, while occupied by these important concerns, forgot not its pleasures and intrigues. The empress passed from the council to the ball-room, and from the senate to the theatre. She gave audience to the ministers of foreign powers, received her courtiers, dictated a law, and wrote a billet with equal grace and facility. Satisfied in her new attachments, she appeared not to remember those that were past. Orloff, after travelling five months, suddenly re-

CATHERINE II.

appeared at Petersburg: his enemies were alarmed; but Catherine, refusing to admit him to her presence, sent him orders to repair to Revel: he was at the same time presented with considerable presents; while his friends were received by the empress with honours and favour. Her motives for a conduct apparently so magnanimous, were to oppose the party of her former favourite to a faction which she had reason to dread was forming under the sanction of the name of the grand-duke.

Victorious over her enemies, respected by Europe, adored by her courtiers, the mind of Catherine was nevertheless a prey to the most poignant disquietudes. While she formed projects for the aggrandisement of her dominions, she trembled for her throne and her life. But, dissembling her feelings, she spoke with confidence of the long career she expected to run: nor did she ever shew herself more tranquil and composed, than one day after finding in her cabinet a paper which gave her notice of a threatened assassination. Ambition enabled her to conquer her emotions, and to preserve self-possession in the most trying and critical circumstances. Whatever might be her sentiments, she always wore the appearance of gentleness, sincerity, clemency, and generosity. The blood of Ivan yet reeked from the ground:

CATHERINE II. 97

Catherine, moved at the fate of a family from which she had no longer any thing to fear, offered liberty to the duke, with the means of retiring into Germany. ' Why should I go,' answered the prince, ' out of the Russian empire, to publish the excess of my miseries, and to excite an useless compassion ?'

The place of favourite, vacated by the banishment of Orloff, had been for some time filled by his successor, who, using his influence with moderation, provoked no enemies: Catherine, praising the prudence of this conduct in her lover, appeared daily more attached to him; when suddenly, in the career of his favour, an order was brought to him to depart to Moscow. He obeyed the mandate, and fresh presents rewarded his docility. His favour had continued during the term of two-and-twenty months.

At this instant, whether secretly recalled from Revel, or wearied of his exile, Orloff once more appeared at court. No censures were thrown on his conduct; 'he was received, on the contrary, with an appearance of pleasure. Elated with the behaviour of the empress, and the recollection of past favours, he doubted not of being able to resume his honours and his influence; which, while possessed, he appeared to contemn, and of which the loss only had taught him the value. Born in obscurity, and trained up in the barracks, his sudden elevation, while it had inflated his pride, had neither altered his taste nor polished his manners : eleven years passed near the person of the empress, in the elegance of luxury and the refinements of voluptuousness, had neither reformed the coarseness of his mind, nor deprived him of his hardy habits. In possession, since his dismissal from his post, of a princely revenue, he yet led the life of an officer in garrison ; he kept an ordinary table, and ate with the commensals of the court : in his amours he was still less delicate ; the emotions excited in his mind by a squalid Finn, a savage Kalmuck, or a court beauty, were in no repect dissimilar.

Jealous of the authority enjoyed by his rivals, and contemplating with envy the throne to which he had aspired, he demanded of the empress to be re-established in his functions, and that he whom he accused as the instrument of his disgrace, the minister count Panin, should be sent into exile. Catherine, in whose heart Orloff appeared to have regained his ascendancy, hesitated not to restore to him his employments : to the banishment of Panin she however refused her assent.

CATHERINE II.　　99

During this period the buildings and embellish-
ments of Petersburg had proceeded without interruption; while works of imperial magnificence
gave dignity and fame to the city. But sumptuous
bridges, palaces, and public offices, were yet contrasted, in the eye of the stranger, with dirty
lanes and wretched huts: the renovation of a
city must necessarily be slow, and its progress
gradual to order and improvement. The various
benevolent and patriotic institutions, planned by
the empress, required new buildings, in the erection of which magnificence and taste were equally
consulted. Moscow, Iver, Toula, Kief, with other
cities, grew also under her forming hand.

Catherine had, in the midst of the Turkish
war, purchased pictures in Holland to the amount
of 60,000 rubles, a collection unfortunately lost,
by the wreck of the vessel in which they were
conveyed, on the Finland coast: others were
brought from France; and from Italy numerous
curiosities and antiques. By her liberality to
Diderot, whose library she purchased at a price
above its value, and returned to its owner, whom,
with a large annual stipend, she appointed librarian, Catherine gained the esteem of literary men.
The expenditure of her court establishment, without including her numerous and magnificent pre-

sents, was reckoned annually at 4,000,000 rubles. The court of Petersburg had, during the reign of the empress, become the most brilliant in Europe; the resort of talents, of wealth, and of accomplishments. The favourites of Catherine were not suffered to influence her in affairs of state. Orloff and Panin held their places in opposition and in defiance of each other. The princess Dashkoff had, after a long absence, appeared again at Petersburg, where she received from the empress a present of 60,000 rubles; and, with other marks of favour, the post of director of the academy of sciences. Panin filled under the empress and her son the most important places, in which he acquired the esteem of both : integrity and indolence were the qualities peculiarly ascribed to him by the public. In his last illness, the tears of his imperial pupil manifested his own sensibility, and the worth of the tutor.

By an impartial observer, who saw her in 1772 and 1773, the empress is thus described. " She is of that stature which is necessary to the perfect elegance of the female form*. Her eyes are blue, large and fine; her eye-brows and hair brown; her mouth well proportioned; her chin

---

* It would be somewhat difficult to fix the standard.

CATHERINE II. 101

round; her nose rather long; her forehead regular and open; her hands and arms round and
white; her complexion not perfectly clear; her
shape rather full; her neck and bosom high; the
air of her head full of grace and dignity. She
rouges high, according to the Russian custom:
she adopts as the model of her dress the usual
habit of the Russian ladies, with some slight alterations which render it tasteful and becoming.
Her rich clothes are reserved for solemn festivals,
when her head and corset are entirely set with
brilliants. In grand processions she wears a crown
of diamonds and precious stones. Her gait is majestic; her form and manner noble and dignified:
in a circle of ladies, though without external distinction, she would be immediately recognised as
chief. In her aspect, and in the features of her
face, authority and command are expressed. In
her character there is more liveliness than gravity:
her manners are gentle, courteous, beneficent, and
extremely devout. She rises at six in the morning, and frequently, even in the depth of winter,
earlier. Without calling any person, she prepares
her own breakfast: she dislikes personal attendance, and dispenses with it as much as possible.
The business of her toilet, during which she signs
orders and commissions of various purport, lasts

not long. Those days on which the council does not meet, she employs herself in her cabinet from eight till eleven; thence she proceeds to chapel, where the service occupies an hour. From twelve till one she receives the ministers of the several departments, and sits down to dinner at half past one; after which she employs herself again for an hour or two as business may require. She then walks, rides on horseback, in a coach, or on a sledge. At six she appears at the theatre, where the drama is performed alternately in Russ and French. If she sups in public, which happens but rarely, the meal is never protracted later than half past ten; usually she retires at ten. Excepting holidays, Sunday is the only court day in the week. On the morning of this day, as the empress passes from chapel to her apartments, the embassadors and foreigners of rank, who have been once presented, receive her hand to kiss: such persons also who have any petitions, or who are desirous to return thanks for favours received, are on this day presented to the empress, whose hand they kiss on one knee. The court begins at six in the evening. A ball or a concert is at the same time usually given. The empress never dances, but sits down to cards, having previously informed the chamberlain in waiting whom she

CATHERINE II.   103

chooses to be of her party. She generally chooses piquet, or some other game at which silence is not necessary. A semi-circle is formed round her card-table, beginning on the left hand with the ladies, and closing on the right with the privy-counsellors. When the game is concluded, the empress rises, and converses indiscriminately with those who form her circle. At ten, and sometimes earlier, she breaks up the party, and retires without form through a side-door. Such is the ordinary routine of her conduct through the winter months, when the court is at Petersburg. When the empress is at Tzar-sko-selo, no court, except on extraordinary festivals, is held.

" Of civil processes, criminal causes, &c. nothing is referred to the empress during the hours of the forenoon, which are allotted to conferences with the minister: but, without previous information delivered to her, no person can be condemned to death ; this punishment is almost always commuted or mitigated. All business relative to the army, navy, finances, taxes, &c. are reported to her by the chiefs of the several departments. Acquainted with all that concerns the administration of government, the empress, in state affairs, acts from herself. As she never interferes in the private concerns of her household, she has sufficient time for public business. The regularity and uniformity with which she apportions her hours, allow her leisure for writing, conversation, company, and exercise. Her constitution is robust and healthy : her mind active, tranquil, and cheerful."

With a view of introducing the practice of inoculation into the remoter parts of the empire, Catherine instituted hospitals in various provinces, even to the extremities of Asia, where it has been since practised with uniform success.

The prosperity of the empress seemed to have reached its height : the horizon was overcast with clouds ; the storm murmured at a distance ; every thing menaced a reverse of fortune. The ancient nobility, disgusted at the arrogance of the favourites, openly murmured ; the clergy cherished vengeance for the loss of their privileges ; while the people groaned under numerous oppressions. The peasants beholding their children successively torn from them to recruit the armies, mowed down by the sword, or perishing by the pestilence, became desperate and outrageous. The Kozacs of the Don gave the first signal of revolt ; several provinces followed, who wanted but a skilful leader to give a new turn to the empire.

A report was spread by the priests that Peter

CATHERINE II. 105

III. was still living, and would quickly appear to reclaim his rights. Several impostors had, under the same pretence, already appeared, and suffered the reward of their temerity : these tragical farces were the prelude of scenes still more sanguinary and threatening. Catherine was destined to witness, in an open rebellion and civil war, the greatest calamity that had yet befallen the empire since her accession to the throne.

Ikhelman Pugatcheff, the son of a Kozac, born at a village on the borders of the Don, having served in several campaigns in the capacity of a soldier, applied for his dismissal from the army : on being refused, he fled to Poland, where he lay some time concealed by some hermits of the Greek confession. In a conversation with these recluses respecting his various adventures, he one day related to them, that when in the army, a Russian officer, after attentively regarding him, had said to him earnestly, 'If the emperor, Peter III. my master, was not dead, I should believe that I once more saw him in you.' The hermits listened to this account without apparent interest ; but some time after, one of their comrades, whom Pugatcheff had not yet seen, suddenly exclaimed, ' Is not that the emperor, Peter III ?' From this time the monks found little difficulty in seducing

him to their purpose. Having prepared their instrument, the impostor, assuming the garb of a
patriarch, and the external of sanctity, supported
by the numerous sectaries of the Greek religion,
began with the air of an apostle to court popularity, and to bestow his benedictions upon the
people. Under the name of the late emperor,
he affected to abjure all interested views, profess-
ing that, weaned from the vanities of the world,
he had devoted his life to piety; that his purpose
was but to place on the throne his dear son, when
he would again retire to the occupations of a her-
mit. These pretences, however gross, his appeal
to the sympathy of the people, with the marvelous
circumstances of his tale, procured him a crowd
of followers. Apprehensive of being detected as
a deserter, he fled to the Kozacs of the banks of
the Yaik, communicated to them his design of
putting himself at the head of a party, and engaged them to accompany him to the mountains
of Caucasus, with an assurance that they would
there find powerful succours. He had not yet
announced himself to them as Peter III.

At Malkoffska he was seized while disposing the
people to revolt, imprisoned, and sent to Kasan to
take his trial. In prison he was visited by the
priests, who furnished him with money, which

CATHERINE II.

having employed in corrupting his guards, he contrived to escape. Having rejoined his old comrades, he penetrated into the desert, where his adherents daily increased. When he conceived his party sufficiently strong, he publicly declared himself to be Peter III., delivered by a miracle out of the hands of his assassins. A soldier who resembled him had, he pretended, been substituted as a victim in his stead : the report of his death, he added, had been fabricated by the court to quiet the people, and to reconcile them to the usurpation. The Kozacs on the borders of the Caspian, a credulous and ignorant race, received this intelligence with honest joy : religious differences with the established faith increased their attachment to their supposed master; whose cause, as it flattered their superstitions, and imposed on their simplicity, they embraced with zeal and ardor.

In the middle of September, 1773, Pugatcheff began his operations. It belongs not to the design of this work minutely to describe his progress; the cruelties which he exercised on several persons of rank who fell into his power, his marches from place to place, his sieges, his battles, and his conquests. The moderation which he at first affected was changed by success to the most sa-

vage brutality : whole hordes, allured by his victories and the hope of plunder, flocked to his
standard : the revolt spread over the provinces,
which it ravaged as a torrent.

Pugatcheff, for a season, strictly adhered to the
lessons of the hermits, and continued to wear the
mask of religion and humility; but, intoxicated
by the rapidity of his successes, he at length threw
off a constraint which he had impatiently endured,
gave a scope to his brutal passions and sanguinary
temper, cooled the enthusiasm of his disciples,
gave time to his adversaries to collect their
strength, and suffered a check in the midst of his
career.

The spirit of rebellion had reached to Moscow, the garrison of which consisted of only six
hundred men : Pugatcheff, by presenting himself
before it, must inevitably have become master of
the place. He neglected his advantage, and by
his negligence lost, with the second city of the
empire, an army of 100,000 vassals, who waited
his arrival to escape from bondage. He wasted
the greater part of the winter in useless sieges :
before Orenburg, he exterminated with the sabre
all the officers and gentry of the country, whose
families were involved in the promiscuous carnage:
he professed himself determined to shed to its

CATHERINE II. 109

last drop the blood of a haughty and despotic nobility. While he thus inhumanly butchered the nobles, he conferred, with curious inconsistency, their vacant titles and ensigns of honour on those of his partisans in whom he most confided. He alienated a number of his adherents by violating those religious principles of which he had affected to be the zealot: though a husband and a father, he had the effrontery to take another wife, a woman of abandoned character, and to celebrate his nuptials with a bacchanal licentiousness.

Catherine, alarmed at a rebellion that menaced her throne, seriously prepared to check its progress. General Bibikoff was recalled from the frontiers of Turkey, and ordered to march, with a considerable army, against the insurgents. Manifestoes were published, which followed close on each other; deserters were invited back to the imperial standard, an amnesty promised, and a reward of 100,000 rubles set upon the head of the usurper.

Pugatcheff, on his side, spared not declarations, to which he affixed the name of Peter III. By one of his manifestoes he affranchised all the boors: he caused rubles to be struck with his effigy and this inscription, " Peter III. emperor

and autocrator of all the Russias:" on the reverse, " Redivivus et Ultor."

The nobles joined the imperial general, bloody
and desperate conflicts ensued, the rebels increased in number and in arrogance, and ravaged an
extent of country of more than six hundred leagues.
The ferocious intrepidity of the insurgents appeared to be directed by officers of superior skill :
in one of these encounters the Russian general
lost his life. The contest continued with various
success ; the steps of the rebel chief were tracked
in blood, and his laurels stained with the most atrocious cruelty. In the town of Dmitrefsk, which
was surrendered by treachery, the governor was,
by his order, impaled alive. The astronomer
Lovitch, member of the imperial academy of
sciences, being employed in the neighbourhood in
taking levels for a canal projected between the
Don and the Volga, was, by the commands of
Pugatcheff, brought into his presence, when he
ordered him to be lifted on the pikes of the soldiers, for the purpose, as he expressed it (adding
insult to barbarity), of being nearer the stars,
and then caused him to be cut in pieces by
the Kozacs. In this monstrous atrocity and
savage insolence the empress perceived her
safety.

CATHERINE II. 111

A peace being concluded between the Russians and the Turks, fresh troops under the command of general Panin (the brother of the minister), were dispatched against the rebels; with these reinforcements their convoys were cut off, their armies deprived of provision, and an attack made upon them, when, loaded with baggage, and encumbered with women, they were entangled in the intricate passes of a mountain. Notwithstanding these disadvantages, they refused to submit; numbers fell on the spot, while many perished in the precipices, and among the steep and rugged rocks, where they sought a refuge. Pugatcheff, having kept the field till all means of defence failed, swam over the Volga, crossed the desert, and found himself nearly at the place where he had first raised the standard of revolt. Here he was joined by many of his friends; but hunger, fatigue, and disappointment, had caused more to abandon him. His power of disturbing the empire was by no means exhausted, when treachery stepped in to precipitate his fall. Antizoff, a chief of the Kozacs, his confident and friend, fell into the hands of the imperial army, who employed his consequence among his people in reducing the Kozacs to obedience.

But to the exertions of colonel Mikelson,

CATHERINE II.

Russia was more peculiarly indebted for its deliverance. This officer, in pursuit of the rebels, suffered almost incredible fatigues; pursuing his march over deserts of trackless snow, without a guide, without succours, and at times nearly without food. In a few months, in the most inclement season, he traversed, with his small band, over the space of 7000 versts. Supported by the confidence his prudence and his bravery had acquired among his troops, always bold, and always victorious, he encountered the rebels, however numerous, wherever they were to be met. The wasted army of the insurgents was shut up by Mikelson in a desert, 500 versts in length, behind Tzaritzin, where distress and famine opened their eyes.

While the miserable chief was in this condition, gnawing the bones of a horse, some of the principal of the Kozacs, running up to him, exclaimed—'Thou hast been long enough emperor!' Pugatcheff, firing a pistol, shattered the arm of the foremost; the rest, having bound him, carried their prisoner over the desert to their seat on the Yaïk, where they sent to the commandant of the place, informing him 'of what they had done. Hence he was at length delivered over to general Panin, when Mikelson, who was still pursuing the enemy through the deserts, received

CATHERINE II. 113

news of his capture. On this intelligence, having conducted his troops to Saratoff, and left them to repose after their fatigues, he repaired to Panin, from whom he experienced a generous and noble reception; and whence Catherine recalled him to bestow on him the recompence of his services and his merit. Thus terminated a rebellion which cost the empire 100,000 men. Pugatcheff was, by the order of the general, conveyed in an iron cage to Moscow, together with several of his principal accomplices.

The empress, informed of what had past, appointed a commission, in unison with the senate, for the trial of the impostor. It was recommended to the judges to be satisfied with the confession of his guilt without applying the torture, and without exacting the names of his accomplices. The czarina dreaded the obligation of multiplying punishments, which might involve the nation in new calamities. The sentence passed on Pugatcheff was, to lose both his hands and feet; and, having been shewn to the people in this condition, to be quartered alive. This horrid sentence was not fulfilled; whether by an order from the empress, or by the mistake of the executioner, the criminal was first mercifully decapitated, after which his body, divided into quarters, was exposed in different parts of the city; five of his accomplices suffered with him; three were hanged, and eighteen, having undergone the knout, were banished to Siberia. Pugatcheff arrived at Moscow in September, 1774, and was executed in the January following. He acknowledged the justice of his sentence, the deception he had used, with his true name and condition, and submitted to his fate with undaunted resolution.

In the midst of these rapid and important events, Catherine, firm and self-possessed, calmly selected the most judicious measures, which she as resolutely applied : her sagacity and fortitude, on the most trying occasions, secured her authority, commanded the respect of her friends, and extorted admiration even from her enemies. In the convulsions which agitated the state, she forgot not its internal welfare : the arts of peace followed in her train, while of science and literature she continued the beneficent patroness. Shortly after the execution of Pugatcheff, a new occasion occurred for the display of her clemency; the public money had been embezzled, but the depredators were not even brought to trial. Catherine had, from the lessons of philosophy, conquered the impetuosity of her temper : ' What I cannot

CATHERINE II.

overthrow,' she was accustomed to say, ' I under-
mine and root up.' She had not been prevented
by the heavy burthens of foreign and domestic
war from taking off most of the taxes that had
been levied for their support; a number of the
ancient taxes, considered as burthensome to agriculture, or partially oppressive, were also abolished. It seemed as if the resources of the government increased with its expences. In the same
spirit of policy and benevolence, large sums were
lent out, interest free, for a specified term of years,
to those provinces which the revolt had ravaged;
while a strict prohibition was laid against any re-
criminations or reproaches on the subject, which
was condemned to perpetual oblivion.

Various other regulations were also established,
in a spirit equally enlightened: pernicious distinc-
tions were weakened, ruinous monopolies destroyed, the severity of punishments mitigated,
impolitic restrictions removed, absurd prejudices
softened, and mankind brought nearer to an
equitable equality in the several ranks of society.
A pardon was granted to criminals who, by long-
suffering, had already expiated their guilt; imprisoned debtors were, in certain circumstances,
and under certain limitations, released from confinement: the heirs of debtors to the crown were

wholly discharged from their bonds and obligations. The affairs of Russia were conducted on a liberal system, and all her acts were in a great style: she sat between Europe and Asia, often dictator to both, as a rising empire, not yet arrived at the summit of its growth, with vigor and animation circulating through every part.

Ambition, the vice of strong minds, was that of Catherine's; the period of peace left her not the leisure which it had at first seemed to promise; too large a share of her attention was engrossed and absorbed by foreign affairs. Alliances, guarantees, leagues, preparations, plans for future enterprises, all which the thirst of power can suggest, alternately engaged her thoughts; if she forgot not the interest of her people, if new life and improved organisation rose beneath her forming hand, this external attention disturbed the tranquillity of the nation, and again kindled a war, which, though triumphantly concluded, emptied the exchequer and wasted the force of the nation. A generous scorn of foreign fame would have reflected on the empress a truer and more lasting reputation.

But, amidst the dreams of ambition, she neglected not the security and happiness of the empire, by an attention to the regulation of its civil police: Peter the Great had done much for his

CATHERINE II. 117

country, but it remained for Catherine to give to Russia a constitution. The ordinances out of which it arose, acknowledging the rights of mankind, breathe throughout a wise, a benign, and an enlightened spirit. The public security of Petersburg was great in proportion to its population and extent: robberies and murders were seldom known in the city; the passenger, at all hours in the night, and in the most obscure parts, might walk in safety. The police of Petersburg is a simple and competent system, in which there is no spies: it is also peculiarly obnoxious to gaming; no sports or games are allowed, except such as require bodily exertion and dexterity, or consist of a due proportion of skill and hazard. In prohibited games the police has regard to the motive of the gamester; all complaints and demands relative to play debts are declared null. No tax, corrupting the principles of the people, in the form of a lottery, is permitted in the Russian empire. Work is found with facility in Petersburg, in which no beggars were to be seen, the high price of labour leaving indigence without excuse. For those really incapable of procuring a subsistence, a poor-house, on an excellent plan, was provided. A house of correction was likewise appointed for delinquents condemned to labour, in which their punishment was rendered beneficial to the state.

It would be greatly exceeding the limits of the present work, which have, in this interesting life, been already encroached upon, to extend the details of the various institutions and regulations of Catherine, for the better security of the lives, the health, the morals, and the property of her people. Every law, promulgated by the autocratic authority, and subscribed by the empress, must be transmitted to the police-office, and entered, with its particulars, in the proper books. If it be sent for publication, the crown-advocate of the police office is called, and his legal opinion taken; if any doubtful point appear, it must be represented in the place appointed; if none arise, a resolution is made concerning its publication. The preceding faint sketch may suffice to give a general outline of the ordinances and conduct of a *despotic* sovereign. It is thus that the most unnatural and odious prerogatives are ameliorated by an enlightened mind.

Gregory Orloff had been from policy reinstated by Catherine in his post of favourite; but a passion once extinguished is rarely revived: she lavished on him favours, but to the possession of her affections nothing could restore him. The

CATHERINE II.   119

dismission of Vassiltschikoff had not, as he believed, been a sacrifice to Orloff. On the day of
the revolution of 1762, Catherine had been struck
by the gallantry and noble air of Potemkin, a
young officer, who, riding up, as she mounted her
horse, had presented her with the plume from his
hat. The empress having resolved at length to
become better acquainted with him, he had found
means to secure an ascendancy over her heart.
Elate with success, his pride and presumption,
which had kept pace with his prosperity, received
at length a severe check. One day being engaged
at billiards with the brother of Orloff, he impru-
dently boasted of the favour he enjoyed with
Catherine ; while he asserted, with arrogance, that
it depended only on him to remove from the
court any persons whom he disliked. Alexius
Orloff answered his boast with disdain ; a quarrel
ensued between them, which led to blows, the
consequence of which to Potemkin was the loss
of an eye. Nor was this his only disaster ; Gregory Orloff, informed of what had past, hastened
to the empress, and requested of her the removal
of his presumptuous rival.

Potemkin retired to Smolensk, his native city,
where, remaining a year in solitude, he expiated
his vanity and folly. At the end of that period he

was recalled by the empress, in consequence of his contrition and entreaties, and reinstated at court, whence the reproaches of his rival proved insufficient to remove him.

The post of favourite had been, during the preceding reigns, for many years in Russia an established court etiquette: it was the business of the person on whom this office was bestowed, and who occupied an apartment in the palace, to attend the empress on parties of amusement, at the opera, at balls, and promenades; nor was he allowed to leave the palace but by express permission. When his attendance became no longer agreeable, he had orders to travel; but was assured of finding, at the place of his destination, a consolation for his dismission in the munificence of his sovereign.

It ought to be observed, in justice to Catherine, that since the sword had been sheathed in Poland, her conduct had been, compared with that of Prussia and Austria, moderate and just; instead of new and endless claims, she had observed the treaties; she had even been the advocate and mediatrix of this injured people, and preserved them from farther outrages. Some time after the conclusion of the peace with Turkey, she had remitted to the king of Poland, as a compensation for that part of his dominions which had fallen into her hands, 250,000 rubles. Commissioners were appointed to settle the limits between the territories of the republic and the partitioning powers; but the demands of the latter were too exorbitant to admit an adjustment. An unlimited toleration on religious subjects, the leading principle of the court of Petersburg, was more particularly insisted upon by the empress, as a measure which both policy and justice required.

In tranquillity, abroad and at home, Catherine employed herself in cultivating the arts of peace, in the improvement of the country, and in enlightening the minds of the nation. In these occupations Potemkin became so useful as to acquire an influence almost despotic. To him the courtiers looked as to the source of honours, and the people as the dispenser of benefits: nor did he fail to abuse his good fortune. The empress studied to preserve the peace between her favourite and the Orloffs, whose petition to retire was rejected, lest they should carry with them sentiments that might become dangerous to the empire. Gregory Orloff, piqued and incensed at this refusal, expostulated with Catherine, and recalled to her remembrance his boasted services, his fidelity, and his zeal. Having listened with temper to his complaints, she soothed his resentment, and assured him that the empress was always his friend. She wished, by opposing him to the petulance of his rival, to check the presumption of Potemkin, and to balance them against each other.

Orloff experienced new mortification in the resolution of the empress to visit Moscow, a measure advised by his rival, and against which he remonstrated in vain. Aware of the bigotry of the provinces through which she must pass, Catherine disdained not to flatter the popular superstitions : she carried with her a number of small figures of saints, which she caused to be distributed among the churches and chapels on the road. A large picture, richly decorated with gold and diamonds, was also prepared for the cathedral at Moscow, and, placed on a carriage, followed in the train of the empress. Six hundred men from each regiment of guards, who had preceded her arrival at the ancient metropolis, drawn up in arms, waited to receive her.

Catherine entered Moscow, under triumphal arches, with a brilliant retinue, amidst a crowd of spectators : order and magnificence prevailed on every side. The populace, more surprised than

CATHERINE II.   123

affected, exhibited no symptoms of joy. All was silent, though a diminution of imposts had been proclaimed previous to the ceremony. But the homage which was withheld from the mother was lavished upon the son. It is pretended, that a courtier, struck with the contrast, thus address-ed the duke, into whose sentiments he wished to penetrate : ' Your imperial highness sees how much you are beloved. Oh ! if you would . . . . .' Paul, to his honour, is said to have answered this insinuation only by a severe look. Some days after her arrival at Moscow, Catherine performed a pilgrimage on foot, attended by her court, to a convent situated forty versts from the city. Count Panin only was omitted in the invitation to this act of devotion.

Panin had become negligent of his duties both as a courtier and minister : Potemkin, who, in succeeding to the post of Orloff, had succeeded to his ambition, took advantage of this remissness to prejudice him in the favour of the empress. The favourite, who aspired to the hand and throne of Catherine, stood in awe of the frankness and in-fluence of the minister.

With these views Potemkin, whose disregard and contempt of religion had been notorious, suddenly assumed the exterior of piety. At the

G 2

beginning of Lent, to the astonishment of the court, he renounced those luxuries to which he had been attached, and practised the most rigid austerity. He confessed regularly every day, and wearied the saints with prayer : his table was furnished with roots, and his drink was water. To the confessor of Catherine, to whom he chose to unburthen his transgressions, he disclosed the scruples of his conscience respecting his intercourse with the empress, since it had not received the sanction of the church. The monk, from whatever motive, entered into the views of his penitent, and acquitted himself of the commission he had received. Catherine, perceiving the source of this pretended delicacy, sent for Potemkin, to whom she addressed herself with mingled tenderness and firmness. She gave him to understand, without entering into any explanations, that, notwithstanding her regard for him, she was still mistress of her passions ; and that if he was no longer disposed to fill the post of favourite, she could resolve without difficulty to put another in his place.

Potemkin, confounded and abashed, was unable to conceal his vexation : he talked of taking orders, and causing himself to be consecrated archbishop. But the empress returned to Petersburg ; the new

CATHERINE II. 125

convert followed in her train, and left at Moscow his resentment and his scruples.

During the stay of Catherine in the ancient capital, marshal Romantzoff returned in triumph from the Turkish war, of which he had been the hero. He was received with distinction as the most illustrious supporter of the throne, covered with honours, and laden with benefits. Rewards apportioned to their rank and merit, and to the munificence of the sovereign, were distributed among his officers, with large gold medals struck for the occasion. Several noblemen were at the same time recalled from their exile in Siberia. Various taxes were abolished and regulations planned, in a spirit of true policy, beneficence, and wisdom. The empire was divided, for the better administration of the laws, into governments or viceroyalties; the interior provinces were also by this measure refined and civilised: the rich salaries and example of the civil officers, the erection of a public theatre, and other incitements to improvement in dress and manners, gradually softened the national ferocity. In this division of the empire its old constitutions were completely altered; all was simple, uniform, and novel.

Two institutes in every government-department

are deserving of mention: the college of general provision, which took cognisance of affairs relative to schools, infirmaries, work-houses, mad-houses, &c. and the court of conscience, which, in cases where judicial proofs were not to be had, pronounced according to equity, and before which the governor himself might be cited by the most obscure individual. Every college had its peculiar members, and the members their stated rank; an exact gradation, which contributed to the maintenance of order, prevailed through the whole. The inhabitants of distant provinces in this immense empire had, before the appointment of these institutions, been compelled to travel to Moscow or Petersburg in pursuit of justice. A right was however preserved to the appealing party, to refer the cause adjudged by the provincial tribunal to the senates, or to the council of the sovereign. If the original judgment was in this case confirmed, the appellant forfeited a fine. Joy was diffused among the inhabitants of Siberia, and their commerce revived, which languished under the scarcity of a circulating medium, by the establishment of a bank.

The attention of Catherine was more especially occupied by extending and encouraging the general trade of the empire, which she justly considered as the foundation of her greatness. No im-

CATHERINE II. 127

portant change had, since the conclusion of the war, taken place in Poland: under the order preserved by the strong grasp of power, the country began to recover from devastation : its plains once more rewarded the labours of the husbandman. The moderation of the court of Petersburg produced some effect on the conduct of its allies, who relaxed from their former rigor and violence. To excite emulation, and to confer a dignity on those of her subjects who should devote themselves to commerce, Catherine published an edict, or ukause of grace, freeing them from the capitation, and the necessity of drawing lots for supplying recruits to the army and navy : the free boors were also permitted, on condition of paying one *per cent.* annually to the crown for the capital which they should employ in traffic, to enrol themselves in one of the mercantile classes. With the same commercial views, the treaty with England was renewed : the empress was also declared patroness of industry and agriculture. New manufactories were, by her direction and encouragement, every-where established ; workmen were employed to rebuild the villages, and repair the devastation of the late rebellion : happy had it been for Russia if those to whom Catherine entrusted the execution of her plans had imbibed a portion of her own enlightened spirit!

The advantages offered to foreigners, added to the inducement of an unlimited religious toleration, contributed to people those vast deserts, which, in many parts, required only cultivation, to become the sources of animal life and happiness. Twelve new colonies, comprehending more than 6000 families, were already established on the borders of the Volga. To facilitate the communication and commerce with China, endeavours were used to form a cultivated tract through the regions which separated the two empires.

The inhabitants of the newly acquired provinces having solicited to have their taxes remain on the former footing, Catherine, with a liberal policy, granted more than their request, and reduced their imposts to the half of their existing rates. Various other regulations were also established, which had for their end the security and happiness of the subject. The attention paid to the increase and improvement of the navy bespoke the design of government of advancing speedily into the first class of maritime powers. But of all the projects

CATHERINE II. 129

of Catherine, that of joining the remote and inland Caspian with the far-distant Frozen ocean
was the most stupendous: this plan, if ever executed, will exhibit an extraordinary instance of
human industry.

Though incessantly occupied with great designs, Catherine nevertheless found time for
amusements; if constant in her ambition, she was
fickle in her attachments; by those who admire
her as a sovereign, she cannot be defended as a
woman. While she continued to lavish benefits
and dignities upon Potemkin, her inclinations had
already selected another object. Zavadoffsky, a
young Ukrainian, was favoured in private with
the smiles of the empress. At first appointed her
secretary, he was shortly after openly preferred.
This arrangement gave occasion at court to a singular scene. It had been the invariable custom
for the discarded favourite, when superseded by
a rival, to receive orders to travel, and these orders, without excepting the ferocious Orloff, had
been as invariably obeyed. Potemkin only presumed to contemn them. On the day after he
had received this command, with which he at first
affected a compliance, he repaired to the palace,
and, with great tranquillity, placed himself opposite to the empress, as she was sitting down to

G 5

cards. Catherine, without appearing either discomposed or offended by his boldness, presented him with a card from the pack, observing, at the same time, that he always played with fortune: his departure was no more spoken of; he preserved his posts, his honours, and his interest, and from the lover became the friend of the empress. If the Ukrainer possessed the art of pleasing, Potemkin knew how to render himself useful; his talents, more analogous to the genius of Catherine, uninterruptedly preserved their ascendant.

Prince Orloff, presuming too suddenly on the disgrace of his rival, hastened to Petersburg, whence, having made his appearance and kissed the hand of his sovereign, he as hastily returned to Moscow. The courtiers were perplexed between the two favourites, to determine which was the happy lover; they could not be persuaded that Potemkin would surrender his interest in the affections of his mistress; they neglected to consider that love is with most men, after the first periods of youth, silent in the presence of ambition.

The party of Panin, whose habitual indolence had nearly degenerated into apathy, was solicitous that the grand-duke should lay claim to the throne, of which he was the rightful heir; but the mo-

CATHERINE II. 131

deration of Paul, and his reverence for his mother, impeded their views in his favour. Catherine was not on this subject free from inquietude, though she mistrusted the power of the prince rather than his inclinations. These fears were observed by the king of Prussia, who failed not to apply them to his own benefit. Aware of the effectual support which it was in his power to give to the duke, he used his advantage to bend the empress to his purposes. To preserve the friendship of Frederic, Catherine hesitated not to make many sacrifices.

The grand-duke had a friendship for count Razumoffsky, in whom he placed an entire confidence: the empress, acquainted with the enterprising spirit of the count, was alarmed at this intimacy, which she determined to break. With this view, she availed herself of some symptoms of intelligence which she had remarked between the count and the grand-duchess, to infuse suspicions into the mind of Paul. But the prince, unwilling to distrust his consort or his friend, withdrew not his kindness from the latter, while to the former he recommended a more cautious behaviour. The grand-duchess, however, whether already disposed to favour Razumoffsky, or piqued by the restraints laid upon her, continued privately to correspond with the count. It was even believed, that, from vindictive motives, she entered into political intrigues against the empress. Whatever might have been her views, a premature death precluded their development. She expired in childhood, and the circumstances of her fate reflected some imputations on the conduct of Catherine.

The czarina, overwhelmed by this event with real or pretended grief,, retired with the duke, whom a sincere affliction had seized, to Tzar-sko-selo. After the sorrow of Paul was somewhat calmed, he found, in searching among the papers of his deceased consort, letters from Razumoffsky, which he carried in wrath to his mother, whom he conjured to avenge herself upon a man who had thus dared to violate her commands. The empress yielded in part to the instances of her son; but, unwilling to punish with too much severity the son of a man to whom she was in a great degree indebted for the crown, contented herself with banishing him to Venice, under the title of her envoy-extraordinary. The count hesitated not to accept a mission, the motives of which were but too apparent. After remaining at Venice some time, he was appointed minister at Naples, where he resided when Paul, travelling

CATHERINE II. 133

into Italy, passed through the place, when the count was forbidden, on pain of death, to appear before him.

About this period (1776), prince Henry of Prussia, commissioned by his brother to confer with the empress on the affairs of Poland, made a second visit to Petersburg. In a conversation which took place between them, respecting the obstacles which still opposed themselves in Poland to the confederate powers, the prince, in reply to some objections raised by Catherine, thus expressed himself :—' Madam, there is one sure method of obviating every difficulty; a method which may perhaps, on the account of Poniatoffsky, be displeasing to you. Nevertheless you would do well to approve it, since a compensation may be offered to that monarch more valuable than a tottering throne :—The remainder of Poland must be partitioned.' The ambition of Catherine was gratified by the idea, and the annihilation of Poland was determined.

The death of the grand-duchess had left the empire without a successor to Paul, a matter of too much importance to be subject to the control of punctilio and form. The obsequies of her daughter-in-law were scarcely performed, when Catherine employed her thoughts on the selection of a new consort for her son. She informed the prince of Prussia, that, for this purpose, she had cast her eyes on his niece, the princess of Wirtemburg Stutgard. This lady was already betrothed to the hereditary prince of Hesse-Darmstadt; but her uncle, judging the alliance with Russia to be more advantageous, scrupled not to take measures for dissolving the contract.

Frederic entered with facility into the views of his brother, regardless of the attachment which subsisted between the young people : availing himself of his ascendancy over the mind of the prince, he persuaded him that his duty and reputation combined to demand of him the sacrifice of his passion. Every difficulty thus removed, the grand-duke was invited to pay a visit to Berlin, that he might judge in person of the qualifications of the lady.

Satisfied with these arrangements, Catherine made preparations, with her usual magnificence, for the departure of her son. Marshal Romantzoff was recalled on this occasion from his government in the Ukraine, and appointed to attend the duke to the court of Berlin :—' It is only,' said the empress, ' to the friendship of prince Henry, and to the most illustrious supporter of my throne, that I can consent to trust my son.'

CATHERINE II.   135

It was towards the close of summer when the duke, accompanied by prince Henry, quitted Petersburg: Catherine appeared much affected by their departure, and addressed to the travellers on their journey several letters. Paul received at Berlin the honours due to the heir of the Russian empire. He was presented by prince Henry to the king, who met them at the entrance of his apartment. At the conclusion of a speech studied for the occasion, the duke expressed his pleasure in having the opportunity of beholding ' the greatest of heroes, the admiration of the age, and the astonishment of posterity.' ' Instead of which,' interrupted the king, ' you see, my prince, a hoary-headed valetudinarian, who could never have wished for a superior happiness to that of welcoming within these walls the hopeful heir of a mighty empire, the only son of my best friend, the great Catherine.' The Prussian monarch then turning towards Romantzoff, welcomed politely the ' conqueror of the Ottomans.'

After half an hour's conversation with Frederic, the duke was conducted to the presence of the queen and the assembled court, among the ladies of which he beheld the princess of Wirtemburg. Prince Henry having, in the name of the empress of Russia, demanded in form the hand of the princess, the marriage contract took place on the same day. An extraordinary court, attended by the foreign ministers and every person of distinction, followed, when the whole company supped with the queen in great magnificence, and dined with her on the ensuing day. Feasts, entertainments, and military spectacles, succeeded. The troops of Frederic, to the delight of marshal Romantzoff, performed in their manœuvres an imitation of the battle of Kayal, when a complete victory was gained by the Russians over the Ottomans. Prince Henry afterwards accompanied the grand-duke to Rheinsburg, where he entertained him four days with scenes of festivity equally elegant and splendid. After quitting Rheinsburg, Paul took leave of the royal family, and, laden with presents, returned to Petersburg. Thither the princess soon followed him, and, having embraced the Greek religion with the usual formalities, adopted the name of Maria Feodorovna, and gave her hand to the duke. The marriage was celebrated with solemn pomp. Twenty years after, the imperial pair ascended together the throne of Russia.

Catherine, having given to her son a second consort, extended the bounds of her empire, and extinguished the flames of rebellion, might at

CATHERINE II.   137

length be expected to repose in tranquillity; but
quiet was little suited to her restless and enterprising temper.   Sacrificing to distinction, and thirsting for fame, when her armies had ceased to
astonish Europe with their conquests, she aspired
to other triumphs.   Her brilliant acts of munificence, her encouragement of the sciences and
arts, her liberalities to foreigners, and her numerous internal institutions, were re-echoed from
court to court, and celebrated in every nation.
The civilisation and improvement of Russia, re-
generated by Peter the Great, made rapid advances
during the reign of Catherine : by legislation and
the erection of schools she completed the plans
of her great predecessor, and carried them to an
extent upon principles, and in a period so near
his own, which it was not possible for him to
conceive.   Directed by her hand, the mass of
knowledge, which had been confined to Petersburg and kept for ostentation rather than for use,
distributed in a thousand channels, pervaded the
whole empire, fructifying the soil through which
it flowed.   According to an imperfect survey, in
thirty-one places of education 6800 children of
both sexes were trained up at the expence of
government.   The sums appropriated to this purpose are said to amount to 754,335 rubles per

annum.   But to return to the affairs of the
court.

Orloff, who had, without being recalled, come
back to Petersburg, became habituated to the pre-
eminence of Potemkin, who occupied the place
nearest the throne.   Proud of his influence and
insatiable of power, the latter left to Zavadoffsky
the quiet possession of the affections of Catherine.
For a year and a half this subaltern favourite appeared content with his fortune ; but ambition at
length divided his heart.   Fired by the example
of Potemkin, like him he aspired to pass from the
cabinet of the empress to the post of first minister.   But for this purpose it was necessary not
merely to possess the talents, but to supplant the
object of his envy, a project in which he engaged
with greater ardor than skill.   He began his operations by an attempt to render the despotism of
his rival odious to the sovereign, in which design
he obtained the concurrence of envious courtiers,
discontented officers, and artful women.   Potemkin, informed of these intrigues, and conscious of
his superior powers, resolved to crush at a blow a
competitor whom he despised.   An opportunity
for effecting this design soon presented itself.

Zoritch, a young Servian, an officer of the
hussars, possessed the qualities calculated to at-

CATHERINE II. 139

tract the notice of the empress : Potemkin gave
him a captain's commission, and threw him in her
way; the scheme failed not to prove successful
with the voluptuous and inconstant Catherine :
Zavadoffsky, who, like Phaeton, owed to his ambition his fall, was presently dismissed, and Zoritch
promoted to his place. Zavadoffsky, however,
departed not without the usual marks of the
bounty of his mistress. The new favourite, un-
educated and inexperienced, could give no umbrage to the haughty minister ; content with his
advantages in the favour of Catherine, he used
his influence but in the service of his benefactor.
It was with Potemkin only that the empress balanced the concerns of Europe.

An account of the relation between Russia and
Denmark, the arrogant conduct of the Russian
ministers at Copenhagen, the pretensions of Catherine, and the politic conduct of Bernstoff, the
Danish minister, by which they were defeated,
would extend this article to an unreasonable
length, and perhaps be foreign to the present purpose.

The revolution which took place about this
period (1776) in Sweden, and which diminished
the influence of Petersburg, gave great umbrage
to Catherine. Her agents were ordered to restore

the government overturned by Gustavus; but their efforts to this purpose proved ineffectual. Some explanations having terminated with harshness, Russia fitted out at Cronstadt a fleet of galleys, which excited at Stockholm great alarm. Gustavus demanded in vain the cause of these preparations; no satisfactory answer was to be obtained: disquieted by appearances so hostile, he determined personally to confer with the empress respecting the measures she meant to adopt.

On the 16th of June, 1777, the king of Sweden arrived at Petersburg, under the title of count of Gothland, accompanied by several of his courtiers. The Swedish minister only had been apprised of his intention: Gustavus alighted at his hotel, and presently afterwards visited count Panin. Towards evening, he proceeded to Tzar-sko-selo, where he had an interview with the empress: expressions equally cordial and equally sincere were, on this occasion, lavished on both sides. Catherine, to impress the Swedish monarch with her magnificence, entertained him sumptuously, while, with her usual penetration, she studied his character, of which presumption appeared to her the prominent feature.

By qualities more brilliant than solid, by his

CATHERINE II. 141

popular manners, and by the pleasures which he provided for his people, he had conciliated their affections. A reputation resting on a basis thus precarious, a moment's imprudence might overthrow; the purposes of Catherine were to accelerate that moment, by prompting him to embark in some hazardous enterprise.

With this view, she talked to him of the impediments experienced by sovereigns in their attempts to advance the civilisation of their subjects; the difficulty with which changes were effected, even in things apparently insignificant and unimportant; while mankind, the slaves of habit, obstinate in error, and averse to change, behold with distrust every innovation. She illustrated these observations, just in themselves, by the example of Peter the Great, and the resistance opposed to him by the Russians, when he wanted them to part with their beards. These artful insinuations roused, as was foreseen, the vanity of the Swedish monarch, who contended warmly that such failures originated with the sovereign rather than with the people; that men sacrificed willingly their habits to their fortunes; and that the king who made himself beloved would triumph without difficulty over obstacles like these. To this he added, that, on all occasions, there was a fitness of times and seasons, which must be skilfully chosen; and also a *manner* of executing a design that required qualities to which Peter the Great was a stranger. Catherine, in reply, supported her arguments with additional proofs, till the pride of Gustavus was irritated to prove by facts the verity of his assertions. The challenge being provoked and given, the monarch undertook to induce the Swedes to adopt a new mode of dress.

After his return to Stockholm, Gustavus, in consequence of this debate, introduced the theatrical dress still worn by the Swedish court. Without enforcing this change as a law, he contented himself with directing the governors of the provinces to recommend it as a fashion by gentleness and persuasion. He pretended that this fantastic habit of his own invention was similar to that worn by the ancient Swedes : he proposed it only to the courtiers, the military, and the superior classes of the people ; the lower ranks, with a view of piquing their pride, were not even invited to adopt it ; nevertheless, they insensibly and gradually advanced towards the reigning mode. The visit of Gustavus to Petersburg had not augmented his esteem for the empress, while her desire of humbling a young and turbulent rival became

CATHERINE II. 143

strengthened and confirmed. The Swedish monarch had, notwithstanding this mutual distrust, received on his departure fresh tokens of the magnificent spirit of Catherine.

In the autumn of 1777, Petersburg was visited with a dreadful calamity: an inundation, to which the city was at times liable, produced the most terrible and destructive effects.

Some new disputes and hostilities which had arisen between Russia and the Porte, were (in 1778) terminated by the interposition of the French embassador at Constantinople, through whose mediation a treaty was signed in the ensuing spring. The zeal of the French minister on this occasion originated in the desire of the court of Versailles to deprive England of the support of Russia; an attempt that proved in some measure successful. The alliance between the courts of London and Petersburg, if not broken, was greatly weakened: the French assured themselves, that a power indebted to them for its peace, would not lightly take up arms against them. Catherine testified her satisfaction with the treaty, which favoured her ambition, and extensive commercial projects, by magnificent presents to her own minister at Constantinople, and to that of France. The grand-seignor, the favourite sultana, and the principal members of the divan, experienced on the same occasion proofs of the munificence of the empress. Proud of her victories, and elate with her advantages, jealousy of the superiority claimed by the British flag had contributed to detach the czarina from Great Britain, whose trade she was nevertheless anxious to retain ; but, while refusing assistance to the English, she was lavish to them of civilities, inviting them, on the loss of their colonies, to fetch from her ports the commodities they could no longer obtain from America : she saw, with pleasure, from year to year, their vessels become more numerous in the port of Archangel. The American ships received from her the same encouragement, while, in despite of the British minister, she granted to them the free navigation of the Baltic. A treaty had also, a few years before, been concluded with Versailles, which admitted the establishment of a French factory at Archangel.

The anniversary of the accession of the empress to the throne, and the birth-day of the grand-duke, were this year (July 9th, 1779) celebrated with extraordinary splendour. The several festivals of the orders of chivalry were not less distinguished by pomp and magnificence. Catherine consented to discharge the functions of

CATHERINE II.   145

sovereign of the order of the Bath, by conferring its badges on sir James Harris*, to whom they had been sent by the British monarch. Having struck him on the shoulder with a sword richly set with diamonds, and, in conformity to the statutes of the order, exhorted him ' in the name of God, to be a good and loyal knight,' she presented to him the sword, with the following address : ' To testify my satisfaction with you, I present to you the sword with which I have stamped you with the order of knighthood.' A few days previous to this ceremony, a grand entertainment was given to commemorate the conflagration of the Turkish fleet, with a superb masquerade and supper in the summer gardens.

The riches and splendor of the court of Petersburg, during the reign of Catherine, combined with the profusion of Asiatic pomp the refinements and taste of European luxury. On court days, and more peculiarly on festivals, the company which surrounded the empress were resplendent with jewels ; men and women appeared to vie with each other in the sumptuousness of their ornaments, and the prodigality of their

---

* Lord Malmesbury.

riches : the people of fashion were covered with diamonds, with a profusion unexampled in the courts of Europe. This passion for precious stones descended even to private individuals : the wife of a Russian burgher would sometimes ruin her husband for a girdle of pearls or a head-dress of jewels.

On days of ceremony the empress dined in public, on which occasion she usually wore a diamond crown of immense value ; the ribands of St. Andrew and of St. George, both over one shoulder, with the collars of St. Alexander Nefsky, St. Catherine, and St. Vladimir ; also two stars on her breast, the one above the other, as grand master of the two first-mentioned orders. The courtiers, who follow the example of their sovereign, emulated this brilliant exhibition. There are five orders of chivalry in Russia : St. Andrew, St. Catherine, St. Alexander Nefsky, and St. Vladimir ; to these may be added, the order of St. Anne of Holstein, conferred only by the grand-duke, as duke of Holstein. The order of St. Catherine was instituted in 1714, in memory of the assistance received by Peter the Great from his consort in the camp at Pruth. This order is appropriated to the ladies, who wear, as its badges, a narrow red riband, edged with silver,

CATHERINE II. **147**

to which the figure of the saint, set with diamonds, is suspended; on the left breast is worn
a silver star of eight points, with the inscription,
" *Amore et fidelitate.*" In 1790 their number was
twenty-five.

The two orders of St. George and St. Vladimir
were founded by Catherine II. The former, a
military order, in 1769 ; it is divided into four
classes : its badges are a black riband, with a
George and Dragon. Its holiday is the 26th of
November. A specific number of each class
enjoy pensions of 100 to 700 rubles. The order
of St. Vladimir was instituted September 22d,
1782, the twentieth coronation-day of the empress. The badges, an eight-pointed star of gold
and silver, having a red area, bearing a cross, with
the Russian letters, C. P. K. B. i. e. the holy
apostle-like prince Vladimir. Round it the words,
in Russ, " Utility, Honour, and Fame :" with a
riband of two black and one red stripes. Beside
these, were ladies of the Portrait, who wore the
miniature of the empress, set with diamonds.

During the winter, masquerades were given by
Catherine at the palace, to which persons of all
ranks might be admitted. Twenty magnificent
halls, splendidly illuminated, afforded ample room
for the company. In the midst of one of these

spacious apartments, an enclosure, more adorned than the rest, appropriated to the nobility and the courtiers, was made by a low balustrade. The apollo, an elegant room of an oval form, received those burghers who had not been presented at court; card-tables, with tea and refreshments, were placed in another apartment, in which the company were served without ceremony or distinction. Every person had liberty to keep his mask or to lay it aside, as best pleased him. The nobility universally wore dominoes. The inferior classes of Russians appeared at these balls in the usual dresses of their respective provinces, somewhat more decorated. These various and singular habits produced an amazing and diversified effect. The empress usually came to the rooms at seven, and retired at eleven, in the evening.

Catherine, who, about this period, had reason to expect a new rupture with the Turks, was desirous of animating by her presence the zeal of her mariners. With this view she embarked in a yacht at Peterhoff, and visited the squadron cruising between Cronstadt and Krasna-gorca.

A great part of the city of Iver having been consumed by fire, the empress granted to the relief of the inhabitants 100,000 rubles.

Petersburg also experienced a this time a

CATHERINE II. 149

disaster, which the bounty of its sovereign was unable to repair. One of the farmers of the brandy duties, who had made an immense fortune by his contract, proposed to give to the inhabitants of the city a feast in testimony of his gratitude. The victuals, beer, and brandy served on the occasion cost 20,000 rubles. The populace flocked in crowds to partake of this repast, when, in despite of precautions, a contention respecting pre-eminence arose among them. From struggles and noise they proceeded to blows; several persons were killed, while others, who in a state of intoxication fell asleep in the streets, perished by the severity of the frost. Five hundred persons were computed to have lost their lives on this occasion.

Catherine, amidst political and military cares, found leisure for liberal acquirements and the arts of peace. She employed herself with her pen, not merely in framing laws for her people, but in contributing to their recreation and improvement. She had a facility in arranging her thoughts upon paper, an employment in which she took delight. She attacked fanaticism, enthusiasm, and superstition, in comedies, with which, mingling reflection with satire, she enlightened the minds of the people.

In her private attachments she appears to have been true to the sentiment of love, rather than to the object: Zoritch, after filling his station of favourite for a twelvemonth, was suddenly dismissed. Hastening to his protector, Potemkin, who, little jealous of his fortune, had given him his support lest a more dangerous rival should be promoted to his place, he complained of the reverse he had experienced. Potemkin presumed to enquire of the empress for what cause she had discarded her humble friend: ' I loved him yesterday,' replied she, ' but to-day I love him no longer. Perhaps if he were better informed I might regard him still; but his ignorance puts me to the blush. He can speak no other than the Russ language : let him travel into France and England and learn other tongues.'—Potemkin acquiesced in the caprice of the sovereign, and Zoritch set out on his travels.

Potemkin, who was busy in looking out for a successor to the favourite, beheld with astonishment the same evening, at the hermitage, a chamberlain of whom he had not the least knowledge behind the chair of Catherine. From the humble rank of a serjeant in the guards, Rimsky Korzakoff was suddenly raised to that of aide-de-camp general to the empress, in which he received the

CATHERINE II. 151

usual testimonies of her munificence. A fine stature and a handsome figure were the recommendations of Rimsky, nor had Potemkin any thing to apprehend from his talents or attainments, of which the following anecdote may afford a proof.

Having obtained the post of favourite, Rimsky believed that, among other arrangements necessary to his new dignity, it would be proper to provide himself with a library. A principal bookseller of Petersburg was accordingly sent for, and informed of the business on which he was summoned. ' What books,' enquired the bookseller, of the favourite, ' would you please to have ?' ' That is your business,' returned he ; ' you understand that matter better than I do. You know the proper assortments, which I have destined a large room to receive. Let there be large books at the bottom, and smaller and smaller up to the top, in the manner in which they are placed in the library of the empress.'—' How did you contrive to find a sufficient quantity of large books for the purpose, since folios are out of fashion ?' said a person, who had heard this anecdote, to the bookseller. ' Oh ! I went to my warehouse, and drew out old German commentators on the bible, and writers on jurisprudence, where they had lain in

quires since they were sent to my predecessor for
a bad debt. I took care to put them in new coats.
In conspicuous parts of the library I have placed a
set of Voltaire, of Rousseau, of Buffon, for the
inquisitive visitor; and as for the rest, their shewy
outsides, as is common in the world, must be a
passport for any deficiency within.'

Military preparations were made by Russia,
during this year, against Austria, whose minister
at Constantinople had irritated Catherine by some
successless efforts to involve her anew in hostilities
with the Porte. The cloud, however, passed over
without bursting. Vienna, occupied in a contest
with the Prussian monarch respecting the affairs
of the Germanic empire, deprecated the wrath of
the empress, which it dared not to provoke, by
inviting her, in concert with the court of France,
to be the mediatrix between Austria and Prussia.
Catherine accepted the office allotted to her, and
converted the general whom she had destined as
the instrument of her vengeance into a minister
of peace : the treaty was conducted upon equitable principles, and a war, which had threatened
the most important consequences, early and happily terminated.

But while in the north of Europe all was tranquil, the most terrible convulsions agitated the

CATHERINE II. 153

south. England, Holland, France, and Spain, tinged with blood the seas of the two hemispheres, in deciding the fate of the American colonies. The commerce of the north was benefited by the contest: Catherine wisely availed herself of the occasion for extending and improving the trade of her empire. To increase its activity, she had abolished the extraordinary duties on corn, the exportation of which was permitted from Archangel to Riga. Her pride was hurt by the English, who paid no respect to the vessels freighted in her ports, and even sometimes stopped those which sailed under her flag. To this motive was added another, that determined her to protect the navigation of the north; a measure to which she was implored by the merchants of Hamburg, of Bremen, and of Lubeck. Vergennes, the French minister, had formed a project worthy of a great statesman, the plan of the Armed Neutrality, in which he successfully engaged almost every potentate of Europe, and which he found means to render acceptable to Catherine. Resolved to employ her force for the protection of her ships, she proposed to the courts of Copenhagen and Stockholm to equip each of them a squadron, which, combined with hers, should defend the neutrality. This confederacy was to be wholly maritime, and confined to the protection of commerce. Prussia, Austria, and Portugal, concurring in the measure, the sovereignty of the seas, so long maintained by England, appeared to be endangered.

The British minister * at Petersburg had left no means unessayed to dissolve the league, and induce the empress to abandon her purpose, when his efforts were frustrated by a singular stratagem. A long memorial against the project was given by the minister to Potemkin, whose interest he had secured, and who had promised to recommend his paper to the empress. The partisans of the neutrality became informed of this circumstance, and, by means of a girl in the suite of Potemkin's nieces and in habits of familiarity with the uncle, contrived to possess themselves of the memorial, which they enriched with marginal notes, calculated to overthrow the arguments of the British minister. Thus embellished, the writing was, with no less success, returned to the place whence it was taken.

The empress, on perusing the paper, attributed the notes to Potemkin, and became confirmed in her predeliction for the neutral powers. Sir

---

* Sir James Harris.

CATHERINE II. **155**

James Harris, informed of the methods practised against him, sickened with mortification and disappointment.

The favour of Potemkin had reached its summit, his honours and his riches appeared daily to accumulate. The court and the army alike did homage to his power; ministers, generals, and favourites, were appointed or removed at his pleasure : under a rude exterior, he concealed a subtle spirit; while, domineering over the empress, he appeared to exist but for her service : those whom he could affront with impunity, however respectable their names and office, were sure of being insulted, while he fawned on others whose spirit or intrigues he had reason to apprehend. Marshal Romantzoff only, of all the generals, refused to bend to the favourite, who dreaded the inflexibility of the conqueror of the Turks in the same proportion as he envied his glory. This aversion he extended to the sister of the general, countess Bruce, with whom Catherine lived in friendship and confidence. Chance threw in the way of Potemkin the occasion he sought of destroying this lady's interest at court.

Rimsky, the subordinate favourite of the empress, made up of frivolity and ostentation, attracted the attention of the countess : Potemkin flattered her predeliction, and kindly favoured her interviews with the minion, whom he hesitated not to involve in the disgrace which he was preparing for the sister of Rómantzoff.

The plan was successful; Catherine discovered the perfidy of her favourite and her friend; the former was sentenced to travel, and the latter exiled to Moscow. From that period the empress made no more confidants : with a favourite she found it less convenient to dispense : the same day her choice was made; Lanskoï, one of the chevalier guards, a fine and interesting figure, was selected to occupy the vacant post. This youth, who was of all the lovers of Catherine the most tenderly regarded, appears to have best merited the affection he inspired.

The mind of Potemkin was not wholly occupied by court intrigues; led by ambition, he aspired to the honour of causing his sovereign to be crowned at Constantinople; a project which could not fail to meet with her approbation. Panin, who opposed in council a plan so replete. with danger, found himself over-ruled by Potemkin : grieved at this opposition, he fell sick and retired from business, while count Osterman, who filled the place of vice-chancellor, performed the duties of his office.

CATHERINE II. 157

The plans which now occupied the thoughts of Catherine rendered a conference necessary with the emperor Joseph II. whom she requested to join her in Poland. The empress, during her frequent journeys, never entrusted to her son either the government of Petersburg, or the administration of affairs: though by birth generalissimo of the Russian armies, he never led a regiment to battle: though grand-admiral of the Baltic, he was never permitted to visit the fleet. Panin, accustomed to represent the sovereign when absent, had retired from court; worn by care, and oppressed by chagrin, he tottered on the verge of the grave. Field-marshal Alexander Gallitzin was therefore, on the present occasion, appointed governor of the residence.

Catherine reached Mohilef, May 30th, 1780; whither the emperor Joseph had arrived before her. The pomp by which she was surrounded, with the luxury of the Polish grandees, formed a striking contrast with the simplicity affected by the emperor. Joseph, who travelled under the title of the Count Von Falkenstein, entreated the empress to spare him the necessity of ceremony and vain etiquette, a request which was cheerfully granted. After several private conferences, it was agreed that they should attack the Ottomans in concert, share between them the spoils, and re-establish the ancient republics of Greece. To determine the emperor to her views, Catherine consented to patronise the barter of Bavaria for the Austrian Netherlands, excepting the counties of Namur and Luxemburg: also to support him against Prussia, and the princes of the empire. These stipulations were, by a treaty at Peters-burg, shortly after confirmed and settled. Joseph was invited by his imperial ally to visit Russia: fond of travelling, and eager to acquire know-ledge, he took the route of Moscow, while the empress returned directly to Petersburg.

Previous to their separation, Catherine offered to her visitor a suite of splendid apartments in the palace. The emperor, whose aversion to the for-mality of courts formed a distinguished trait in his character, declined the compliment, adding, that unless her majesty would allow him to fix his quarters at an inn, however desirous he might feel of prolonging his visit, he must deny himself the satisfaction he had anticipated. The empress, in compliance with the whimsical singularity of her guest, gave orders to the English gardener, on her return to Tzar-sko-selo, to convert his house into an inn by hanging out a sign, and to provide accommodations for the royal traveller. A Ca-

CATHERINE II. 159

therine-wheel was accordingly painted on a board, below which was written, in German characters, "The Falkenstein arms." Here the fictitious count Falkenstein put up on his arrival, and was perfectly satisfied with the behaviour of his host. Several comic adventures occurred during the emperor's stay, from the singularity of his situation.

Catherine, in despite of the repugnance manifested by her guest, forbore not to display to him the magnificence of her court; but these entertainments appeared to have no attractions for the emperor, who philosophically preferred useful establishments, and curious monuments of art. At Moscow he had seen the Kremlin, the Khitaigorod*, the monasteries, the library, the archives of the history of the north, reduced to admirable order by Muller, the learned professor. At Tula the hardware manufactory, on which Catherine had spared no expence, attracted his attention. At Petersburg he sought for all that was curious, or worthy observation. At Cronstadt he examined the arsenals, the dock-yards, and the various manufactories. He received every-where flattering marks of the empress's attention. On enter-

---

* The Khitaigorod, or Chinese town, in which is carried on a trade in furs, and other merchandise.

160   CATHERINE II.

ing the academy of sciences, he was presented with a volume of geographical maps, among which was already engraven that of his journey from Vienna to Petersburg. At the academy of arts a collection of engravings was laid before him, in which was his own portrait, with the following inscription from Horace:

Multorum providus urbes
Et mores hominum inspexit.

Joseph at length took leave of Russia, not less astonished at the mixture of refinement and barbarism which it presented, than at the various character of its sovereign. The hereditary prince of Prussia soon after made a visit to Petersburg. Catherine determined that the grand-duke should, in imitation of these princes, visit foreign countries. Paul and his duchess, in consequence of this resolution, travelled to Italy, through Poland and Austria, whence they returned by the way of France and Holland. Every day during their tour, which lasted fourteen months, a courier was dispatched to inform the empress of their situation and employments. The ducal pair, equally desirous of knowing what was passing at Petersburg, found their curiosity more difficult to gratify. The chamberlain, Bibikoff, who, disre-

CATHERINE II. 161

garding the will of the sovereign, presumed to
address letters, containing exact intelligence, to a
gentleman in the train of Paul, suffered for his
temerity. The letters were intercepted at Riga,
and the writer condemned to expiate his rashness
in the deserts of Siberia.

Various circumstances combined to disturb the
tranquillity which had for some time subsisted between Russia and the Porte. The navigation of
the Euxine, the opening of the gates of the Dardanelles and Bosphorus, for the admission of a
free intercourse from the White Sea to the Euxine,
the affairs of the Krimea, with those of the Greek
dependent provinces, afforded grounds for dispute
which seemed to render a war inevitable.

The Ottomans, thinned by pestilence, enfeebled
and oppressed, exasperated by the triumphs and
advantages of their adversary, split into divisions,
and torn by factions, prepared vigorously for hostilities, which their situation appeared but ill
calculated to sustain. Russia, content with its
successes, with the benefits of the late treaty,
afraid of the plague, and conscious, amidst its
splendor, of some internal weaknesses, shewed
less ardour for war, and seemed willing to accept
a mediation by which its dignity might be preserved. France availed herself of this situation;

the French minister became again the successful negociator, and received once more the reward of his services.

This arrangement, in which mutual concessions had been made, gave time to the Porte to settle its affairs ; while to Russia it afforded leisure for the object of its constant ambition, an interference with the politics of Europe. The armed neutrality continued to display its flag on the northern seas ; the coasts of the Mediterranean were visited by the Russian squadrons ; and commerce protected in every quarter. Catherine, in the spirit of her predecessor Peter the Great, directed her attention to the improvement of the marine. Ship-builders and seamen were procured from England for the purpose of improving the unskilful Russians. Europe had beheld with surprise the Russian eagle in the Archipelago, and the Ottoman fleet annihilated by a squadron from the north.

The empress at length completed the division of her provinces, all of which participated in the benefit of her regulations : salutary institutions and fresh conquests marked every successive year of her reign.

That she had distinguished herself as an author has been before intimated. " Miscellaneous

CATHERINE II.   163

Pieces, or the Library of the Grand-dukes," the most interesting production of her pen, was written for the benefit of her grand-children, and contained instruction blended with pleasantry, national history enlivened by the description of manners. It is worthy of admiration to behold a great sovereign relaxing from affairs of state in attention to the education and improvement of her successors. The " Tale of the Tzarrevitch Chlor," is at once calculated to delight the child and gratify the more mature understanding. Catherine was respectable in the circle of her family ; mingling tenderness with severity, she cultivated the affections and the talents of her grandsons : she conversed with the tutor in their presence, and, in their absence, wrote marginal remarks on their lessons, sometimes addressed to the pupil, and sometimes to the preceptor ; of which the following instance may afford a specimen. The subject of the morning lecture had been the nature of the government in Switzerland, on which the tutor had displayed his usual liberality of sentiment. The ensuing day, on returning to their studies, they found, in the hand-writing of the empress, the following sentence at the bottom of the exercise : " *Monsieur l'Harpe, continuez vos leçons de cette sorte ; vos sentimens me plaisent beaucoup.*"

This year, 1782, was marked by the inaugura-
tion of the famous statue of Peter I.; a work executed by the genius of Falconet, invited to Petersburg from Paris for the occasion. The design
conceived by the artist was sublime and grand,
but of difficult execution : to indicate to posterity
the obstacles surmounted by the heroic legislator,
he wished to substitue for the pedestal of the
statue a huge and rugged rock. The idea could
scarcely fail of approbation ; it remained only to
find a mass of stone which in form and bulk might
be suited to realise it. Chance favoured the undertaking. Near a village in Karelia, a rock was
found corresponding with the conception of the
artist : its height, taken from the horizontal line,
twenty-one feet by forty-two in length, and thirty-
four in breath. The difficulty of removing this
enormous mass was, in the reign of Catherine, no
obstacle ; a project for the purpose, worthy of ancient Rome, was presently formed. In removing
the ground to discover the foundation of the rock,
which it was expected to find deep sunk in the
earth, the workmen were not less surprised than
pleased to find the stone absolutely detached, and
lying on the ground as if prepared for their purpose. To this discovery another succeeded equally
singular : neither stone, gravel, nor sand, nor any
substance analogous to the mass, or adapted to

CATHERINE II. 165

form its constituent parts, was to be found in its neighbourhood. The interior of the rock afforded a new phenomenon : on one side it had been damaged by a stroke of thunder; on knocking off the shattered fragments, instead of homogeneous particles, a collection of precious stones appeared : chrystals, agates, granites, topazes, cornelians, amethysts, presented to the curious a magnificent spectacle, and to the naturalist an object of interesting enquiry. Thousands of these, and other parts of the mass, being cut and polished into rings, bracelets, snuff-boxes, and other ornaments, found through the empire a rapid sale. So many circumstances, combined by nature, afforded powerful motives for transporting from its place a production thus wonderful, for a monument worthy to perpetuate the memory of a hero. The mechanism for its conveyance was invented by count Carburg : a solid road was made from the rock to the shore; under the stone were inserted brass slips, to go upon cannon balls of five inches diameter in metal grooves, by windlasses worked by four hundred men, every day two hundred fathom towards the shore. The water transport was performed by camels (so called in the dock-yards of Petersburg and Amsterdam), by which ships of war are lifted over shallows, or bars of sand. The distance of the shore from the spot chosen for the monument was eleven versts, or 41,250 English feet. The rock had, on its way, to pass heights, morasses, swamps, and rivers, and, falling down the Neva, to be disembarked and drawn by land to the place of its destination. The weight of the mass, geometrically calculated, amounted to three millions two hundred thousand pounds. The largest known obelisk, that which Constantius son of Constantine the Great caused to be conveyed from Alexandria to Rome, weighed not a third part of the rock of Petersburg.

Such is the pedestal of the equestrian statue of the Russian legislator: the statue is in itself a master-piece of art. The hero, the features of whose countenance are admirably expressed, appears on horseback, in the act of ascending a steep rock, the summit of which he labours to attain. Dressed in an Asiatic robe and crowned with laurels, he extends his right arm with dignity; in his left he holds the bridle of his horse, whose beautiful figure and elegant attitude captivate the beholder. He stands on his hinder feet, in the posture of a fiery courser straining to attain the summit of the rock. The artist, by an ingenious device, combines strength with beauty: the brazen serpent,

CATHERINE II. 167

upon which the horse tramples, emblematical of the obstacles opposed to the monarch, serves also to give an equipoise to the statue; the point of bearing, the full and flowing tail of the courser, gently falling on the serpent writhing with pain, is by this means unperceived. The model of the head of Peter, a performance of singular excellence, in which the artist disclaimed all merit, was the production of a lady, mademoiselle Collot, afterwards married to Peter Falconet, the son of the artist. The whole was grounded on piles closely driven. On the side towards the admiralty, in letters of cast metal, is the following inscription : PETRV PERVOMU EKATERINA VTORAIA. 1782. On the side next the senate, in Latin : PETRO PRIMO CATHERINA SECVNDA.

On the 7th of August, the day on which the monument was disclosed to the public, the empress, appearing in the balcony of the senate-house, solemnised the event by the distribution of medals in gold and silver; also, by an ukause, or grace, which put an end to every process of more than ten years standing, discharged all debtors who had been five years in confinement, and remitted all debts due to the crown below the sum of 500 rubles. The expence of the whole undertaking amounted to 424,610 rubles. Mademoiselle Collot, in consequence of the reputation she acquired on this occasion, gained by her industry, during her stay in Russia, a competency of 50,000 rubles : she was engaged to make a bust of the empress in marble, and employed by the nobility in similar designs.

The treaty of pacification, so lately concluded between Russia and the Ottomans, promised no long duration : perpetual subjects of dispute occurred, which the pestilence, that through the summer and autumn of 1782 ravaged the frontier countries, had hitherto restrained from breaking out into hostilities. The Porte had the mortification to perceive, in the pride and impatience of its powerful neighbour, but little disposition for tedious negociation : its remonstrances were accompanied by every preparation for enforcing their effect.

The emperor of Germany now, plucking off the mask, avowed his design of supporting with his own the claims of Russia, while the engagements of the two empires were declared to be reciprocal. Towards the close of the year, two strong memorials were presented from the united courts, when their armies appeared on the frontiers of Turkey. The Porte, however desperate its situation, having no part to choose, contented

CATHERINE II.　　　169

itself with preserving an appearance of dignity. Russia had experienced from her late conquests a rapid increase of her commerce ; her vessels passed the Dardanelles, proceeded to Aleppo and Smyrna, and traded in the ports of Italy. The foundation of the city of Kerson, on the shores of the Dniepr, was laid by Catherine, and the work accelerated by the activity of Potemkin. Kerson already counted within its walls 40,000 inhabitants, while from its yards were launched vessels of commerce and ships of war, destined to strike terror into the Ottoman empire. The empress and Potemkin felt with these advantages their ardour rekindle : they desired with equal fervour the conquest of a country so long the object of their ambitious projects. It was resolved to begin their operations by detaching the Krimea from Turkey : the fertility of the country is disputable, but it promised, in a resource to the armies and in its commercial advantages, benefits less equivocal.

Reinforcements were sent to the armies in Poland and the Ukraine, while every thing announced a speedy declaration of war. The Russian minister at Constantinople had orders to extend his demands, and to extort from the divan a promise not to interfere in the fate of the Krimea. The divan, feeble and disunited, yet incensed at these pretensions, murmured instead of flying to arms. Pretences for injustice are seldom wanted by powerful states: an insurrection was by the emissaries of Russia stirred up in the Krimea, while the troops of Catherine, under pretence of assisting the Khan, found means to possess themselves of the country. In justification of an invasion, in which every law of nations and every principle of honour were alike violated, a manifesto was published, in which the Turks were accused of having broken the treaty of Kaïnardgi.

The pacific disposition of the Porte proved of little avail in producing an accommodation with its ambitious adversaries: their demands were so exorbitant, that it became a question with the prudent whether it were not better to put every thing to hazard. All sides prepared for decisive hostilities, and the preparations of each were immense.

The year 1783 exhibited an apparatus of war, in the northern and eastern borders of Europe, unprecedented even in those martial regions. The Danube groaned under the weight of artillery and stores, which the emperor forwarded to the frontiers from his hereditary states. The Russian forces advanced at the same time through different parts of Poland, and through the coun-

CATHERINE II. 171

tries from the Don to the Dniepr, to the scene of action. The armies of the Porte, which had drawn into Europe great bodies of Asiatic troops, already exceeded 150,000 men. A number of European officers, particularly from France, among whom were several engineers, had been attracted into their service. The janissaries and soldiers shewed on this occasion a singular docility: misfortune, joined with the example of their rulers, appeared to have softened their prejudices, and changed their character.

The manifesto published by Catherine in justification of her conduct in the Krimea, was answered by the Porte in a masterly style. The English minister * is said to have lent his pen on this occasion: the perfidy and injustice of the court of Petersburg it was by no means difficult to prove. But of what avail is truth in the causes of sovereigns, which can be pleaded effectually only by the sword?

Apprehensive lest the king of Sweden should take advantage of the absence of her armies, Catherine endeavoured to form with Gustavus a new treaty of alliance, and, on the failure of a ministerial negociation, resolved on a second interview

---

* Sir Robert Ainslie.

with the Swedish monarch. Frederiksham, a frontier town, being appointed for the meeting, the empress repaired in a yacht to the place of rendezvous. Among the ladies who attended her was the princess Dashkoff, who had for some time past apparently regained her friendship and confidence. Two contiguous houses, furnished with great elegance, and a gallery of communication constructed between them, had been previously hired. One of these was occupied by Catherine, the other served as quarters for Gustavus, during the four days they remained at Frederiksham.

Peace having been signed some months before, there appeared no longer any reason for keeping in arms the neutrality of the north; a position to which the king of Sweden assented. A neutrality during the war with the Turks was also proposed to him, while he was assured that, after its termination, he should be assisted by Russia in gaining possession of Norway. Flattered by this idea, Gustavus complied with all that Catherine demanded: they parted mutually satisfied, their minds occupied with different projects of conquest. The empress, on their separation, displayed her munificence in presents to the Swedish officers: Gustavus emulated this example; the favourite Lanskoï was decorated by him with the

CATHERINE II. 173

order of the polar star, and a diploma presented to the princess Dashkoff, as member of the
academy at Stockholm.

The Porte beheld with anxiety the preparations
of the enemy, which seemed to assure them of
victory. Seventy thousand men, under the command of Potemkin, were assembled on the frontiers of the Krimea : forty thousand, at the head
of whom was prince Repnin, were in readiness to
back them : marshal Romantzoff, with a third
army, held his quarters at Kief. The squadrons
of the Euxine were armed, while ten sail of the
line, with several frigates, waited the signal for
proceeding to the Mediterranean.

The court of London tried in vain to rouse the
divan to arms, which France and Austria, with
more success, laboured to prevent. Negociation
was, as a safer mode, preferred by the Porte. By
a new treaty, signed at Constantinople, the empress retained the sovereignty of the Krimea, of
the isle of Taman, and a great part of the Kuban,
while her right was acknowledged to the dominion
of the Euxine, and to the passage of the Dardanelles. Catherine thus acquired, without the necessity of a battle, an immense territory, with
1,500,000 new subjects. She restored to the
Krimea and to the Kuban their ancient names of

Taurida and Caucasus. The example of the khan of the Krimea deterred not other princes from accepting the perfidious protection of Russia, whose presents dazzled their eyes.

While extending the dominions of his sovereign, Pótemkin neglected not his personal interests. Estates and honours were lavished upon him. The surname of Tavritschesky * was conferred upon him by the empress, who, with the rank of grand-admiral of the Euxine, gave him the government of Taurida, and built for him the magnificent palace in Petersburg, which bears the name of Tavritschesky.

Count Nikita Ivanovitch Panin, and prince Gregory Orloff, died about this period; the one at Moscow, the other at Petersburg. Panin died of chagrin, a malady to which discarded ministers are liable. Orloff, though in possession of numberless benefits heaped on him by Catherine, and the husband of a young and beautiful wife, found the presence of the new favourites insupportable. He had passed in travelling the latter years of his life. In 1782 he lost his wife at Lausanne, and on her death sunk into deep melancholy. On his return to court, he presented to his friends a

---

* The Taurian.

CATHERINE II. 175

sad spectacle of insanity : at one moment he gave himself up to an extravagant gaiety; the next, bursting into reproaches against the empress, he struck horror into those who heard him, and filled Catherine with terror and grief. Having at length retired to Moscow, remorse revived with tenfold force : the bleeding shade of the murdered Peter incessantly haunted his imagination, and pursued him in every retreat : night and day, in his distracted fancy, it appeared to aim at him an avenging dart. Death at last relieved him—he expired in the agonies of frenzy and despair.

In the former periods of his favour he had received from the empress a medallion surrounded with brilliants, on which was her portrait, which he constantly wore. After his death, the miniature was presented to Catherine, who returned it to Alexy Orloff, the brother of the deceased, and the actual murderer of Peter III. An affecting present * !

About 1780 it happened that, after presenting some gentlemen at court, the English minister and

---

* The sequel to the revolution of 1762 was performed in 1797, after the death of the empress, when Alexy Orloff resided at Moscow. The emperor Paul, on coming to the crown, caused the corpse of his father Peter III,

his countrymen were favoured by a conversation with the empress. Prince Baratinsky standing near her, she exclaimed in her lively manner*, ' *Voilà un homme qui m'a rendu le plus grand service dans le moment le plus critique de ma vie.*' Every

---

interred in the church of St. Alexander Nefsky, to be taken up and brought to the palace, to receive there similar honours with that of the empress his wife. In the printed ceremonial, prince Baratinsky † and count Alexy Orloff were ordered to officiate as chief mourners. The ceremony of coronation having been omitted by Peter during his life, the imperial crown was placed on his coffin, as it lay beside that of his consort. Over both was a kind of true-love knot, with the following inscription in Russ: "-Divided in life, united in death." The chief mourners took their station in presence of the assembled court ; amidst sable hangings, lighted tapers, and all the solemnity of imperial woe. The strong nerves of Orloff endured the scene, unshaken : his companion, with a heart less inaccessible, fainted beneath his emotions, and could scarcely support his station, during the three hours ordained by the ceremonial, with the aid of volatile salts and other stimulative applications. Alexy, without requesting it, received afterwards permission to travel in foreign parts, while Baratinsky was spared the trouble of a future attendance at court.

† The assistant of Alexy Orloff in the murder of Peter.

* ' Behold a man who rendered me the greatest service in one of the most critical moments of my life.'

CATHERINE II.   177

one present heard this expression with astonishment, as the particulars of the revolution were one of those *secrets* which are known to all the world. Catherine immediately added, perhaps on recollection, that in stepping from her carriage her foot had twisted at the ancle, when Baratinsky catching her at the instant prevented her from falling upon her face to the ground.

This anecdote is thought by many to afford a presumption of the ignorance of the empress respecting the manner of her husband's death: otherwise, say they, it could scarcely be expected, from her acknowledged prudence, that she would have hazarded an expression thus equivocal.

The vicinity of the Caspian invites the Russians to trade with Persia; and by Persia a commerce with India can easily be prosecuted. They had accordingly long profited by these advantages. The fleet maintained in the Caspian by Catherine cruised along the Persian coasts, burning all the vessels and even floats of timber which they happened to meet. The commanders received orders to sow discord between the several khans, and to support the weak against the strong; a method found but too successful in Poland and in the Krimea. In 1782, the empress determined on executing the project formed by Peter I. against

I 5

Persia, of extending the Russian dominion on the western shores of the Caspian sea. The dissensions which laid waste those fertile regions appeared to favour her design, which unforeseen obstacles nevertheless opposed.

The trade carried on by the Russians in China, not less beneficial than that of the Caspian, had received a check by their arrogance and ill conduct. Catherine found means to appease the Chinese, and to revive the spirit of commerce : an archimandrite, with several young Russians, was at the same time sent to study the language of China. Maritime expeditions to Kamtschatka were also set on foot.

There was yet another country with which the empress was desirous of a commercial connection, when an incident occurred that favoured her purpose. Some shipwrecked Japanese, sixteen sailors and the master of the vessel, had saved themselves on the northern coasts of Russia, which approximated to Japan. The master was, in 1792, brought by professor Laxmann to Petersburg. Catherine received him graciously, and gave him instructors, who, while they taught him the Russian and Tartarian languages, learnt enough of the Japanese to enable them to form some commercial arrangements. If no great success has

CATHERINE II. 179

hitherto attended this enterprise, there is no reason to doubt that, at some future period, Russia may share in the profits made by the Dutch at Japan.

While Catherine was in every quarter extending her dominions, and grasping all the territory on which she could seize with impunity, every accession of power to her rivals alarmed her fears and awakened her jealousy. The increasing fame of Frederic II. and his preponderance in Europe, more particularly disquieted her. From the first partition of Poland, Frederic had been daily encroaching on the privileges of Dantzick, which, pressed by his power, was nearly compelled to surrender itself or relinquish its commerce. Catherine, who had herself coveted Dantzick, was the more exasperated at this conduct. Its magistrates were, by her minister, artfully invited to implore her protection. Her mediation was in consequence offered to the king of Prussia, which retarded for a while the fate of the city.

A disturbance of a different nature agitated, at the same time, another quarter of Europe. A design of opening the Scheldt had been formed by Joseph II. This measure was opposed by the Dutch, who left no means unessayed to engage Frederic to support by force their pretensions.

CATHERINE II.

Catherine having declared on the side of Germany, Holland, dreading to be excluded from the ports of the Baltic, wisely forebore hostilities, and had recourse to negociation. The attention of Europe became interested in a question which, however apparently simple and limited, gave rise to various conclusions. Nature and justice appeared to be on the side of the emperor, whose arguments were forcible, open, and plausible. The states opposed facts and existing circumstances to the reasoning of their adversaries. ' What an extraordinary scene,' said they, ' would Europe exhibit, if compelled to recur to original principles, and to acknowledge the law of Nature ! What would be the fate of its different powers, when obliged to relinquish those possessions and privileges which fraud or force, war or treaty, through the revolution of ages, have enabled them to acquire ?' Arguments like these, however they might affect the philosopher, must to the spoilers of Poland be allowed unanswerable.

The Dutch had for their tenacity a better motive than these ostensible pleadings. The Scheldt by its different branches intersected their dominions, and communicated with their rivers : many of their principal cities, their harbours, docks, and naval arsenals, even the whole interior of their

CATHERINE II.   181

couhtry, would lie upon and exposed to the pos-
sessor of the Scheldt. Their very existence therefore, as a nation, was concerned in this dispute.

The history of this contention, however interesting in itself, belongs not to the present memoir. Let it suffice to say, that in the summer
of the following year, the negociations between
the emperor and Holland were resumed at Paris.
Towards the end of June, a deputation from the
republic set out from the Hague to the court of
Vienna, whose object seems to have been merely
to make such concessions on the part of Holland
as might accord with the emperor's ideas of dignity, and open the way to accommodation.

While Catherine was securing the external
peace of the empire, cabals and intrigues were
reviving in her court. No means were unessayed
to incite the grand-duke against his mother, and
irritate the mother against her son. Paul was accustomed to pass the autumn at Gatshina, a seat
eighteen versts from Tzar-sko-selo. A report
suddenly arose, that he designed to build there a
town, and to give liberty to all who should make
it their residence. The peasants flocked in crowds
to partake of these benefits, from all parts of the
empire. Paul beheld them with surprise, and
with great prudence kindly dismissed them. An

incipient revolt was thus stifled, from which great effects had been anticipated.

Bezborodko, who succeeded to Panin, and who seemed to have inherited his sentiments, became, by his perspicacity and zeal, necessary to the empress. Connected with the family of Vorontzoff, he was the secret opponent of Potemkin, who, disdaining his enemies, openly braved them, or made them his sport with peculiar address.

Lanskoï the favourite, attached to Potemkin, by whom he was affectionately regarded, grew daily more dear to Catherine. His education having been neglected, she took on herself the improvement of his mind, which she enriched with useful knowledge. Through his capacity and docility, he soon became not less distinguished for his acquirements and manners, than for the graces of his person. The affection of the empress for this youth appears to have been tender and sincere : she admired in him her own creation. But her satisfaction, however genuine, proved to be transient. A fever seized her beloved pupil, who, in the flower of his age, expired in the arms of his friend and sovereign. Catherine, till the last moment of his existence, continued to lavish on him the most passionate attentions. She abandoned herself on his decease to grief and regret: shutting her-

CATHERINE II.   183

self up in her chamber for several days, she refused all sustenance, and remained three months,
without going out, in her palace of Tzar-sko-selo.
She erected, in the gardens of the palace, a superb
mausoleum to the memory of Lanskoï, which
appeared through the trees from the windows of
her private apartments. Two years after this
event, while accidentally walking near this monument of her tenderness, she was observed by the
courtiers to shed a flood of tears. The fortune of
Lanskoï, which was estimated at 3,000,000 rubles, and which he had bequeathed to the empress, she returned to his sisters, reserving to
herself only the right of purchasing the pictures,
the medals, the library, the plate, and one landed
estate, valued at 400,000 rubles, of which she had
made him a present.

Potemkin took upon himself the care of con-
soling the empress for the loss of her favourite :
he only could presume to penetrate the retirement
in which she passed her hours. His influence
over her mind appeared daily to increase, and,
whether from gratitude or from attachment, she
determined, it is said, to unite him to herself by
secret but indissoluble ties. The obligations of
marriage, if indeed they existed, appeared to im-

pose but little restraint on the future conduct of either party.

The place of favourite, vacated by the death of Lanskoï, excited the ambition and intrigues of the court. Princess Dashkoff earnestly sought to obtain it for her son, and for a moment promised herself success. The young prince Dashkoff, tall and of an advantageous figure, flattered himself with being able to atract the attention of the empress. But Potemkin, aware of his designs, without affecting to oppose them, contrived to render him ridiculous in the eyes of Catherine, and to introduce a competitor in her favour. Yermoloff and Momonoff, two subaltern officers in the guards, were with this view charged by him with some trifling commission to the empress, who, having attentively observed them, decided in favour of the former.

A ball was given at court, in which prince Dashkoff, unconscious of what had passed, displayed an extraordinary magnificence. The courtiers, believing his triumph at hand, already paid to him their homage ; while Potemkin artfully redoubled his complaisance to the princess. Deceived by his duplicity, she wrote to him a note on the following day, requesting him to admit her nephew, the

CATHERINE II. 185

young count Butterlin, into the number of his aides-de-camp. Potemkin maliciously replied, that the places were full, the last having been already bestowed on lieutenant Yermoloff, whose name and person were alike unknown to the princess. The same day she became acquainted with both, on perceiving him at the Hermitage take his station behind the chair of the empress.

In 1785, a new source of jealousy and discord had opened in Germany, respecting the proposed exchange of an ancient and great electorate in the heart of Germany, for the Austrian Netherlands. The king of Prussia, who became upon this occasion the guardian and protector of the Germanic rights and liberties, and who regarded the alliance between Austria and Russia as highly formidable, invited the electors and princes of the German empire to unite for the defence of the Germanic constitution. The king of Great Britain, as elector of Hanover, was one of the first who entered the confederacy; a measure which gave great displeasure both to the empress and to Potemkin.

The court of London, desirous of renewing its treaty of commerce with Russia, had sent for the purpose to Petersburg a minister-plenipotentiary. Catherine, though with no design of interrupting a trade beneficial to both countries, thought proper, as a testimony of her resentment against the court of England, to delay the renewal required.

The French embassador at Constantinople had instigated the court of Petersburg to act in concert with that of Versailles. The count de Ségur was appointed embassador upon this occasion, a young negociator peculiarly suited to his mission, who, to talents and extensive erudition, added prepossessing manners with the most frank and insinuating address. Thus qualified he failed not to acquire the favour of Catherine and the esteem of Potemkin, who, rough and haughty, was yet capable of appreciating merit.

The empress was desirous of visiting the famous canal of Vishney-Volotshok, which, joining the Volga with the Ilmen lake, and the lake with the Ladoga, unites the Caspian with the Baltic sea. Prince Potemkin, Yermoloff, and the foreign ministers, accompanied her on this expedition. The embassador of France going one day to speak with Potemkin, found him particularly incensed against the court of London. Ségur, artfully taking advantage of this disgust, represented to Potemkin the benefit that would result to Russia from a direct commerce with France, without the agency of England, which reaped the

CATHERINE II.

profits from both countries. Potemkin having listened to him with attention, engaged him to commit his observations to paper, promising to communicate them only to the empress. The minister immediately returned to his barge, where, finding count Cobentzel and Mr. Fitzherbert amusing themselves with backgammon, he borrowed of the latter his inkstand, and, with the pen of the English embassador, drew up the plan of a treaty of commerce between France and Russia. The paper was immediately, through Potemkin, conveyed to Catherine, who gave to it her assent. This done, it was returned to Ségur, to be presented in the customary form to Osterman the vice-chancellor.

Osterman, on the receipt of the paper, ignorant of what had passed, and devoted to the English, informed the French minister that he could not presume to flatter him with success. Ségur made no reply. The plan was submitted to the council and immediately ratified. Such was the origin of the treaty of commerce between France and Russia. Previous to signing the treaty, an expectation was signified by the Russian ministers, that France should declare her adhesion to the armed neutrality. This was consented to, on a proviso, that the court of Petersburg should promise to conclude no treaty with any other power but on a similar condition. This clause, inimical to the interest of England, retarded for a long time the renewal of the treaty solicited by its minister.

Towards the close of the same year, 1785, a treaty of commerce was concluded with the emperor, highly advantageous to his people, and calculated to produce between the two empires an hereditary and permanent friendship. Similar negociations also took place with various other nations, while the commercial treaty with England was suffered to expire.

Catherine, before she returned to Petersburg, made a visit to Moscow ; and, time having nearly effaced the remembrance of her usurpations, was less unfavourably received than on former occasions. Among those who appeared at her court was Gudovitch, the friend of the late czar, the simplicity of whose dress distinguished him from the crowd of courtiers, and whose presence recalled to every mind the image of his unfortunate master. Countess Vorontzoff, the mistress of Peter, had been long recalled from exile, and was married to the admiral Paliansky. She was never invited to court, but her daughter had been sent for by the empress, and admitted into the number of her maids of honour.

The spirit of toleration was a distinguished and singular feature in the administration of Catherine : during the whole of her reign, not a single instance occurred of religious penalty or prohibition. Persons of all countries and persuasions, lutherans, calvinists, moravians, papists, mohammedans, and infidels, if deemed worthy, might alike aspire to any place under government, whether civil or military. This liberal spirit became, in its most comprehensive sense, not merely the characteristic of the government, but of the whole empire. Professors and teachers of the several religions communicated with each other in the bonds of strict fellowship and social union ; neither jealousy nor hatred existed among them ; no one erected his own into a *standard-mind*, or assumed the office of inquisitor into the faith of his neighbour. The empress, not satisfied with having appointed a catholic bishop, established at Mohilef a seminary of jesuits, supported islamism in the Krimea, and gave annually to her people some solemn instance of her protection granted to liberty of conscience. On the day of the benediction of the waters, her confessor, by her orders, invited to his house the ecclesiastics of every denomination, to whom he gave a grand entertainment, styled by Catherine the ' dinner of toleration.' The clergy of eight different forms of worship have been seen associated at this philosophical festival. The offices of religion, it has been calculated, were performed in Petersburg in fourteen different languages.

The empress had laboured, through the whole of her reign, to diffuse knowledge among her people. With this view, houses of education had been founded in the several towns, and at length distributed through the countries. A commission of public instruction was erected, at the head of which was placed Zavodoffsky, her former favourite, who was also appointed secretary of the cabinet and governor of the Lombard or loan-bank, which had been opened on a singular principle. Instead of borrowing money from her subjects, Catherine reversed the usual order of things, and became the great money-lender to the empire. This bank also acted as an insurance-office against losses by fire: in it likewise both foreigners and natives were permitted to deposit their money, for the security of which the imperial word was pledged.

The empress was perpetually sending notes to

CATHERINE II.   191

the committee of public instruction, to which she
attached great importance, communicative of her
ideas for the improvement of the institution;
while, during the performance of the lessons, she
was frequently present. A learned German had
consented to become professor of history and
geography, in the Russ language, of which no
native was found capable. Catherine being one day
present at a lecture, delivered by the professor to
the several tribes that inhabit Siberia, bestowed
great praise on his knowledge and zeal. She
afterwards proposed an objection to some of his
observations, to which he replied in a clear and
satisfactory manner. Zavodoffsky, unaccustomed
to hear a literary man oppose an opinion against
that of the sovereign, appeared irritated by the
presumption of the lecturer. The empress, earnestly interrupting him, acknowledged that she had
been mistaken, and thanked the professor for the
ability he had displayed in rectifying her ideas :
but, observing the wrath of Zavodoffsky not yet
allayed, she embraced the opportunity offered her
by the moment in which he led her to the carriage, to order him to repeat to the lecturer her
satisfaction and her thanks. The president, less
candid and liberal than his sovereign, found
means, notwithstanding what had passed, to

punish the professor for his courage by depriving him of his place.

In the latter part of this year, 1785, great havoc was made by the Russians among the Ruban Tartars : a Tartar khan, two of his sons, and a nephew, were captured and brought prisoners to Petersburg.

Yermoloff, when arrived at the pinnacle of favour, fell by his own imprudence. Jealous in his temper, he treated with caprice and ingratitude the man to whom he owed his fortune; and eagerly seized every opportunity to lessen him in the opinion of the empress. Potemkin perceived in the coolness of Catherine's manner the perfidy and influence of the favourite. An uncle of Yermoloff had been, not undeservedly, dismissed by Potemkin from the service in disgrace, in consequence of a quarrel at play. The nephew complained to the empress, who, at his instigation, reproved Potemkin. ' Madam,' replied he, haughtily, ' there is but one alternative ; you must dismiss Yermoloff or me : for so long as you keep that white negro *, I will not set my foot within the palace.' The same day Yermoloff received orders to travel, and was succeeded by Momonoff.

---

* A term alluding to the fairness of his complexion.

CATHERINE II.   193

These intrigues were scarcely heard beyond the precincts of the court, while Catherine's love of glory was universally known. If her character as a *sovereign* was great, as a *woman* it admits of no palliation.

The professor Pallas had, during his travels in the interior of Russia, collected various natural curiosities, with which he had formed a valuable cabinet. This was purchased of him by the empress, as were also the libraries of d'Alembert and Voltaire.

Several persons had, at various times, by order of Catherine, traversed the northern Archipelago, and the remotest of the Russian provinces. In 1785, she sent others towards Caucasus, and to the frontiers of China, for the purpose of exploring those parts of the empire which were yet unknown. The only fruit of their discoveries made public, was the account of a small colony of strangers and Christians, found in the most sequestered parts of the wilds of Caucasus, and whose manners exhibited a primeval simplicity. These people appeared ignorant of their own origin; but, from an affinity in their language and other circumstances, were supposed to be descendants of a colony of Bohemians, who, flying from persecution, towards the close of the fifteenth

194   **CATHERINE II.**

century, found refuge from their oppressors in these remote deserts.

A marine expedition was formed about this time, for the purpose of ascertaining, or of extending, those discoveries which had before been unsuccessfully undertaken or imperfectly achieved. But the work which reflects yet greater honour upon Catherine, is the navigable canal in the province of Iver, which, by opening a communication between the rivers Ivert and the Msta, will, if ever completed, not only establish an inland navigation through the countries between the shores of the Caspian and the Baltic, but actually unite those distant seas: an union unparalleled in the annals of history.

The czarina, desirous of augmenting the population of her newly-acquired provinces, published a manifesto, inviting foreigners to resort thither. By another manifesto, which appeared a few months after the former, she declared to the inhabitants of Russia and Tartary, that it was no longer required of them, in their addresses to the throne, to style themselves *slaves* but *subjects*. Arts of popularity like these are laudable, and reflect credit upon such as adopt them. Whether from inclination or policy, Catherine endeared herself to her people by the attention she paid to

CATHERINE II. 195

their children, of whom she always had a number in her apartments, whose caresses she returned with extreme complacence, and who enjoyed in the palace the same liberty with the princes her grandchildren.

Munificence and grandeur were the characteristics of her court, which in splendor and magnificence was formed upon the Asiatic rather than the European model.

In the beginning of the year 1786, the empress publicly announced her design of making a progress to Kerson and the Krimea, for the purpose of being crowned sovereign of her new conquests. The procession, whether by sea or land, was to be suited to the grand concluding ceremonial, when the empress was to be crowned queen of Taurida, and declared protectress of all the Tartar nations. A fleet of galleys, built for the occasion, were ordered to be furnished with every necessary convenience, and elegant accommodation, fitted to a luxurious and magnificent court. The sum of 7,000,000 rubles * is said (probably with some exaggeration) to have been dedicated to the mere expence of presents to be

---

* 1,500,000*l.*

K 2

distributed at the coronation. In this lavish magnificence a political object was in view: terrified by the power, or allured by the pomp, displayed on this occasion, the adjoining nations, it was believed, would flock from all parts to do homage to the new sovereign of the east, who would thereby enlarge and secure her dominion, without the hazard of war or the expence of conquest.

But the grand political object of Catherine in this intended display, after having taken the sceptre of the Krimea, and awed the surrounding nations, was to conduct her grandson Constantine to the gates of the eastern empire; to the sovereignty of which she had destined him from his birth. Greek nurses had, with this view, been procured for him from the isle of Naxos: dressed in the Greek fashion, and surrounded by children of that nation, he had acquired their language, which he spoke with facility. It was for him that the Grecian cadet-corps of two hundred cadets was established. The preparations were nearly completed, and all was in motion, when the prince unfortunately sickened of the measles, and was obliged to be left at Petersburg. This event, combined with other circumstances, more particularly the account of some serious altercations between the Russians and Tartars, occasioned

CATHERINE II. 197

considerable alterations in the projected progress. Narrowed in its design, and disencumbered of its magnificence, the coronation and the new titles were given up, the expected military force did not attend, neither did the procession take place at the time proposed : the empress was content with shewing herself to her new subjects, and appearing to take some kind of formal possession of Kerson and the Krimea. The inhabitants of those unknown regions, alarmed rather than dazzled by the report of the intended progress, and considering it as a signal of general danger, cemented their forces, and united for resistance. This effect of a vain pomp soon became apparent, while the war of the Krimea grew daily more serious.

The conferences held on this occasion between Catherine, the emperor, and the king of Poland, were beheld by the Ottomans with anxiety and suspicion. However insignificant Poland might appear as an ally, in the scale of hostile exertion, its situation between the two empires, which it was capable of uniting, with its valuable productions, rendered it, in the eyes of the Porte, a formidable accession to the strength of their enemies. It was even rumoured, that, on this memorable progress, the friendship of the king, limited as was his authority, had been purchased by a sum of money; a report that exposed him to a charge, at the ensuing diet, of having entered into conditions inimical to the republic.

The ambition of Catherine had roused the jealousy and the fears of the Turkish empire; a distrust which a thousand circumstances, added to her views respecting her grandson (views rendered but too apparent by his name and education) sufficiently justified. The grand object attributed to her, to which every other was said to be in subordination, was the establishing in her family two mighty empires, capable of subverting Europe and Asia. The ruined Tartars, driven from the Krimea, complained loudly of the pusillanimity of the Porte, and implored heaven and earth for vengeance. The intended enthronement of Catherine was regarded by all as fixing to her usurpations a final seal.

On the 18th of January, 1787, the empress commenced her journey, attended by her court, her friends, and favourites, with the ministers of Austria, of France, and England. The sledges travelled night and day. At every station a number of horses had been previously collected: great fires were lighted at the distance of every thirty fathom; while a concourse of people, whom cu-

CATHERINE II. 199

riosity had attracted, skirted the road. Potemkin, who had gone on before, joined Catherine at Kief, where she was also met by the Polish princes and nobles who were in the Russian interest.

Fifty galleys had been disposed on the Dniepr for the reception of the empress, who embarked at the beginning of the spring, attended by a numerous suite. On the following day the fleet cast anchor opposite to Kanieff, when the king of Poland, under the title of Count Poniatofsky, went on board the galley of Catherine. On their first meeting, after an interval of three-and-twenty years, the empress appeared to be in some degree affected, while Stanislaus, preserving more presence of mind, discoursed with great composure. They remained alone, in private conference, more than half an hour, after which they dined together. Catherine decorated her former favourite with the riband of the order of St. Andrew. Potemkin appeared to be charmed with the Polish monarch, whom he beheld for the first time: to this favourable impression made upon the Russ by Stanislaus, the preservation of his crown for some years longer is ascribed. He retired in the evening highly satisfied with his reception, and the fleet pursued its course.

At Krementshuk the empress found an army of

12,000 men, in new uniforms, who performed before her a mock fight. It was on this occasion, while distributing her favours on all who pressed forward to receive them, that Catherine, addressing Suvaroff, said, ' And you, general, do you want nothing ?'—' Only that you will order my lodgings* to be paid, madam,' answered he.

The shores of the Dniepr were covered with villages, constructed for the occasion, with peasants elegantly dressed, tending numerous flocks, who, by cross roads, came to different parts of the coast by which the fleet was to pass, and thus were incessantly reproduced to the voyagers. The beauty of the season, added to the effect of this spectacle, spread an enchantment over regions nearly desert.

Joseph II. had arrived at Kerson some time before the empress, whom he set out to meet. Catherine landed at Kaïdak, and, accompanied by the emperor, proceeded to Kerson, already an opulent city. Upon a gate towards the east, the empress read as she passed, a Greek inscription to the following purport :—" By this, the way leads to Byzantium."

---

* The rent of the lodgings was two rubles per month.

CATHERINE II. 201

Foreigners of all nations, drawn by-curiosity, or by the desire of paying homage to Catherine, were assembled at Kerson. Among others, Miranda, a fugitive from the Havannah, was presented to her by Potemkin: obliged to fly his own country, he sought and found an asylum in Russia. Among the ladies who resorted to the court of the empress, appeared a Grecian, whose charms triumphed over the heart of Potemkin.

A message sent to the divan, before the departure of Catherine from Petersburg, announcing her journey and softening its purport, had failed in disarming the distrust of the Porte; who, considering the progress in itself as an aggression, took measures to repel it. Four Turkish ships anchored at the mouth of the Borysthenes, while the empress remained at Kerson. Beholding them with scorn, and turning to her courtiers— ' Do you see ?' said she: ' one would suppose that the Turks had no recollection of Tschesmé.'

It was at Kerson that Joseph II. received intelligence of the rebellion that had broken out at Brabant. He nevertheless followed Catharine in her visit to the interior of the Krimea, where she was received by the principal myrzas, whose troops in her presence made various evolutions. On a sudden the carriages were surrounded by a

Memoirs of Women Writers, Volume 7

thousand Tartars, who formed themselves into an escort. Joseph, who had not been apprised of this manœuvre, expressed some uneasiness, while the empress preserved her usual tranquillity. This Tartar escort had been appointed by Potemkin, who, not far off, had an army of 153,000 men.

Catherine, having made her entry with great pomp, was lodged with her suite in the palace of the Khan. In the evening she was entertained with the spectacle of a mountain which, artificially illuminated, appeared as on fire. Every exertion was made to entertain her with agreeable objects, while, in her turn, she omitted no art of conciliation to engage the affections of the people. She allotted funds for the building of two mosques, and distributed considerable presents among the myrzas, who testified towards her an ardent devotion, and in six weeks afterwards declared for the Turks.

On her way back the empress was conducted to Pultowa, where, on her arrival, two armies appearing, approached, engaged, and gave a lively and exact representation of the famous battle in which the hero of Sweden was defeated by Peter the Great. Joseph II. delighted with this spectacle, prepared by Potemkin, expressed his sa-

CATHERINE II. 203

tisfaction, while he deplored nevertheless the fate of the Swedish hero. Gratified by the conduct of Potemkin, and charmed by the behaviour of the empress, he entered into all her measures, and expressed his inclination to assist in causing her grandson to be crowned at Constantinople. At Moscow the imperial friends parted: Joseph, taking leave of the empress, rapidly crossed Poland, and returned to his dominions, while Catherine pursued the road to Petersburg.

Potemkin, however desirous of war both from public and private motives, was anxious that hostilities should be commenced by the Turks. Burthened with honours and titles, he was still solicitous to add to his dignities the grand riband of the order of St. George. To obtain this, it was necessary to command an army, and to gain a victory. A hecatomb of victims was without remorse to be offered at the shrine of his ambition.

The Russian troops made a licentious use of the privileges granted to them by the Porte: a variety of intrigues were set on foot; while the court of Petersburg gave perpetual countenance to the violation of treaties. The Porte, irritated at this conduct, and at the discovery of a correspondence between one of the rulers of Cairo and the Russian minister, gave orders for quelling the disturbances in Egypt. A conference was a few days afterwards demanded of the minister, and a memorial presented to him, stating the causes of complaint.

The embassador requested time to consult his court; a petition readily granted: but, on a second meeting, the divan resolved that it was unnecessary to wait for an answer. War * was accordingly declared in Constantinople, and the minister shut up in the castle of the Seven Towers. The injuries and insults of which the Porte complained, were certainly neither few nor imaginary.

The embassadors of Vienna and France united their efforts to obtain from the divan the liberation of the Russian minister: their remonstrances proved ineffectual: the English embassador, entering warmly into the interests of his court, which resented the treaty of commerce between Russia and France, opposed to theirs his influence.

The Turks prepared with alacrity for war: a formidable army advanced to the shores of the Danube, while the standard of Mohammed was prepared to be unfurled. The progress of the empress to Kerson had been beheld with rage by

---

* August 18th, 1787.

CATHERINE II. 205

the people, who repined at the supineness of their governors. All Europe wondered, on seeing the Porte prepare for war, at its forbearance on this occasion.

To increase the confidence of the army and the reverence of the nation, the grand-vizier was entrusted by the sovereign 'with extraordinary powers, which received a sanction in the joy and approbation of the people. A squadron of sixteen ships of the line, eight frigates, and several galleys, entered the Euxine, under the command of the capadan-pacha. The old admiral had but recently returned from Egypt, where he had subdued the rebellious beys, and collected a tribute of twelve millions of piastres. Humble amidst his success, he recollected with grief the disaster of Tschesmé, while he harangued the fleet on the subject of their expedition. ' I am going in quest of battles,' said he, ' firmly resolved to conquer or die.—Should there be any one among you who wants courage to sacrifice himself in the glorious conflict, let him speak freely. He shall find favour before me, and receive his dismission. But those who neglect to execute my orders in the hour of battle, must hope for no excuse. I swear by Mohammed, and the life of my sultan, their heads shall pay the forfeit of their disobedience.

But on him who performs his duty a liberal reward shall be bestowed.   Let those who on these
conditions are willing to follow me, rise up, and
swear to obey me faithfully.'   The commanders
having on this address all risen, swore to conquer
or die with their leader. ' Go,' returned he, ' my
brave and faithful companions, return to your
ships, receive the oaths of your crews, and hold
yourselves in readiness for sailing to-morrow.'
The Turks having disarmed the Greeks, of whose
fidelity they were doubtful, invited the Tartars,
who regretted their old masters and detested
their new ones, to return to their allegiance.   In
vain the empress loaded them with presents; in
vain she caused mosques to be erected, and Korans
to be printed ; the Tartars, beholding in her
merely the Christian, yearned after their mussul-
man prince. The myrzas met and elected a khan,
who soon beheld under him an army of 4000
men.

The news of the war, which, foreseen by the
empress, had been impatiently expected at Petersburg, was received with transports of joy.   The
preparations were already made : prince Potemkin,
commander in chief of the forces, had under his
orders a number of generals, among whom was
Suvaroff, afterwards so celebrated.   Marshal Ro-

CATHERINE II.   207

mantzoff, unwilling to be an instrument to the glory of Potemkin, excused himself on account of his age from accepting the command, of which some remains of a forced respect had procured him the offer. His son joined the army. A fleet was equipped in the Euxine, and two strong squadrons were in readiness at Cronstadt to sail for the Mediterranean. Joseph II. not less solicitous than Catherine for a war with the Turks, afforded to her a powerful support. Eighty thousand Austrians were on their march to Moldavia; every thing seemed to announce the ruin of the Ottoman power.

A manifesto was published by the empress in the usual style: the Turks were accused in lofty terms of the infraction of treaties, while a catalogue of charges was brought against them.— " Perfectly innocent of all the calamities engendered by war," Catherine, relying on the justice of her cause, asserts her claim to the providence and protection of God, and to the prayers of all the christian world. This manifesto was followed by a second, which declared—" That the Porte had been so arrogant as to insist on a categorical answer to its absurd demands : that the empress, forced to repel the aggression of the enemy of the christian name, armed herself with confidence under the protection of that righteous God *, who had so long and so powerfully guarded the Russian empire."

In support of these memorials, which were to move heaven and earth against the Ottomans, means were employed yet better adapted to the superstition of the Russians. Papers were printed, in which prophecies predicting the speedy ruin of Constantinople were published and circulated.

On the side of the enemy also, an angel appeared to the Sheik Mansour, in the midst of a wood, and empowered him to collect an army against the Russians from among the hordes of mount Caucasus. Thus encouraged, the Sheik, supported by some neighbouring tribes of Tartars and scattered Turks, entered the Russian frontiers at the head of 8000 men, but paid dearly for his temerity: the Tartars struggled in vain against superior numbers, arms, and discipline.

---

* The king of Prussia acted with more good sense in his attack upon Silesia. *Pro Deo et Patria,* was proposed as the device for his standard. He erased *Pro Deo,* saying it was improper to confound the name of God with the quarrels of men, and that he was going to fight for a province and not for religion.

CATHERINE II.   209

To detail the particulars of the war is not the business of this narration; suffice it to say, that the advantage was on the side of the Russians, and *Te Deum* was sung in the churches of Petersburg. The minister of France was earnestly solicited by the empress to engage his court to unite with her in the dismemberment of the Ottoman empire; in return for which service she proposed to cede to France the possession of Egypt, of the conquest of which she believed herself secure. This temptation proved insufficient to overpower other considerations nearer and more impressive: the government of Petersburg already threatened to disarrange the equilibrium of Europe; while interest and policy combined to render France adverse to the ruin of the Turks.

In her efforts to incite christendom against the Porte, Catherine could scarcely flatter herself with success; her growing power must necessarily become an object of distrust, and awaken the jealousy of the surrounding nations. Prussia could not be expected patiently to suffer the aggrandisement either of Russia or Austria; while England excited the Ottomans to resistance. But what appears to have been unforeseen by the empress, was the resolution of Gustavus III. to declare against her immediate war.

Russia thus found herself suddenly involved in new and unexpected difficulties, the consequences of which were not in her original calculations. As a nation, Sweden wanted not cause of resentment against Russia; the sense of past injuries was still keen, while from her present boundless ambition she had every thing to dread. The revolution in the government of Sweden had produced between the two courts mutual jealousy and dislike: that Sweden should ever recover her rank among nations was contrary to the policy and to the interest of Russia: since the visit of Gustavus to Petersburg, whence he departed suddenly, as it was reported, without taking leave, and returned precipitately to his dominions, the breach between the two courts had been gradually growing wider. In a pamphlet written by Gustavus on the situation of public affairs, his offered mediation is stated between Russia and the Porte; an office for which he was particularly qualified by the friendship subsisting between Sweden and Turkey. The scorn with which this proposal was received and rejected, appears to have been sensibly felt by the royal writer. A similar offer from Great Britain, supported by Prussia, was treated with little less ceremony. To the pertinacious adherence of Catherine to her designs, the king attributes his subsequent conduct, which he justifies on the principle of self-defence. The ministers also of Russia had successfully employed themselves in sowing dissensions among the Swedish nobles, who were but too much inclined to listen to their insidious counsels.

Gustavus, resolved on revenge, formed a treaty with the Ottomans: Prussia supplied him with money, while England promised to assist him with a fleet. Thus supported, he determined to march against Frederiksham, to attack the town on two different sides, and take it by assault.

The inhabitants of Petersburg were seized with surprise and consternation : the Russian soldiery having been sent off against the Turks, the empress at the moment of alarm had only some invalids, with a few detachments of her guards, to send to the relief of Frederiksham. That Gustavus would get possession of the place, and proceed to lay siege to the residence, no one appeared to doubt. Catherine preserved, amidst extreme anxiety, the exterior of tranquillity : the French embassador entering the palace at this critical moment, she enquired of him what news was talked of ?—' That you, madam, are going to set out for Moscow,' replied he.—' It is true,' said she, ' I have given orders for a number of post-horses to be kept in readiness ; but it is for the purpose of bringing soldiers and cannon.'—In reality, the few troops dispersed among the less distant garrisons were collected and sent into Finland to join the detachments already there. The command of this incomplete army was given to an inexperienced general, whose military reputation was ill calculated to alleviate the apprehensions of the people. The empress hastily published a declaration, in which, complaining of the conduct of the king of Sweden, she dissembled the weakness of her troops, pretending that the garrisons had been reinforced by way of precaution, long before the aggression of the Swedes. The Swedish minister was at the same time ordered instantly to quit the empire.

Hostilities were commenced in Finland, in which the advantages were on the side of the Swedes. Their fleet in the mean time paraded about the gulf; and even, advancing within sight of the batteries of Cronstadt, appeared to defy the Russian armament, which had received sailing orders for the Mediterranean; but the appearance of the Swedish vessels occasioned them to be recalled.

The near approach of an enemy could not fail to alarm the capital, who knew of war only by report. Troops were drawn from all quarters for

CATHERINE II. 213

its defence, and every possible precaution of security adopted. The younger branches of the imperial family were sent to Moscow, while the empress unappalled awaited the bursting of the storm. All the Kozacs within reach were hastily collected, to be turned loose, when occasion should serve, upon the provinces of Sweden; while admiral Greig, a Scotsman, a brave and distinguished seaman, sailed with a strong fleet from Cronstadt to counteract the designs of the enemy by sea, on the side of which only they could yet menace Petersburg.

It should seem as if, from the supineness with which Europe had beheld the dismemberment of Poland, with the perfidy and violence practised on the occasion, Russia and Austria had in their present system been lulled to security; they appeared to take it for granted, that the subversion of a great and ancient empire, with the division of its spoils, would be observed by the nations with equal indifference: but this inertness no longer existed; attention had been roused, jealousy was excited, and Europe took the alarm. The claims, pretensions, and designs of the allied empires, were now regarded with a general coldness, an implied or declared disapprobation. Genoa only afforded an exception, by granting a loan to

Russia and the use of her ports; she engaged likewise to furnish the Mediterranean fleet with stores and supplies. Prussia, from its situation, its interest, and its power, was the most formidable adversary to the allied empires; its monarch, whose policy was not yet to be fathomed, beheld the gathering tempest with a steady eye, as if waiting to behold it burst before he took his resolutions.

Such was the aspect of public affairs, and so unfavourable was the appearance of Europe to a war, which its partisans firmly believed would terminate in the subversion of the Ottoman empire. The favour and concurrence of England, on which the court of Petersburg had multiplied disobligations, was of peculiar importance in this conjuncture: but while Russia depended for assistance on the commerce and manufactures of Great Britain, she neglected to conciliate her favour, and refused to renew her treaties. The agents for the empress in London had agreed for the hire of ships to serve as tenders to the Russian fleet, in the conveyance of stores, arms, and ammunition, when a proclamation in the London Gazette, prohibiting British seamen from entering into the service of any foreign power, &c. put a sudden stop to their proceedings.

CATHERINE II. 215

This disappointment was followed by a second of a similar nature in the republic of Holland; a measure which was attributed by Russia to the influence of Great Britain. The court of Petersburg, however exasperated, was ultimately benefited by these impediments, which, by occasioning the delay of her fleet, preserved her capital from the attacks of her neighbour the king of Sweden.

The Russian squadron, commanded by admiral Greig, having put to sea, the hostile fleets approached each other in a fog off the island of Hoogland. A desperate conflict ensued, the horror of which was augmented by darkness, by inclement elements, and the dangers of a narrow sea, studded with islands, rocks, and shoals. The event was undecisive, victory being claimed on both sides. Admiral Greig, from the accession of fresh ships, and the vicinity of the great naval magazines and arsenals, was in a short time able again to put to sea with an acquisition of strength. Coming suddenly upon the Swedes when, unapprehensive of an attack, their situation and circumstances rendered them incapable of defence, he assailed them furiously and threw them into disorder: the Gustavus Adolphus, of 60 guns, abandoned as a sacrifice for the rest, was taken and burnt by the Russians. From this event till the end of the campaign, the Swedes, shut up in the harbour of Sveabourg, were precluded from the means of refitting, while the Russian fleet rode triumphant mistress of the seas.

The joy at Petersburg on this sudden turn of affairs, was in proportion to its late panic; while the favours shewn to the admiral proved the importance of his service. A letter was written to him by the empress, in her own hand, full of praise and acknowledgment: to this honour were added the substantial benefits of a large sum of money, and an estate in Livonia. Not more fortunate in his life than honoured in his death, which took place towards the close of the year, his funeral was, by the orders of the empress, celebrated with pomp, and adorned by those appropriate naval and military honours, which by the martial nations of Europe are assigned as a tribute to the manes of the brave.

Offers of accommodation were proposed to Catherine by the king of Sweden, who, adopting a high tone, sensibly wounded her pride. It was required by Gustavus, that count Razumoffsky, the Russian minister at Stockholm, should be punished for his intrigues and machinations; that a part of Finland and Karelia, ceded to Russia by former treaties, should be restored to Sweden;

CATHERINE II. 217

that the court of Petersburg should, under the mediation of Sweden, make peace with the Pope; that the independence of the Krimea should be established, and that Russia should immediately disarm, while Sweden should remain in arms till after the conclusion of the treaty.—'What language!' exclaimed Catherine indignantly; 'if the king of Sweden were already at Moscow, I would even then shew him what a woman-like myself, standing on the ruins of a mighty empire, is able to do.'

Instead of making any reply to the proposals of Gustavus, the empress recalled general Mikelson, who was fighting against the Turks, and conferred upon him the command of her army in Finland, which she reinforced with 20,000 men. Beside which, she reckoned on the defection of the officers of Gustavus, nor did she miscalculate. The king of Sweden, destined to mortification, beheld the fortune of Russia predominate: in his endeavours to free his country from foreign control, and to restore in some degree her ancient glory, he experienced only accumulated and bitter disappointments. To produce in Sweden a counterrevolution, which, gratifying the ambition and venality of its nobles, would subject it to the domination of a foreign minister, was the determined

policy of Russia : for this her measures were so artfully planned, that she appeared to calculate with
certainty upon their success. Confiding in a well-
constituted army, and in the courage and discipline
of his troops, Guftavus flattered himself with carrying terror to the gates of Petersburg; when he had
the mortification to discover that no confidence
could be placed in the soldiers, that the officers
were disaffected, and that a traitorous correspondence was carried on with the enemy. At
the siege of Frederiksham, his misfortune and his
disgrace became apparent: under pretence that
the war had been undertaken without the consent
of the state, and contrary to the constitution of
Sweden, the officers refused to lead on the attack;
while the troops, to whom Gustavus appealed, laid
down their arms, to his utter surprise and dismay.

The defection of the Swedes was more than a
victory to Catherine, who, not satisfied with this
advantage, called upon Denmark for succours.
The court of Copenhagen, however averse to war,
was faithful to its engagements with Russia: a
fleet was ordered to be equipped, while the prince-
royal, accompanied by prince Charles of Heffe*,

---

* Viceroy of Norway, and father-in-law to the prince
of Denmark.

CATHERINE II. 219

proceeded to Norway, and put themselves at the head of the troops. The Norwegians, a simple and generous nation, heard not in vain the signal of war: entering the western provinces of Sweden, and capturing every place in their course, they proceeded to lay siege to Gothemburg, the second city of the kingdom.

Gustavus was in the most imminent hazard of destruction, when the interference of England and Prussia, whom policy directed to preserve the equipoise and protect the liberties of the north, averted the present danger. The English minister at Copenhagen, informed of the siege of Gothemburg, rapidly crossed Sweden and repaired to the Danish camp. Having summoned the prince to raise the siege, he declared to him, that unless he evacuated the territory without delay, England would lay an embargo on the Danish ships in her ports, and send a squadron to bombard the castle of Kronenberg. These menaces, seconded by the remonstrances of the minister of Prussia, finally prevailed: a truce was concluded, and the army of the Danish prince returned peaceably to Norway.

The Russian fleet was in the mean time gaining frequent advantages against the Turks and Tartars: during an engagement an incident took

220   CATHERINE II.

place in which the courage inspired by national
pride was displayed even in the conduct of slaves.
The Turkish admiral's ship having caught fire, a
sailor rushed through the flames to save the flag:
a Russian seaman, not less intrepid, observing the
action, leaped into a canoe, and climbing on board
the ship on the point of blowing up, seized
the flag which the Turk was employed in un-
fastening, took him prisoner, and carried it off in
triumph.

Immense armies were preparing in Russia for
the field: nothing that might tend to ensure success was withheld from Potemkin, who governed
the war department, and whose influence was absolute. In the distribution of kingdoms and empires, it was expected that a sovereignty, under
whatever title, would at least be allotted to his
share. Those who cherished patriotic sentiments
were not without apprehension of the consequences of vesting so exorbitant a power in the
hands of an individual. The scene of action in
which the war was to be exhibited, presented the
most calamitous and deplorable aspect: famine
and pestilence had, with a long and cruel war,
combined to desolate the Tartar countries, and
lay waste the frontiers of the contending empires;
excepting in the single article of green forage, it

CATHERINE II. **221**

was necessary that the provision of the armies should be brought from an immense distance.

The Russian forces, estimated at 150,000 men, under the orders of Potemkin and general count Romantzoff, assisted by prince Repnin, Suvaroff, and other officers, appeared, in despite of these difficulties, on the banks of the Bogue, on their way to the Euxine. This force was supported by corresponding preparations of artillery, cannon, mortars, engines, &c. destined for the siege of Otchakoff. During the siege, Potemkin, whose personal courage some one had ventured to call in question, passed repeatedly for several days, with great coolness, under the very cannon of the ramparts. A general officer who accompanied him in one of these walks, having had his thigh carried away by a cannon ball, suffered some cries to escape him.—' What do you cry for?' said Potemkin coolly *. The officer was silent from respect, but expired the next day.

The place was carried by assault: the lieutenant of Potemkin (who remained with his mistresses in his camp) rushed into the town, and spread carnage and desolation on every side. Po-

---

* This speech respecting the sufferings of another exhibited brutality rather than courage.

temkin absented himself from this assault, because it presented no extraordinary opportunity for signalising himself. The Turkish soldiers defended themselves with bravery : the greater part of them fell with their weapons in their hands ; the rest, with the majority of the inhabitants, were put to the sword. The town was given up to plunder, when every species of horror and profligacy ensued. The scenes of riot and slaughter lasted three days, during which more than 25,000 Turks perished. The Russians lost in the assault 12,000 men.

These conquests, little less fatal to the victors than to the vanquished, failed to abate the ardor of Catherine for the continuance of the war. Fresh recruits were by her orders levied through the empire : men began to grow scarce in Russia ; the wilds of Siberia were therefore ransacked for exiles, who were brought to be incorporated in the troops.

Gustavus during these events was meditating revenge against Catherine ; the dissensions fomented in Sweden by her agents were injuries that he could not pardon. A lieutenant-colonel, by an atrocious plan, administered to the animosity of his master. The Russian squadron was detained by the ice in the road of Copenhagen : under the pretence of a speculation in commerce, a vessel was purchased and freighted, filled with casks of brandy, and well pitched within and without. O'Brien, a native of Ireland, of whom the ship was bought, was left as commander, with orders to take advantage of the first north-east wind and set fire to his vessel : by this means it was intended to consume not merely the fleet of Russia but that of the Danes also. O'Brien indiscreetly mentioned his engagement to a friend, who, struck with horror at the project, went in haste to report what he had heard : the Danish ministry thus alarmed, sent people to search the ship and take the commander into custody. The original contriver, suspecting the failure of his design, escaped in the livery of a domestic from the house of the Swedish minister, whither he had repaired for refuge. The minister himself, foreseeing the odium that would follow on the discovery of the plot, timely withdrew. This atrocious attempt was not calculated to reconcile the courts of Stockholm and Petersburg. Gustavus was at length finally compelled, by the superior force of Russia, to evacuate Finland.

Conquered but not discouraged, he desisted not from attempts to annoy his enemy. The

Swedish and Russian fleets continued to skirmish with various success. The prince of Nassau, who had with superior force given battle to the Swedes, and by his unskilfulness suffered an entire defeat, thus wrote to the empress :—' Madam, I have had the misfortune to fight against the elements, against the Swedes, and against the Russians *. I hope that your majesty will do me justice.' The empress replied—' You are in the right, because I am resolved that you shall be so. This is highly aristocratic, but it is therefore suitable to the country in which we live. Depend always on your affectionate Catherine.' This engagement had cost the Russians half their fleet, with more than 10,000 men. To the Swedes, who had formerly taught them to fight by land, they returned the obligation, by teaching them in turn to vanquish in this new and severe mode of deciding the fortune of war.

This defeat, which went near the heart of Catherine, accelerated a peace : Gustavus, sensible of his imprudence, and conscious of the disordered state of his affairs, accepted the terms proposed to him by the empress. The minister of Spain, who

---

* Implying that the Russians had suffered themselves to be beaten, to tarnish his glory.

CATHERINE II. 225

offered his mediation on the occasion, engaged that Gustavus should turn his arms against the French. Catherine, in the hope of seeing him entangled in a new and distant adventure, affected magnanimity ; and, feigning to pardon him, required only the re-establishment of former treaties and a total oblivion of the late hostilities.

The war of Finland afforded to the empress occasions for the display both of severity and clemency. Some Swedish officers, employed as teachers in the cadet-corps at Petersburg, ventured to correspond with their countrymen, and to speak of Catherine with great freedom. These letters were intercepted and read by the empress. The Swedes were arrested, tried, and found guilty. Catherine had, on their examination, joined with the head of the secret commission, who was a man of savage and sanguinary temper, a worthy military officer, for the express purpose of moderating his colleague. The punishment for the crime proved was death ; but the empress, with a lenity that did her honour, contented herself with sending the delinquents into the interior provinces, where she continued to them the whole of their appointment, and on the conclusion of the peace sent them back to their own country.

About the same period Radischeff, a director of

the customs at Petersburg, published the narrative of a journey from Petersburg to Moscow, in which he feigned to have had a dream, wherein Truth, appearing to him, dictated representations (which he was commanded to deliver) by which the unbounded authority of Potemkin was forcibly displayed, and even the conduct of Catherine attacked. This was the first printed libel that ever appeared at Petersburg. Notwithstanding the strict regulations of the press, it was sold by hawkers in the exchange for two days, with the *imprimatur* of the public licenser upon it, before it attracted the notice of government. Enquiries having been made respecting it, the officer of the police, whose business it is to license publications, alleged in his excuse, that, having looked at the manuscript and seen it to be the narration of a journey to Moscow, he had stampt it with his *imprimatur* without farther consideration. The author had printed the pamphlet in his own lodgings, with the types of the custom-house press: he was nevertheless discovered, and, on being interrogated, simply replied, that he conceived there was no harm in publishing a dream; that if people saw in it their own resemblance, he was no more to blame than a man who should hold up a mirror for every person to look into that pleased.

CATHERINE II. 227

The empress, so moderate on the former occasion, was so much incensed at this impertinence as to send the writer to Siberia. The princess Dashkoff and her brother, the known patrons of Radischeff, were suspected of having instigated him to this publication. It is possible that, in her generosity to the Swedes, Catherine was solicitous of gaining partisans among their countrymen, as it is certain that to the nations already in her power she could sometimes assume a terrible aspect.

That the peace should occasion joy at Stockholm is little surprising, when even at Petersburg the testimonies of public satisfaction were carried to an extreme. The pride of the nation, and the contempt so recently affected for its adversary, were not perfectly consistent with these rejoicings. A grand *Te deum*, at which the empress in person assisted, was performed in the church: during one day and night the whole court exhibited the most splendid gala; while the city, in a blaze of illuminations, re-echoed with acclamations of joy. The negociators of the peace on both sides were magnificently recompensed by Catherine; a conduct which seemed to testify the interest she took, in the event.—But to return to the Ottoman war, from which the conflict with the Swedes necessarily led.

Abdul Achmed IV. the grand-signior, a man of admirable qualities and possessing an enlightened mind, dying suddenly, was succeeded by his nephew under the name of Selim III. It was generally believed that, failing in her grand scheme of driving the Turks out of Europe and placing her grandson on the throne of the Greek emperors, the next object of Catherine was to erect into an independent sovereignty, for her favourite Potemkin, the provinces of Moldavia, Valakia, and Bessarabia. The power and influence of Potemkin, already supreme, spread jealousy and alarm through the nation. Compelled to abandon this design by the opposition of the allies, the empress soothed for the present the ambition of her favourite, by appointing him hetman of the Kozacs, an office wearing the semblance of sovereignty, and the highest in the empire.

Respecting Otchakoff, the Krimea, the Euxine, and other points of her claim, she remained inflexible. This perseverance, resented by the allies, had nearly involved Russia in a war with Great Britain and Prussia : an event only prevented by the powerful opposition raised in England against the intentions of the government. Such a measure at one period must have produced extraordinary consequences in favour of Sweden, whose warlike

CATHERINE II. 229

monarch, supported by Prussian armies and English fleets, might have carried fire and sword into the heart of the Russian empire. It became therefore to the court of Petersburg a circumstance of the utmost importance, to draw off Gustavus from an alliance thus formidable.

Of the great events depending on the capture of Otchakoff, Catherine was fully sensible : her rewards to the conquerors on this occasion exceeded even the limits of her usual magnificence. The spirit of emulation thus roused in the Russian armies, every step was marked by triumphs, and victory followed victory. The Austrian army, pressed hard by that of the grand vizier, was already retreating before the Turks, when Suvaroff at the head of 8000 Russians flew to their assistance. ' My friends,' cried he to his soldiers, (who found 30,000 of the allies pursued by 100,000 of the enemy) 'never look at the eyes of your adversaries. Fix your view at their breasts : it is there that you must thrust your bayonets.'— This intrepidity turned the fortune of the day; the Turks were routed with a horrible carnage, and Suvaroff remained master of the field. This victory, gained near the river Rimnik, procured for the conqueror the surname of Rimniksky, with the double title of Count of the Russian and of the Holy Roman empire. The capture of Tutukay in Bulgaria followed: Suvaroff, who affected brevity of style, wrote to the empress on this occasion four lines of Russ poetry, signifying —" Glory to God ! Praise to Catherine ! Tutukay is taken ! Suvaroff is in it !"—Town after town submitted to the victorious Russians : Bender surrendered at discretion. Ismaïl still held out.

This city had been for seven months besieged by Potemkin : living in his camp like one of the ancient satraps, whose luxury he equalled if not exceeded, surrounded by a crowd of courtiers and women, he became nevertheless impatient of delay. One of his mistresses, pretending to read in the arrangement of a pack of cards the decrees of fate, predicted that the town would be taken at the end of three weeks. Potemkin answered, smiling, that he was possessed of a method of divination yet more infallible. At that instant he sent orders to Suvaroff to take Ismaïl within three days. Suvaroff having made himself ready, on the third day drew up his soldiers.—' My brothers,' said he, ' provisions are dear ! No quarter'—The assault was immediately begun. Twice the Russians were repulsed with great loss. The third attack they scaled the ramparts, forced their way into the town, and put to the

CATHERINE II. 231

sword all who opposed them. Fifteen thousand Russians purchased with their lives the bloody laurels of their leader, who wrote to the empress with his usual brevity—' The haughty Ismaïl is at your feet!'

Several French officers distinguished themselves in the attack, among whom was Roger Damus Langeron. Some days after the taking of Ismaïl, Potemkin, discoursing with Langeron respecting the revolution in France, spoke with great contempt of the efforts of the people, whose struggles for liberty he considered as a crime.— ' Your countrymen, colonel,' said he, ' are a pack of madmen. I would only require my grooms to stand by me; and we should soon bring them to their senses.'—Langeron, though an emigrant, could not patiently suffer this language.—' Prince,' replied he boldly, ' I do not think you would be able to do it with all your army.' Potemkin, rising in great fury at this retort, threatened his opponent with exile to Siberia. Langeron, instantly quitting his presence, and crossing the Seret which divides Moldavia from Valakia, entered himself into the Austrian camp.

Catherine, elated with the news of these successive victories, accosted Sir Charles Whitworth, when he next appeared at court, with an ironical smile—' Sir,' said she, ' since the king your master is determined to drive me out of Petersburg, I hope he will permit me to retire to Constantinople.'

Potemkin, impatient to enjoy his triumphs, after making the necessary dispositions for leaving his army in safety, hastened his return to Petersburg. He was received by the empress with transports of joy, while honours and emoluments were showered upon him. She presented to him another palace, contiguous to her own, in the fitting up of which 600,000 rubles had been expended : to this gift was added a coat laced with diamonds, valued at 200,000. The pomp and magnificence which he affected was lavish and excessive : the expence of his table only, furnished with the rarest fruits and most exquisite dainties, was, on ordinary days, estimated at 800 rubles. In the depth of winter he forestalled all the cherries produced by a tree in a green-house at a ruble each. He possessed an immense quantity of jewels, some of which he had scarcely seen and little regarded since the moment they were brought to him. During a fit of caprice, he one day, affecting a dislike to his diamonds, had them all sold : some time after, the desire of possessing them having returned, he

CATHERINE II. 233

ordered that they should be bought in, on all sides, at whatever expence. His levee was more crowded than that of the empress : all Russia was at his feet. Seated among twenty ladies, like a sultan in his haram, with a sullen and downcast look, he spoke to no one, except at long intervals and in monosyllables. Among the princes of Russia, superior to him in birth, his title was *the prince* by way of excellence. *The prince,* as has been related, had a defect in one of his eyes : a report was one day sent to him by the hands of a one-eyed colonel ; this accidental circumstance he interpreted into a designed insult, and resented with puerile extravagance. A foreigner, a major in the Russian service, having in a poetical compliment praised, in the same stanza with the sultana of *the prince,* the mistress of his secretary, received from the indignant lover a violent box on the ear. All those who paid their court to him were treated with great arrogance : in public he has sometimes taken a Russian general by the collar, and sometimes inflicted blows on his general officers. Yet he knew where liberties might be taken with impunity, and when to command his passions. Major-generals performed for him the offices of valets ; but this, if they were content to pay the price, proved no obstacle to their

Memoirs of Women Writers, Volume 7

promotion. Of the army he was absolute lord. A lady, known at Petersburg, whose husband had a place at court, said that she meant to pass the summer at Yassy with *the prince*, who had presented to her an estate of 2000 rubles per annum. He discovered a childish eagerness in procuring every thing the most costly of its kind: he possessed ten or twelve violins of exorbitant price, one of which was valued at 6000 rubles: yet he never in his life had played on a violin: after the moment of their purchase they were no longer regarded, but were left to be spoiled by the dust or gnawed by the rats. Some person speaking before him of a library, he boasted the possession of one more valuable than could be shewn by the most learned man in Europe. A bookcase was accordingly thrown open, in which appeared several shelves of books: on examination they were found to be boxes gilt and lettered on the backs, filled with bank assignats, and rouleaux of imperials and ducats to an immense amount. Surfeiting in prosperity, he thirsted, like the fabled Tantalus, amidst the waters by which he was nearly overwhelmed.

Though severe towards the officers, he flattered the soldiery, among whom he relaxed all discipline; if by the former he was detested, of the

CATHERINE II. 235

latter he was the idol. It is pretended that this conduct was a concerted scheme between Potemkin and the empress; aware that in Russia the soldiery only can effect a revolution, discord was sown between the officers and the troops, that the former might, on an emergency, be sacrificed at the first signal.

Extraordinary projects of aggrandisement have been attributed to Potemkin, among which may be mentioned that of excluding from the throne the grand-duke and his sons, and of placing on the head of the eldest of the grand-duchesses the imperial crown, espousing her, and reigning in her name. During his stay at Petersburg in 1791, between four and five months, he expended more than 1,200,000 rubles. An entertainment which he gave at his palace (since his death called the Pantheon) realised in splendor and effect the tales of enchantment, and is worthy of a particular description.

A month was employed in preparations : artists of every kind were engaged; whole shops and warehouses were exhausted for the occasion. Hundreds of persons assembled daily to rehearse their several parts ; each day was in itself a grand spectacle. The moment of exhibition at length arrived. Notice was given that the empress and the imperial family would honour the entertainment with their presence : the court, the foreign ministers, the nobility, and people of condition in the city, were invited as guests. The company, in masquerade habits, assembled at six in the evening. On a signal given, as the empress ascended her carriage, the treat for the populace was opened before the palace. Piles of clothing of every article, pyramids of provisions, and a plentiful supply of liquors, were surrendered to a general scramble. As Catherine entered the vestibule of the Tauridan palace, loud music, struck up from the lofty galleries, resounded through the saloon and spacious halls. The orchestra consisted of six hundred performers, who mingled their voices with the instruments. The empress, advancing to the great saloon attended by a brilliant concourse, took her seat on a gentle elevation, decorated with transparent representations; the company dividing among the colonades and boxes. Four-and-twenty couple of noble and beautiful youths of both sexes, among whom were the grand-dukes Alexander and Constantine, commenced the dances with a quadrille. Habited in white, the dresses of the dancers were distinguishable only by the colours of their scarfs and girdles. The value of their habits was estimated at ten millions of rubles. Vocal and instrumental music accompanied the dance: a solo by the celebrated la Picque concluded the scene.

The company then proceeded to a hall hung with tapestry of the most costly kind: an artificial elephant, decorated with rubies and emeralds, was here exhibited. The Persian who led him struck upon a bell as a signal for a new scene; when a curtain, flying up as by magic, discovered a theatre magnificently adorned, where a dramatical piece and two ballets, afforded to the spectators a splendid entertainment. The music, the dancing, the pomp, and grandeur, the diversity of national dresses, in their most pleasing costume, gratified at once every sense. After the play, the company divided into several apartments: magnificent illuminations every-where charmed and dazzled the eye: the columns and walls appeared to glow with variegated fires, in lamps of every colour: large mirrors, artfully disposed in the form of pyramids and grottoes, multiplied the splendors: every room was a blaze of glory.

Six hundred persons sat down to a table furnished with suitable magnificence, while the remaining company were entertained at side-boards: the covers and utensils were universally of silver or gold. Various coloured vases, in which lamps were inserted, lighted the table. Servants and

domestics superbly habited attended the company : nothing which could gratify the palate of
the epicurean, or flatter the most refined voluptuary, was wanting.

The empress did honour to her host by infring-
ing her general rule, and remaining at the entertainment till midnight, that she might not disturb
the enjoyments of the company. On her return
through the vestibule, the choir of voices chanted
a hymn to her praise. Surprised and affected at
this circumstance, Catherine turned to the prince,
who, overpowered by his emotions, fell at her
feet, and, seizing her hand, bedewed it with his
tears. A gloomy foreboding seemed to shake his
frame, an expression of anguish overspread his
countenance : his fortunes arrived at their height,
a presentiment appeared to seize him that his glory
was passing away, and that this was the last moment which he had to spend in the magnificent
theatre of his grandeur, the last tribute of gratitude he should pay in presence of the assembled
court, at the feet of his august benefactress.

Wearied with prosperity and pleasure, satiated
with the attainment of every wish, his spirits were
exhausted : hope was extinct in fruition ; the spirit
of activity was fled ; languor clouded his intellects ; depression enfeebled his mind ; and life
itself became to the minion of fortune, the spoil-

CATHERINE II. 239

ed and enervated votary of voluptuousness, a loathed burthen. During the long evenings of winter, he would sit alone, and, like an infant, occupy himself for hours in placing and replacing his diamonds on a table covered with black velvet: sometimes he would weigh them, sometimes pour them from one hand to the other, or, throwing them carelessly from him, would pace for hours up and down his apartment, biting his nails, absorbed in thought, or lost in vacuity, though twenty persons might be present. His house, with all its splendor, exhibited a scene of confusion : the visitor might wander through a suite of apartments without meeting a single domestic to take his name ; neither bread nor water was at times to be had in his kitchens, but of *petit-patés* and champagne there was always an abundant supply. This picture may afford to the voluptuary and the prosperous a striking lesson, and to the philosopher an interesting subject of reflection.

Yet Potemkin was a man of talents, had grand and extensive views, and his death was a real loss to the empress. He possessed a thorough knowledge of his country and his countrymen, and a penetration that seized at once the character of his own and of foreign nations, though he had never been out of the Russian empire. In ceasing to be the favoured lover of Catherine, he lost not his influence, but through life maintained himself in absolute power. His ascendency over the mind of his sovereign was not to be weakened by the cabals of his successors; in a country prone to revolution he stood alone, firm and self-supported. His character has the praise of uniformly patronising his friends, while with the ruin of an enemy no one could charge him.

Some time in the year 1787, having ordered Plutarch to be read to him, he listened with attention to the life of Agesilaus and the narration of his conquests. ' Think you,' said he, interrupting the reader, after appearing thoughtful for some moments ; ' think you that, at some future period, I could go to Constantinople ?' ' If the sovereign pleases,' replied the person addressed, ' there is no *impossibility* to prevent you from doing so.' ' That is enough,' returned the prince ; 'if any one should come to-day and tell me that I *could not* go thither, I would shoot myself through the head.' He even meditated an attack on China : it was his opinion that a body of 10,000 Russians could march through the Chinese empire. But death put a stop to his extravagant projects and insatiable ambition.

He discovered no small degree of political dexterity in detaching France from Turkey, and in inducing her to concur with Russia. The news of the French revolution, respecting which he was sometimes observed talking to himself, with great eagerness and gesticulation, and in broken sentences, appeared deeply to affect him.

After a stay of five months in Petersburg, Potemkin quitted it, with a presentiment that he should never return, and repaired to the army: his forebodings, without having recourse to a miracle, were sufficiently justified and accounted for by the irregularity of his life, and the consequent depression of his spirits. Satiated with prosperity, sickened with grandeur, and weary of triumph, he was listless and disquieted; his sighs betrayed the sadness of his mind: the bounties of his sovereign, and the flatteries of his courtiers, served but to irritate rather than to gratify him: the presence of the new favourite, Plato Zuboff, had also become odious to him.

Momonoff, the predecessor of Plato, had not made to the partiality of his sovereign an adequate return: his heart wandered to the charms of a young damsel of the court. This fair-one had also been distinguished by Potemkin: Momonoff, alarmed at the idea of so formidable a rival, threw off the reserve he had hitherto maintained, pleaded his cause before the lady, and obtained the preference. Their connection became known to the court. Catherine only remained in ignorance of the infidelity of her lover ; to which, however, her attention was, by the jealousy of the courtiers, speedily directed. Though offended by this discovery, she concealed for a time her sentiments. These events occurred during the summer of 1789, when the court was at Tzar-skoselo, where the daughter of count Bruce, one of the richest heiresses of the empire, had just been presented.

Catherine, availing herself of this opportunity, informed Momonoff that she intended he should marry the young countess Bruce. The favourite, alarmed at the intimation, implored her not to insist on his compliance with this proposal; and, on her insisting to be informed of the reasons of his reluctance, fell at her feet, confessing that he had already plighted his faith. Catherine desired no farther explanation : the lovers were married on the next day, when they set off for Moscow.

A curious story is added to this account. Momonoff, bound to the empress by every tie of gratitude, dishonourably and indiscreetly imparted to his wife circumstances of delicacy which respected his connection with the sovereign : these the lady divulged with unpardonable levity. This imprudence is said to have been severely expiated.

CATHERINE II.   243

When Momonoff and his bride had, on the night of their nuptials, retired to their chamber, the master of the police at Moscow suddenly entered the apartment, where, having shewn the new married pair an order from the empress, he left them in the hands of six women, and retired to an adjoining chamber. These six women, or rather six men habited as women, ministers of the wrath of Catherine, seized the lady, and, in the presence of her husband, whom they compelled to witness on his knees the ceremony, inflicted on her with rods the discipline of flagellation—an admirable but severe cure for tattling and scandal! The chastisement concluded, the police-master re-entered : ' This,' said he, ' is the method by which the empress punishes a first indiscretion. For the second, Siberia awaits the delinquent.'

On the day of the marriage of Momonoff, the post of favourite was conferred on Plato Zuboff, an officer in the horse-guards. Potemkin heard with concern on whom the election of Catherine had fallen, and in a letter to her majesty, employed every argument to dissuade her from her choice. But, from the period of his elevation, Zuboff was too assiduous to please to fear a rival. The suit of Potemkin was rejected, though he desisted not for some time from his importunities.

By the death of the emperor Joseph II. Russia was left to contend alone with the Ottomans: the successor of Joseph, yielding to the solicitations of Prussia, and to the exigencies of his people, was in haste to conclude with the Porte a separate peace. Deserted by her ally, Catherine began to perceive that her victories were ruinous; while, too proud to sue for a peace of which she felt the necessity, her armies continued their conquests. Great Britain, which had incited the Turks to declare war against Russia, now proposed to itself an advantage in being the mediator of an accommodation. Catherine, on this occasion, maintained the same character of haughty independence which she had supported through the war; and, though determined on concluding a peace with the Turks, managed to obtain the most advantageous conditions. Mr. Fawkener, the English minister, felt her power, and was baffled by her address.

During this negociation, a traveller, connected both by blood and friendship with the illustrious leader of the opposition party in the British parliament, appeared at Petersburg. The empress seized this opportunity of shewing a marked disrespect to the English minister. To the traveller she gave, in the presence of his countryman, the place of honour on her right hand; and, on the

CATHERINE II.   245

arrangement of the peace, her presents to the relation of Mr. Fox, of whom, as an orator and a statesman, she expressed her admiration, exceeded in number and value those conferred upon the embassador. The preliminaries of peace were signed January 9th, 1791. It has been calculated, that Austria lost in this war 130,000 men, and expended three hundred millions of florins. Russia 200,000 men, with two hundred millions of rubles. The Turks 330,000 men, with two hundred and fifty millions of piastres. At such an immense expence of blood and treasure are the games of sovereigns decided. The empress, after signing the treaty, gave up, by an act of imperial generosity, her claim to the twelve millions of piastres which the Porte had stipulated to pay to her, as an indemnification for the expences of the war.

Potemkin was prevented from being present at the conclusion of the peace, by an epidemical fever, with which he was seized at Yassy, where the congress met. On the news of his sickness, the empress sent from Petersburg to his assistance two of the most experienced physicians. But the prince, disdaining advice, would conform to no regimen. His intemperance was singular and excessive : the greater part of a smoke-dried goose from Hamburg, slices of ham or hung-beef, with a quantity of wine and liquors, was his ordinary breakfast. He dined with equal voracity: in every species of gratification his appetites were uncontrolled. Sterlet-soup was his favourite dish; which at all seasons must be procured, however enormous the price. This prelude to his dinner frequently cost him 300 rubles. He one day, in a fit of caprice, dispatched a major from Yassy to Petersburg, for a tureen of his favourite soup, made by the hand of a capital artist. The dish, before it reached the prince, had travelled post near 2000 versts. His officers have been frequently sent from the Krimea to Petersburg, and even to Riga, for oysters or chinaoranges, on their first arrival at those ports.

That the fever should gain ground with this intemperance is little wonderful, but he hoped to escape it by removing from Yassy. Having set out for Nicolayeff, a town which he had built at the confluence of the Ingoul with the Bogue, he had scarcely proceeded three leagues, when his disorder becoming aggravated, exhibited the most fatal symptoms. He alighted from his carriage in the midst of the highway, threw himself on the grass, and expired under a tree, in the arms of the countess Branika, his favourite niece. His death took place in his fifty-third year, October 15th, 1791. His remains were transported to

CATHERINE II. 247

Kerson, where they were interred : an hundred thousand rubles was allotted by the empress for the erection of a mausoleum.

His character appears to have been no less singular than the circumstances in which he was placed, and to have united in itself apparent contrarieties. He was at once ostentatious and avaricious, despotic and popular, beneficent and inflexible, haughty and affable, frank and politic, superstitious and profligate. Lavish to his favourites, while his creditors and his household remained unpaid. Depending on women, yet always unfaithful, The activity of his mind was equalled only by the indolence of his body. Nothing could appal his courage, nothing compel him to abandon his projects ; while, in success, disgust invariably seized him. Wearied at all he performed, and sickening at all that was performed by others, he loathed existence as an intolerable burthen. He neither loved occupation, nor enjoyed repose : without order and without method, all his pursuits were desultory. In society, while he appeared himself embarrassed, his presence imposed on every one a constraint : morose to those who depended on him ; familiar and caressing where his interest was concerned. Promising every thing, never forgetting, yet seldom keeping his word. Without reading, his knowledge, though not profound, was extensive: he conversed with scholars, with artists, and with mechanics; drew forth the talents of each, and appropriated them to himself. Without penetrating into any deeply, he spoke well upon all subjects.

His conduct was not less various than his character; ambition and retirement, war and policy, building up and pulling down, business and pleasure, avarice and prodigality, by turns employed his thoughts, and occupied his time. Ever actuated by caprice, his actions and his inclinations had no apparent cause. His singularities and his humours alternately offended and interested the empress: in his youth he flattered her passions: in his maturer years, he aided her ambition, and soothed her pride. As a lover, he had performed all the extravagancies which the most romantic passion could inspire: banished by his rival from the presence of his sovereign, he ran to meet death in battle, and returned with glory. He had put out one of his eyes to free it from a blemish which diminished his beauty. When no longer acceptable to his mistress as a favourite, he became her friend, her confident, her minister, and her general. The alliance of Catherine with Joseph II. was the consequence of his persuasions; the subsequent conquests in the Krimea,

CATHERINE II. **249**

the splendid progress of the empress, the victories over the Ottomans, the conquest of Otchakoff, were all the instruments and the triumphs of his ambition: the grand riband of St. George, the only decoration wanting to his vanity, crowned the career of his prosperity, and the termination of his life was not far distant. He died almost by a sudden stroke. His death, lamented by a small number of friends, while his rivals eagerly divided his spoils, was in a little time remembered no more: his triumphs and his services sank in oblivion.

" His life," says the artist, by whom his portrait was drawn, " resembled the rapid passage of a meteor; dazzling, but unsubstantial. He began every thing, completed nothing, disordered the finances, disorganised the army, depopulated his country, and enriched it with new deserts. In his mind, as in his country, were cultivated districts and barren plains : it partook of the Asiatic, of the European, of the Tartarian, and of the Kozac; the rudeness of the eleventh century, and the corruption of the eighteenth; the surface of the arts, and the ignorance of the cloister; an outside of civilisation amidst the traces of barbarism.—He had great defects, but without them, probably, he would never have obtained the ma-

stery of his sovereign, nor that over his country.
He was made by chance precisely what he ought
to have been for preserving so long his power over
a woman of so extraordinary a character."

On the death of her favourite Lanskoï, Catherine, abandoned to sorrow, and indifferent to the
world, shut herself up in her apartment: on that
of Potemkin, she also retired from company, but
it was to employ herself in the administration of
the empire. She was busied for fifteen hours in
dividing among her ministers the affairs and employments which had belonged to the deceased
prince. Plato Zuboff, her last favourite, till this
period an utter stranger to business, was now solicitous to take a part in the ministry. On this
occasion, Markoff undertook to be his guide, and
was recompensed by the favour of the sovereign,
added to the confidence of the favourite. It was
in a council composed of Zuboff, Markoff, the minister of war, and others, that the annihilation of
Poland, long since proposed by Catherine, as an
offering to her pride and her revenge, was finally
determined. The ministers promoted with eagerness the plan, in the hope of sharing the spoils
of the unhappy Poles. Catherine had never for-
given Poland the diet of 1788, by which the constitution, dictated by force, of 1775, was abro-
gated. To this offence, those of the alliance with

CATHERINE II.   251

Prussia, accepted in contempt of her own, and
the constitution of 1791, decreed at Warsaw,
were added. The moment of vengeance was arrived: Bulgakoff, her minister at Warsaw, had
orders solemnly to declare war against the Poles.
The declaration was received in the diet, not
merely with firmness, but a generous enthusiasm.
The sentiment diffused itself through the nation;
even the king affected the same indignant ardour.
The sickening details of the various actions by
which the plains of this ill-fated country were
drenched in blood, must here be briefly passed
over; suffice it to say, that in their disunion the
unhappy Poles found their destruction. It was
in these conflicts that Kosciusko displayed talents
that, obtaining the confidence of the nation, and
exciting the admiration of Europe, provoked the
hatred of Russia.

Catherine, in effecting her purpose, called in
negociation to the aid of force: to Frederic William she proposed the definitive partition of Poland; while she secretly brought over to her
party those whose interests appeared to favour her
views. To Stanislaus Augustus she insisted, that
he should make a public declaration of the necessity of yielding to the Russian arms: the miserable monarch submitted to this indignity, which
procured for him no greater indulgences.

CATHERINE II.

At Grodno the confederated partisans of Russia assembled; when the Russian general seated himself under the canopy of the throne which he was about to overthrow. The minister of Catherine published, at the same time, a manifesto, in which he declared the resolution of the empress to incorporate with her domains all the territory of Poland which her arms had conquered. Her soldiers, dispersed among the provinces, committed ravages of which history furnishes but few examples, while Warsaw became a theatre of their excesses. The disorders of the troops were connived at by their general, who made the country groan under his barbarous arrogance. Their property seized upon, themselves reduced to servitude, the wretched inhabitants, rendered desperate by calamity, once more determined on resistence. Having assembled together, an invitation was sent to Kosciusko, who had retired to Leipsic with three friends, to return and place himself at their head.

These four Poles hesitated not to accept the call of their countrymen; but, to succeed, they felt it would be proper to commence their operations by giving liberty to the peasants, who had been treated in Poland like beasts of burthen. Their measures were planned and taken; the Russian yoke was borne with impatience; every

CATHERINE II. 253

thing seemed ripe for insurrection. Kosciusko was received by the Poles as their deliverer, and, joined by some officers, proclaimed general of their scanty forces. Three hundred peasants, armed with scythes, ranged themselves under his standard. To this little army, consisting of 3000 infantry and 1200 horse, 7000 Russians having opposed themselves, they were defeated and put to flight. On this check, the Russian general arrested all those suspected of being concerned in the insurrection; a measure which served but to irritate the people. The rebellion broke out, and two thousand of their tyrants were slaughtered by the Poles. The general, besieged in his house, and refusing to capitulate, found means to escape to the Prussian camp. The provinces followed the example of the capital, but their vengeance was less terrible and sanguinary.

Kosciusko strained every nerve to augment his army: to inspire the peasants, among whom he got recruits, with emulation, he wore their dress, partook of their diet, and distributed encouragements among them. These men, degraded by slavery, and distrusting the nobles, were not yet prepared for freedom. Stanislaus caballed in favour of Russia, whose troops, strengthened by the Prussians, poured into Poland. Frederic

William, at the head of his forces, fought against
Kosciuski, whose talents, courage, and despair,
were unavailing against multiplied and increasing
numbers. The greater part of his army were cut to
pieces, or compelled to lay down their arms : himself, covered with honourable wounds, fell senseless on the field, and was captured by the enemy.
The remnant that escaped the conquerors, shut
themselves up in the suburbs of Prague, whither
they were pursued by Suvaroff. The siege was
short, and the carnage horrible : without distinction of age or sex, every inhabitant was mowed
down by the sword: twenty thousand persons
satiated with their blood the savage conqueror of
Ismael, who, trampling on the necks of its inhabitants, and reeking from the gore of their countrymen, entered Warsaw in triumph. Such are
the trophies of despotism—such the triumphs of
ambition !

The courts of Petersburg and Berlin divided at
their pleasure the remains of this unhappy country; while the courtiers of Catherine shared among
them the possessions of the proscribed. The pa-
geant monarch, the creature of her power, was
sent to Grodno, and condemned to live obscurely,
on a pension granted to him by the empress;
while the Russian governor of the usurped pro-

CATHERINE II. 255

vinces displayed ostentatiously the pomp and· the pride of a sovereign.

The friends of the brave and generous Kosciusko were, with their general, conveyed to Petersburg, and shut up in dungeons. Among these was the young poet Niemchevitch, distinguished for his valour and his talents, the friend of Kosciusko, with whom he was wounded and taken. His offence against Catherine had been two-fold; he had not only dared to defend his country, but, with all the boldness and energy of satire, he had presumed to compose verses against its destroyer. In the citadel of Petersburg, and afterwards under severer durance at Schlusselburg, he had leisure to repent his temerity.

Catherine, greatly interested in the French revolution, appeared full of apprehension lest its principles should find their way into Russia, and subvert the sentiments on which her authority was established: to the emigrants she gave a welsome reception, while she proscribed those who dared to avow bolder and more novel opinions. The king of Sweden received from her the promise of an annual subsidy, and 12,000 soldiers, to assist in restoring to his dignity the French monarch. This engagement, made with a view -of accelerating the moment of the confederation

of kings, and of exciting her rivals to mutual destruction, she however found means to elude.
The assassination of Gustavus precluded the execution of his chivalrous enterprise, and quieted
for ever his restless spirit.   A short time previous
to this catastrophe, the emperor of Germany,
Leopold II. died also at Vienna.

The French emigrants, distressed by the loss of
these chiefs of the confederacy, fled in numbers
to Petersburg, where they implored assistance,
but obtained only promises.   The embassador of
France quitted Petersburg : Catherine, while she
censured his opinions, did justice to his talents,
to his virtues, and to the amenity of his manners.
' I am an *aristocrat,*' said she to him, on his taking
leave, ' for I must carry on my business.'   She
recalled her embassador from Paris, refused the
chargé d'affaires of France access to her court,
and prohibited his conferences with her ministers.
Her animosity extended even to Colonel l'Harpe,
preceptor to the young princes, a Swiss and a philosopher, who cherished in his heart the love of
freedom.   The bust of her favourite Voltaire was
degraded, nor was that of the English patriot suffered to keep its place.   The French in her dominions were compelled, like Hannibal, to swear
immortal hatred against the new republic ; and to

CATHERINE II. 257

take an oath of allegiance to the pretender to the French monarchy. It is yet a curious fact, that the son of count Esterhazy, an emigrant, used, at the desire of Catherine, to sing the French patriotic songs at the Hermitage; which sometimes resounded with the *Carmagnol* and *Ça ira.*

Two parties divided the court; at the head of one was the old count Osterman, the Vorentzoffs, &c. who sheltered themselves under the name of the grand-duke. The other was supported by Zuboff, Markoff, &c. The father, the three brothers, and the sister of the favourite, were all provided for by the bounty of the sovereign. Ministers, generals, embassadors, as the most effectual means of conciliating the favour of the empress, paid their court to Zuboff, who, with the most servile adulation, united in himself all the privileges and authority of his predecessors. Catherine, notwithstanding her advanced age, kept a vigilant eye over her cabinet; and employed herself some hours every day with her ministers, in attending to affairs of the state.

About this period (1794), she concluded with Great Britain a new treaty of commerce; and, by the publication of two edicts, prohibited the importation of French merchandize. The English obtained even yet more, the promise of a Russian squadron to join their fleet.

The marriage of one of her grand-daughters with the young king of Sweden, a prince of great promise, had become with Catherine a favourite project. The death of the king his father, the regency of the duke of Sudermania during the minority of the prince, and the intrigues of the court of Petersburg in Stockholm, had produced a breach between the two courts, which appeared to be aggravated from day to day. An union was even negociated between the young Gustavus and a princess of the house of Mecklenburg. Catherine on this occasion testified great displeasure, while the misunderstanding seemed to arrive at its height. At this instant, a French emigrant made his appearance at Stockholm, charged with secret powers to bring about an accommodation. His negociation proved successful; an embassy from the empress followed; the young king was disposed to repudiate the German princess, and to espouse the grand-daughter of Catherine. As a preliminary to this measure, he was engaged not to exact of his consort a conformity to the Swedish church: to this was added an invitation to visit Petersburg.

CATHERINE II.   259

The empress was gratified; the king, attended
by the regent, the minister, and a train of courtiers, repaired to the court of Catherine, who entertained them with her accustomed magnificence.
She appeared at their first interview delighted
with the young Gustavus; who, seventeen years
of age, tall, finely formed, with an air at once
sensible, noble, and mild, united to the graces of
youth, the dignity and intelligence of maturer
years.   His manners were simple, courteous, and
manly; he appeared to speak with reflection, and
displayed knowledge and information beyond his
age.   On his presentation to Catherine, he attempted to kiss her hand—' No,' said she, withdrawing it, ' I cannot forget that the count Von
Haya is a king.'—' If your majesty,' replied Gustavus gallantly, ' will not give me permission as
empress, at least allow me this favour as a lady
to whom I owe so much respect and admiration.'
The king appeared affected by the kindness of the
empress, but his sensations became yet more interesting in the presence of the young grand-duchess.   Alexandra Paulina had scarcely completed her fourteenth year, her tall and elegant
figure, fair complexion, light flaxen hair waving in
ringlets on her shoulders, regular features, and
modest aspect, made a lively impression on the

heart of the young monarch; which her innocence, candour, sensibility, and talents, on a farther acquaintance, contributed to strengthen. The princess of Mecklenburg was quickly forgotten; proposals of marriage were immediately made, and a day fixed for the celebration of the espousals.

The only difficulty which presented itself on this occasion was that of religion: Catherine consulted the archbishop, whether her grand-daughter might abjure the orthodox faith:—' Your majesty is allpowerful,' was the only answer. The national pride of Russia was to be flattered by making a queen of Sweden of the Greek church. The regent appeared to be gained, and the enamoured king completely dazzled; a retreat was scarcely dreaded. With this persuasion Catherine left to her favourite ministers the drawing up of the contract.

In the mean time the day arrived for the public betrothment of the enamoured pair. The young princess, in her bridal attire, the empress and her court were already assembled; the bridegroom only was missing, whose tardiness was a subject of surprise. The contract and articles of alliance had been purposely withheld till an hour previous to that appointed for the solemnity. But Gusta-

CATHERINE II. 261

vus perceived and resisted the snare: he declared that no restraint should be imposed on the conscience of the princess; but insisted on an outward conformity to the established laws of Sweden. The conflict was severe; the moment critical; but the principles of the youthful monarch triumphed over his passions: a noble and rare example. The importunities of the Russian ministers, the solicitation of the Swedes gained over to the cause, by whom he was surrounded; even the interference of the regent, failed in shaking the resolution of the young hero!—' No, no; I will not; I cannot; I will never sign them,' exclaimed he; and, vexed at their pertinacity, after again repeating his determination never to violate the laws of his country, hastened from them, and shut himself in his apartment.

The court had assembled at seven in the evening, nor separated till ten, when all hope of accommodation appeared at an end. Catherine sickened at the disappointment and mortification; her speech faltered, she was near fainting, and even had a slight fit, the precursor of one more fatal. The young princess abandoned herself to the most lively grief, which was followed by a serious illness. Pleasure and festivity was at an end; all was restraint, gloom, and embarrassment.

A compromise was attempted but produced little effect. The lovers were separated; Gustavus quitted Petersburg. Catherine remained overcome with chagrin; while the heart of the young Alexandra experienced the bitterness of the first sorrows of love.

One half of Poland, the Krimea, the Kuban, and a part of the frontiers of Turkey, had yielded to the arms or the intrigues of Catherine; but for the usurpation of another rich and populous country she had no need of battles: for the conquest of Courland and Semigallia her intrigues proved sufficient. The nobles were gained over by her emissaries; the people, to elude her oppressions, with which they were wearied out, accepted her protection. The reigning duke, under the pretence of an important conference, was seduced to Petersburg; when advantage was taken of his absence to subjugate his domains. The possessions of the proscribed were bestowed on the courtiers of Catherine, and her favourites were enriched with the spoils. The acquisition of Courland proved, from its corn and timber, and its ports on the Baltic, a valuable prize to Russia.

Unsatiated with empire, perpetual measures were taken by Catherine for the annexing to her dominions new kingdoms and states, whose mi-

CATHERINE II. 265

serable inhabitants were, on resistance, despoiled of the heritage of their fathers, and driven from their native soil.

The empress was at length induced, by the solicitations of her favourite, to fulfil her promise of assistance to the powers confederated against France. A squadron was appointed by her to join the English navy, yet not without a view to the interest of Russia. Her ships were, by a stipulation, to be provisioned at the expence of her ally, and returned back in thorough repair: by this treaty her raw mariners were disciplined, and her crazy vessels, which would scarcely bear the sea, completely refitted.

Her grandson Alexander having been married by Catherine to the princess Louisa of Baden Durlach, she became also desirous of choosing a wife for Constantine. With this view the three daughters of the prince of Saxe-Coburg were invited to her court, and the youngest selected for the consort of the prince.

But in quiet usurpations, in treaties, and alliances, her restless mind remained unsatisfied. Thirsting for conquest and inured to the din of war, she turned her arms against Persia. At the head of a numerous force, the brother of the favourite penetrated into Daghestan, and laid siege to Derbent; the keys of which were delivered to him by the commandant, a venerable old man, 120 years of age, the same who, at the commencement of the century, had surrendered Derbent to Peter I. This triumph received some alloy in a subsequent defeat by the Persian army. But Catherine, not discouraged, gave orders for the reinforcement of the troops, not doubting of their ultimate success.

The hope of obtaining a greater triumph also flattered her pride: the new treaty concluded with Austria and Great Britain secured to her the assistance of these powers against Turkey: elated with this idea, the period seemed approaching for the accomplishment of her darling plan, that of driving the Ottomans out of Europe, and of reigning in Constantinople. Already, in idea, arrived at the summit of her ambition, her visions of greatness experienced a sudden check.—The magnificent Catherine was not immortal.

On the fourth day of November, 1796, the empress displayed, in what was called her *little hermitage* (a small party), uncommon cheerfulness and vivacity. By a vessel from Lubeck she had received news of the French, under Moreau, having been obliged to repass the Rhine. She wrote on this occasion the following humourous note

CATHERINE II. 265

to Cobenzel, the Austrian minister: " I hasten to inform your excellent excellence, that the excellent troops of the excellent court have given the French an excellent drubbing." She amused herself with rallying and laughing at her grand-ecuyer and first buffoon: but retired somewhat earlier than usual, assigning as a reason, that too much laughing had given her slight symptoms of the colic. She arose the next morning at her accustomed hour, and transacted business with her secretaries: on dismissing the last, she told him to wait in the antichamber, whence she would presently recal him. The secretary, having waited for some time, and hearing no noise in the apartment, began to grow uneasy. He at last opened the door, and beheld, to his surprise and terror, the empress stretched on the floor, between the two doors leading from the alcove to her closet. She was already without sense or motion. The secretary, on this spectacle, ran to the favourite, whose apartment was above: physicians were sent for, and an universal consternation prevailed. A mattress was spread near the window, on which Catherine was laid: bleeding, bathing, and every means usually resorted to on such occasions, were employed, by which some effect seemed to be produced. She was still alive, but without

any other perceptible motion or sign than the
beating of her heart. Every one was eager to
dispatch a messenger to Paul: the brother of
the favourite was the person employed in this
service. The situation of the empress was, till eleven o'clock, her accustomed hour of seeing her
family, kept secret from the grand-dukes and
from the houshold: every one feared to mention
his apprehensions; her death was considered as
the epoch of some extraordinary revolution; the
court first, and presently the city, were in a state
of the most alarming agitation.

The grand-duke was absent on the arrival of
the messenger: six couriers met nearly in the
same instant: Paul was, with his court, gone a
few miles to inspect a mill constructed by his
orders. On receiving the intelligence, he appeared to be affected; asked a thousand questions,
gave instant orders for his journey, and proceeded
rapidly to Petersburg; where, arriving with his
consort at eight in the evening, he found the palace in confusion. The courtiers crowded around
him; the favourite, a prey to grief and terror,
had relinquished the reins of empire.

Paul, accompanied by his family, repaired to the
chamber of his mother; who, without shewing
any consciousness, still existed. The young princes
and princesses, dissolved in tears, formed around

CATHERINE II. 267

their grandmother an affecting groupe. The grand-duchesses, the gentlemen and ladies of the court, remained through the night waiting the last sigh of the empress: the following day passed in the same anxious solicitude. Catherine, still breathing, remained in a kind of lethargy; she even moved one of her feet, and pressed the hand of one of her women. About ten in the evening she appeared suddenly to revive; a terrible rattling was heard in her throat; the family crowded around her; when, uttering a piecing shriek, she expired, thirty-seven hours after her first seizure. She betrayed no symptom of pain till the moment before her decease: a prosperous life was terminated by a happy death.

Zuboff, the favourite, was, by this event, which hurled him at once from the pinnacle of power to his original obscurity, overwhelmed with an unfeigned sorrow. The young grand-duchesses bewailed in their grandmother the source whence all their pleasures flowed. The ladies and courtiers who had enjoyed her private society, and experienced the captivation of her manners, paid a tribute of tears to her loss : the happy evenings of the hermitage, the freedom and pleasure which Catherine so well knew how to diffuse, were contrasted by them with the military constraint and formal etiquette which were likely to succeed. The domestics of the empress sincerely mourned a good and generous mistress, whose mild and equal temper, superior to petty caprices or sudden gusts of passion, whose noble and dignified character, had rendered their services equally easy and pleasant. Catherine, as the mother of her family and household, as the patroness of her court, and the benefactress of her friends, merited the tears that embalmed her memory. The changes that followed under the administration of her son made her still more regretted.

She still retained, though seventy years of age, the vestiges of beauty. She was of the middle stature, and, carrying her head high, appeared tall : her hair was auburn, her eye-brows dark, and her eyes blue : her countenance, though not deficient in expression, never betrayed what passed in her mind ; a mistress of dissimulation, she knew how to command her features. She became corpulent as she advanced in years, yet her carriage was graceful and dignified. In private she inspired, by her conciliatory manners, confidence and good humour; youth, playfulness, and gaiety appeared to surround her. But in public, and on proper occasions, she knew how to assume the empress, to appear " *the Semiramis of the*

CATHERINE II.   269

North," and to awe by her frowns. She usually dressed in the Russian mode. She wore a green gown or vest *, with close sleeves reaching to the wrist: her hair lightly powdered, and flowing upon her shoulders, was crowned with a small cap covered with diamonds: in the later periods of her life she put on a great quantity of rouge. In her habits and diet she was strictly temperate: she took a light breakfast, ate a moderate dinner, and had no supper.

The estimate of her character must be formed from her actions: her reign was perhaps for her people rather brilliant than happy. Within the circle of her influence, her government was moderate and benign; at a distance, terrible and despotic: under the protection of her favourites, justice, order, and law, were sometimes violated, and the most odious tyranny practised with impunity. Her situation in the empire, delicate and often critical, restrained her judgment; it was by suffering her power to be abused that she was enabled to preserve it; she knew how to reward, but dared not always punish.

For her licentiousness as a *woman* no excuse can be offered; as a sovereign she must be allowed the title of *great*. If her love of glory too often

---

* Green is the national colour of Russia.

assumed the features of a destructive ambition, the praise of an enlightened and magnanimous mind cannot be denied to her.

It has been well observed, that the splendor of her reign, the magnificence of her court, her institutions, her monuments, and her victories, were to Russia what the age of Louis XIV. had been to Europe: as an individual, the character of Catherine had a better title to great. The French formed the glory of Louis, Catherine that of the Russians : she reigned not like him over a polished people, nor had she his advantages. She had a nation to form, and her measures were her own : however deceived or seduced, she suffered not herself to be governed. Humane and generous, cheerful and amiable, she constituted the happiness of those who surrounded her. Her active and regular life, her firmness, courage, and sobriety, were moral qualities of no mean value : corrupted by prosperity, and intoxicated with success, her crimes of a darker hue were those of her station rather than of her heart. The barbarous country over which she reigned, the grossness of its manners, and the difficulties with which she had to struggle, must not be forgotten in forming an estimate of her character. Whatever may have been her faults, and doubtless they were great, her genius, her talents, her courage, and her success, must ever entitle her to a high rank among those women whose qualities and attainments have thrown a lustre on their sex.

She aspired to the character of an author, to which by her celebrated *Instructions for a Code of Laws*, her dramatic pieces and proverbs, her tales and allegories for the improvement of her grand-children, she is justly entitled. Among the productions of her pen, her Letters to Voltaire are accounted the most interesting. She composed also for the imperial family a plan of education, compiled principally from the writings of Locke and Rousseau, which reflects infinite credit on her liberality and discernment.

There are few reigns more interesting than that of Catherine, more strictly biographical; few that involve more important principles, that afford a wider scope, or that more forcibly tend to awaken reflection. Let this be an apology for a diffuse-ness that may seem to form an exception to the limits allowed to individuals by the nature of the present work.

Life of Catherine II.—Secret Memoirs of the Court of Petersburg, &c. &c.

LADY ELIZABETH CAREW.

THIS lady, the author of a dramatic piece entitled " Mariam, the fair Queen of Jewry" (4to. 1613), lived in the reign of James I. and is supposed by Oldys, in his MS. notes on Langbaine, to have been the wife of sir Henry Carew. The works of several of her contemporaries are dedicated to lady Carew.

SUSANNAH CENTLIVRE.

SUSANNAH, daughter of Mr. Freeman, a gentleman of Holbeach in Lincolnshire, was born in 1667. Her father, a dissenter zealously attached to the parliament, was at the period of the restoration compelled to fly into Ireland, when his estate, which was considerable, was forfeited. Her mother was the daughter of Mr. Markham, a gentleman of fortune at Lynn Regis in Norfolk, who, in consequence of his political principles, was involved in the same calamity. It is uncertain whether Susannah was born previous or subsequent to the flight of her family. She unhappily

SUSANNAH CENTLIVRE.   273

lost her father in the third year of her age, nor did her mother survive many years. Before she had completed her twelfth year, Susannah found herself an orphan.

At a very early period of life she discovered a propensity to poetry, and is said to have composed a song before she was seven years of age. Having been treated with unkindness and severity by those under whose care she had been placed, she determined to leave the country, and to seek in London a happier destiny. Some obscurity at this period involves her life, to which an air of romance is given. She attempted, it appears, to put in practice her perilous enterprise alone and on foot, the consequences of which were such as might have been expected and foreseen. On the road she met with Anthony Hammond, esq. (father of the celebrated author of the elegies), then a member of the university of Cambridge. Struck with her youth and beauty, this gentleman offered to her his protection. Induced by her forlorn circumstances and inexperience in life to accede to his proposal, she accompanied him to Cambridge, her sex disguised by the habit of a boy,. and was introduced by her protector to his college acquaintance, as a relation desirous of spending with him some time in the university.

She remained with her seducer for some

N 5

274   SUSANNAH CENTLIVRE.

months, till, either wearied with his conquest or apprehensive of a discovery of the sex of his companion, he prevailed on her to go to London, for which purpose he provided her with a considerable sum of money, and a recommendatory letter to a lady of his acquaintance. On their parting, he gave her an assurance of speedily meeting her in town and renewing their intercourse.

This promise he however neglected to perform, yet, notwithstanding the disadvantages of her introduction into life, she married, in her sixteenth year, a nephew of sir Stephen Fox. This gentleman died within two years after their union. Soon after his decease, the youth and charms of his widow attracted a new lover, an officer of the name of Carrol, with whom she formed a second matrimonial engagement, and who was killed in a duel about a year and a half after their marriage. To this gentleman she seems to have been tenderly attached, his death for a time overwhelmed her with affliction.

During her second widowhood, she was, by the narrowness of her circumstances, induced to become a candidate for dramatic fame. Her earlier pieces were published under the name of Carrol. Her first tragedy, "The Perjured Husband," was performed at Drury-lane, in 1700, and published

SUSANNAH CENTLIVRE. 275

in 4to. the same year. In 1703 she produced " The Beau's Duel, or a Soldier for the Ladies," a comedy. Also " Love's Contrivances," principally translated from Moliere. The succeeding year she brought out " The Stolen Heiress, or the Salamanca Doctor outwitted," a comedy. In 1705, her comedy of " The Gamester" was acted at the theatre in Lincoln's-inn-fields, with great success. This piece has been since revived at Drury-lane. The plot was in great measure taken from *Le Dissipateur*, a French comedy. The prologue was written by Mr. Rowe.

Not satisfied with her fame as a dramatic writer, she became ambitious of making a figure on the boards. In this department, it is probable, she proved less successful, as it does not appear that she ever exhibited at the theatres in the metropolis. In 1706 she performed at Windsor, where the court then resided, the part of Alexander the Great, in Lee's " Rival Queens." She captivated in this character the heart of Mr. Joseph Centlivre (principal cook to queen Anne), to whom she soon after gave her hand, and with whom she passed the remainder of her life in tranquillity.

She produced the same year the comedies of " The Basset Table," and " Love at a Venture." The latter was represented by the servants of the duke of Grafton, at the new theatre at Bath. Her

276   SUSANNAH CENTLIVRE.

most celebrated performance, " The Busy Body," was acted at Drury-lane in 1708. This play, afterwards so popular, was refused by the managers, nor were they prevailed upon to let it appear till towards the close of the season. Mr. Wilkes, even then, threw down at the rehearsal the part of sir George Airy with contempt on the stage, while he declared ' That no audience would endure such stuff.' Notwithstanding these prognostics, the piece was received by the public with unbounded applause, and is still occasionally performed.

In 1711, " Marplot, or the Second Part of the Busy Body," was brought out. This performance, though inferior to that which had preceded it, was well received. The duke of Portland, to whom it was dedicated, presented the writer with forty guineas. In 1717, " A Bold Stroke for a Wife" was performed in Lincoln's-inn-fields. In the composition of this comedy the author was assisted by Mr. Mottley, who wrote one or two entire scenes. It was well received, and still keeps possession of the stage, in despite of the verdict pronounced against it by Mr. Wilkes, who in strong language swore, that not only the play would be certainly damned, but that Mrs. Centlivre herself deserved damnation for writing it.

Several other dramatic pieces were also written

by this lady. In 1707, " The Platonic Lady," a comedy, was acted at the Haymarket, and published in 4to. The prologue was composed by Mr. Farquhar. " The Man's bewitched, or the Devil to do about her," a comedy, was also acted at the Haymarket, and printed in 4to. in 1710. " The Wonder, a Woman keeps a Secret," one of Mrs. Centlivre's best pieces, was performed at Drury-lane, in 1714. Mr. Garrick revived this comedy, with some alterations, and played himself the part of Don Felix. " Bickerstaff's Burying, or Work for the Upholsterers," a farce of three long scenes, was acted at the Haymarket, printed in 4to. in 1717, and dedicated "to the magnificent company of Upholsterers." " The Perplexed Lovers," a comedy, printed in 4to. 1712, was acted at Drury-lane. " Gotham Election," a farce of one long act, never performed, was printed in 12mo, 1715, and dedicated to Mr. Secretary Craggs, who complimented the author with twenty guineas. " A Wife well managed," a farce, acted at Drury-lane, was printed in 12mo. 1715. " The Cruel Gift, or Royal Resentment," a tragedy, was performed at Drury-lane, and printed in 12mo. 1717. " The Artifice," a comedy, acted at Drury-lane, was printed in 8vo. 1721.

In the Biographia Dramatica, it is observed of

Memoirs of Women Writers, Volume 7

Mrs. Centlivre that, as a writer, it is not easy to estimate her rank. Her plays, of which the language sometimes is feeble and incorrect, do not abound with wit. But her plots are busy and well managed, and her characters natural and marked. If she is not, it is added, allowed to rank as the first female dramatist, she deserves a place next to Mrs. Behn, her predecessor.

Mrs. Centlivre enjoyed the intercourse and esteem of many of the most eminent wits of her time, particularly of sir Richard Steele, Mr. Rowe, Dr. Sewell, and Mr. Farquhar. Eustace and Budgel were also of the number of her acquaintance. She unfortunately provoked the resentment of Mr. Pope, by having, as it is reported, written a ballad against his Homer before it appeared, in consequence of which she had a place in the Dunciad.

She died December 1, 1723, in Spring-garden, Charing-cross, and was interred at St. Martin's-in-the-fields. She possessed considerable personal beauty, great vivacity in conversation, with a benevolent and friendly temper. She appeared to inherit from her family their political principles: she professed herself in the most dangerous times of the whig party, and manifested a zeal for the House of Hanover which, breathed in her writings, procured her some friends and more

SUSANNAH MARIA CIBBER.　279

enemies. Her acquirements were, amidst many disadvantages, the result of her own application : she is said to have understood the French, Spanish, and Dutch languages, and to have had some acquaintance with the Latin. A knowledge of men and manners is displayed in her dramatic productions. Her dramas were collected in 1761, and printed in three vols. 12mo. She composed also several poems, on various occasions, which, with a miscellaneous production, entitled " Letters of Wit, Politics, and Morality," were published by Mr. Boyer.

Biographia Britannica—Biographia Dramatica.

SUSANNAH MARIA CIBBER.

THIS admirable actress, sister to the celebrated Dr. Thomas Augustus Arne, was the daughter of an upholsterer in Covent Garden. She first appeared on the stage as a vocal performer, when the sweetness of her voice, and the correctness of her judgment, rendered her a distinguished favourite with the public. In 1736 she made her *debut* as an actress, in the character of Zara, a tragedy written by Mr. Hill, at its first representation in Drury-lane. Her performance on this occasion

surprised and delighted her audience : the promise
which she gave by her powers of being a valuable
acquisition to the stage, was more than verified
by her future excellence.   Her figure, light and
youthful, was formed with exquisite symmetry
and grace; her countenance was agreeable and
expressive, and her voice flexible, plaintive, and
melodious.   She possessed in an eminent degree
that sensibility of character, and flexibility of
muscles, which enabled her to conceive and express in her features every variety of passion,
whether of tenderness or of rage, of softness or of
pride.   In every cast of tragic character she was
exquisite, but in comedy her attempts were
less successful.

In April, 1734, she gave her hand to Mr. Theophilus Cibber, to whom she was the second wife.
The indiscretion and extravagance of her husband
produced an embarrassment in their circumstances,
through which, in the year 1738, they were obliged
to make a short tour to the continent.   Mrs. Cibber had formed an attachment with a young man
of fortune, a friend of her husband's, who was
suspected of having connived at his own dis-
honour, through base and interested views   On
his return from France he first thought proper to
notice this correspondence, and, having laid his
damages at five thousand pounds, commenced a

SUSANNAH MARIA CIBBER. 281

suit against the gentleman. So many circumstances of an equivocal nature, which respected
the plaintiff, appeared on trial, that the jury gave
a verdict only for ten pounds.

The creditors of Mr. Cibber, on this event,
pouring in upon him, he was arrested, and, laden
with public odium, thrown into the King's Bench
prison. Mrs. Cibber continued to perform with
increasing excellence, high reputation, and favour with the public. She afforded great delight
whenever she appeared : in the latter periods of
her life she engaged at Drury-lane.

A disorder, the nature of which appears not to
have been ascertained by her physicians, and for
which she was treated improperly, occasioned frequent interruptions to her performance. More
than once her death was publicly announced by
the papers. About a month before her malady
terminated fatally, the comedy of " The Provoked
Wife" was ordered by the king. Mrs. Cibber
was solicitous on this occasion to shew her respect for the royal family, by performing her favourite part of Lady Brute. Her exertions in the
infirm state of her health were thought to have
accelerated her death. But she was still more
hurt by sea-bathing, injudiciously advised by her
physician, and to which she had a decided aversion. Her disorder was by the medical men sup-

posed to be a bilious colic, but was discovered, after her desease, on the opening of the body, to have been occasioned by stomach worms.

She expired January 30, 1766, and was buried in the cloisters in Westminster-abbey. On hearing of her death, Garrick declared ' that tragedy died with her.' She brought on the stage an elegant little piece from the French, entitled " The Oracle," in one act, printed in 8vo. 1752.

Biographia Dramatica.

MARY CHANDLER.

MARY CHANDLER was born at Malmsbury in Wiltshire, in 1687. Her father was a dissenting minister at Bath, whose narrow circumstances rendered it necessary that his daughter should be put in a situation that might enable her to provide for her own subsistence. She was accordingly placed with a milliner. Mr. Chandler, nevertheless, neglected not to pay attention to her education, and to superintend with more especial care the moral culture of her mind. From her childhood Mrs. Chandler shewed a talent for poetry; she was accustomed to compose riddles in verse for the amusement of her young companions:

MARY CHANDLER. 283

Herbert's Poems were at that period of life her favourite study. As her judgment matured, she applied herself to the perusal of the first poets, both ancient and modern. She preferred Horace to either Virgil or Homer, because his subjects were less fabulous and came nearer to nature and common life. Her poem upon the *Bath* received the approbation of the public; but, by the praise of Mr. Pope, with whom she was acquainted, she was still more gratified.

Her figure was deformed, but her countenance was sweet and engaging: she refused several solicitations of marriage on account of her personal disadvantages. She died, after two days' illness, September 11, 1745, in the fifty-eighth year of her age. The following extract from her poem on *Solitude* is characteristic of the qualities of her mind and heart:

" Sweet solitude, the muses' dear delight,
Serene thy day, and peaceful is thy night ;
Thou nurse of innocence, fair virtue's friend !
Silent, tho' rapt'rous, pleasures thee attend.
Earth's verdant fcenes, the all-surrounding skies,
Employ my wand'ring thoughts, and feast my eyes :
Nature in every object points the road,
Whence Contemplation wings my soul to God.
He 's all in all, his wisdom, goodness, pow'r,
Spring in each blade, and bloom in ev'ry flow'r,

284   **MRS. CHAPONE.**

Smile o'er the meads, and bend in ev'ry hill,   ⎫
Glide in the stream, and murmur in the rill :   ⎬
All nature moves obedient to his will.   ⎭
Heav'n shakes, earth trembles, and the forests nod,
When awful thunders speak the voice of God."

            Biographium Fæmineum.

MRS. CHAPONE.

T HE respectable family of Mrs. Chapone, whose maiden name was Mulso, were natives of Northamptonshire. The married life of this lady, which was short, appears not to have been happy. Her circumstances, when left a widow, were scanty and limited. She possessed in her youth a fine voice and great taste in music. Without an acquaintance with classical learning, the style of her compositions was elegant and correct. She was acquainted with the modern languages, and made some translations from the French. She was fond of conversation, and possessed conversible powers, with an occasional talent of humour. From having associated in early life with polite circles, Mrs. Chapone had acquired easy and polished manners. She was long known to the public as an elegant and moral writer. Among her first productions were the interesting story of *Fidelia* in the *Adventurer*, and a poem prefixed to

MRS. CHAPONE. 285

the translation of Epictetus by her friend Mrs. Carter. Her "Letters on the Improvement of the Mind, addressed to a Young Lady," and printed in 1773, made her name known. The following character of this work is given by a lady * highly and justly esteemed in the republic of letters. " It is distinguished by sound sense, a liberal as well as a warm spirit of piety, and a philosophy applied to its best use, the culture of the heart and affections. It has no shining eccentricities of thought, no peculiarities of system ; it follows experience as its guide, and is content to produce effects of acknowledged utility by known and approved means. On these accounts it is perhaps the most unexceptionable treatise that can be put into the hands of a female youth. These letters are particularly excellent in what relates to regulating the temper and feelings. Their style is pure and unaffected, and the manner grave and impressive. Those who choose to compare them in this respect with another widely circulated publication †, addressed about the same time to young women, will probably be of opinion that the dignified simplicity of the female writer is much more consonant to true taste than the affected prettinesses and constant glitter of the preacher."

---

* Mrs. Barbauld.   † Dr. Fordyce's Sermons.

Mrs. Chapone published soon after a volume of miscellanies, containing some elegant poems, and one or two moral essays. This performance did not obtain the notice it merited.

The loss of a beloved niece, the lady to whom the letters were addressed, and of a brother yet dearer, to whom similarity of taste had affectionately united Mrs. Chapone, affected her health and spirits, and hastened prematurely the infirmities of age. Having withdrawn herself from society, she gradually declined and expired, at Hadley, in Middlesex, December 25, 1801, in the 75th year of her age.

CHARIXENA.

CHARIXENA, a learned Greek lady, the author of several compositions both in prose and verse; particularly of a poem entitled "Crumata." This lady is mentioned by Aristophanes.

Biographium Fæmineum—Plutarch.

CHELONIS.

CHELONIS was the wife and daughter of two kings of Lacedemon. Leonidas her father was

CHELONIS. 287

deposed by a faction, who placed on the throne Cleombrotus her husband. Chelonis, on this occasion, refusing to share the fortune of her husband, retired with her father into a temple in which he had taken sanctuary. In this retreat the father and daughter appeared as suppliants, in a state of humiliation and dejection. Leonidas some time after was permitted to retire to Tagea, whither Chelonis accompanied him.

But in the fluctuation of human events, and the levity of popular favour, the former circumstances were reversed. Leonidas was restored to the throne, and Cleombrotus reduced in his turn to take refuge in the sanctuary. Chelonis now forsook her father, and attached herself to the adverse fortunes of her husband.

Leonidas with an armed force repaired to the sanctuary, where he passionately reproached Cleombrotus for his usurpations, and the injuries he had made him suffer. Cleombrotus listened in silence to the accusations of his father-in-law ; but Chelonis, with tears and protestations that she would not survive him, obtained from her father the life of her husband, with liberty that he should choose the place of his retirement. To the affectonate entreaties of Leonidas, that she would continue with him and forsake Cleombrotus, she returned a resolute refusal, and putting one of her

CHRISTINA.

children into the arms of her husband, and taking
the other in her own, she accompanied them into
exile.

Biographium Fæmineum, &c.

CHRISTINA,

QUEEN OF SWEDEN.

CHRISTINA, daughter of the great Gustavus
Adolphus, king of Sweden, and of Maria Eleonora of Brandenburg, was born December 18,
1626. During the pregnancy of the queen her
mother, it was predicted by the astrologers,
whose pretensions were at that time held in high
estimation, that to Gustavus a son was about to
be born destined to maintain the glory of his
father. This prediction, added to some other
circumstances, misled the women who attended
the queen on her delivery, to misrepresent the
sex of the child. Gustavus, on being informed
of the mistake by Catherine his sister, smilingly
replied—' Let us however thank God ; this girl,
I trust, will prove not less valuable than a boy :
she has already, by deceiving us, given a presage
of her ingenuity.'

CHRISTINA.　　289

Gustavus attached himself to the child, which he carried with him in all his journeys. Christina, when about two years of age, was taken by her father to Calmar, the governor of which hesitated whether to give to the king the usual salute, lest the infant should be terrified by the noise of the cannon. Gustavus being consulted upon the occasion, exclaimed, after a moment's pause—' Fire! the girl is the daughter of a soldier, and should be accustomed to it betimes.' The salute being given, the princess clapped her hands, and, in her infantine language, cried— ' More, more !' Delighted with her courage, Gustavus afterwards caused her to be present at a review—' Very well,' said he, perceiving the pleasure she took in the military show—' Very well, you shall go, I am resolved, where you shall have enough of this diversion.' Gustavus was prevented by death from executing his promise. Christina laments, in her Memoirs, that she was not permitted to learn the art of war under so great a master. She also expresses regret, that, during her life, she never marched at the head of an army, nor even witnessed a battle.

The tears which she shed at parting with her father, on his German expedition, were regarded by the superstitious as an ill omen. She had been

taught a complimentary address, which she was
to repeat to Gustavus at parting. Absorbed in
thought, the monarch appeared abstracted while
his daughter performed her lesson : the child, observing his inattention, pulled him by the sleeve,
and began again to repeat the address. The king,
affected by her perseverance, burst into tears,
caught her in his arms, and, after holding her in
silence some moments to his breast, delivered her
to an attendant.

After the death of Gustavus the states of
Sweden assembled, when the marshal of the diet
proposed the crowning of Christina, in conformity
to a decree by which the female posterity of
Charles IX. the father of Gustavus, were declared
capable of succeeding to the throne.—' Who is
this Christina ?' exclaimed Larfsen, a member of
the order of peasants ; ' let us see her, let her be
brought out to us ?' The marshal retiring, returned
with the young princess in his arms. The pea-
sant coming up to her, considered her attentively.
—' Yes,' cried he aloud, ' this is she herself; she
has the nose, the eyes, and the forehead of Gustavus :—we will have her for our queen.' Christina, who was immediately seated upon the throne,
and proclaimed queen, appeared from that moment to take a pleasure in the regal dignity.

Russia having soon after deputed its embas-

sadors to ratify the treaty with Sweden, it was
feared by the court, that the appearance of these
strangers, their number, their beards, their un-
couth habits, and rude manners, would alarm the
young queen; but these apprehensions proved to
be unfounded. Christina received the embassadors with mingled firmness and dignity, as
became the daughter of a hero and a king.

She discovered while in her childhood a distaste
for the society and occupations of her sex; in
which, it is said, she betrayed all the awkwardness
and incapacity of a boy; while she delighted in
violent exercises, in exertions of strength and feats
of activity. She possessed also a taste for abstract
speculations, for the severer sciences, the acquisition of language, the study of civil polity, of legislation, and of history. Thucydides, Polybius,
and Tacitus, were among her favourite writers.

While the queen was employed in cultivating
her talents and improving her mind, her generals,
Neymar, Manier, Wrangel, and Torstenson, were
desolating Germany in the thirty-years' war.

Christina, having on the 18th of December
1644, completed the eighteenth year of her age,
assumed the reins of government; to the conduct
of which she proved herself fully equal. The
sovereign of a great kingdom, the princes of

Europe aspired to her hand: the kings of Portugal, of Spain, and of the Romans; don John of Austria; Sigismond of Rakocci, count and general of Cassonia; Stanislaus, king of Poland; John Cassimir, his brother; the prince of Denmark, the elector Palatine, the elector of Brandenburg, and Charles Gustavus, duke of Deux Ponts, of the Bavarian Palatinate family, son of the sister of her father, and first cousin to Christina; were among the number of her suitors.

Their proposals were uniformly rejected by the queen, who caused Charles Gustavus her cousin to be appointed her successor. Political interests, contrariety of religion, and diversity of manners, were pleaded by Christina as the motives of her conduct; the true cause of which perhaps is to be sought for in her love of independence and impatience of control. From childhood she expressed a distaste to marriage.—' Do not,' said she to the states, ' compel me to make a choice: should I bear a son, it is equally probable that he might prove a Nero as an Augustus.'

The magnanimity of Christina was, while yet in early youth, at the commencement of her reign, displayed by a singular incident. A preceptor of the college, disordered in his intellects, conceived a design of assassinating the queen. For this purpose he repaired to the chapel of the castle of

CHRISTINA. 293

Stockholm, where Christina, with the principal noblemen of the court, was attending religious service: the assassin made choice of that moment for the perpetration of his design, when the assembly were engaged in what is termed by the Swedish church an act of recollection; in which each individual, kneeling, and covering his face with his hand, performs a silent and separate devotional service. At this instant, the lunatic rushing through the crowd, ascended a balustrade, within which the queen knelt. Baron Brahi, chief-justice of Sweden, being first alarmed, cried aloud, while the guards crossed their partisans to bar the approach of the madman; who, furiously striking them aside, leaped the barrier, and, with a knife which he had concealed in his sleeve, aimed a blow at the queen. Christina, evading the stroke, pushed the captain of the guards, who, throwing himself upon the assassin, seized him by his hair. All this passed in a moment of time; the man was known to be deranged, and therefore not suspected of having accomplices. They satisfied themselves with putting him under restraint; and the queen, without any apparent emotion, returned to her devotions. The people, with a lively interest for the fate of their sovereign, shewed great alarm and agitation.

One of the most important events that occupied the attention of Christina, during her reign, was the peace of Westphalia. Two plenipotentiaries were commissioned by her to the congress; Oxenstiern, whose father the grand-chancellor had enjoyed the favour of Gustavus, and who had with absolute power governed Sweden during the minority of the queen, till she became, at length, weary of the yoke; and Salvius, lord privy-seal, in whom she placed entire confidence, and who, by her desire, forwarded the pacific measures, against which Oxenstiern, who foresaw in the peace the diminution of his own and of his family's importance, opposed every possible obstacle.

His opposition, however, proved abortive : a peace so desirable, and in which so many jarring interests were conciliated, was finally determined in October, 1648. Christina was, by the success of the Swedish arms, rendered mistress of the treaty, which confirmed to Sweden the possession of many important countries. The services of Salvius on this occasion were rewarded by his mistress with the dignity of senator; a prerogative which had till then belonged to birth, but to which the queen rightly judged merit afforded a juster claim.

During the remainder of her reign, a wise administration and a profound peace afforded none

CHRISTINA. 295

of those striking and terrible events which dis-
tinguish more stormy periods : the happiness, the
confidence, and the love of her people, reflect upon
Christina a higher and less equivocal praise than
can be derived from subtle negociations, or conferred by successful wars. Learning and the arts
flourished under her administration ; while all that
was distinguished in genius and acquirements,
were attracted by her liberality to the Swedish
court. Among characters illustrious for their talents about this period, may be named Grotius,
Paschal, Bochart, Descartes, Cassendi, Saumaise,
Nande, Vossius, Heinsius, Meiborn, Sauvery,
Menage, Lucas, Holstenius, Lambecius, Bayle,
Fillicaca, and madame Dacier, who returned the
notice and patronage of Christina by celebrating
her praises. In the following Latin epigram, a
parallel is drawn by Bochart between the queens
of Sweden and of Sheba :

Illa docenda fuis Salomonum invisit aboris ;
Undique ad hanc docti, quo doceantur, eunt.

It has been alleged against Christina, that the
distinction she bestowed on merit was not always
apportioned with strict discrimination ; or, in other
words, that her judgment was human and fallible,
sometimes misled by imagination, and sometimes

betrayed by partiality and affection. She is accused of having disgusted Descartes by withhold-
ing from him the meed due to his superiority.
The acute feelings attendant on genius might perhaps render the philosopher unreasonable, or possibly make his patroness unjust.

A heavier charge is brought against her, respecting the rapid fortunes acquired under her
protection by Michon (i. e. Bourdelot), who
seems not to have merited her liberalities and
countenance. Introduced at court by Saumaise,
sprightly and little scrupulous in the subjects of
his mirth, without pretention to erudition, he superseded for a time, in the favour of the queen,
the satellites of literature, whose endowments he
treated in his licentious mirth with but little respect. Compelled at length by the public indignation to banish her favourite, Christina lavished
on him marks of confidence. The glory of Bourdelot, like a meteor, glittered but for a moment,
and sunk in obscurity. His favour with the queen
survived not his presence : as if ashamed of the
transient infatuation, she soon ceased to remember
him but with aversion and contempt. His qualities amused for an instant, but afforded no basis
on which to found esteem. Christina preserved
no other correspondence with him than to render
him subservient to her taste for letters, by em-

CHRISTINA.   297

ploying him to collect for her in France, of which
he was a native, and to which he retired, the most
valuable productions as they successively appeared.
During the ascendancy of Bourdelot over the
queen, he supplanted in her favour count Magnus
de la Gardie (son of the constable of Sweden),
her relation, favourite, and reputed lover.

Madame de Motteville, who conversed with
the count when on an embassy to France, speaks
in her Memoirs of his attachment to the queen,
of whom (says she) he talked in a manner
so respectful and passionate, that every person
who heard him suspected his eulogiums were excited by a sentiment more ardent than duty. His
disgrace is said to have arisen from his ambition
of usurping too much power in the state ; while
Bourdelot, without awakening the jealousy of the
queen, knew how to flatter and amuse the *woman:*
his humorous sallies, and flights of imagination,
by affording to his patroness a careless relaxation
from the burthen of state affairs, secured his ascendancy over her mind.

Scudery, having obtained permission to dedi-
cate to Christina his Alaric, she required him to
erase from the poem a compliment inserted to her
fallen favourite, the count de Gardie. The poet,
with a becoming spirit, that implied a reproach on

the little magnanimity displayed by the queen in this request, generously replied, ' That he would never destroy the altar upon which he had sacrificed.'

An accident happened about this time which reflects upon Christina greater credit. Some ships of war had been built at Stockholm by the orders of the queen, which she was desirous of inspecting. As, for this purpose, she crossed a narrow plank, led by admiral Herring, his foot slipped, and, drawing the queen with him, he fell into water ninety feet in depth. Anthony Steinberg, first equerry to Christina, plunged instantly into the sea, caught hold of the queen's robe, and with such assistance as the by-standers could afford, drew her to the shore. Christina preserved through the whole of this transaction her recollection and presence of mind. ' Take care of the admiral,' cried she, the moment her head was raised above water. When brought on shore, she neither expressed fear nor betrayed any emotion ; but, dining in public on the same day, gave a humorous turn to the adventure.

The rank, which by its splendor and power had at first flattered her imagination, she at length began to feel as a burthen: she sighed for freedom and leisure, and, after mature deliberation, determined on abdicating the throne. In 1652, she

CHRISTINA. 299.

communicated her resolution to the senate, who remonstrated against its execution; in which remonstrance the people unanimously, and even Charles Gustavus, nominated by her to the succession, warmly joined. Yielding to their importunities, she sustained the weight of the crown two years longer, when she resumed her purpose of abdication, which she carried into effect.

It appears by a letter from Christina, addressed to M. Canut, the French embassador, in whom she placed confidence, that she had meditated this design for more than eight years, and had five years previous to its execution communicated it to him. The ceremony of the abdication afforded a solemn and affecting spectacle: in the tears of the people Christina read at once their attachment and regret: while every heart was moved, and every eye overflowed, she alone appeared firm and tranquil.

Having thus discharged the debt due to the public, and transferred to Charles Gustavus its future welfare, she hastened in pursuit of science to a country more favourable to its cultivation. Whether, in resigning the cares of state, and claiming freedom, the birth-right of every human being, Christina merited censure or applause, must be left to casuists to determine. The voluntary abdication of power affords a phenomenon in the history of sovereigns that has rarely been exhibited. ' How great,' exclaimed the prince of Condé, and many perhaps will sympathise with him—' How great was the magnanimity of this princess, who could so readily yield that for which mankind are perpetually practising mutual destruction; and which so many make, though with little prospect of its attainment, the pursuit of their lives !'

The abdication of Christina gave to Europe a new subject of speculation. In quitting the scene of her regal power, she appeared as if escaped from imprisonment: having arrived at a small brook which separates the countries of Sweden and Denmark, she alighted from her carriage, and leaped over the stream : ' At length,' cried she, ' I am free, and out of Sweden, whither I hope never to return.' Dismissing with her women the habit of her sex, she assumed that of the other. ' I would become a *man*,' said she; ' but it is not that I love men because they are men, but merely that they are not women.' Masculine in her habits no less than in her endowments, she affected on all occasions a contempt for her sex : she seems not to have been aware, that the tenderness, the sensibility, and the gentleness of woman, combined with the reason and fortitude of man, affords the perfection of human character.

With the sovereign authority, Christina also

CHRISTINA.　　301

abjured the faith in which she had been educated.
On the evening of the day on which this ceremony
took place, a comedy was acted. ' Is it not
just,' said the protestants, who doubted of the
sincerity of this conversion, 'that a comedy should
be given by the catholics in the evening, to her
who exhibited to them a farce in the morning ?'
Some time previous to the abdication of Christina,
Anthony Macedo, a jesuit, was chosen by John
IV. king of Portugal to accompany his embassador into Sweden. In some conversation between the queen and the jesuit, with whose talents and address she was greatly pleased, she
imparted to him her design of entering the Romish church. Macedo was dispatched to Rome
with letters from the queen to the jesuits, in
which she requested that two of their society
might be dispatched to her, Italians and learned
men, with whom she might confer on religious
subjects. This request was instantly and gladly
complied with. Francis Maline, professor of divinity at Turin, and Paul Casatus, professor of
mathematics at Rome, were accordingly commissioned to the queen, whose predilection for their
tenets being thus confirmed, she embraced the
faith of the Roman church; that grand and affecting superstition, the study and the labour of ages,
so fitted to allure the senses, to captivate the

imagination, and to triumph over the affections of
the human mind.

The Lutherans, while they censured the insta-
bility, mourned the defection of the royal convert;
whom Rome received in triumph with open arms.
The ceremony of her abjuration took place at
Brussels, where she met the great Condé, who
had there sought an asylum. ' Cousin,' said she
to him, ' who, ten years ago, would have thought
that we should have met at this distance from our
countries ?' This interview, earnestly desired by
both parties, from sentiments of mutual respect,
a trifling etiquette was suffered to disturb. The
prince demanded to be received by the queen with
honours similar to those she had shewn to the
arch-duke Leopold. This she refused. Condé
determined therefore to see her incognito, and
entered her apartment among the crowd of common visitors. Christina, discovering him by a
picture in her possession, was about to pay him
the honours suited to his rank, but the prince,
perceiving her intention, precipitately prepared
to withdraw. Perceiving the queen follow him,
with a view of inducing him to return, he cried.
out laconically, turning his head :—' All or nothing, madam.' Having thus said, he instantly
quitted the room. From this time they met but
by accident with mutual reserve and disgust.

CHRISTINA.   303

A restless temper, or a fondness for travelling, prevented Christina from remaining long in any place : from Brussels she went to Rome, into which, as the capital of the christian world, her entry was made with all the pomp of a triumph. The pope declared, that more honour was reflected upon Rome by this conquest over error, than by all her ancient warlike achievements. Many days passed in festivity and joy; after which Christina gave herself up to her taste for letters, for the sciences, and the arts. The jesuits affirmed that she ought to be placed by the church among the saints, by the side of St. Bridget of Sweden. ' I had rather,' said she, with vivacity, when informed of the honour designed her, ' be placed among the sages.'

Having left Rome she visited France, whence she returned to Rome, and afterwards repaired to Sweden; where it does not appear that she was well received. Leaving Sweden for Hamburg, where she continued a year, she passed again to Rome, then back to Hamburg, and once more to Sweden; where being received with still less respect, she returned again to Hamburg, and thence to Rome. Another journey to Sweden was projected, and also an expedition to England, where Cromwell seemed not disposed to receive her. Neither of these designs were executed : Christina, after many wanderings and purposes of wandering, died at Rome, April 15th, 1689.

It is affirmed by some historians, that, after the decease of Charles Gustavus, in 1660, Christina was desirous of resuming the throne, from which, by the laws and constitution of Sweden, her religion excluded her. Upon this conviction, she confirmed anew her abdication, reserving only for herself and her attendants, in case of her return to her native country, the free exercise of the religion she had chosen. Others, without mentioning this circumstance, allege as a motive for her frequent journeys to Sweden, that her appointments were ill paid. It is certain that she repeatedly confirmed her abdication to the states.

That human consistency is rare, and that habits are not easily broken, are trite observations: Christina is accused of disturbing the quiet of the places which she visited, by exacting those regal honours which she had voluntarily resigned, by refusing to conform to common modes and customs, and by exciting and fomenting political intrigue. While on the throne, she had been ambitious of taking the lead in the affairs of Europe ; the same active, enterprising spirit, followed her in her retreat. During the faction of the *Fronde* in France, she addressed letters to the parties interested, offering her mediation ; an interference that was

CHRISTINA.   30.5

regarded as equally absurd and mischievous. She gave disgust to the court by violating its forms, by persevering in wearing the dress of the other sex, and by the contempt with which she treated her own. Yet, while ridiculing the manners of the ladies of the court, she busied herself in their cabals. She flattered the passion of Lewis XIV., then in early manhood, for mademoiselle de Mancini, niece to cardinal Mazarine. ' I would fain be your confidant,' said she to them : ' if you love, you must marry.' A still more serious accusation is brought against her, respecting the murder of Monaldeschi, her master of the horse, and entrusted with her confidence, over which a mystery seems to hang, and of which the following particulars are given by *Père Bell*, who confessed the unfortunate victim in the royal palace of Fonairebleau, where the transaction took place.

" On the 6th of November, 1657, at nine in the morning, I was sent for by the queen of Sweden, to attend her at the *conciergerie* of the palace, where she was lodged, the messenger having first enquired whether I was the superior of the convent. Having accompanied me to the door of the anti-chamber, he left me a few minutes, and then returning, conducted me to the apartment of the queen, whom I found alone. After paying my respects, I desired to know her majesty's com-

mands. She invited me to attend her to the gallery of *Cerfs*, that we might converse with more
freedom. She asked me if, on any former occasion, she had ever spoken to me. I had been
once, I informed her, presented to her majesty,
and graciously received. ' You bear sir,' said
she, ' a habit which implies confidence ; you hold
the seal of secresy, and are worthy of being entrusted—are you not ?' In these respects I assured her I was both deaf and blind. She then
put into my hands a packet, sealed with different
seals, and without superscription, and desired me
to minute down the place, day, and hour, in which
I had received it from her hands, requesting that
I would preserve it till called for. After promising punctual obedience to her commands, I retired, leaving her alone in the gallery.

" On Saturday the 10th of the same month, a
valet of the queen came to desire my attendance
on his mistress. I accordingly, taking with me
the packet, obeyed her summons, and was conducted by the valet into the same gallery. On
entering, the servant shut to the door with a vehemence that surprised me. In the middle of the
gallery I found the queen in conversation with a
gentleman, whom I afterwards found to be the
marquis Monaldeschi : three other men stood at
a small distance. ' My father,' said Christina (as

I approached) in an exalted tone of voice, and with a majestic air, ' give me the packet of letters which I entrusted to your charge.'—I did so. She paused after having received them, then, opening the cover, she took out several, gave them to the marquis, and desired he would read them. In a firm and steady voice, she asked him if he knew them not. He denied any knowledge of their contents. ' And really, sir,' said she, with an ironical pleasantry of manner, ' do you not remember these letters ?' They were in fact copies of his own, transcribed by the queen from the originals, which she then produced, calling him a traitor, and declaring that his blood should atone for his perfidy. She questioned him severely, while he endeavoured to palliate his conduct by throwing the blame on others. At length, perceiving himself clearly detected, he sunk on his knees, and at her feet implored pardon and grace. The three men, in the mean time approaching, drew their swords from their scabbards. The marquis, rising from his knees in terror, took the queen to a distant corner of the gallery, and thence to another, apparently supplicating her in humble terms for mercy. She heard him with patience, and without any symptoms of passion or emotion. She then returned to me, the marquis still pressing her to hear him farther. ' My father,' said she, pointing to her victim with a small ebony stick which she held in her hand, ' observe that I do not deny, or withhold from that perfidious traitor, any time which he might reasonably desire to justify or acquit himself of the great offences of which he has been guilty.' Having thus said, she desired the marquis to deliver up some papers which he possessed, with two or three small keys. Taking them from his pocket, he accidentally scattered about the room some small pieces of money.

" More than an hour passed in conference, when the marquis being unable to justify his conduct, the queen addressed me with a dignified manner, and in an elevated voice : ' My father,' said she, ' I shall retire, and leave you to prepare that man for death, and pray take care of his soul.' Greatly shocked at hearing such a sentence so solemnly pronounced, we both fell at her feet, and besought her pardon. Refusing to hear our prayers, she declared the marquis to be a traitor of the most atrocious kind, adding, that he deserved to die upon the wheel, having divulged the most important secrets of state, entrusted to him in the confidence she had reposed in him. Turning from us, she retired to her private apartments, leaving me to confess the prisoner, and the three executioners to perform the bloody deed.

CHRISTINA. 30**9**

" The marquis, on his knees, entreated me to follow the queen, and to solicit her grace and favour. The three men, calling upon him to confess to me, placed the points of their swords to his back, while I exhorted him, with tears, to recommend himself to God, to implore his mercy, and the remission of his sins. The chief of the three men, however, went himself to the queen, to enquire if she persisted in having the sentence executed. He returned presently, bringing her positive orders for the death of the marquis, whom he exhorted to offer up his prayers to Heaven. The miserable victim, at these words, again prostrated himself befoie me, conjuring me to implore once more the queen's mercy.

" I complied with his request, and, going to her apartment, found her alone, with a composed and serene countenance, apparently free from any of those emorions which at such a time it was so natural to expect. Kneeling, I entreated her, with weeping eyes and a bleeding heart, in the name of our Redeemer, and for the sufferings he had borne for us, to follow that god-like example, and to make me, an humble servant of the Deity, the messenger of comfort. She heard me impatiently ; and, by repeating again and again the crime of the marquis, convinced me that, by this mode of proceeding, nothing was to be gained. I then ventured humbly to hint, that an act of a nature so extraordinary, to be committed in a royal palace of the king of France, deserved her most serious consideration; that it was not merely unexampled, but a business in which the whole world was interested; and though within her own dominions, her right to execute justice on her subjects and domestics was undoubted, yet, I begged leave to observe, that herself, with the marquis, were now under the protection of another prince, and in a foreign empire; adding, that I could wish her majesty would proceed against the criminal by a regular process, and not put him to death in a manner so precipitate.

" I almost repented having thus spoken, for I perceived I had urged the queen too far. Before I took my leave, I therefore observed, that the high honour and esteem with which she had inspired the French nation, would not, I hoped, be sullied by a too hasty punishment of so great an offender. The king, I was persuaded, would, on application, direct a formal process to be carried on, and justice to be executed on the marquis; in which case her majesty would preserve that admirable character to which her actions had so justly entitled her,

" ' What,' said she, ' shall I who preside absolute over my own subjects, be reduced to solicit

CHRISTINA. 311

justice against a domestic traitor from another prince ? I have proved his perfidy : he stands convicted under his own hand, and he *shall* suffer for his treason and infidelity.' ' True, madam,' replied I, ' but your majesty being a party so deeply interested—and—' ' No, no, my father,' said she, interrupting me, ' I will make my reasons known to the king. Return, I beseech you, and take care of his soul ; I cannot in conscience comply with any of your requests.'

" The change which I perceived in her voice and manner convinced me that every effort must prove fruitless. Yet, I cannot but think, that in any other place, where there had been no danger lest the marquis should escape, nor hazard of her own life, that she would have deferred the execution of so singular a design. For my own part, duty and charity constrained me to return to the prisoner, and to prepare him for his fate."

This narration by no means removes the obscurity in which this affair is involved : whatever might have been the crime of Monaldeschi, or the rights of Christina, humanity must shudder at the preceding account of a transaction, difficult to extenuate, and impossible to excuse. The temper of Christina appears on all occasions to have been vindictive : educated in despotism, and accustomed to govern, she knew not how to resign with

her rank the mischievous privileges which that
rank had bestowed. ' If you fail in your duty,'
said she to her secretary, whom she sent after her
abdication to Stockholm, ' the power of the king
of Sweden, though you should take shelter in his
arms, shall not save your life ?' In asserting the
rights of the franchises, she thus wrote to the
officers of the pope: " Believe me, those whom
you have condemned to die, shall, if it please God,
live some time longer. Should it happen that
they die a violent death, be assured, that they die
not alone." A musician had quitted her service
for that of the duke of Savoy. Transported with
resentment, she wrote—" He lives only for me,
and if he does not sing for me, he shall not long
sing for any body. It is his duty to live only in
my service, and, if he does not, he shall surely
repent it." Bayle was also threatened by Christina, for having said, that her letter on the revocation of the edict of Nantes was a remain of pro-
testanism*; but, having appeased her by his apologies and submissions, she thus wrote to him:
" You shall not get off so cheap as you imagine.
I will enjoin you a penance; which is, that you
shall henceforth take the trouble of sending me all

---

* Nouvelles de la République de Lettres. Juin, 1686.

CHRISTINA.

curious books, that shall be published in Latin, Italian, Spanish, or French, on whatever subject or science, provided they are worthy of being looked into. I do not even except romances or satires : and above all, if there are any books of chemistry, I desire you will send them as soon as possible. Do not forget also to send me your journal."

Like all human characters, that of Christina appears to have been mingled. Her wit, her talents, her learning, her activity, her courage, and magnanimity, are worthy of praise. When, speaking of herself, she declares that she is ' ambitious, impetuous, haughty, disdainful, satirical, and sceptical,' we must at least give her credit for ingenuousness. Should it be allowed that her temper was restless, vindictive, and impatient of control, let it be remembered, that early seated on a throne, and accustomed to exercise authority, she was unused to opposition and corrupted by power. Subject, like all ardent temperaments, to extremes, in her emulation of the severer virtues of one sex she lost sight of the delicacy and decorums of the other : in common discourse she was profuse of oaths, she laughed aloud, and walked with precipitate strides. ' I had rather,' says she, speaking on this subject, ' emancipate myself all at once,

314   LADY MARY CHUDLEIGH.

since I was not born to be a slave.' Glory was
her ruling passion, which she sought alike in the
possession and in the relinquishment of power:
but in the pursuit of this *ignis fatuus* she was often
seduced or misled by appearances. Virtue and
heroism must be loved for their own sakes, or
they will not reward their votaries: those only
who obey with simplicity their dictates, without
looking to what is adventitious and extrinsic, are
truly great. Christina, after having relinquished
the crown of Sweden, intrigued for that of Poland with a levity that degraded her. Those who
withhold their praise till they meet with consistency of character must, it is to be feared, deal
only in satire.

The letters to the king of Prussia, published at
Amsterdam 1759, and at Geneva 1761, said to
be written by Christina, are since known to be
spurious.

Biographium Fæmineum—Encyclopediana, &c. &c.

LADY MARY CHUDLEIGH.

MARY, daughter of Richard Lee, esq. of Winslade, Devonshire, was born in August, 1656.
She received from education no particular advantages; but a passion for books, great activity of

LADY MARY CHUDLEIGH. 315

mind, and habits of application, enabled her to make a considerable progress in literature, and to acquire distinction and celebrity. She devoted herself more particularly to poetry and the *belles lettres*. She married sir George Chudleigh, of Ashton, bart. to whom she bore several children.

She composed a poem to the memory of a favourite daughter, who expired in the bloom of life, entitled, " A dialogue between Lucinia and Marissa." A short time after, she gave another specimen of her poetic talents in " The Ladies' Defence; or, the Bride-woman's Counsellor answered; a Poem. In a Dialogue between Sir John Brute, Sir William Lovell, Melissa, and a Parson." This production, occasioned by an illiberal sermon preached against the sex, has been several times republished.

The devotion of lady Chudleigh to the muses did not prevent her from cultivating the severer studies of philosophy; as was proved by the publication of some essays, in verse and prose, 1710, dedicated to the princess Sophia, electress and dowager of Brunswic. The princess acknowledged the merit of the writer by a very obliging letter, written in French. The subjects of these essays are " Knowledge, Pride, Humility, Life, Death, Fear, Grief, Riches, Self-love, Justice,

316   LADY MARY CHUDLEIGH.

Anger, Calumny, Friendship, Love, Avarice, Solitude." They are said to be written with purity
and elegance, and to evince the knowledge and
piety of the author, who contemned the frivolous pursuits of her sex. " The Song of The
Three Children, paraphrased," was, with a collection of poems on various occasions, published in
1722, 12mo. This work went through several
editions.

Lady Chudleigh, after having been confined to
her chamber a considerable time with the rheuma-
tism, died in the fifty-fifth year of her age, at
Ashton, in Devonshire, December 15th, 1710.
She left in manuscript two tragedies, two operas,
a masque, some of Lucian's dialogues versified,
Satirical Reflections on Saqualio, in imitation of
a dialogue of Lucian; with several other poems,
which are preserved in her family. At the end
of the second volume of the duke of Wharton's
poems, are five letters from lady Chudleigh, addressed to Corinna*, and to the rev. Mr. Norris of
Bemerton. Also, in a collection of poems by eminent ladies of Great Britain and Ireland, several
pieces of lady Chudleigh's are preserved, which display strong powers of understanding, and a facility

---

Mrs. Elizabeth Thomas.

LADY MARY CHUDLEIGH. 317

of versification, rather than a poetic imagination. This lady, not less distinguished for her exemplary conduct than for the powers of her mind, was an ardent advocate for the improvement and cultivation of female talents. Her " Defence of the Ladies," in which she deprecates with some severity the usurpations of man, and contends for intellectual rights and privileges of her sex, was several times reprinted. The following lines are selected as a specimen from this performance :

" Yours be the fame, the profit, and the praise ;
We'll neither rob you of your vine nor bays :
Nor will we to dominion once aspire ;
You shall be chief, and still yourselves admire.
The tyrant man may yet possess the throne,
'T is in our minds that we would rule alone :
Those unseen empires give us leave to sway,
And to our reason private homage pay.
Our struggling passions within bounds confine,
And to our thoughts their proper task assign.
This is the use we would of knowledge make,
You quickly would the good effects partake," &c.

This lady's claims are a little too modest : light on some occasions serves but to make darkness visible. Happy is the slave who remains unconscious of his bonds !

[318]

MARGARET CLEMENT.

MARGARET CLEMENT, niece to sir Thomas
More, was born in 1508, and educated in the
family of her uncle, with his daughters, whom
she emulated in learning and science. This lady,
who corresponded in Latin with Erasmus, is
praised by him for good sense, and a chaste correct style. She is mentioned by Mr. More, in
his Life of sir Thomas, as a woman of singular
acquirements and learning. She was greatly attached to her uncle, whose virtues she reverenced ;
she was accustomed to say, that she had sometimes committed wilful errors, from the pleasure
she experienced in his mild and affectionate re-
proofs.

She carefully preserved the linen, stained with
the blood of sir Thomas, in which he was executed, and also his shirt of hair.

In 1531, she married her tutor, Dr. John
Clement : their nuptials were celebrated by Mr.
John Leland, the antiquarian poet, in a Latin
epithalamium. One daughter, Winefrid Clement,
was the fruit of this union, a learned and ingenious woman, who married Mr. William Rastall,

a man of talents and literature and an eminent lawyer.

Dr. Clement and his wife left England to avoid a religious persecution, and settled at Mechlin, in Brabant, where Mrs. Clement died, July 6th, 1570, in the sixty-third year of her age, and was interred near the tabernacle, in the church of St. Rumbold.

Ballard's British Ladies—Biographium Fæmineum.

CLEOBULE.

CLEOBULE, or CLEOBULINE, daughter of Cleobulus, prince of Lindus, was celebrated among the ancients for her enigmatical sentences, or riddles, composed for the most part in Greek verse.

CLEOPATRA.

PTOLEMY AULETES, who reigned in Egypt fifty-one years before the Christian æra, bequeathed at his death the sovereignty to his eldest son and daughter, who, according to the custom of the country, were to be united in marriage, and reign jointly.   Cleopatra, the eldest, being only seventeen years of age, was, with her brother, committed, by the will of her father, to the care and tuition of the Roman senate.

Posthinus, the eunuch, with Achillas, general of the Egyptian army, and Theodotus, a rhetorician, preceptor to the prince, ambitious and aspiring men, contrived to get into their hands the young king, who, by their counsel and persuasions, raised a force for the assistance of Pompey, in the disputes which had taken place between him and Cæsar.   In recompence for this service, Pompcy procured a decree of the senate to vest the government of Egypt solely in the hands of the prince.   But after the battle of Pharsalia, Pompey, flying for refuge to Egypt, was, by the intrigues of these very men, basely murdered.

Cæsar, after this catastrophe, coming to Alexandria, while Cleopatra, with her sister Arsinoe, were collecting in Syria troops for the recovery of their rights, the decision of the dispute between the prince and his sisters was referred to his tribunal, and advocates on both sides appointed to plead before him.

Cleopatra, on this occasion, aware of the frailty of her judge, and confiding in her personal charms,

CLEOPATRA. 321

formed the project of an interview with Cæsar, whose passions she doubted not to interest in her favour. Arsinoe and her younger brother had obtained an easy admittance into Alexandria; but Achillas, the general of Ptolemy, jealous of the address and talents of Cleopatra, sought to prevent her from entering the city. But the princess, fertile in expedients, having obtained from Cæsar permission for the solicited conference, eluded the precautions of her enemy, by causing herself to be secretly conveyed in a small galley, in the dusk of the evening, by Apollodorus the Sicilian, to the port of Alexandria, and landed near the palace; whence she was carried, folded in a mattress, through the gates of the castle, into the presence of Cæsar. Her enterprise produced the effect she had foreseen: Cæsar, captivated by her youth, her beauty, and her address, granted all her demands, and purchased her favours by the sacrifice of integrity and justice.

On the ensuing day, her brother was exhorted to accede to the terms demanded by his sister; but Ptolemy, finding in his judge a prejudiced advocate, appealed from his decision to that of the people. An entire exclusion of the prince from the throne had been the purpose of Cæsar; but, to appease the murmurs of the populace, the destiny of Ptolemy was mitigated to a participation with Cleopatra of the regal dignity, according to the will of their father. In this situation he was incited, by the turbulent and aspiring temper of Achillas, to raise new commotions and tumults, which terminated in a war. After various disputes and skirmishes, a decisive battle was at length fought, in which the fortune of Cæsar prevailed. The unhappy Ptolemy, seeking safety in flight, was drowned while endeavouring to regain, in a boat, his ships in the Nile. On this catastrophe, a younger brother of Cleopatra, a youth only eleven years of age, was associated with her in the government.

Cæsar, plunged in voluptuousness and luxury, continued near twelve months a guest in the Alexandrian court. Soon after his departure, Cleopatra was delivered of a son, to whom, with the permission of his father, she gave the name of Cæsarion.

On his return to Rome, the emperor caused a statue of the queen of Egypt to be placed with that of the goddess in a temple dedicated to Venus. Cleopatra, accompanied by her brother, followed her lover to Rome, where, to the great disgust of the people, she was lodged in an apartment of the palace. A war which raged in Spain compelling the emperor to quit Rome, he prevailed upon his mistress, whom he was unwilling

CLEOPATRA.

to expose during his absence to popular insult, to return, laden with magnificent presents, to her own dominions.

Cleopatra, from political motives, had contrived to leave her brother in Italy, where, jealous of his future interference with her authority, she caused him to be dispatched by poison. The unhappy youth having expired in a foreign country, far removed from his adherents and friends, no inquisition was made into the manner of his death, or the arts to which he fell a victim.

Cleopatra had scarcely reached Alexandria, when tidings arrived in Egypt of the assassination of Cæsar in the senate: on this intelligence, far from consuming her time in fruitless sorrow, she formed with the eldest son of Pompey, the most inveterate enemy of her deceased lover, an immediate treaty, in expectation of the revival of the interest of his family at Rome. During the civil war that ensued, the queen of Egypt, with a view of securing the favour of the victorious party, afforded to the contending factions alternate aid : while she sent troops to the assistance of Dolabella in Syria, Serapion, her lieutenant in Cyprus, had orders to declare in favour of Cassius.

After the battle of Philippi, when Augustus

and Mark Antony shared the world between them, Antony came into Cilicia, whence he sent Delius to summon Cleopatra before him, to justify herself from the charge of having assisted the enemies of Cæsar. The queen, with a view of discovering the character of Antony, artfully questioned his messenger, and was too well satisfied with the result of her enquiries to doubt the success of the plan she meditated. Delius, overwhelmed by her with obligations and presents, for the purpose of securing his favourable report to his master, was dismissed with answers of humility and acquiescence. But, still farther to excite the curiosity and heighten the impatience of Antony, delays were variously contrived, and excuses framed, to procrastinate the expected interview.

The day at length being appointed, Cleopatra, bearing magnificent presents, embarked in regal pomp on the Cydnus, in a small galley, the head of which was inlaid with gold; the sails were of purple silk, and the oars of silver, which, dashing the waves, kept time to the sound of musical instruments. The queen, habited as Venus, reposed under a canopy of cloth of gold richly embroidered, while beautiful boys, representing Cupids, fanned her on either side: her women, attired as sea-nymphs

CLEOPATRA. 325

and Graces, surrounded their mistress in respectful silence.   Perfumes breathed a fragrance around, wafted by the breeze to the shores, which were crowded by people, who flocked to gaze on a scene so novel and splendid.   Antony, seated on his tribunal in the forum, found himself wholly deserted : Venus, it was said, had arrived to feast with Bacchus, and to consult with him on the common welfare of Asia.

Cleopatra, having landed, was invited by Antony to supper; but, still farther to irritate his impatience, she artfully eluded this request, pleading her privilege, as a woman and a stranger, to be first allowed the honour of entertaining *the greatest man in the world*, to whom, as a Roman senator, all the potentates of the earth owed homage.   Antony, gratified by her flattery, readily acceded to her request, while every preparation which the time would allow was made by her court for his reception.

Soft music, lights advantageously disposed, crowds of beautiful women magnificently attired, every elegance that could charm the fancy, every voluptuous incitement which could fascinate the senses, gave zest and variety to the entertainment. The queen, still more lovely and splendid than her attendants, reclining in a pensive and studied attitude, her head resting on her hand, contrived to be seen by her guest without being supposed to observe him; till, on his nearer approach, rising suddenly to receive him, she fell, as by accident, on her knees before him. As Antony hastened to raise her, she pretended to recover herself; and, addressing him in an elegant compliment, affected to construe her fall into a favourable omen, that her weakness would receive support from his strength, and that he would defend and protect a queen who wholly resigned herself into his power. Still leaning on Antony, she suffered herself to be placed by him in a chair of state, which had by her orders been prepared for her guest, who gallantly seated himself beside her. This interview proved decisive : Antony became fascinated by the beauty and artifices of the fair Egyptian, whose only passion was ambition; and who, by the coldness of her own heart, was enabled the more effectually to triumph over that of her lover.

The following evening Cleopatra was invited by Antony to return his visit, when the festivities were renewed, and the chains of the enamoured Roman completely rivetted. Credulous, ardent, voluptuous, and sincere, Antony was, without difficulty, induced to yield his judgment to the charms that had subjugated his senses : a dupe to the artifices of Cleopatra, he blindly gave credit,

CLEOPATRA.   327

without troubling himself to investigate facts, to whatever she thought proper to assert. By her intrigues and address she separated from him those friends whose integrity gave her umbrage, or whose penetration she feared; while, availing herself of his boundless love of pleasure, she acquired, by her arts and caprices, an unlimited control over his passions. Governing him with a secret but absolute sway, friendship, honour, reason, humanity, and justice, were the sacrifices which she exacted from her victim.

Having long coveted the possessions of her younger sister, to whom, in conjunction with her deceased brother, the kingdom of Cyprus had been allotted by Cæsar, she induced Antony, by her insinuations, to stain his hands in the blood of Arsinoe, whose death, to throw from herself the odium of the crime, she afterwards affected to deplore. Her sister had indeed, she pretended, conspired against her life and dignity, nevertheless she would have pardoned her, and must ever remain inconsolable for her fate. To appease her grief, and to reward her magnanimity, Antony presented to her the kingdom of Cyprus, the object of her cruel ambition.

She gave a new instance of her power over her lover, in leading him back with her to Alexandria,

CLEOPATRA.

while his presence was indispensable at Rome, where Fulvia, his wife, maintained with Augustus an unequal contest. The Parthian troops had at the same time assembled in Mesopotamia, under the command of Labienus, and were ready to enter Syria. In vain the friends of Antony exhorted him to disentangle himself from the toils of this Armida : held in voluptuous bondage, he wholly disregarded their entreaties and representations. Cleopatra gloried in thus holding in her chains one of the masters of the world: it was of his power rather than of his person that she was enamoured; she dreaded his absence, lest he should escape her fascinations; above all, she feared the influence of Fulvia, a woman of high and masculine spirit, who had fomented the disputes between Augustus and her husband for the purpose of detaching him from the spells of her rival. Cleopatra exhausted her invention in devising new pleasures and spectacles for Antony, with a view of detaining him in her snares. An order, the members of which bore the title of the *Inimitable Livers,* was instituted at Alexandria, the grand rule of which was, by varying their enjoyments, to exclude every interval of satiety or reflection.

Of the excessive expence and profusion attending these festivals, the following curious instance

CLEOPATRA. 329

is related by historians.—A young Greek, who
came to study physic at Alexandria, had the curiosity to procure himself admission into the kit-
chen of Antony; where, among other provisions
in preparation for a repast, he beheld eight wild
boars roasting whole, at the same time. Having
expressed his surprise at the great number of guests
which he supposed must be expected to partake of
the feast, one of the officers smiled, and informed
him that ten only were invited, but as the moment
when Antony would choose his supper was uncertain, and it was necessary that the table should
be served in the utmost perfection, not one only
but many suppers were always prepared. To this
it is added, that it was the custom of Antony
and Cleopatra to present to their guests the gold
and silver vessels in which the entertainment was
served up.

The queen, aware that to an enchantment
which depended on caprice serious thought was
the most formidable enemy, surrounded her captive by the creatures of her power, carefully
excluding from him his real friends. Festivals,
carousals, gaming, hunting, warlike amusements,
and voluptuous repose, alternately occupied and
diversified their hours. When Antony exercised
in arms, his mistress was near him; he was by
turns her Hercules, her Hector, or her Alexander.

At other times, habited as gods, they caroused on ambrosia and nectar; or, as the caprice seized them, strolled disguised through the city on nocturnal rambles, amusing themselves in wild frolics and dissolute mirth. Every casualty which seemed to threaten an interruption to their pleasures, served, by the wit and ingenuity of Cleopatra, but to improve and heighten their zest. Sometimes, dissolving in softness, she overwhelmed her lover with caresses; then, in fits of feigned anger, compelled him to sue for her returning smiles. By keen and delicate strokes of satire, she would frequently contrive to rouse his anger and alarm his pride, when, by the most artful and ingenious turns, she would suddenly convert into compliment the implied censure.

Antony, one day on a fishing party, being irritated by ill success, gave secret orders to the fishermen to cause divers, under water, to fasten to his hook fishes newly taken: the scheme succeeded; the fish were drawn up, and Antony triumphed in his skill. Cleopatra, suspecting the cause of this suddenly acquired dexterity, privately imparted her suspicions to the courtiers, whom she invited to be present on the ensuing day, to witness the catastrophe of the adventure. Every thing being prepared accordingly, Antony again let down his line, assured of prey, and again in a few minutes

CLEOPATRA.

drew it forth exulting ;—when behold a salted fish, of a species originally taken in the Pontic sea, appear' suspended to the hook. Confounded by the burst of mirth which this incident produced, he reddened with indignation; when the queen, approaching him with a smiling countenance,—' Leave the line, brave general,' said she, in a soft tone of voice, ' to us, the poor inhabitants of Pharos and Canopus: kingdoms, provinces, and cities, are your nobler game.'

Cleopatra, by holding the passions of her lover in perpetual agitation, by the varied pleasures and vivid emotions she prepared for him, maintained undiminished her ascendancy over his mind: a stranger to genuine tenderness, it was her pride to display her power to an indignant world, in the degradation of the man whom she pretended to love. By her management, his faithful servants were driven from the presence of their master, whom, with Circean arts, she retained as in a magic circle : his reason, his affections, his glory, were sacrificed to the enchantress, for whom he contemned a prostrate world. Intoxicated with the success of her spells, Cleopatra sported with deceit, and wantoned in new inventions, with which she daily beguiled her fascinated victim.

Yet, amidst the intoxications of pleasure, she omitted not to cultivate the sciences and elegant arts. In the place where the celebrated Alexandrian library had suffered destruction, she erected a new one; to the augmentation of which Antony considerably contributed, by presenting her with the libraries of Pergamus, which contained more than two hundred thousand volumes. Her collection of books was not merely ostentatious; she delighted in literature: there were few nations, however barbarous, to which she needed an interpreter; with the languages of the Ethiopians, Troglodytæ, Arabians, Syrians, Medes, and Parthians, she was familiar, nor was she unacquainted with those of several other nations; while the greater part of the sovereigns of Egypt who preceded her, wrapt in profound ignorance, had been unable to acquire even the language of Egypt.

Antony was at length roused from his voluptuous trance by messengers from Rome, from whom he received information, that Lucius Antonius his brother, and Fulvia his wife, had, after many disputes, united against Octavius; and, failing in success, had been compelled to abandon Italy: while Octavius, having made himself master of Gaul, had gained the legions stationed there to his party. From another courier, who arrived at the same time, he learned that the Parthians, under the command of Pacorus the son of their

CLEOPATRA. 333

king, assisted by Labienus and Barzapharnes, had made themselves masters of Syria, and marched to Jerusalem; which having sacked, they carried away Hyrcanus the high-priest, with Phazael the brother of Herod, prisoners; Herod himself having fled for safety to the mountains.

Cleopatra, filled with consternation by these accounts, which threatened to rob her of her captive, and dreading more than all his return to Italy and Fulvia, prevailed on him to turn his attention to the east, and to recover Syria, which she regarded as her own. With this view, she affected to treat lightly the Italian war, and magnified the importance of his presence in the east. After various delays and obstacles, which she opposed to the departure of Antony, for the purpose of displaying her power in his weakness, two hundred ships, with a considerable army, were collected to oppose the Parthians. Cleopatra omitted no artifice, on this separation, to convince her lover of the sacrifice she made of her tenderness to his glory, in suffering him to depart.

But her triumph received an alloy, when, some time after, intelligence arrived from the spies she had placed about him, that Antony had steered his course for Italy, and had already reached Athens, where he had been joined by Fulvia.

Stunned by a blow thus unforeseen, her first idea was to repair to Athens, and to dispute with Fulvia the heart of her husband; but farther reflection induced her to abandon a project, which, in its possible failure, would overwhelm her with humiliation. Her apprehensions were in some degree softened when she learned that Antony and his wife passed their time in mutual reproaches; Antony upbraiding her with the war she had kindled at Rome, and Fulvia retorting upon him his inglorious captivity in Egypt, to which she imputed the calamities that had taken place. Encouraged by this intelligence, and by the consciousness of superior charms, a comparison which she believed her lover could not fail of making in her favour, Cleopatra addressed to him an epistle, in which, after artfully insinuating her claims, her passion, her sufferings, and the sacrifices she had made to him, she ridiculed, with poignant satire, the age, the person, the character, and the privileges of her rival; while, with mingled flattery, she affected to rally the respect of Antony for the conjugal tie. This address concluded with exaggerated expressions of her despair in his absence. The letter produced the effect intended by the writer, who, on the return of her messenger, received from Antony the

CLEOPATRA.

tenderest assurances of affection and fidelity. She had also the satisfaction of learning that, on hearing of the nuptials of Octavius with Scribonia, he had advanced towards Italy, without taking leave of Fulvia, whom he left at Scyon, or shewing any concern for an indisposition under which she then laboured. A valuable present was at the same time sent by Antony, as a testimony of his love, to his mistress. Fulvia survived not long this new instance of her husband's contempt, while her rival rejoiced at an event which she fancied secured to her for ever the heart of her lover.

Antony having made a league with Pompey against Octavius, the queen of Egypt flattered herself that he would be enabled to lay the world at her feet. Ventidius, his lieutenant, recovered for him Parthia and Syria, while Antony was besieging Brundusium, the gates of which had been shut against him by the order of Octavius, whose troops murmured at being compelled to turn their arms against their former commander; a disposition which promised to facilitate to Antony a victory or an honourable peace.

In the midst of these flattering prospects, an event took place that appeared to give to the hopes of Cleopatra a mortal blow. Through the interposition of Julia, the mother of Antony, he became reconciled to Octavius, from whom he received, as a pledge of their union, the hand of his sister Octavia. Octavius and Antony, leading Octavia between them, had entered Rome in triumph, amidst the acclamations of the army and people. A new division was made of the empire, by which the western provinces, including Gaul, were given to Octavius, while to Antony was allotted the empire of the east. Codropolis, a town of Illyria, on the confines of Macedon, was appointed the boundary between their domains: Africa was to remain in the possession of Lepidus, and the dominion of Sicily to be continued with Pompey. In token of his entire satisfaction with these measures, Antony accepted the priesthood of the temple newly erected in honour of Julius Cæsar by Octavius his successor.

The queen of Egypt, filled with surprise and anguish, was, on the first tidings of what had taken place, nearly deprived of sense and life. On the recovery of her faculties, fury succeeded to grief; she struck the messenger of the unwelcome news, and would have stabbed him to the heart, had he not saved himself by a precipitate flight. She vented her passions, unaccustomed to control, in rage and execration; while all who surrounded her suffered the effects of her vehemence and disappointment. The tumult of her feelings

CLEOPATRA. 337

having abated, she sought to learn the character
of a rival, the report of whose youth and beauty
had filled her with dismay. In the description of
the mild, unassuming virtues of Octavia, she
found some alleviation to her despair: acquainted
with the temper of Antony, she felt a conviction
that his passions, accustomed to a stronger stimu-
lus, would languish in the possession of a woman
whose simple goodness and unaffected graces
could but feebly affect a vitiated taste, and a heart
exhausted by voluptuous excesses. To this confidence in her own discernment, and in her knowledge of her lover, other circumstances were
added, which tended to cherish a latent and almost expiring hope. Antony had, on a frivolous
pretence, caused Marsius to suffer death ; a man
who, by freely censuring his connection with the
queen of Egypt, had exasperated Fulvia, and occasioned the war which the present alliance had
so happily terminated. He also loaded with favours an astrologer whom, at the recommendation
of Cleopatra, he had brought with him from Egypt,
and who, with a view of ensnaring him to return,
perpetually declared, that his fortune, however
glorious, was overshadowed by that of Octavius,
from whom it behoved him to remove to a distance. ' Your genius,' he was accustomed to re-

peat, ' is menaced by his ; in his absence you are great ; in the presence of your rival, you sink into comparative littleness. In every contention, even in every game, you are vanquished by Octavius.' Antony, disgusted and humbled by these representations, which were not without a foundation in truth, resigned, after a time, to Octavius the regulation of Rome ; and, quitting Italy, repaired with his wife to Athens.

Here he again gave the reins to his inclinations, and plunged into dissipation and pleasure : yet, at intervals, emerging from these excesses, he courted the society of the learned ; while Octavia, by her virtues, conciliated the popular esteem. To fill up the measure of his extravagance, Antony assumed the title and insignia of Bacchus, under which he caused himself to be worshipped by the Athenians in a temple near the city. He also ordered a throne to be erected in a grotto, to which was given the name of the Cave of Bacchus ; and where, enervated by soft music, he indulged in voluptuousness. To his effeminacy was added an insatiable rapacity : the Athenians having supplicated their new deity to take to wife Pallas, their tutelary goddess and protectress, he consented to their request, but stipulated that the goddess should bring to him, as her dowry, a thousand talents. The servile crowd, alarmed by the consequences of their absurd and licentious superstition, hesitated at this unexpected demand, while they alleged in reply, that his father Jupiter had exacted no portion with his mother Semele. ' True,' answered their new god; ' my father was rich, but I stand in need of money.' The ridiculous festival of the nuptials of Bacchus with Pallas was kept in all the Peloponnesian towns; each, in its proportion, contributing to defray the expences. Antony, charmed with his new dignity, which had proved more than an empty title, ordered the name of Bacchus to be inscribed at the feet of every statue which had been raised to his honour.

From Athens he sailed to Syria, for the regulation of his affairs, and thence returned to Athens; where, irritated by some reports concerning Octavius, he remained but a short time. Having departed for Italy with a fleet of an hundred sail, and being refused harbour at Brundusium, he sailed indignantly to Tarentum. From Tarentum, Octavia, who accompanied her husband, and who was then pregnant, prevailed on him to suffer her to repair to her brother. Having met Octavius on the road, she held with him a conference in the presence of two of his friends, by her tears and representations softened his anger, induced him to yield his resentments, to accompany her

back to Tarentum, and to make an amicable visit
to Antony. It was in this interview mutually
agreed, that Octavius should give to his brother-
in-law two legions, and one thousand foot soldiers,
to serve in the Parthian war, while Antony should
leave with him one hundred armed galleys and
twenty brigantines. After parting on terms of
cordiality, Octavius prepared to dispute Sicily with
Sextus Pompeius; while Antony, leaving with
her brother his wife and family, sailed for Asia.

Cleopatra, who had been watchful of his steps,
seized this occasion to allure her captive back to
her arms. She had entrusted with one of her
spies a letter to be put into the hands of Antony
whenever he should be separated from Octavia.
This letter, containing a mixture of submission and
tenderness, of insinuations and reflections, calculated to touch the heart, and rouse the pride of him
to whom it was addressed, could scarcely fail of its
purpose. Should Antony, it intimated, shew
compassion for the only woman who had really
loved him, and who was ready to expire the victim of his neglect, Octavius, to whose power
and fortune respect was certainly due, would, it
was but too probable, vindicate the cause of his
sister. The vain and feeble-minded Antony, softened by the recollection of his former mistress,
and the images which she had conjured up of her

CLEOPATRA. 341

passion and of her despair, and piqued at the supposition of his being held in vassalage by the brother of his wife, determined, by the sacrifice of his principles, to assert his courage and independence. The queen of Egypt (learning from her agent the impression which her epistle had produced) continued daily to importune him with messages; till, on his arrival in Syria, Antony, against the remonstrances and entreaties of his friends, sent to her to join him.

This summons was heard with exultation, and obeyed with facility. Antony advanced to receive his mistress on her way, and to conduct her himself to his palace. On their meeting, she affected an air the most humble and submissive, and prostrated herself before him; when he raised and embraced her in a transport of joy and passion.

The purpose of Cleopatra thus accomplished, and her triumph over her rival complete, she resumed her former artifices; banished from the presence of Antony his friends; and, plunging him in dissolute pleasures, barred, by her insinuations, and by the whirl of dissipation, in which reflection was drowned, every avenue of his heart against the virtuous Octavia. Apparently watchful of his interest and safety, new alarms of plots and treacheries were daily fabricated; while by multiplied confiscations her rapacity was gratified, and the hearts of the people alienated from Antony. Lysanius, whom he had made king of Chalcis, and for whose spoils she thirsted, was sacrificed by him to the avarice of his mistress: Cyrene, Cyprus, Cœlo-Syria, Iturea, and Phenicia, with great part of Cilicia and Crete, were added to her dominions. The kingdoms of Judea and Arabia, over which Herod and Malchus reigned, became objects of her ambition: to possess herself of their territories, she brought an accusation of tyranny and mal-administration against Herod; while Malchus, she affirmed, had favoured the enemies of her lover.

These affairs were yet undecided when the season of the year called upon Antony to quit Antioch, and to march towards Armenia. Cleopatra, afraid of trusting him out of her presence, accompanied him to the banks of the Euphrates; where, by her caprices, dissipating his attention, and occupying his time, she caused him to neglect the warlike preparations indispensable for the occasion. It was here that, apprehensive lest the chance of war might deprive her of the advantages which she derived from his infatuation, she again importuned him to grant to her the kingdoms of Judea and Arabia. Herod and Mal

CLEOPATRA. 343

chus attended at Laodicea the summons of the triumvir, to clear themselves from the charges preferred against them. The injustice of the process appeared so manifest, that, notwithstanding the arts and solicitations of their formidable adversary, Antony contented himself with dismembering their dominions. Jericho and the balsam gardens were taken from Herod; and from Malchus, Arabia Nabath, famed for its perfumes.

The profusion of Antony, however lavish, was insufficient to gratify his venal mistress. On being reproached for his extravagant donations—— 'The greatness of the Roman empire,' replied he, with a specious magnanimity, ' consists in bestowing, rather than in conquering, kingdoms.'

Cleopatra, compelled at length to leave her lover to the prosecution of the Parthian war, omitted no artifice before her departure that might tend to insure his return. To beguile the time during the interval of his absence, she passed through the principal towns of Syria; and, coming to Judea, was received by Herod, who sought, with respectful attentions, to procure her favour and interest. She is accused of having been prompted by vanity, during her stay in the court of Judea, to rival his beloved Mariamne in the affections of Herod, who, either blind to the charms of the Egyptian, or aware of the danger of contesting a heart with Antony, affected to overlook her advances ; while he confined his behaviour to a distant and respectful homage. Mortified by the coldness or the prudence of Herod, rage succeeded to coquetry in the heart of the vindictive queen, who silently meditated the future destruction of the man who contemned her attractions. With a view of softening the malignant spirit of his guest, Herod, on her departure, attended her to the boundaries of Egypt; where, on taking his leave, he loaded her with magnificent presents.

On her return to Alexandria, Cleopatra received intelligence, that Octavius having made a glorious campaign, had conquered Sicily, whence he had driven Sextus Pompeius ; also that he had compelled Lepidas to renounce the dignity of a triumvir. That the senate of Rome, lavishing honours on its hero, had decreed to him and to his family a festival in the capitol. At the same time, a messenger arrived from Antony with news of an opposite nature : his impatience to return to Egypt, had, notwithstanding his formidable power, which had spread throughout Asia terror and dismay, rendered his campaign disastrous : harassed and defeated in all his projects, having lost in the expedition more than thirty thousand of his best troops, he had been com-

CLEOPATRA. 345

pelled to make an inglorious retreat. To this intelligence was added, that having with difficulty reached Leucone in safety, he there impatiently awaited his mistress. The mortification which this account produced was in some degree softened to Cleopatra by the reflection, that it was to the power of her charms that the discomfiture of Antony might be attributed; her presence and her fascinations having robbed him of his accustomed activity.

Couriers succeeded to couriers to hasten her departure, the impatience of her lover enduring no delay: while he waited her coming, anxiety and grief evidently preyed upon his health. Cleopatra was, by an earnestness so flattering, induced still to procrastinate her journey; wantoning in her power of giving pain, and gratified by the extravagance and infatuation of her lover. When she at length joined him, his transports knew no bounds: having brought with her clothing and presents for the troops, magnificent liberalities were added to her gift by Antony, who contrived to give to his mistress all the honour. By her advice, he softened and falsified, in a letter to the senate, his unsuccessful campaign, of which the truth had already reached them. Octavius, nevertheless, on the receipt of his letters, or-

dered thanks to be offered to the gods for his success.

Octavia, who had remained at Rome during
this interval, now solicited permission of her brother to depart in search of her husband. Her
request was the more readily granted, as Octavius foresaw, in the indignity with which she
would be treated by Antony, a pretence for a
rupture, which he had for some time meditated.
Carrying with her magnificent presents from her
brother, Octavia immediately commenced her
journey.

Cleopatra, alarmed by the purpose of her rival,
prevailed, by her insinuations, on Antony to sig-
nify to his wife, that she should wait at Athens,
till the embarrassments of his affairs should allow
him the satisfaction of joining her. Octavia, but
too sensible of the truth, appeared to acquiesce
in these pretences, and, resigning herself with respect to the commands of her husband, entreated
only to be informed in what manner she was to
dispose of the money and horses, the presents
for his friends and officers, and the clothing for
his soldiers, with which she was charged. She
had also brought with her two thousand chosen
soldiers for recruiting the prætorian cohorts, which
had suffered during the campaign. Nieger, a
friend of Antony's, was deputed with this mes-

sage, who concluded his commission with high and just praises of the virtues and conduct of Octavia. In this panegyric, the queen of Egypt, who was present, affected to join, yet not without artful allusions to the relationship which she bore to the victorious and powerful Octavius.

The purpose of Antony was, in union with the king of Media, once more to take the field against the Parthians; but Cleopatra, apprehensive *lest he should,* when so near, visit Athens and Octavia, redoubled her efforts to turn him from his design. She affected to deprecate his absence in transports of grief and passion; while she sought to persuade him that the moment of their separation must inevitably be that of her death : by refusing to take nourishment, and by a studied negligence in her air and dress, she contrived to appear wasted by sickness and sorrow: when Antony entered her apartment, she would assume an air of grief and surprise; and with eyes bathed in tears, which she yet seemed to struggle to suppress, appear, when he quitted her, to sink into anguish and despondency. Her creatures, by whom she had surrounded him, aided her views by their arguments, their representations, and their appeals to his passions. A dupe to the blandishments of a vain and capricious woman, whose tenderness was a fiction to cover her

venal purposes, Antony became entangled in the
toils which encompassed him, through which he
wanted firmness to break : his projects were abandoned, and, while Octavia awaited him at Athens,
he suffered himself to be led in triumph, the scorn
of an indignant world, by Cleopatra back to Alexandria.

Yet, unsatisfied with her victory, she left no
means unessayed to prevail on her lover to treat
with indignity his blameless wife ; and, without
admitting her to his presence, to order her back
to Rome.   By irritating his pride and his jealousy
of Octavius, whose power she extolled and magnified, she at length brought him to her purpose.
To assert his independence, and humble his rival,
Antony heroically determined to insult and outrage his admirable wife.   Cleopatra, by seeming
to oppose it, strengthened his resolution, till her
design was fully completed.   Octavia received
the commands of her husband, in which a studied
contempt was mingled with asperity, to quit
Athens, and to return to Rome.   Without
condescending to contest with her rival, she
meekly obeyed the mandate, and prepared for her
departure.

Sextus Pompeius, who had about this period
been driven from Sicily by Octavius, sought protection from Antony ; and, at the same time, lest

his negociation should fail, had, by his embassadors, endeavoured to secure for himself a refuge
with the Parthians. This duplicity, which had
been betrayed to Antony, Pompeius sought to excuse on the plea of necessity and distress. The
queen of Egypt, with a view to strengthen her
party against Rome, espoused the cause of Pompeius; but, persevering in a crooked policy, he at
length fell into the hands of his enemy Titius,
who, having against him a personal pique, put a
period to his life, by a pretended mistake of the
orders of Antony. On this event, disappointed
in her plans, Cleopatra induced Antony to turn
his arms against Artabazes, the king of Armenia,
whose dominions she thirsted to annex to her
own. Artabazes, pretending to be the ally of
Antony, had, during the Parthian war, treache-
rously withdrawn his troops, the consequences of
which had been fatal to the campaign.

While Antony was absent on this expedition,
Cleopatra heard with rage and mortification of the
fortune of Octavius in Illyria, who, crowned with
success, carried the glory of the Roman arms
where, till now, its name had been unknown. To
this intelligence it was added, that he had, with
the spoils of the Illyrian war, raised a magnificent portico, ornamented with pictures and statues of inestimable value, on which was placed

the standard taken from the enemy, and which he
had consecrated to the honour of his sister Octavia. To increase the anguish and malignity of
Cleopatra, she also learned that her rival, on her
return to Rome, resisting the entreaties of her
brother to abandon the house of her unworthy
husband, had declared, that no injuries from Antony should induce her to forget the duties of a
wife, to which it was her determination, in every
instance, to adhere. Remaining in his house, she
had, in conformity to this resolution, devoted herself to the cares of his family, and reared, with
her own children, those of Fulvia, his former wife.
His friends were also received by her with kindness, while she promoted their interest and preferment with her brother. In the most cruel species of widowhood, she lived at Rome, amidst the
sympathy and affection of her family, and the respect and admiration of the people.

Cleopatra sickened at the virtues and magnanimity of her rival, whose superiority she could
scarcely conceal from herself: incapable of a generous emulation, she determined to leave no effort unessayed to shake her fortitude, and tarnish
her reputation.

Addressing herself to Antony, she implored his
return, and exhorted him, should force or stratagem prove ineffectual for the conquest of Arme-

CLEOPATRA. 351

nia, to delay his operations till another season. To this request was added a declaration, that she was unable longer to endure their separation.

A civil war with Octavius was the project now revolving in the thoughts of Cleopatra; her restless ambition aspired to the empire of the world, in the humiliation of the family of her rival. Occupied with these plans, she gave the reins to her imagination, indulging in fancied triumphs in the capitol of Rome, where she seemed already in idea to trample her adversaries under her feet. Dazzled with vanity, and frenzied with passion, she beheld no obstacles to her wishes: every difficulty receded before her ardent fancy, while she waited in breathless expectation the return of Antony, in whose presence she saw the accomplishment of her daring plans.

Hastily obeying her summons, he arrived in Alexandria, having adopted the insidious policy recommended to him by his mistress, of betraying into his power, under fair pretences, and by solemn engagements, the king of Armenia, whom, with his family, he brought back with him in chains. His entrance into the city was by a triumphal procession in the manner of the Romans, in which Artabazes and his family, their misfortunes aggravated by insult and mockery, preceded the chariot of victory. The procession, which in

Rome terminated at the temple of Jupiter, ended
in Egypt at the foot of the throne; where Cleopatra, surrounded by the people, received, as a goddess, the homage of the victor. The royal cap-
tives, presented in fetters to the queen, having
refused with sullen dignity the prostration demanded of them, experienced, in their subsequent
treatment, the vindictive malice of a mind to which
magnanimity was a stranger.

A short time after his return, Antony gave a
festival to the Alexandrians, whom he afterwards
assembled in the place of public exercises; where
seated, with their queen, on a throne of gold, he
declared Cæsariò, the son of Cleopatra and Julius
Cæsar, in conjunction with his mother, sovereign
of Egypt, Cyprus, Lybia, and Cœlo-Syria. Among
the three children which she had borne to himself, he divided the remainder of his dominions
in the east; to Alexander, the eldest, he gave
Armenia, Media, Parthia, and the country which
should be yet subdued from the Euphrates to India. To Cleopatra, his twin sister, he gave Lybia and Cyrene; and on Philadelphus, the younger,
he bestowed Phenicia, Syria, Cilicia, with the
countries of the Lesser Asia, from the Euphrates
to the Hellespont; while he conferred on each the
title of king of kings. The princes, in the appropriate habits of the respective countries bestowed

CLEOPATRA; 35:

upon them, rising from their seats as the ceremony concluded, approached the throne, and, putting one knee to the ground, kissed the hands of Antony and Cleopatra. A retinue suited to their new dignities was assigned to them, with regiments of guards drawn from the families of the principal nobility.

To the queen was given the name of Isis, while Antony assumed to himself that of Osiris, the tutelar deities of the Egyptians. They appeared in public in the habits of these divinities; while, in a studied oration, Antony made the panegyric of his mistress, acknowledging her as the lawful wife and widow of Julius Cæsar, to whose rights her son was justly entitled. The eldest son of Antony and Fulvia, present on this occasion, was passed over with entire neglect.

This youth had been brought to Egypt at the request of Cleopatra, who, humbled by the generosity of Octavia, was desirous of withdrawing from her protection the children of Antony. Having, by her blandishments, prompted the prodigality of her lover towards her children, she had, at the same time, instigated him to assert the legality of the birth of Cæsarian, with a view of irritating Octavius, by raising to him a rival in the empire, to an incurable rupture with Antony.

But, amidst her aspiring projects, she omitted

not, by inexhaustible varieties of luxury and pleasure, to rivet her chains on the voluptuous Anthony.   At a splendid feast which he had caused
to be prepared for her, she affected to undervalue
the entertainment, boasting that she would, in her
turn, provide for him a supper, on which should
be expended more than a million of sesterces*.
Antony, mortified at her raillery, dared her to
the performance of her engagement.   The evening was accordingly appointed, and the supper
served up, in which there appeared to be nothing
extraordinary.   Antony smiling, called for a bill
of the amount.   Cleopatra, with an appearance
of good-humour, suffered his raillery for some
time in silence : at length, taking from her ear a
pearl of immense value, and dissolving it in vi-
negar, she swallowed it, inviting her lover to
pledge her with that which remained†.   Lucius
Blancus, who stood near the queen, snatched from
her hand the gem, declaring the wager to be already

---

* Centies, H.S. Hoc est centies centena millies sester-
tiûm.   52500 *l.* sterling.   ROLLIN.

† The remaining pearl was afterwards consecrated to
Venus by Augustus, who carried it to Rome, on his return from Alexandria ; and, having caused it to be cut in
two, its size was so extraordinary, that it served for pen-
dents in the ears of the goddess.

CLEOPATRA.   355

decided. For a moment Antony appeared confounded, till Cleopatra, laughing gaily, assured him, that not only these pearls, transmitted to her from a long race of illustrious ancestors, but the world itself, were it at her disposal, should, to afford him one moment's gratification, be lavished without regret. Transported by a compliment thus extravagant, Antony was careful to return, by a profuse magnificence, the gallantry of his mistress.

The contest between the rival heroes now drew near to a decision; the rendezvous of the fleet was appointed at Ephesus, whither Antony sailed with the queen of Egypt. His force consisted of eight hundred vessels. Egypt supplied for the maintenance of two hundred of these twenty thousand talents, with provision for the whole army, during the continuance of the war. The friends of Antony pressed him to send back Cleopatra to wait in Alexandria the event of the battle; but, dreading lest she should be made the sacrifice of a new reconciliation between the chiefs, she left no means untried to secure her stay. Canidious was bribed by her to plead her cause with Antony, and to paint to him the injustice of depriving, of her share of the glory, the woman who had so largely contributed to the charge of the expedition. To this he added a

356   CLEOPATRA.

representation of the impolicy of disgusting the
Egyptians, who composed a great part of the naval
force, and concluded by commending the talents
and prudence of their queen. Cleopatra entering
during this remonstrance, completed, by her blandishments, the seduction of her lover, who yielded
blindly to all her demands.

From Ephesus they sailed to Samos, where the
allies of Antony were to bring the stores stipulated for his use. While he appeared thoughtful
for the event of so important a contest, Cleopatra,
alarmed lest he should be meditating a compromise with Octavius, invited to Samos every art
and every diversion, that could beguile anxiety or
dissipate apprehension. The allies emulated each
other in gallantry and magnificence ; spectacles
occupied the day, and carousals shortened the
night ; Samos became a new Alexandria, while
every thing wore the aspect of triumph and joy.
' How,' said the reflecting few, ' will they celebrate their victories, who commence a war with
such useless expence ?'

In despite of the enchantments of his Circe, a
cloud still hung on the brow of the chief ; he became morose, suspicious of those who surrounded him, and distrustful even of the queen herself.
He appeared restless with undefined apprehensions, and would take no sustenance till it had

CLEOPATRA.   **357**

first been tasted. Cleopatra, solicitous to cure him of these inquietudes, and, more than all, hurt by his apparent distrust of herself, determined to convince him, by a stratagem, of her power and his injustice. She caused the tops of a garland, which they were accustomed, on festivals, to wear on their heads, to be dipped in a subtle poison, and, in the midst of the entertainment, when wine had banished all care, proposed as in sport that the flowers should be thrown into the bowl. With this frolic, Antony, accustomed to her caprices, immediately complied, and, raising the vessel to his lips, was about to pledge her in the poisoned liquor.—' Hold, my friend,' said she, seizing his hand, ' I am the poisoner, against whom you employ these useless precautions. If it were possible for me to live without you, judge whether I should want the opportunity or provocation to render them fruitless.' She then, having sent for a criminal, obliged him to drink from the bowl, when he instantly expired at her feet. Antony seemed for some moments lost in astonishment, till Cleopatra, observing his features soften, burst into a passionate flood of tears, and with difficulty suffered herself to be appeased by his apologies and caresses.

From Samos they directed their course to Athens, where the queen, jealous of the respect paid by the Athenians to Octavia, courted, by her allurements and powers of insinuation, popular favour. Skilled in the arts of address, she ensnared by her attractions the fickle Athenians, and triumphed over their prejudices : a deputation of the citizens, led by Antony, to whom the freedom of the city had been presented, attended her at her palace, and public honours were decreed to her. But her restless jealousy was yet unsatisfied, while Octavia remained with his children in the house of Antony : with unprincipled malignity, she endeavoured to give the colour of guilt to the virtues of her rival, and to persuade Antony, that her forbearance and magnanimity were affected for the purpose of aggravating his faults, by thus contrasting them with her ostentatious virtue. Antony, eager to avail himself of a supposition which seemed to lighten the load of his own infamy, caught at the barbarous suggestion, of the reality of which he chose not to doubt.

An officer was commissioned to drive with contumely Octavia from the house of her husband : bursting into tears from a reflection on the probable consequences which would ensue from this outrage, she meekly obeyed the mandate, and took with her the children of the unworthy Antony, whose conduct she laboured to palliate to her brother, leaving no means unessayed that might

CLEOPATRA. **359**

tend to allay his anger, and soften his sense of the indignities she had suffered.

But to the jaundiced eye of Antony, whose heart, corrupted by an artful and unprincipled woman, had perverted his judgment, the mild heroism of his wife appeared but as a new evidence of her guilt and duplicity.

The facility with which Cleopatra moulded the character and abused the affections of her lover, rendered her caprices unbounded, and drove from him every person whose aid or counsel might, in the critical posture of his affairs, have proved beneficial. She engaged him to confirm by a will his gifts to her and her children, and again solemnly to declare the legitimacy of the birth of Cæsarian. The body of Antony, should he fall by the chance of war, was directed to be conveyed to Alexandria, and interred by the queen of Egypt. This testament, witnessed by Minucius Plancus and his nephew, was deposited in the hands of the vestal virgins. Disgusted by the weakness of Antony, and irritated by the caprices of his mistress, the secret of the will was afterwards revealed by the witnesses to Octavius, who, having found means to get it from the vestals, read it publicly in the senate. A dependent of Octavius gave him, at the same time, information that Antony had bestowed on Cleopatra the library

of Pergamus, which contained two thousand volumes : to this intelligence, various anecdotes
were added in proof of the blind infatuation of
the triumvir, and his contempt of decorum.   He
was accused of having risen abruptly, in the midst
of a solemn feast, to attend an assignation with
his mistress ; of having suffered the Ephesians to
salute her as their queen ; of having, during public
audiences to princes and embassadors, received
and read openly messages of gallantry, inscribed
on tablets of onyx and crystal.   Also, that on
Cleopatra's passing the hall of audience in her
chair, while Turnius, a Roman of distinction was
pleading, Antony, as under the power of magic,
had, to attend her, left the cause unfinished.   It
was likewise alleged, that he had assigned to her
a Roman guard, who bore her name on their
targets.   That, in their progress through the
towns and cities, he followed on foot her magnificent car, undistinguished from her train of
attendants.   That the favourite oath of Cleopatra
was, ' by the right of commanding the capital,'
which she trusted would shortly be hers.   No
submission of her infatuated lover, no caprice,
however wild or absurd, was omitted in this detail, which failed not to provoke the astonishment
of the grave and indignant senate.

The friends of Antony at Rome deputed to

CLEOPATRA. 361

him Germinius to inform him of the state of affairs, to exhort him to greater discretion, to warn him that his government and office of consul were about to be taken from him, when he would be declared the enemy of Rome. The queen of Egypt exerted all her arts to prevent a conference between Antony and Germinius, whose purpose she suspected, and whom she sought, by persecution and insult, to drive from the camp. But, perceiving him determined to defeat her efforts, she prevailed on Antony to invite him to a supper, and to interrogate him publicly on the affairs with which he was charged. Germinius, in reply to a demand thus imprudent, declared that his business was worthy a serious conference.—One part of it, however, he should deliver without reserve, which was, ' that the affairs of the consul would wear a less menacing aspect, should the queen of Egypt return to Alexandria.'—Antony, as Cleopatra had foreseen, was disgusted by this abruptness. ' You have done well,' said she, scornfully, to Germinius, ' to confess, without the rack, this important secret.' Aware of the temper of the woman whom he had the temerity to insult, and who meditated against him a cruel revenge, Germinius wisely retreated and returned to Rome.

The warlike preparations of Antony were in such advance, that had he promptly and vigorously attacked his opponent, his advantage would have been inevitable ; but, immersed in luxury and dissipation, he suffered the opportunity to escape, and, by his delays, gave time to Octavius to collect and assemble his forces.

War was, however, at length declared in form, but in the declaration, which spoke only of the queen of Egypt, the name of the consul was omitted. Antony, whom it was said a woman ruled, or rather an enchantress fascinated by her powerful spells, was pronounced incapable of his offices.—It was not against their consul that the Romans professed to exercise hostilities, but against Mardion the eunuch, Photinus, Iras, and Charmion, the women of Cleopatra, whom Antony had adopted for his ministers and counsellors. On the part of the Romans, two hundred and fifty galleys, well equipped, were prepared, with twelve thousand horse, and eighty thousand foot. On that of Antony, five hundred ships of war, of extraordinary size and structure, with high towers on their heads and sterns, as for show and triumph : but, unable to procure a sufficient number of mariners for this equipment, the vessels were ill manned, with husbandmen, artificers, and persons void of experience. On board this

CLEOPATRA. 363.

fleet were two hundred thousand foot, and twelve thousand horse. The galley of the queen of Egypt was resplendent with gold, its sails of purple floated in the wind, while trumpets and instruments of war swelled prematurely with notes of joy and victory. Eleven kings attended Antony as allies. Herod had provided an army for the occasion, but, for the private interest of Cleopatra, was, by her advice, ordered to turn his arms on Malchus king of Arabia, who, taking advantage of the present situation of affairs, had withheld from the queen of Egypt the tribute extorted from him.

The tract of land between the Euphrates and the Ionian sea, with great part of Illyria, was under the government of Antony. That of Cæsar comprehended from Illyria to the western ocean, and thence along the Tuscan and Sicilian seas. In the division of Africa, the coast opposite to Italy, with Gaul and Spain, were allotted to Octavius. To Antony the provinces from Cyrea to Ethiopia. The fate of the world was thus about to be decided by the ambition of a woman, who had determined to be mistress of its undivided empire, or to perish miserably in the attempt.

The celebrated battle of Actium now drew near. The friends of Antony laboured to per-

suade him to rely for success on his land forces,
which surpassed in strength those of his adversary, while his navy was but inadequately supplied. But the counsel of Cleopatra prevailed,
who believed that in a naval victory more honour
would redound to the Egyptians, of whose vessels
the greater part of the fleet was composed, while
a defeat by land would more immediately expose
to the conqueror the safety of Alexandria, and of
her own person. The engagement having commenced in sight of both armies, drawn up on the
shores, Agrippa, who commanded the left squadron of Octavius, extended his wing, with a view
of hemming in the enemy. Publicola, who commanded the right wing in conjunction with Antony, observing this manœuvre, found himself, to
oppose the design of Agrippa, compelled to occupy a greater space. By this motion he left the
main body weakened, which, pushed at the same
time vigorously by Arruntius, was considerably
discouraged. Cleopatra, from the disposition of
the fleet, conceiving the victory to be doubtful,
was seized with consternation; and, intent only on
escaping, or in the last resort of making her peace
with the conqueror by betraying her lover, she
crowded her sails, and, flying across the vessels
engaged, disordered the fleet of Antony, by compelling it to open and give way, as she steered her

CLEOPATRA. 505

course, followed by the whole Egyptian squadron, towards Peloponnesus. Antony, struck by
this circumstance with confusion and despair,
threw himself, with Scellius and Alexander of
Syria, into a galley of five banks of oars, and
precipitately pursued his mistress. Cleopatra, full
of the project of appeasing Octavius, by abandoning to his destiny the man who for her had scorn-
ed a prostrate world, saw him not till the galley
had nearly overtaken her bark. Perplexed how
to act in this critical conjuncture of affairs, her
first thoughts were to refuse him admission;
till the suggestions of interest, yielding to those of
pride and shame, to the fear of infamy, and the
possible contempt even of the victor himself, to
whom she meditated submission, induced her to
receive Antony into the vessel.

In silence, and without deigning to cast a
glance towards her, he placed himself in a desponding attitude, his head reclining on his hands,
at the stern of the bark, where he continued for
three days, till his arrival at Tenarus. In the midst
of this distress, Cleopatra yet felt a secret satisfaction in the sacrifice paid to her vanity, when
Antony, before a gazing world, abandoned its
prospects and dignities, his friends, his interest,

his principles, and his honour, to be the partner
of her ignominious flight.

At Tenarus she determined, in despite of the
injuries he had sustained, to effect with him a reconciliation. For this purpose, she caused her
women to represent to him the excess of her contrition and sorrow, and to attribute her error to
the softness and timidity of her sex. To these
representations was added an affecting picture of
her tears and her beauty, which even grief could
not rob of its lustre. Perceiving Antony softened by the images they had presented to his imagination, her attendants, to whom their lesson had
been taught, artfully availed themselves of the generosity of his temper, which, they insinuated,
must prevent him from loading with additional
sorrows the partner of his misfortunes, whom
disappointment had already overwhelmed. The
reconciliation was at length accomplished, in
which Antony was brought to act the part of a
suppliant, and to receive with gratitude the favour
which his mistress, with the dignity of an offended queen, deigned to yield him.

The vessels and friends of Antony, which had
escaped the wreck of his fortunes, now arrived:
their accounts of the bravery and fidelity of the
fleet, which refused, till abandoned by its officers,

CLEOPATRA. 367

to listen to the agents of Octavius, gave a pang
even to the heart of Cleopatra, who at length began to suspect that she had betrayed her own
cause. The land forces, consisting of eighteen
legions, and two-and-twenty thousand horse, still
remained unbroken, under the command of Canidius; but, on finding themselves abandoned by
their generals, they surrendered to the Romans,
who received them with open arms.

Antony, vanquished and desponding, attended
only by two friends, wandered through various
parts of Africa, while the queen of Egypt, no
longer solicitous for his presence, returned to
Alexandria, meditating how she might sacrifice
him to her safety. To deceive the Alexandrians,
she sailed into port with crowns on the prows of
her vessels, as denoting victory : but, finding by
her spies that suspicions of the truth were already
entertained, and murmurs heard, several of the
popular nobles became the victims to her jealousy.

Antony, deserted and an exile, received information, to fill up the measure of his calamities, that
the commander whom he had appointed in Lybia,
to whose charge his remaining troops had been
committed, was gone over to the enemy. Despair, on this intelligence, prompted him to put
an end to his misfortunes with his life; but, with-

held by a friend from his desperate purpose, his heart once more turned towards Alexandria, where Cleopatra was meditating how to elude his return.   Occupied with her plan of conciliating his rival, or of escaping for the present his power, she formed a project of abandoning Egypt. Between the Egyptian and the Red seas, a small neck of land, thirty-six miles over in its narrowest part, separated Asia and Africa.   Over this isthmus she proposed that twenty galleys should be carried or drawn, and launched into the Red Sea: in these vessels she designed to embark with her treasures, and seek a remote country, where by her arts or resources she might retrieve her ruined fortunes.   The first galleys, after having been successfully conveyed over the neck of land, were destroyed and burned by the Arabians of Petra: on this event, the enterprise was abandoned, and orders issued for fortifying the avenues to the kingdom.

Antony, on his arrival at Alexandria, met a reception so cold and repulsive, that he was compelled to retire to the isle of Pharos, where, having erected a house on the seaside, he gave to it the name of *Timonium*, intimating that, like the Athenian Timon, he was in his adversity forsaken by his friends.   At this crisis, Cleopatra received an intimation, that Herod had sent to advise An-

CLEOPATRA. 369

tony, as the only remedy for his broken fortunes, to deprive of her dominions the perfidious queen of Egypt, to punish her with death, and to return to Octavia, through whose mediation he might yet make his peace with her brother. Cleopatra, alarmed by this account, and haunted by the idea of the possible triumph of her rival, sent messengers to Antony, excusing what had past, and pressing his return to Alexandria. The weak Roman, falling into the snare, was again plunged in revels and debauchery, which by their intoxicating effects precluded the possibility of reflection, and lulled his senses into a fatal torpor. The order of *The Inimitable Livers* was dissolved, and that of *The Diers Together* substituted in its place, with no less luxury, splendour, and profusion. Doubtful of the success of her intrigues with the conqueror, Cleopatra determined to be prepared for their failure; and, rather than swell the Roman triumph, to perish by a voluntary death. With this view, she caused experiments of every species of vegetable or animal poison to be made on criminals, the consequences of which she personally witnessed, to ascertain the speediest and least painful death. Among these the venom of the asp obtained the suffrage, the effect of which was to operate as a narcotic, without spasm or apparent pain. She likewise ordered to be constructed, adjoining to the temple of Isis, several tombs and monuments of stupendous height and exquisite workmanship : to these she removed her treasures, consisting of gold and silver, emeralds, pearls, ebony, ivory, and cinnamon; to which was added, by her order, a considerable quantity of aromatic wood, flax, and torches.

Octavius, whose affairs had called him to Rome, alarmed at these preparations, of which he was informed, and which threatened to deprive him of the reward of his toils, resolved on dissembling, and encouraging, by external marks of respect, the hopes of the Egyptian queen. Embassies, with flattering offers and promises, arrived daily at Alexandria, hostilities having been suspended at the approach of winter.

On the return of spring, the conqueror, by long and hasty marches through Syria, approached the capital of Egypt. Cleopatra, agitated by contending interests, and unable to determine on the course proper to pursue, deputed embassadors to the victor, to petition that Egypt might be left to herself and her children, while Antony desired leave to remain there, or to retire to Athens in a private station. The queen transmitted, at the same time, privately to Octavius, a golden sceptre, crown, and chair. To the request of Antony no

CLEOPATRA. 371

answer was vouchsafed, but the couriers of Cleopatra were commissioned to assure her, that, on the condition of sacrificing Antony, no reasonable indulgence would be refused to her. By her subtle questions to the emissaries of the conqueror, she perceived cause to distrust the sincerity of his propositions, which she yet hesitated to fulfil. In the sacrifice of her lover she would have found little difficulty; but, aware of the cold and crafty temper of Octavius, she doubted not but that, having first made her infamous by the desertion of the man she had ruined, he meditated to allure her into his power, to swell the pomp of triumph, and gratify the supposed rage of her rival. In this conviction, she boasted to Antony of her devotion to his cause, and determination to share his destiny. Transported by these assurances, her credulous and generous lover offered to Octavius, on condition of securing to Cleopatra her possessions, to perish by his own hand. This proposition was received in silence, on which Antony sent, by his son Antyllus, a third embassy, accompanied by a present of gold, to the Roman camp, to which the same taciturnity was preserved.

To Cleopatra, promises and threats were renewed, with a view to divert her mind from the execution of any desperate purpose. Thyreus, a

man of address and insinuation, was more particularly deputed to the queen, to hint to her that
the conqueror, captivated by her beauty, was disposed to lay his laurels at her feet. Intoxicated
by a flattery so according with her confidence in
her charms, she loaded Thyreus with favours and
presents, while, by the frequent and long conferences in which she indulged him, she roused
the suspicions of Antony, who, having caused
him to be chastised, dismissed him ignominiously
from court. The queen, still judging it necessary
to preserve appearances, lest a return to his wife
should reconcile her lover to Octavius, and defeat
her meditated plans, found means to appease the
jealousy of Antony, and to lull to repose all his
suspicions. The anniversary of the day of his
birth was celebrated by her with splendour and
magnificence, while that of her own she affected
to overlook. Her fascinations produced their
usual success; Antony, transported by these
marks of her affection, exceeded on the festival
she had instituted to his honour his usual profusion, and enriched his guests with a lavish
bounty.

While thus acting on the passions of her lover,
Cleopatra was secretly and earnestly negociating
with his enemy. Seleucus, her governor in Pelusium, was ordered to surrender the citadel to

CLEOPATRA. 373

the Romans, while, to veil her perfidy, she basely sacrificed to the vengeance of Antony his wife and family. No sooner had he possessed himself of Pelusium, than Octavius directed his force against Alexandria : the citizens, whom Antony sought to encourage to repel the foe, had private orders from the queen to lay down before him their arms. The spirit of Antony, in the first sally, notwithstanding prevailed ; the horse of the enemy was routed and driven back to their entrenchments, while, returning in arms to the palace, he saluted the queen, and recommended to her notice an officer who had distinguished himself in the engagement. As his reward, the officer received from the hands of Cleopatra a helmet and cuirass of gold : the favour was enhanced by the winning grace of the donor, who having, by her smiles and her sweetness, ensnared the intoxicated youth, engaged him to favour her purpose of surrendering the city to Octavius.

Antony defied his rival to decide their cause by a single combat, but received from him an intimation, as in scorn, that if he was weary of life, there were other methods by which he might rid himself of the burthen. Cleopatra seized the moment of indignation which this sarcasm produced, to urge her lover to a last and desperate effort, for the failure of which she had taken care to pro-

vide. In compliance with her counsel, Antony
prepared himself to make on the ensuing day a
general attack both by sea and land. This intelligence was, by the young soldier whom the queen
had seduced by her smiles, conveyed to Octavius;
to which an assurance was added, that the fleet
and army should be surrendered into his hands.
The interval was not passed by Cleopatra without
great inquietude; the flatteries and promises of
Octavius having failed to allay a sentiment of distrust which still lurked at the bottom of her heart.

The morning at length arose, when Antony,
marching out of the city, met the fate prepared
for him. He had posted his infantry on a rising
ground, whence he beheld his fleet moving towards the enemy: as he continued to gaze, in
expectation of the conflict, how great was his consternation and surprise, in beholding the hostile
vessels salute, mingle, and, with united force, proceed towards the city! Turning with horror from
a sight thus unexpected, he perceived on the other
side, his cavalry wheel off and join the enemy,
while the infantry separated in disorder. Struck
with the truth, which now darted through his
mind, he drew back towards the city, exclaiming,
that he had been betrayed by her in whose cause
only he had contended. Cleopatra, informed of
the event, fled to the monument, under pretence

CLEOPATRA. 375

of terror at the Roman arms, but in reality to avoid the despair of the man whom she had betrayed and destroyed. Having taken measures for her personal safety, she ordered Antony to be informed, that, preferring to a shameful captivity an honourable death, she had perished by her own hand : by this means she hoped to elude the first bursts of his indignation, or to urge him, perhaps, on his fate.

She received at this period, an intimation from Cornelius Dolabella (a favourite of the conqueror), whom, by her allurements, she had engaged to her interests, that the reserve of Octavius rendered it difficult to penetrate his purposes, but that she would do well to be guarded, and to distrust his proffers. Roused by this hint to a sense of her conduct, its probable consequences rushing on her mind, she determined, by a parade of sympathy for Antony, to avert impending shame : she judged aright, that to expire with him would be less humiliating than to swell the triumph of his adversary. Under this impression, she dispatched to Antony a messenger, who had orders to persuade him that, in despite of appearances, she yet lived only for him, and impatiently expected him at the monuments, whither she had retired for safety.

This conciliating message arrived too late; Antony, on being informed of the death of his mistress, had in broken exclamations declared, that, having lost the only object for which he had cherished life, he had no more business in the world. Having thus said, he commanded Eros, a faithful servant, from whom he had extorted a vow to put an end to his existence whenever his misfortunes should become irremediable, now to fulfil his engagement. Eros, to evade his promise, chose rather to die in the presence of his beloved master, who, following the example given him by his servant, plunged his sword in his breast and sunk beside him. At this instant the messenger from the queen of Egypt arrived: Antony raising himself, and reviving at the intelligence brought to him, eagerly desired to be taken to the monument. The entrance having been fastened to prevent surprise, he was drawn up through the window with cords, by the queen and two female attendants, the only persons whom she dared to trust. The spectators melted into tears, when they beheld the dying Antony, covered with blood, stretching out his hands to Cleopatra, and raising his body as if to aid her efforts: even the callous heart of the queen was at length touched for the fate of a hero, whose passion for her had proved his destruction: having placed him on a bed in the monument, she wept over him with unfeigned and impassioned sorrow, while her soul was rent by a too late remorse. Generous even in death, Antony seemed to have lost in his efforts to console her the sense of her guilt and of his own condition, while, without uttering either reproach or complaint, he exhorted her to use every means for her security; and, among the friends of Octavius, to trust only Proculeius. Calling for wine, he implored his mistress rather to rejoice in the recollection of his past felicity, than to afflict herself with the present reverse of his fortunes. His speech failing him, he grasped the hand of Cleopatra in his, and, fixing his eyes tenderly on hers, while death seemed deprived by love of its pangs, he gently breathed his last.

It was at this instant that Proculeius, whom Octavius had deputed to confer with the queen of Egypt, arrived before the monument: at the sight of the sword yet reeking with the blood of Antony, and at the recital of what had past, he dissolved into tears. Octavius, desirous of seizing the person of Cleopatra to grace his triumph, and apprehensive of losing her immense treasures, had, by his agents, spared no insinuations that might tempt her ambition or flatter her pride. Cleopatra demanded that her kingdom might be secured to her children; in reply to which she was

exhorted by Proculeius to confide wholly in his
master. A second officer arrived charged with
new proposals, and having contrived to fix the attention of the queen, who conversed with him
through an aperture in the monument, Proculeius,
in the mean time, by the aid of a scaling ladder,
entered through the window by which Antony
had been admitted. One of the attendants turning
and perceiving him, exclaimed aloud, ' Wretched
Cleopatra, thou art now indeed lost !' The queen
attempted suddenly to plunge into her bosom a
dagger which hung from her girdle, but Proculeius, seizing her hands, wrested from her the
weapon, and shook her robe lest poison should be
concealed in its folds. Epaphroditus was then
commissioned by Octavius to take charge of the
royal captive, whom he had orders strictly to
guard from the means of self-destruction, and to
treat with all possible gentleness and respect.
The gates of Alexandria now opened to the conqueror, who entered the city, conversing familiarly
with the philosopher Ariæus, upon whose arm he
leaned : he refused to suffer the prostration of the
people, to whom he granted a pardon, first, as he
declared, on the account of Alexander their founder ; secondly, for the beauty of their city ; and
thirdly, for the sake of Ariæus, to whom it had
given birth.

CLEOPATRA. 379

The body of Antony was solicited by various kings and sovereign princes, who desired to honour it with funeral rites ; but, at the earnest request of Cleopatra, the privilege of interring it was granted to her, an office which she performed with imperial magnificence and expence. She received an intimation soon after the funeral, that Octavius designed her a visit: foreseeing in this interview the decision of her fate, she prepared for his reception with a beating heart. Having caused her apartment to be adorned with various pictures of Julius Cæsar, his predecessor, she attired herself in a thin, loose, mourning robe, disposed with studied, yet negligent grace, and, reclining on a couch in an attitude of pensive sadness, waited the coming of Octavius. Starting, on his entrance, from her position, with dishevelled hair and eyes swimming in tears, her air languishing, her voice faultering and tremulous, she sunk half fainting at his feet. Octavius, touched with compassion, raised and supported her to a seat; while, addressing him by the title of her lord and master, she implored his compassion in a speech prepared for the occasion, reminded him of his predecessor, to whom she owed her crown and dignity, lamented the loss of his protection, and flattered herself with seeing him restored in his adopted son and successor. Octavius listened with downcast

eyes, while, essaying every art to move him, she
affected to excuse her conduct towards Antony,
on the plea of constraint and fear. Her justification being interrupted by her guest, whose
patience began to be exhausted, she had recourse
to submission, prayers, and tears, offering to put
into his hands an inventory of her treasures, and
to throw herself entirely on his mercy. One of
her treasurers, present at the interview, accused
her, with a view of making court to the victor, of having secreted many of her most valuable jewels. Thrown off her guard by a
temerity to which she had been so little accustomed, she seized the treasurer by the hair,
and repeatedly struck him in the face. Octavius, smiling at her transport, endeavoured to
pacify her; when, recollecting herself and apolo-
gising for her vehemence, she added meanness to
duplicity, and protested that she had reserved
only some female ornaments, as presents to his
wife and his sister Octavia, through whose inter-
cession she hoped to receive clemency. Persuaded from this circumstance that she had relinquished any design against her life, Octavius
sought to sooth and encourage her, by declaring,
that whatever she had thought proper to reserve
should be left to her discretion, and that she might
assure herself of honourable treatment. He then

CLEOPATRA. 381

departed, pleased with the interview, and persuaded that he had imposed on the discernment, and quieted the apprehensions, of his captive.

Cleopatra, feeling herself less satisfied, suspected the sincerity of her visitor: shortly after she received a new intimation from Dolabella, that his master, about to return into Syria, proposed to send her before him, accompanied by her children.

The dread of being led in triumph to Rome again seized her, and once more she determined to die. Having requested to be allowed to make a last oblation at the tomb of Antony, her demand was complied with, and she was conducted with her women to the place of his interment; where, having made a theatrical show of sorrow, and adorned the monument with garlands, she ordered a bath to be prepared and a splendid supper. After the entertainment, one of her domestics, disguised as a countryman, obtained leave of the guards to present to her a basket of figs, under the leaves of which an asp was concealed. Cleopatra received the fruit, rewarded the bearer, addressed a letter to Octavius containing an entreaty to be interred with Antony, and applied the asp to her veins.

Thus perished in her fortieth year, twenty-two years after her elevation to the throne, a woman who, perverting the bounties of nature, found in an inordinate selfishness the destruction she

laboured to avert, and received, in the consequences of her duplicity and perfidy, the just recompence of her crimes. The statues of Antony
were overthrown, but those of Cleopatra were
suffered to remain ; Archibius, who had been long
in her service, having given to Octavius a thousand talents, on condition of their being spared.
After her decease, Egypt was reduced to a province of the Roman empire, and governed by a
præfect sent thither from Rome.

> *Rollin's Ancient History—Biographium Fæmineum—*
> *Lives of Cleopatra and Octavia, by the author of*
> *David Simple, &c.*

ANN CLIFFORD,

COUNTESS OF PEMBROKE, DORSET, AND MONTGOMERY.

ANN, daughter and heir of George Clifford,
third earl of Cumberland, was born January 30th,
1589, in Skipton-Castle, in Craven. Her father
had, under the reign of Elizabeth, distinguished
himself by his naval expeditions, on which he had
expended a great part of his patrimony. In return for his services, he was appointed by the
queen her champion in tilts and tournaments,
where his dignity, skill, and address, equally excited
admiration   Lady Ann Clifford was, on the death

ANN CLIFFORD. 883

of her father, only ten years of age; but his loss was supplied to her by the care and attention of an excellent mother, a daughter of the earl of Bedford; who, aided by her aunt, the countess of Warwick, superintended her education. Mr. Samuel Daniel, a poet and an historian, was by these ladies appointed preceptor to their charge, who under his tuition made a considerable progress in literary attainments.

Lady Ann, in February, 1609, married lord Buckhurst, earl of Dorset, a gallant and accomplished nobleman, with whom she lived fifteen years. In March, 1624, she was, by the decease of her husband, left in a state of widowhood, with two daughters, Margaret and Isabel, who were afterwards espoused to the earls of Northampton and Thanet. Six years after this period, she gave her hand to Philip Herbert, earl of Pembroke and Montgomery. This nobleman, through the favour of James, who had succeeded to Elizabeth, possessed, as a reward for his skill in hawking and hunting, a large estate of eighteen thousand per annum, on which he lived in a style of magnificence. His stables are said to have vied with palaces, and his falconry, in which he chiefly prided himself, was furnished at an immense expence. In his private life he was characterised by gross ignorance and vice, while his public cha-

ANN CLIFFORD.

racter is, by the noble historian of those unfortunate times, branded with ingratitude and tergiver-
sation.

Of the inducements of lady Ann for forming a
connection with a man so worthless, there is no
account: it is certain that, for near twenty years,
her life was by his conduct considerably embit-
tered; and that by his dissolute manners she was
at length compelled to separate herself from him;
till, in January, 1649, death relieved her from fetters which had become nearly intolerable.

About this period she became possessed of an
ample fortune. Her succession, on the decease
of her father, to the Clifford estates, had been dis-
puted by an uncle, who inherited the title: an
award, to which she had never submitted, had, on
this occasion, been given against her by James I.
The fortunes, on the demise of her uncle and
his son, reverted to her, increased by the large
jointures which she had received from her mar-
riages. Having sketched a plan for her future
life, she determined to retire to the north, and ex-
pend her income on her own estates.

Five noble castles had in ancient times been
possessed by the earls of Cumberland, in the three
counties of Yorkshire, Westmoreland, and Cumberland; Skipton, Pendragon, Appleby, Brougham, and Brough: also a sixth fortified seat in

ANN CLIFFORD. 385

which they sometimes resided. These castles, which during the civil war had greatly suffered, were falling to decay. The countess, on coming into the possession of her estates, resolved on repairing and furnishing the fortresses of her ancestors: this design was, during the years 1657 and 1658, completed; when over the gate of each castle was placed the following inscription: " This castle was repaired by the lady Ann Clifford, countess dowager of Pembroke, in the year ———, after the main part of it had lain ruinous ever since 1648, when it was demolished almost to the ground by the parliament then sitting at Westminster, because it had been a garrison in the civil wars. IS. LVIII. 12. LAVS DEO."

Oliver Cromwell was, about this period, at the head of the state: his usurpations and his hypocrisy had inspired the countess with an aversion to his character, which she took little pains to conceal. Her friends, aware of the jealous temper of the protector, advised her to be less lavish in building, hinting, that there was cause to fear that her castles would be no sooner rebuilt, than orders would be sent to demolish them. ' Let him,' said she with spirit, ' destroy them if he will; he shall surely find, that as often as he destroys I will rebuild them, while he leaves me a shilling in my pocket.' On another occasion, she likewise manifested her high spirit and contempt for Cromwell. In receiving her rights, she had, by the misconduct or negligence of her uncle, been involved in a tedious suit of law. Cromwell, informed of the affair by the opposite party, offered his mediation, which was by the countess haughtily rejected. 'What,' said she, 'does he suppose that I, who refused to submit to king James, will submit to him?' Whether from respect to her character, or from the influence of her numerous friends, it is certain the protector shewed no resentment on these occasions: the castles and estates of the countess remained uninjured. Her aversion to Cromwell seems to have originated in principle rather than in party: being pressed by her friends, after the restoration, to appear at court, she testified an unqualified dislike to the spirit of the government of Charles; 'By no means,' replied she to their intreaties, 'unless I may be allowed to wear blinkers.'

Another instance of her independent spirit is worthy of being perpetuated. Sir Joseph Williamson, when secretary of state to Charles II. named to the countess in a letter, a candidate for the borough of Appleby. Disdaining to be dictated to on such an occasion, she returned him the following spirited and laconic reply : " I have

ANN CLIFFORD. 3ᵮ7

been bullied by an usurper, I have been neglected by a court, but I will not be dictated to by a
subject. Your man sha'n't stand. Ann Dorset,
Pembroke, and Montgomery."

The churches belonging to the villages on her
estates having been beaten down, or converted to
other purposes, she repaired and rebuilt them.
Her expences in building were estimated at forty
thousand pounds. She divided the year into periods, residing in turn at each of her castles, thus
superintending the whole of her estates, and carrying blessings in her train. The patroness of
the distressed, her ear and her heart were open to
their complaints ; her expanded mind and liberal
fortune were in unison ; none implored relief
from her in vain. To occasional acts of beneficence she added permanent endowments, among
which she founded two hospitals.

By the side of the road between Penrith and
Appleby, appears an affecting monument of her
filial gratitude. On this spot she had last parted
with a beloved mother, a separation she was accustomed to recal to her mind with tender sorrow, and in commemoration of which she erected
a pillar, its base a stone table, known in the country by the name of *Countess Pillar*, on which were

engraven her arms, a sun-dial, and the following inscription :

" This pillar was erected in the year 1656, by Ann, countess dowager of Pembroke, for a memorial of her last parting in this place with her good and pious mother, Margaret, countess dowager of Cumberland, on the second of April, 1616. In memory whereof she hath left an annuity of four pounds, to be distributed to the poor of the parish of Brougham, every second day of April for ever, upon the stone table placed hard by. LAVS DEO !"

The establishment of the countess's household accorded with her liberal mind ; her servants were the children of her tenants, who, if they behaved well, were sure of a provision : to her women, when they married, she gave small portions. She was a lover of learning, and a patroness of learned men. In gratitude to her tutor, she erected a monument to his memory in the church at Beckington, near Philips-Norton, Somersetshire. She also raised a monument to the memory of Spenser. Her liberality was experienced by several of the ejected ministers, among whom may be mentioned King, afterwards bishop of Chichester ; also Duppa and Morley, both afterwards bishops of Winchester, to each of whom she al-

ANN CLIFFORD. 3·9

lowed four pounds per annum. During their distresses abroad, being informed that a sum of money would be more serviceable to them than the annuities, she remitted a thousand pounds to be divided among them.

At Bearmky she restored and repaired an alms-house, built and endowed by her mother. On the 23d of April, 1651, she laid the first stone of an hospital, founded at Appleby in Westmoreland, for a governess and twelve widows, which was finished in the three following years ; and for the endowment of which she purchased the manor of Brougham, and the lands of St. Nicolas, near Appleby. This establishment being completed, the pensioners were placed by the countess in their several apartments, in which their benefac-tress frequently dined with them : she also enter-tained them once a month at her own table, and conversed with them with an engaging familiarity.

At Temple Soureby in Westmoreland, she pur-chased lands, value eight pounds per annum, for repairing the church, school-house, town-hall, and bridge at Appleby. At the rebuilding of the church at Appleby, she caused a vault to be made at the north-east corner of the chapel for her own sepulture, on which she expended seven hundred pounds, and over which was erected a monument

of black and white marble. Having repaired a
part of the steeple and church at Skipton in Craven, she raised there a superb monument to the
memory of her father.

Her prudence in the management of her affairs
was exemplary: bishop Rainbow, speaking on
this subject, calls her " a perfect mistress of fore-
cast and aftercast." Her economy and exactness
in her acconnts were the support of a generosity
truly deserving of the name. In each of her castles
was an office where her receipts and disburse-
ments were entered with commercial punctuality.
The account of her more private benefactions was
kept by herself with so much precision, that, on a
comparison with her public accounts, she had at
once a complete view of the state of her affairs.
To vain and frivolous gratifications she allowed
nothing : the regular form in which the expences
of her family ran, under the article *necessaries,*
made every year a check upon that which succeeded it. The spirit and firmness with which
she defended her rights, doubtless preserved her,
in those fluctuating and relaxed times, from many
contentions. A lesser instance after those before
mentioned, may serve still farther to illustrate this
observation.

Among the tenants on her estate, it was an
annual custom, after paying their rents, to present

ANN CLIFFORD. 391

a *boon-hen*, generally considered as the steward's perquisite, and ever acknowledged as a just claim. A rich clothier from Halifax, whose name was Murgatroyd, having taken a tenement near Skipton, was called upon by the steward for his boonhen. This he refused to pay; the countess therefore commenced a suit against him, which, the parties being alike inflexible, was carried into length. The countess established her claim at the expence of two hundred pounds, when, the affair being decided, she invited the defendant to dinner. The hen was served up as a first dish. ' Come sir,' said the countess, drawing it towards her, ' let us now be friends; since you allow the hen to be dressed at my table, we will, if you please, divide it between us.'

The understanding of this lady had received considerable cultivation; of her it was said humourously by Dr. Donn—' that she knew how to converse on all subjects, from predestination to slea-silk.' Her chief delight was in the study of history, by which she was led to examine that of her ancestors. There had been few scenes of public life, in which her progenitors, the Veteriponts and Cliffords, an active race of men, had not been engaged. The countess employed learned men, at a great expence, to make collections

from the records in the Tower, the rolls, and
other depositories of public papers, towards materials for a history of those two powerful northern
families, which, being fairly transcribed, filled
three large volumes. This work, containing a
great variety of original characters engaged on
important occasions, is still at Appleby castle,
among the family records.

While thus intent on perpetuating the honour
of her ancestors, she instituted a severe restraint
on her own actions: an entrance of the transactions of every day was made under her inspec-
tion, in a large folio volume, kept by a confidential
secretary; a work still extant, and in the hands
of the earl of Thanet. A regular attention to the
forms of religion occupied a great part of her
time; she was particularly conversant with the
Scriptures, and exemplied in her conduct the benevolent morality of Jesus Christ. Brought up in
the church of England, she rigidly adhered to its
ceremonials, amidst menaces of sequestration from
the ruling powers, whom on this, as on other occasions, her lofty spirit held at defiance.

Her manner of living was simple, and nearly
parsimonious: abstemious in her diet, she was accustomed to boast that she had scarce ever tasted
wine or physic; her active and temperate life preserving the vigour and soundness of her constitu-

ANN CLIFFORD. 393

tion. Her dress, in the later periods of her life, was a close habit of plain black serge. Her retinue, calculated for use rather than for parade, bespoke the same moderation. Two ladies, well educated, constantly resided with her, in whose conversation she relaxed from her graver pursuits. In her library, stored with the best writers, she gratified a liberal curiosity, and indulged her ardour for knowledge.

Her rational and exemplary life was extended to an advanced period; she survived her second husband twenty-six years, a blessing and an ornament to her country, and expired in her castle at Brougham, March 23d, 1675, after a few days' illness, in the eighty-sixth year of her age. She was interred April 14th, at Appleby, in Westmoreland, under the monument she had erected. Her funeral sermon was preached at Appleby, by Dr. Edward Rainbow, bishop of Carlisle, from a verse in the Proverbs of Solomon—" Every wise woman buildeth her house." In her ended the Clifford family, whose estates, by the marriage of her daughter Margaret to the earl of Thanet, reverted to the family of Tufton.

Lady Ann Clifford is described by Mr. Pennant*

---

* In his Tour.

s 5.

as the most eminent character of her times, for intellectual accomplishments, for spirit, magnificence, and benevolence. He also mentions two
portraits of this lady, both full length, in a family
picture in Skipton castle. In one she is drawn at
thirteen years of age, in the other during middle
life in her widowhood. In the first of these pictures is a representation of the books read by persons of rank and fashion at that period, among
which are Eusebius, St. Augustine, sir Philip
Sidney's Arcadia, Godfrey of Boulogne, the
French Academy, Camden, Ortelius, and Agrippa
on the Vanity of Occult Sciences. Above are the
heads of Mr. Samuel Daniel, her tutor, and
Mrs. Ann Taylor, her governess. The books in
the second picture consist of the Bible, Charron on
Wisdom, and pious treatises: also a treatise on
distillation and medicine. From this enumeration the studies of the countess in the different
periods of her life may be inferred.

A narrative, or rather journal, of her own life
was left by the countess, consisting principally of
minute details of the petty occurrences of a retired life, the greater number of which are tedious,
uniform, and but little interesting. In this manuscript she describes her own mental and personal endowments: " I was very happy," says
she, " in my first constitution both of mind and

ANN CLIFFORD.

body. I resembled equally both father and mother: the colour of my eyes was black, like my
father's, the form and aspect of them quick and
lively, like my mother's. My hair brown and
thick, and so long that it reached the calf of my
legs, with a peak of hair on my forehead, and a
dimple on my chin. Full cheeks, like my father,
and a round face like my mother's. An exquisite
shape of body resembling my father. But now
time and age have ended all these beauties, to be
compared to the grass of the field.—I have passed
the sixty-third year of my age. The perfections
of my mind surpassed those of my body. I had
a strong and copious memory, a sound judgment,
a discerning spirit, and an imagination so strong
that many times even my dreams and apprehensions beforehand proved to be true; so that old
Mr. John Denham, a great astronomer, who lived
in my father's house, would often say that I had
much in me in nature to shew, that the sweet influence of the Pleiades and the bands of Orion,
mentioned in Job, were powerful both at my conception and nativity." She goes on to speak of
" sucking from her dear mother the milk of goodness, which made her mind grow strong against
the storms of fortune." She informs us that in
her childhood, by means of her aunt Warwick,
she was much beloved by queen Elizabeth.

Her escape from various perils is thus recorded: " In my infancy and youth, and a great part of my life, I have escaped many dangers, both by fire and water, by passage in coaches and falls from horses, by burning fevers, and excessive extremity of bleeding, many times to the great hazard of my life. All which, and many wicked devices of my enemies, I have passed through miraculously, and much the better by the help of the prayers of my dear mother, who incessantly begged of God for my safety and preservation."

The following account of her marriage life may not be unacceptable to the reader. " I was born a happy creature in mind, body, and fortune, and those two lords, to whom I was afterwards by the Divine Providence married, were worthy noblemen as any then in this kingdom ; yet it was my misfortune to have contradictions and crosses with both. With my first lord about the desire he had to make me sell my rights in the lands of my ancient inheritance, which I never would consent to, insomuch as this was the cause of long contention ; as also for his profuseness in consuming his estate, and some other extravagances. With my second lord because my youngest daughter, the lady Elizabeth Sackville, would not be brought to marry one of his youngest sons, and that I would not relinquish my interest in five

ANN CLIFFORD. 397

thousand pounds (being part of her portion) out of my lands in Craven : nor did there want divers malicious ill-willers to blow and foment the coals of dissension between us.—So as, in both their life-times, the marble pillars of Knowle in Kent, and Wilton in Wiltshire, were to me oftentimes but the gay arbor of anguish. A wise man, that knew the insides of my fortune, would often say, that I lived in both these my lords' great families as the river of Roan runs through the lake of Geneva, without mingling its streams with the lake ; for I gave myself up to retiredness as much as I could, and made good books and virtuous thoughts my companions, which can never discern affliction, nor be daunted when it unjustly happens. And by a happy genius I overcame all these troubles, the prayers of my blessed mother helping me therein."

On the 18th and 20th of January, 1616-17, the countess was brought before king James, in Whitehall, to give her consent to the award which James intended to make (and afterwards executed) of the lands of her inheritance. This having refused to do, she was involved by her opposition in many difficulties and vexations.

Soon after the decease of her first husband, she had the small-pox, from which, after the most imminent danger, she escaped with life, but with the destruction of her beauty.

In speaking of the characters of her two husbands, " The first," says she, " was in his nature of a just mind, of a sweet disposition, and very valiant in his own person. He had great advantages in breeding, by the wisdom of his grandfather, Thomas Sackville, earl of Dorset, and lord-high-treasurer of England, who was held one of the wisest men of his time, by which means he (i. e. her husband) was so good a scholar, in all manner of learning, that in his youth, when in the university of Oxford, of which his grandfather was the chancellor, there was none of the young nobility or students that excelled him. He was a good patriot to his country, and well beloved in it ; much esteemed by the parliaments that sat in his time ; and so great a lover of scholars and soldiers, that, with excessive bounty towards them, or any of worth who were in distress, he did much diminish his estate, also with prodigality in housekeeping, and other noble ways at court, as tilting, masqueing, and the like. By prince Henry, then alive, and much addicted to these noble exercises, he was well beloved."

Her second husband, who died 1650, is thus described by her : " He was no scholar, having

CATHERINE CLIVE. 399

passed but three or four months at Oxford, when he was taken thence, after his father's death, in the latter end of the reign of Elizabeth, to follow the court, judging himself fit for that kind of life when not passing sixteen years old. Yet he was of quick apprehension, sharp understanding, very crafty withal, of a discerning spirit, but a choleric nature, increased by the office he held of chamberlain to the king. He was never out of England but two months, when he went into France with other lords, in 1625, to attend queen Mary, when coming over to marry king Charles. He was one of the greatest noblemen of his time in England, and well beloved throughout the realm."

Ballard's British Ladies—Gilpin's Account of a manuscript life of Mr. Sedgewick (written by himself), secretary to the countess of Pembroke.

CATHERINE CLIVE.

MR. WILLIAM RAFTON, the father of Catherine, a native of Kilkenny in Ireland, was educated for the law; but, having attached himself to the fortunes of James II. and entered into his service when James was in Ireland, he forfeited to the crown a considerable paternal estate. After the battle of the Boyne, he still adhered to his master, through whose recommendation, and his own merit, he obtained a captain's commission in the service of Lewis XIV. Having afterwards procured a pardon from the English court, he came to London, where he married the daughter of a respectable citizen. Several children were the fruit of this union.

Catherine, who was born in 1711, gave early promise of talents for the stage. Her humour, and agreeable manner of singing lively, spirited, songs, recommended her to the notice of Colley Cibber, then manager of Drury-lane, to whom she had been introduced by some friends. She was immediately engaged by Cibber, on a small salary. She first appeared in boy's clothes, in the character of a page, in the tragedy of Mithridates, king of Pontus, when she merely sung a song, which met with applause. She was at this time (1728) seventeen years of age. During the same season, she attracted particular attention from the audience, in the part of Phillida, in Cibber's " Love in a Riddle." A popular prejudice against the author had predetermined the fate of this play ; on which occasion a compliment was paid to the rising merit of Catherine, which, on the ensuing night, the presence of the royal family could not command : whenever she appeared on the stage, the clamours against the author were suspended.

CATHERINE CLIVE.   401

In 1731 she burst upon the public in the full lustre of comic excellence, in the part of Nell, in " The Devil to pay, or the Wives metamorphosed," a farce, by Colley Cibber. Her success in this character procured her salary to be doubled, established her reputation with the town, and placed the piece in the constant list of acting farces.

In 1732 she married G. Clive, esq. brother to Mr. Baron Clive. These nuptials appear not to have proved fortunate : a separation soon took place : yet, in a situation thus delicate and exposed, Mrs. Clive preserved an unblemished character.

After continuing on the stage, the ornament of her profession, and the delight of the public, more than forty years, she retired with dignity, her powers unimpaired, in 1769. On taking leave of the audience, she spoke an epilogue, written by Horace Walpole, near whom she fixed her residence, at Strawberry-hill, Twickenham. In this situation, she continued to enjoy health, ease, good-humour, and independence.

She introduced upon the stage, at different benefits of her own, several little pieces, not devoid of merit: " Bayes in Petticoats," 8vo. 1753. " Every Woman in her Humour," 1760, not printed. " The Faithful Irish Woman," 1765, not printed. " Island of Slaves," 1761, not printed. The latter is nearly a literal translation of Marivaux's " *Isle des Esclaves*," executed, as confessed by herself, by a gentleman, at her request. She died December 6th, 1785.

Biographia Dramatica.

CATHERINE COCKBURN.

CATHERINE, daughter of captain David Trotter, a native of Scotland, and a naval officer in the reign of Charles II. was born in London, August 16th, 1679. Captain Trotter, distinguished for his probity and integrity by the epithet of *honest David*, was highly favoured by the king and his brother the duke of York. He had served the royal cause both by sea and land, with courage and gallantry, and was styled by James, earl of Perth, lord high chancellor of Scotland, " an ornament to his country." Having been sent to convoy the fleet of the Turkish company, an expedition that it was expected would prove highly advantageous to his fortunes, he was seized at Scandaroon with the plague which raged there, and of which he expired.

His death was an irreparable loss to his family, whom the cupidity of the ship's officers defrauded

CATHERINE COCKBURN.   403

of his effects, to a considerable amount: a gold-
smith, in whose hands the greater part of his remaining property was lodged, becoming a bank-
rupt, completed their distress.   The admiralty,
in consideration of the merit of captain Trotter,
and the misfortunes of his family, settled on them
a pension, by the order of the king, which continued during his life. On his decease, the pension
ceased, for which deprivation the family received
no compensation till the reign of queen Ann, who
granted to the widow the annual sum of twenty
pounds, which was paid by the duchess of Marlborough into the hands of Dr. Burnet, bishop of
Salisbury, till the removal of the duchess from
court, and afterwards through other channels.

Captain Trotter left two daughters, the elder
of whom afterwards married Dr. Inglis, physi-
cian-general to the army.   Mrs. Trotter, whose
maiden name was Ballenden, was nearly related to
the nobleman of that name, and to the families of
Maitland duke of Lauderdale, and Drummond
earl of Perth.   Catherine, the younger daughter,
was, on the death of her father, by which the circumstances of her family were greatly reduced,
still a child.   She had given an early indication
of genius by some extemporary verses on an incident, which, passing in the street, excited her attention.   Several of her relations and friends hap-

pened to be present on this occasion, among whom was her uncle, a naval commander. This gentleman, greatly struck by such a proof of observation, facility, and talent, in a child, observed, with what pleasure would the father of Catherine (who himself possessed a peculiar taste and passion for poetry) have witnessed, had he been living, this unpremeditated effusion.

Catherine, by application and industry, made herself mistress of the French language without any instructor; she also taught herself to write. In the study of the Latin grammar and logic, she had some assistance; of the latter she drew up an abstract for her own use. Though educated in the principles of the reformation, she imbibed, from an early intercourse with some catholic families of distinction, a prejudice in favour of their faith; and, after conferring on the doctrines in dispute with several eminent and learned ministers of the church of England, who failed to convince her, she entered into the Romish communion, in which she remained for some years.

In 1693, being then only fourteen years of age, she addressed some lines to Mr. Bevil Higgons, on his sickness and recovery from the small-pox. She produced also a tragedy, in her seventeenth year, entitled, " Agnes de Castro," which was acted with applause at the Theatre-

CATHERINE COCKBURN. 405

royal, in 1696, and published, but without her name, the following year, with a dedication to the earl of Dorset and Middlesex, in which the author declares, that this offspring of her early muse owed its publication to his lordship's judgment, to which it had been submitted. Agnes de Castro is founded on a French novel printed in Paris, 1688, and translated into English by Mrs. Behn.

In 1697 our youthful dramatist complimented Mr. Congreve, on his " Mourning Bride," in an elegant copy of verses, in return for which she received a very flattering epistle, wherein Mr. Congreve expresses his mortification and regret, that the poem arrived too late to be prefixed to the publication of his tragedy. " All the satisfaction that I can take," adds he, " and all the sacrifice that I make to you, is only to stifle some verses on the same subject, which were printed with it, and which now, I assure you, shall never appear. Since I am deprived of the recommendation you designed me, I will be obliged to no other, till I have some future opportunity of preferring yours." These reciprocal civilities gave rise to an acquaintance between the parties.

In 1698 " The Fatal Friendship, a tragedy, composed by Catherine Trotter," was performed at the New Theatre, Lincoln's-inn-fields, and printed, the same year, in quarto, with a dedication to the princess Anne of Denmark. This play, which is said to possess considerable merit, was received with great approbation. Various complimentary poems were addressed to the writer on the occasion, and prefixed to its publication. Among them was one sent anonymously by Mr. John Hughes, author of " The Siege of Damascus." Mr. George Farquhar likewise expressed his satisfaction with this piece, and soon after complimented the author with a copy of his first comedy, accompanied by a letter written in a high strain of gallantry and panegyric.

On the death of Mr. Dryden, in 1701, Mrs. Trotter united with several other ladies in paying to his memory a poetical tribute, in a joint production, entitled, " The Nine Muses; or Poems written by so many Ladies on the Death of the late famous John Dryden, Esq." In the same year she also produced a comedy, " Love at a Loss, or most Votes carry it;" acted at the Theatre-royal, published in 4to. and dedicated to lady Piers, wife to sir George Piers, an officer of high rank under the duke of Marlborough. This lady, with whom Mrs. Trotter lived in habits of friendship, possessed a taste for literature and the fine arts.

CATHERINE COCKBURN.   407

The author being absent from London, her comedy was so incorrectly printed, that, had it been practicable, she would gladly have suppressed the edition. It was many years afterwards revised by Mrs. Trotter, and considerably altered, with a view of bringing it again upon the stage, under the title of " The Honourable Deceivers, or all right at last." This purpose was never effected. Towards the latter end of 1701, Mrs. Trotter brought upon the stage, at Drury-lane, " The Unhappy Penitent," a tragedy, which was printed in 4to. with a dedication to Charles lord Halifax. The author, in her dedication, expresses a doubt whether love is a passion sufficiently sublime to form a proper subject for the tragic muse. It may be observed, in reply to this scruple, that love, on such occasions, is never pourtrayed unmixed with the severer passions; nor can it be denied that love, in chaste and elevated minds, is an heroic sentiment. Some complimentary lines were prefixed to this performance, by lady Piers.

Mrs. Trotter's attention to the drama did not prevent her from cultivating graver studies. She took a peculiar pleasure and interest in metaphysical enquiries, so captivating to an acute and inquisitive mind; and, enlisting under the banner of Mr. Locke, composed a defence of his Essay on the Human Understanding, in reply to some

anonymous * strictures to which it had given rise.
Mrs. Trotter was at this period only two-and-
twenty years of age.   Her Defence was written
in December, 1701, and published anonymously
in the following May.   The writer concealed her
name, lest the knowledge of her sex and youth
should produce a prejudice against her performance.   She seems also to have felt an apprehension of being known to Mr. Locke, under the
presumptuous title of his defender : in a preliminary address to him, she calls her performance
" a bold unlicensed undertaking," and declares
she had not ventured its publication " without
much apprehension and awe of his displeasure."
In a letter to George Burnet, esq. of Kemnay, a
gentleman with whom she frequently corresponded, she writes—" I am more afraid of appearing
before him I defend, than of the public censure ;
and, chiefly for the honour I bear to him, resolve
to conceal myself."

Her precautions, as is usual in these cases,
proved ineffectual ٬ her name was discovered, when
she received from Mr. Locke, through the hands
of his cousin, Mr. King, afterwards lord chancellor, a present of books, and a letter of praise
and acknowledgment.   " Give me leave to assure

* By Dr Thomas Burnet, master of the Charter-house.

CATHERINE COCKBURN.   409

you," says Mr. Locke, " that as the rest of the world take notice of the strength and clearness of your reasoning, so I cannot but be extremely sensible that it was employed in my defence. You have herein not only vanquished my adversary, but reduced me also absolutely under your power, and left no desire more strong in me, than that of meeting with some opportunity to assure you with what respect and submission I am, &c." Mrs. Trotter, in her "Défence of the Essay on the Understanding," endeavours to prove that the doctrine of materialism was not inconsistent with that of revelation, nor with the hope of a future existence, which rested not on the notion of an immaterial soul.

Mrs. Burnet, wife to the celebrated prelate of that name, addressed Mrs. Trotter on her *Defence*, and assured her of the approbation which her performance had received from the bishop, Mr. Norris, and other excellent judges. " It is not," she adds, " without difficulty some can believe, that any one not bred to science, and logic in particular, could be capable of such clear and close reasoning."

Mrs. Trotter, while on a visit at Salisbury, at the latter end of the year 1701, thus writes to Mr. George Burnet, in a letter dated December

9th : " The bishop goes next week, whom I saw last night, being at his palace to wait on his lady. I am much obliged to them both, and have not a little reason to be vain upon the advantageous things they have said of my last plays, especially the comedy. At least I may prefer the judgment of two such persons, to the rash censures of a giddy multitude. My lord's character is universally known ; but give me leave to tell you, upon my particular observation of his lady, what every body that knows her does allow, that she has an extraordinary clear and solid judgment, the truest goodness and prudence, and the most charming affability in her behaviour ; in short, I have met with no such perfection in any of my sex.... You desired news from me, but this place affords none ; and I keep no correspondence with intelligencers. I can only tell you of an unexpected pleasure I had here. Abel came this way to the bath, and complimented the bishop with a concert, where I was charmed with him enough to ride six miles after him to lord Arundel's, for the same pleasure, which has only increased my desire of hearing him."

Mrs. Trotter still continuing her attachment to the Romish church, injured her health by a too strict conformity to the severities which it enjoins. Her physician, Dr. Denton Nicholas, a learned and ingenious man, advised her, in a letter dated October 19th, 1703, to dispense with the rigorous fasts which she had imposed upon herself, and which were destructive to a constitution originally weak. He desires her to communicate his letter, for their satisfaction, to her friends and confessor.

In the beginning of the year 1704, Mrs. Trotter addressed a letter to her friendly physician, upon the truth of the christian religion, in reply to which he observes; " That she had proved unanswerably what she had undertaken, and had done it more clearly and effectually in half a sheet, than Grotius in a whole volume : though he differed from her in one point, where, from her prejudices in favour of popery, she lessened the authority of the Scriptures, making way for the traditions of the church, &c." This gentleman is presumed to be the physician of whom she speaks in a letter to Mr. Burnet, as having been her instructor in geography; and by whom she had been kindly furnished with maps, books, and globes.

Notwithstanding her predilection for the catholic church, she treated those who differed from her in opinion with great candour and moderation. " I am sorry, sir," says she, in a letter to Mr. Burnet, " the difference there is between us in the controverted points of religion, should abate any thing of the little happiness you could find in my company. For my part, I consider nothing in the opinion of my friends, but what is likely to influence their morals; and provided they worship the true God, and acknowledge the doctrines and authority of Jesus Christ, I think we are sufficiently united in religious sentiment for all the purposes of friendship. To say truth, I have of late almost forgotten all distinction of churches: for having had some occasion of observing more than before the great growth of infidelity; that there are many who disbelieve, and more who doubt that there ever was any divine revelation; I have employed myself much in considering the proofs, and defending the truth of the christian religion, which has so entirely engaged my concern, that when I am with those who sincerely submit to the authority of Christ, what sense soever they understand him in, I am satisfied, and really think myself with one of my own communion." These sentiments, it must be allowed, are liberal for a member of an infallible church.

Mr. Burnet continued to correspond with Mrs. Trotter during his travels. He was received at Berlin by Sophia Charlotte, queen of Prussia, daughter to the princess Sophia, with respect and distinction. To the latter princess he wrote in

CATHERINE COCKBURN. 413

terms so advantageous of Mrs. Trotter, that in a
reply to him from Hanover (dated July 29th,
1704), she expressed herself " charmed with the
agreeable picture which he had drawn of the new
Scotch Sappho, who seemed to merit the praise
he had bestowed on her."

Mrs. Trotter addressed some lines to the duke
of Marlborough, in 1704, upon his return from
Germany, after the battle of Blenheim. This
poem was honoured with the approbation of the
duke and duchess, and of the lord treasurer Godolphin. In 1706, after the battle of the Ra-
millies, she addressed to the duke a second con-
gratulatory poem. In the same year was acted,
at the theatre in the Haymarket, " The Revolution of Sweden," a tragedy, printed in 4to. with
a dedication to lady Harriet Godolphin, eldest
daughter of the duke of Marlborough. In this
dedication the writer observes, that poetry, as an
instrument of virtue, may be called *a divine art*,
that it has been cherished by the best governed
commonwealths, and is worthy of the protection
of the wise and good. That the particular tendency of the present piece was " to incite a dis-
interested and resolute care of the public good."
Three years before the representation of this tragedy, the first sketch had been communicated by

414   CATHERINE COCKBURN.

the author to Mr. Congreve, who returned it with some remarks upon the conduct of the drama, which were published by Dr. Birch. The plot turned upon the Revolution in Sweden, under Gustavus Erickson.

Doubts had, previous to this period, suggested themselves to the mind of Mrs. Trotter, respecting the Romish religion; these doubts led her to investigate the principles of her belief, to consult the writers on either side, and to confer with freedom on the subject. The result of this examination was a conviction of the absurd pretences of one church, and a return into the bosom of the other. This change took place in the beginning of the year 1707. During the remainder of her life she continued to adhere to the doctrines of the Reformation. In the course of her enquiries, she discussed, in two letters, the question respecting " a guide in controversies." This discussion was published under the title of " A Discourse concerning a Guide in Controversies, in two Letters, written to one of the Church of Rome by a Person lately converted from that Communion." A preface was prefixed to this performance by bishop Burnet, who commends the judgment and perspicuity of the writer, with the strength and clearness of her reasoning. A second edition of the letters was printed at Edinburgh, 1728, in 8vo.

CATHERINE COCKBURN. 415

Part of the summer of 1707 was passed by Mrs. Trotter at Oakham-mills near Ripley, where she frequently met with a Mr. Fenn, a respectable young clergyman, on a visit to his friends in the neighbourhood; who, becoming enamoured of her fine qualities, offered to her his hand and heart. She was induced to decline this proposal, from a prior attachment to Mr. Cockburn, with whom she had been for some time in the habits of friendship and correspondence.

In the beginning of 1708 she gave her hand to Mr. Cockburn. The graces of her person, her talents, and amiable manners, had, previous to her marriage, procured her several opportunities of an advantageous establishment; but, superior to mercenary motives, and, from the purity of her mind and habits, disgusted with the profligacy of the age, she determined to be guided in her choice by those principles of reason and virtue which she conceived afforded the best foundation for domestic happiness. " As piety and virtue," says Dr. Birch, " were the ground of their mutual affection, so their chief view in their union was the improvement of themselves in the principles of all religious and moral excellence."

Mr. Cockburn was the son of Dr. Cockburn, a learned and eminent clergyman of Scotland, at-

tached to the court of St. Germain; an attachment which he at length relinquished from his
adherence to the protestant religion.   He was
some time after minister of the episcopal church
at Amsterdam, whence he was collated to the rectory of Norshaw in Middlesex, by Dr. Robinson,
bishop of London, at the recommendation of
queen Anne, by whom he had been intended for
one of the bishops of the plantations in America.
Mr. Cockburn, his son, a man of extensive learning, published in the Weekly Miscellany, a defence of prime ministers, in the character and
under the name of Joseph.   He was also the author of a treatise on the Mosaic deluge, published
after his decease.   A short time before his marriage, he had taken orders in the church; he received soon after the donative of Nayland, in Suf-
folk, whither he immediately repaired, leaving
Mrs. Cockburn for some time in London.   In a
letter to Mr. Burnet (dated London, September
10th, 1708) she mentions her husband's journey
to Nayland in the preceding June.   " Our affairs,"
adds she, "have not yet suffered me to go to him,
so that we have been separated near three months,
excepting one week, that he was so kind as to
come and stay with me, when I was ill.   I am
now pretty well recovered, and am hastening to
him as fast as I can; but I have a great deal of

CATHERINE COCKBURN. 417

trouble, and some business yet to bustle through, before I can compass it. We have a house in the country to furnish, for which I must purchase most things here—a new work to me, and a very expensive one. However I hope to be at Nayland in less than a fortnight."

They continued at Nayland but a short time, Mr. Cockburn removing thence to London, to be curate of St. Dunstan's church, Fleet-street; where he remained till the accession of George I., when, doubtful respecting the propriety of taking the oath of abjuration (though he hesitated not to pray for the king and family by name), he was compelled to quit his curacy. He suffered, for the ten or twelve following years, great embarrassments in supporting his family. During this period, he instructed in the Latin language the youth of an academy in Chancery-lane. In 1726, from consulting his father, and the lord-chancellor King, respecting the meaning and intention of the oath, and from reading some papers on the subject, which had fallen into his hands, his scruples were vanquished, and his mind reconciled to the conformity required of him.

In the ensuing year he received an invitation to be minister of the episcopal congregation at Aberdeen in Scotland, which he qualified himself to accept; and, on the day of the accession of George II. preached a sermon to his people on the duty and benefit of praying for the government. This sermon, when printed, gave rise to some animadversions, to which Mr. Cockburn published a reply, with some papers relative to the oath of abjuration. Some time after this circumstance, he was presented by the lord-chancellor King with the living of Long-Horseley, near Morpeth, in Northumberland : by this presentation he was the better enabled to support and educate his family, on which account he was permitted to continue at Aberdeen, till the improper conduct and negligence of the curates whom he had employed at Long-Horseley, obliged Dr. Chandler, bishop of Durham, to call him to a residence on his living. By the necessity of quitting Aberdeen his income was greatly narrowed.

Mrs. Cockburn had, since her marriage, in attention to the more interesting pursuits and occupations of a wife and mother, relinquished her literary pursuits : straitened circumstances, added to the cares of an increasing family, left her but little leisure for study. In a letter to her niece, dated October 6th, 1732, she writes—" Sundays being privileged from the needle, I have found time of late to read three short pamphlets, in an-

CATHERINE COCKBURN. 419

swer to ' Christianity as old as the Creation,' by
Dr. Burnet; which, they say, are the best that
have been written on a subject that has for some
time employed all pens and heads." In another
letter, in the year 1740, she speaks of finding
more time for reading and writing during the
long winter's evenings, than in the summer
months, since she could not work by candle-light.
" In the summer," says she, " I am so much
employed with my needle, that I read little and
write less." In a letter, intended to be sent to
Mr. Pope, she writes—" You had but just began
to dawn upon the world, when I retired from it.
Being married in 1708, I bade adieu to the muses,
and so wholly gave myself up to the cares of a
family, and the education of my children, that I
scarcely knew whether there were such things as
books, plays, or poems, stirring in Great Britain.
However, after some years, your 'Essay on Cri-
ticism,' and 'Rape of the Lock,' broke in upon me.
I rejoiced that so bright a genius was rising on
our isle; but thought no more about you, till my
young family was grown up to have less need of
my assistance; and beginning to have some taste
for polite literature, my inclination revived with
my leisure to enquire after what had been most
celebrated in that kind. I then read your Homer,
&c."

In 1726, eighteen years after her marriage, she
published " A letter to Dr. Holdsworth," in vindication of Mr. Locke, whose material system
exposed him to the imputation of infidelity. Mrs.
Cockburn, in her letter, endeavours to prove that
the system of Mr. Locke was not inconsistent with
a belief in final retribution, a future state of existence, and the resurrection of the body—Whether
of the same body, she contends, is a question of
curiosity, independent of faith in a resurrection,
or the credibility of the christian religion.   This
pamphlet was written in consequence of a sermon
preached by Dr. Holdsworth, a fellow of St. John's
college, Oxford, before the university, from John
v. 28 and 29, concerning the resurrection of the
body. The sermon was afterwards printed; in the
title-page of which the author professes to examine
and reply to " the cavils, false reasonings, and
false interpretations of Scripture, of Mr. Locke
and others, against the resurrection of the same
body."   Mrs. Cockburn remonstrates with Dr.
Holdsworth respecting the uncandid manner in
which he treats his opponents, and hints, that it
is scarcely prudent in the friends of Christianity to
be so earnest in convicting Mr. Locke of infidelity. The zealous divine, in despite of a caution so
sagacious and sensible, persisted in his attack with
equal pertinacity and vehemence. Mrs. Cock-

CATHERINE COCKBURN. 421

burn again replied, in " A Vindication of Mr. Locke's Christian Principles, from the injurious Imputations of Dr. Holdsworth." This pamphlet is said to possess considerable acuteness and merit; but the author finding some difficulties with the booksellers, and being unwilling to publish on her own risk, threw the manuscript aside. It was afterwards printed by Dr. Birch in the edition of her works.

Mrs. Cockburn, in 1732, composed a poem " Occasioned by the Busts set up in the Queen's Hermitage." After some lines containing a panegyric on the taste and liberality of the queen, the poet intimates a wish that her majesty would extend her patronage to her own sex; of whose literary disadvantages she thus speaks:

> " Learning denied us, we at random tread
> Unbeaten paths, that late to knowledge lead :
> By secret steps break through th' obstructed way,
> Nor dare acquirements gain'd by stealth display.
> If some advent'rous genius should arise,
> Who on exalted themes her talent tries,
> She fears to give the work, tho' prais'd, a name,
> And flies not more from infamy than fame.
> Would royal Caroline our wrongs redress. . . .
> *   *   *   *   *
> If not the work, give the attempt applause ;
> And patronise in her the sex's cause."

In this poem, written by Mrs. Cockburn during her residence in Aberdeen, she speaks with regret of her exile from England.—

> " But I, alas! in northern climes grown old,
> No more my native country shall behold."

The poem was to have been presented to the queen, with the author's Defence of Mr. Locke; but the duchess of Hamilton, who had undertaken the presentation, being prevented by illness, and the lord chancellor King having declined the office, it is believed that the verses were never seen by her majesty. They were printed in the Gentleman's Magazine, May, 1737, but with some alterations; of which the writer complained as injudicious and disadvantageous.

Two years afterwards Mrs. Cockburn produced " Remarks upon some Writers in the Controversy concerning the Foundation of Moral Duty and Moral Obligation : particularly the Translation of Archbishop King's Origin of Moral Evil, and the Author of the Divine Legation of Moses: to which are prefixed some cursory Thoughts on the Controversy concerning Necessary Existence, the Reality and Infinity of Space, the Extension and Place of Spirits; and on Dr. Watts's Notion of Substance." These Remarks,

CATHERINE COCKBURN. 423.

to which her name was not prefixed, were " inscribed, with the utmost deference, to Alexander
Pope, by an admirer of his moral character."
The writer professed great reverence for Mr.
Pope, and a desire of being introduced to him.
With this view, she addressed to him a letter *,
which she was withheld by diffidence from sending.   In her remarks, she contends with Dr. Samuel Clarke for eternal and immutable relations,
essential differences, and fitnesses of things. She
treats with great respect the writers whom she
opposes.   This work remained in manuscript
till August, 1743, when it appeared in " The.
History of the Works of the Learned."

In the same year Mrs. Cockburn lost a daughter, of whom she thus speaks in a letter to a friend:
" The loss of my poor child who was so useful to
me, and had been almost all her life with me,
was indeed a severe affliction. She was a long
time every moment in my thoughts. Whatever
I turned my mind to she mingled with it: all that
I found in books was some way or other applied
to her; and still there is not a day but she is frequently the subject of my reflections; nor do I
endeavour to divert them from her, but make the
best use I can of them. I sometimes imagine that

---

* Afterwards published by Dr. Birch.

424   CATHERINE COCKBURN.

I have now a nearer interest in another state than I had, please myself with the hope of joining her spirit there, and finding her rejoicing in her early escape from the evils of this world. Sometimes I consider how graciously Providence often makes our disappointments and crosses in one kind turn to our advantage in another. My Kitty's return to me is an instance of this : had she continued with her brother, how desolate should I have been, when deprived of the only child that was left to me. Sharing each other's grief is a relief and comfort. Besides she is of the greatest use to me ; so that I have reason to be thankful both for her, and the blessing I have in the goodness of my son, though at this distance from me.—I hope God will please to preserve them." Mr. Cockburn, junior, was at this time in Germany, in some office connected with the army : he was afterwards clerk of the cheque at Chatham.

An essay appearing, "On the Nature and Obligations of Virtue," by Dr. Rutherforth, Mrs. Cockburn, notwithstanding the disadvantage of an asthmatic disorder, from which she had suffered some years, and which left her but few intervals of ease, determined on writing a reply. This she executed with spirit and ability. The manuscript was sent to Mr. Warburton, afterwards

CATHERINE COCKBURN. 425

bishop of Gloucester, who took upon himself the care of its publication, and added to it a preface. On this occasion Mrs. C. thus writes to her niece: " I have had a letter from Mr. Warburton, with an encomium on my performance far beyond my expectation, as he says the manuscript was beyond his, when he heard it was written by a lady. He ftyles it ' the strongest and clearest ' piece of metaphysics that ever was written'."

About this period, 1744, Mrs. Cockburn, in a letter dated November 20th, thus expresses herself: " I have very little prospect of tolerable health for any continuance. My cough returned the beginning of September, and held me for two months. It is now succeeded by such a difficulty of breathing, that I do not know which is most grievous; but between them I am reduced to great weakness." August, 1748, she again writes— " There are about nine months in the year when I am unable to write, even to my nearest friends, or on the most important business; much less can I apply myself to abstruse speculations." In a letter to a clergyman (dated March, 1748) who differed from herself in sentiment, and who was prejudiced against the opinions of Dr. Clarke, she writes— " Whenever your affairs will allow you to favour me with a personal conference, I shall esteem it a great obligation, as the advantage must be wholly

on my side; for you will be much disappointed
if you expect to encounter an able disputant.
My companionable capacity, if I may so speak, has
entirely left me; readiness of thought and expression, so necessary to conversation, are no
more; but I can still hear with attention, and consider with impartiality; nor am I yet too old to
learn."

" Remarks upon the Principles and Reasonings of Dr. Rutherforth's Essay on the Nature
and Obligations of Virtue, in Vindication of the
contrary Principles and Reasonings enforced in
the Writings of the late Dr. Samuel Clarke,"
were published in 1747. The opinion of Dr.
Rutherforth, which Mrs. Cockburn laboured to
confute, appears to have been analogous to that
of modern philosophical writers, by which virtue
is defined to be *utility;* or actions considered re-
latively as they affect the community. Man's individual happiness, say they, being the ultimate
end which nature and reason prompt him to pursue, the general approbation given to virtue must
therefore arise out of the general interest, and
not from an intuitive or moral sense. To these
arguments Mrs. Cockburn opposed the eternal
fitness of things, or essential differences in qualities independent of their consequences. In Mr.
Warburton's preface to this work, he declares,

CATHERINE COCKBURN. 427

though he differs somewhat in opinion from the author, " that it contains all the clearness of expression, the strength of reason, the precision of logic, and attachment to truth, which render books of this nature really useful to the common cause of virtue and religion." The acuteness, strength, and vivacity, displayed by Mrs. Cockburn on a subject so abstruse, excited the curiosity of the public, whose admiration received increase from a discovery of the sex and age of the writer, then in her sixty-eighth year.

The reputation which she had acquired by her productions led her friends to propose that they should be collected and published by subscription. Mrs. Cockburn, encouraged by the approbation of several persons of distinguished literary taste, was induced to acquiesce in this plan, which she lived not to execute. The task of editor was, after her decease, undertaken by Dr. Birch.

January 4, 1748-9, when in the seventy-first year of her age, Mrs. Cockburn lost her husband, nor did she long survive a shock so severe. May 11, 1749, after a long and painful illness, sustained with patience and fortitude, she expired, and was interred near her husband and youngest daughter, at Long Horseley. On their tomb is the following short inscription: " Let their works praise them in the gates." Prov. xxxi. 31. She retained her intellects unimpaired till within a few days of her death.

She had been not less distinguished in her youth for beauty and accomplishments than for her talents and genius. Her stature was small, her complexion delicate, and her eyes sparkling and full of animation. Her piety was rational and sincere, her conduct in every relation exemplary, her temper was liberal and benevolent, her conversation pleasing, instructive, modest, and unaffected. She met with universal respect and praise, even from the great, to many of whom she was known; but who, satisfying themselves with barren admiration, made no efforts to relieve her, by a liberal patronage, from narrow circumstances, with which she struggled through life, and which left her little leisure for literary avocations. The disadvantages of her situation, in which she was able to procure but few books, and to which she submitted without repining, rendered her acquirements and efforts more laudable and praise-worthy. Twenty years she devoted to the occupations of her family; yet, after so long an interval, she resumed, amidst increasing infirmities and broken health, her literary pursuits, and applied her powers to the investigation of subjects the most profound and abstracted. In one instance only

CATHERINE COCKBURN. 429

she appears to have suffered from obloquy. Having withdrawn herself from a slight acquaintance with Mrs. Manley, the author of the celebrated Atalantis, whose writings and conduct were equally licentious, Mrs. Manley revenged herself by calumniating the virtues she had neglected to imitate. Convinced at length of the injustice and atrocity of her behaviour, she promised to make to Mrs. Cockburn a personal apology: this humiliation the lady however found means to evade.

In 1751 the works of Mrs. Cockburn were published by Dr. Birch, in two volumes octavo. Of her dramatic performances, " The Fatal Friendship" alone was included in this collection. Two volumes only having been subscribed for by her friends, it was not possible to comprehend in that compass all her productions: to her prose writings it was therefore thought proper to give the preference. In this collection is a letter of advice to her son; also letters between Dr. Sharp, archdeacon of Northumberland and prebendary of Durham, and Mrs. Cockburn, concerning the foundation of moral virtue; likewise letters between Mrs. Cockburn and several of her friends; with short essays in prose; poems, songs, &c. The collection is entitled, " The Works of Mrs. Catherine Cockburn, theological, moral, dramatic, and poetical."

Biographia Britannica.—Biographium Femineum.—The Female Worthies.

[430]

VICTOIRE COLONNE,

MARQUISE DE PESCAIRE.

VICTOIRE COLONNE, passionately devoted to letters, having, while young, lost a husband, distinguished for his valour and martial exploits, devoted the remainder of her life to melancholy and study; and celebrated, in the most tender poetry, the hero whom she had loved.

ANNA COMNENA.

ANNA, daughter of the Greek emperor Alexius Comnenus, flourished about the year 1118. She renounced, in her youth, the amusements and occupations of her sex, to deliver up herself to a passion for study and letters. After acquiring a perfect knowledge of history and the *belles-lettres*, she made great progress in philosophy, through the obscurity in which it was in those times involved. She employed her acquirements in composing a history, in fifteen volumes, of the life and reign of the emperor her father, a work which she entitled " *The Alexiad;*" eight of these books were published by Hæschelius, in 1610; and the whole fifteen, with a Latin version, in 1651. In 1670 the learned Charles du Fresne published another edition with

ANNA COMNENA.

historical and philological notes. Anna Comnena has been accused of partiality in this work, in which the actions of her father appear to greater advantage than in the writings of the Latin historians, who, it is not impossible, might have cherished prejudices against a Greek emperor. The truth is probably to be found in the medium. The *Journal des Savans* thus speaks of Anna in 1675 :

" The elegance with which Anna Comnena has, in fifteen books, described the life and actions of her father, and the strong and eloquent manner in which she has set them off, are so much above the ordinary capacity of women, as almost to excite a doubt whether she were indeed the author of the work. It is impossible to read the descriptions she has given of countries, rivers, mountains, towns, sieges, battles, the reflections she makes upon particular events, the judgment she passes upon human actions, with her digressions on various occasions, without perceiving that she must have been well skilled in grammar, rhetoric, philosophy, and mathematics; nay, even that she must have possessed some knowledge of law, physic, and divinity—studies very rare and uncommon in her sex."

Dictionnaire Histoi ique des Femmes Célébres—TheFemale Worthies.

ISABELLA DE CORDAUD.

This lady, beautiful, rich, accomplished, and mistress of the Latin, Greek, and Hebrew languages, took her degrees in theology, with the title of doctor.

———————————

CHARLOTTE CORDEY.

Of this young heroine of the French revolution, which called forth and displayed so many virtues and vices, but little is known. She was the daughter of a man attached, by his place, to the court. Jacques Adrian de Cordey, her grandfather, married Mary Renée Adelaide de Belleau, lady de la Motte, in the parish of Courtone, near Orbec, by whom he had four sons and four daughters. James Francis de Cordey, sieur d'Ermont, the third of these sons, married Mary Carola Gautier des Antiers. Four sons and two daughters, one of whom was the celebrated Charlotte, were the fruit of this union. The father was living a short time since in the city of Argentan, in the department of l'Orne. The sons, it is believed, were emigrants.

Charlotte having imbibed, with all their enthusiasm, the republican principles, conceived a just indignation at the character and conduct of Marat

CHARLOTTE CORDEY. 433

and, with a truly Roman spirit, meditated a generous sacrifice for the deliverance of her bleeding country. Young, rich, and beautiful, she quitted the bosom of her family and the occupations of her sex, and, armed with a dagger, came to Paris, alone, unprotected, without confidents or accomplices. Under the pretence of business she procured admission to the apartments of Marat, whom, with an unerring arm, and a dauntless spirit, she stabbed to the heart, as, reclining on a sopha, he perused a paper which she had previously presented to him.

She surrendered herself a prisoner with calm intrepidity, and expected, without shrinking, the fate which awaited her. She preserved the same presence of mind, and the same tranquillity, through the whole of her examination and trial, justifying and triumphing in the deed she had committed. At the place of execution, she appeared with an unchanged and cheerful aspect; her pulse beat with a temperate regularity, nor did the colour in her cheeks once vary. She spoke not, but frequently placed her hand on her heart, with an animated gesture more eloquent than words. In the satisfaction of having delivered the earth from a monster, and the anticipation of future glory, all concern for the present seemed absorbed and annihilated.

A curious anecdote is related in connection with

434　　　CHARLOTTE CORDEY.

her death. A young Frenchman, who saw her for the first time as she passed through the streets to the scaffold, struck with her beauty and the dignity of her aspect, conceived for her a violent and enthusiastic passion; and, running wildly through the city, proclaimed, with his sentiments and his despair, his determination of sharing the fate of the object of his admiration, and mingling with hers his blood. He was taken at his word by the satellites of the tyrant demagogues, and hurried to the guillotine.

The following is the translation of a letter addressed by Charlotte Cordey to her father, the evening before her trial, and dated—

" From the prison of the Conciergerie, in the apartment lately occupied by the deputy Brissot.

　　　　　　　　　　　　" July 16, 1793.

" My dear and respected father—Peace is about to reign in my beloved native country, for Marat * is no more! be comforted, and bury my memory in eternal oblivion. To-morrow, the 17th, at seven in the morning, my trial will take place. I have achieved a glorious exploit; I have therefore lived

---

* Charlotte mistook her victim. Marat was sinking into the tomb from disease. It was Robespierre that marked with an indelible stain the cause of liberty and the French name.

CORINNA. 435

long enough. I put you under the protection of Barbaroux and his colleagues, in case you should be molested. Let not my family blush at my fate for, remember, according to Voltaire, ' that crimes beget disgrace, and not the scaffold.'

" Your affectionate daughter,

" Marie Anne Victoire Charlotte Cordey."

While the behaviour of Charlotte Cordey extorts a tribute of admiration, the principle of assassination must ever be reprobated. Private judgment is too much connected with the passions and the imagination to be entrusted with the avenging sword.

Anecdotes of the Founders of the French Republic, &c. &c.

CORINNA.

Corinna, a Theban poetess, daughter of Archelodorus and Procratia, and the disciple of Mirthis, is said to have borne away the palm five times from Pindar, the celebrated lyric poet. She composed five books of epigrams, and was not less celebrated for her beauty than for her genius. She is mentioned by Propertius and other writers. Two ladies of the same name have been distinguished for their talents: Corinna, the Thespian,

436   HELENA LUCRETIA CORNARO.

applauded by Statius, and by the ancient writers. Also the Roman Corinna, who, living in the time of Augustus, was celebrated by Ovid.

The Female Worthies—Dictionnaire Historique des Femmes Célébres.

HELENA LUCRETIA CORNARO.

HELENA LUCRETIA, daughter of Gio Baptisto Cornaro, born at Venice in 1646, received a learned and scientific education, and, after many years spent in study, took at Padua a doctor's degree. She was also admitted a member of the university at Rome. Having determined to devote her life to the sciences, she made a vow of celibacy, from which neither solicitations, nor the offer of a dispensation from the Pope, could induce her to swerve. The title of *unalterable* was given to her at Padua, and that of the *humble* at Rome, of which her fortitude and modesty rendered her equally deserving.

Her profound studies, added to the severity of her devotions, impaired her health and shortened her life. The report of her talents and acquirements attracted the attention of the literati of the age, and of foreigners who passed through Venice, of which she was accounted the greatest curiosity. The cardinals de Bouillon and d'Etrees, having been ordered by

HELENA LUCRETIA CORNARO. 437

the king of France to visit Lucretia, in their way to Italy, and to make a report of the truth of her acquirements, added their testimony to her learning and abilities, which became celebrated throughout Europe. She was particularly skilled in the Greek and Roman languages, in mathematics, and the sciences. Her constitution failing beneath unremitted application, she expired in the beginning of the year 1685. A twelvemonth before her decease, presaging from the symptoms she felt, that her life would not be long, she pointed out to her father, while walking with him in the garden, an old cypress tree, which she desired might be cut down to make her a coffin.

The academicians of Rome, to whose society she had been admitted, composed numberless eulogies and odes to her memory. They also celebrated in her honour funeral solemnities, to which the whole city crowded, in the college of the Barnabite fathers, where they usually assembled. Of these ceremonies, performed with great pomp and magnificence, a description was published at Paris, in 1686, and dedicated to the Venetian republic. A funeral oration was delivered by one of the academicians, in which the fine qualities of the deceased were amply panegyrised, and in which she was extolled above Pompey, who triumphed over three kings, for her

438 **ANONYMOUS.**

conquest over voluptuousness, ignorance, and pride, a victory more praise-worthy, and of more difficult achievement.

Biographium Fæmineum—The Female Worthies—Dictionnaire Historique.

ANONYMOUS.

A DAUGHTER of a Boulognois gentleman, in the 13th century, devoted herself to the study of the Latin language, and of the laws. At the age of three-and-twenty she pronounced, in the great church at Boulogne, a funeral oration in Latin, which obtained, for its eloquence, great applause. At twenty-six, she took the degree of doctor, and undertook to read publicly, at her house, the *Institutions of Justinian*. At thirty, her reputation raised her to the chair of the professor, where she taught the law to a concourse of people of all nations. To masculine knowledge, she added all the elegance of her sex, and it was only when she spoke that her hearers forgot her beauty. The same example was, in the same city, renewed in the 14th century, and again in the 15th. Also, in more modern times, the philosophic chair of Boulogne has been filled with distinction by a woman.

[*439*]

CORNELIA.

CORNELIA, wife to Scipio Africanus, and mother of the Gracchi, gave public lectures of philosophy in Rome. " We are much indebted," says Quintilian, " for the eloquence of the Gracchi to their mother Cornelia, whose unparalleled learning is, in her excellent epistles, bequeathed to posterity." Cicero also thus speaks of her : " Cornelia, had she not been a woman, would have deserved the first place among philosophers." Her reply to the lady who boasted of her jewels, and to whom she presented her sons, as her most valuable ornaments and possession, is well known. A statue was placed on her sepulchre with the following inscription : " Here lieth interred the most learned Cornelia, mother of the Gracchi. She was fortunate in her disciples whom she instructed, though unfortunate in her children."

Biographium Fœmineum—The Female Worthies, &c.

ELIZABETH CROMWELL.

ELIZABETH, daughter of sir James Bourchier (of the same family with the ancient earls of Essex of that name), and wife of Oliver Cromwell, was a woman possessed of an enlarged mind and an

440   JUANA INEZ DE LA CRUZ.

elevated spirit. Though an excellent housewife, she was capable of appearing with dignity in the station to which she was exalted, as wife of the lord protector. She took a profound interest in political affairs, and stimulated her husband in the career of ambition She educated her children with ability, and governed her family with address. She survived her husband fourteen years. On the restoration, she prudently retired, and passed the remainder of her life in obscurity. She died October 8th, 1672.

Letters published by Mr. Duncombe.

JUANA INEZ DE LA CRUZ.

JUANA INEZ DE LA CRUZ, was born in November, 1651, a few leagues from the city of Mexico. Her father, a Spaniard, had sought wealth by an establishment in America, where he married a lady of the country, but of Spanish extraction. Juana, the fruit of this union, displayed in early childhood a passion for letters, and an extraordinary facility in the composition of Spanish verse. At eight years of age, she was placed by her parents with an uncle, who resided in Mexico, and who caused her to receive a learned education. Her talents having attracted notice and distinction, she was patronised by the lady of the viceroy, the marquis de Mancera, and, at the age of seventeen, was received into his family.

JUANA INEZ DE LA CRUZ.   441

A Spanish encomiast of Juana, relates a curious anecdote respecting her, communicated to him, as he affirms, by the viceroy. Her patrons, filled with admiration and astonishment, by the powers and attainments of their young *protegée*, determined to prove the extent and solidity of her erudition. For this purpose they invited forty of the most eminent literary characters of the country, who assembled to examine Juana in the different branches of learning and science. Questions, arguments, and problems, were accordingly proposed to her, by the several professors, in philosophy, mathematics, history, theology, poetry, &c. to all of which she answered with equal readiness and skill, acquitting herself to the entire satisfaction of her judges. To this account it is added, that she received the praises extorted on this occasion by her acquirements, with the most perfect modesty; neither did she, at any period of her life, discover the smallest tendency to presumption or vanity, though honoured with the title of the *tenth muse:* a pious humility was her distinguishing characteristic. She lived forty-four years, twenty-seven of which she passed in the convent of St. Geronimo (where she took the veil) in the exercise of the most exemplary virtues.

That enthusiasm by which genius is characterised, necessarily led to devotion in circumstances like those in which Juana was placed. In the fervour of her zeal, she wrote in her blood a confession of her faith.   She is said to have collected a library of four thousand volumes, in the study of which she placed her delight : nevertheless, towards the close of her life, she sacrificed this darling propensity for the purpose of applying the money, which she acquired by the sale of her books, to the relief of the indigent. However heroic may be the motive of this self-denial, the rectitude of the principle is doubtful : the cultivation of the mind, with its consequent influence upon society, is a more real benefit to mankind than the partial relief of pecuniary exigencies.

Juana was not less lamented at her death, than celebrated and respected during her life : her writings were collected in three 4to. volumes, to which are prefixed numerous panegyrics upon the author, both in verse and prose, by the most illustrious persons of old and new Spain.   It is observed by the Spanish critic, father Feyjoo, that the compositions of Juana excel in ease and elegance, rather than in energy and strength.   This is perhaps in some degree attributable to the age in which she lived, and to the subjects of her productions, which were principally compliments addressed to her friends, or sacred dramas, to which an absurd and senseless superstition afforded the materials.   The following is an imitation in English of one of her poems, in which she complains of what is keenly felt by every

JUANA INEZ DE LA CRUZ.   443

woman of understanding, the injustice suffered by her sex.

" Weak men, who without reason aim
To load poor woman with abuse,
Not seeing that yourselves produce
The very evils that you blame!

" You 'gainst her firm resistance strive,
And having struck her judgment mute,
Soon to her levity impute
What from your labour you derive.

" Of woman's weakness much afraid,
Of your own prowess still you boast ;
Like the vain child who makes a ghost,
Then fears what he himself has made.

" Her whom your arms have once embrac'd,
You think presumptuously to find,
When she is woo'd as Thais kind,
When wedded, as Lucretia chaste.

" How rare a fool must he appear,
Whose folly mounts to such a pass,
That first he breathes upon the glass,
Then grieves because it is not clear.

" Still with unjust, ungrateful pride,
You meet both favour and disdain ;
The firm as cruel you arraign,
The tender you as weak deride.

" Your foolish humour none can please,
Since judging all with equal phlegm ;
One for her rigour you condemn,
And one you censure for her ease.

444　　　　　**CYNISCA.**

" What wondrous gifts must her adorn,
Who could your lasting love engage ;
When rigorous nymphs excite your rage,
And easy fair-ones raise your scorn.

" But while you shew your pride or pow'r,
With tyrant passions vainly hot,
She 's only blest who heeds you not,
And leaves you all in happy hour."

Sketches of the History, Genius, &c. of Woman.

CYNISCA.

AGESILAUS, king of Sparta, to prove his contempt
for the ambition displayed in the races at the Olympic
games, persuaded his sister Cynisca to enter the lists.
The lady was successful, and bore away the prize from
all competitors. She was the first woman who obtained this honour. She consecrated horses of
brass, as a monument of her victory, which were
placed at the entrance of the temple of Jupiter
Olympius. The poet Simonides wrote an epigram
in her praise. Her statue, made by Apelles, and
adorned with several inscriptions, was placed in the
temple of Juno at Elis. The Lacedemonians also
erected to her a monument.

Bayle's Historical Dictionary, &c.

END OF THE THIRD VOLUME.

T. Davison, White-Friars.

EDITORIAL NOTES

p. 6, ll. 20–4: *'Madam ... to ascend it'*: Castéra and Tooke, *The Life of Catherine II*, vol. 1, p. 379.

p. 8, l. 18: *Augustus III*: King of Poland (1696–1763).

p. 10, ll. 9–11: *'Remember ... this affair'*: Castéra and Tooke, *The Life of Catherine II*, vol. 1, p. 401, note.

p. 10, l. 22: *Mokranoffsky*: Andzrej Mokronowski (1713–84), Marshal of Cracow.

p. 10, l. 27–p. 11, l. 3: *'If you must ... lived*: free!*'*: Hays's emphasis. Castéra and Tooke, *The Life of Catherine II*, vol. 1, p. 403.

p. 11, ll. 4–5: *Adam Chartorinsky*: Prince Adam Kazimierz Czartoryski (1734–1823), wealthy man of letters, candidate for King of Poland.

p. 11, ll. 10–16: *'No man ... shall be'*: Hays's emphasis. Castéra and Tooke, *The Life of Catherine II*, vol. 1, pp. 403–4.

p. 16, l. 21: *Vassily Mirovitch*: Vasily Yakovlevich Mirovich (1740–64), executed for attempt to free Ivan VI and organize coup against Catherine.

p. 16, l. 23: *Kozac Mazeppa*: Ivan Stepanovich Mazepa (1639–1709), Cossack hetman who sided with Charles XII (1682–1718), King of Sweden, against Peter the Great in the Battle of Poltava (1709).

p. 16, l. 24: *Charles XII*: King of Sweden (1682–1718).

p. 17, l. 5: *Captain Vlassieff*: Danila Vlas'ev.

p. 17, l. 5: *Lieutenant Ischekin*: Luka Fedorovich Chekin.

p. 18, l. 18: *Jacob Pishkoff*: not further identified.

p. 21, l. 22–p. 22, l. 2: *'I have missed ... prisoner'*: Castéra and Tooke, *The Life of Catherine II*, vol. 1, p. 425.

p. 22, l. 18: *'deep not loud'*: Not further identified, though the surrounding text is taken directly from Castéra and Tooke, *The Life of Catherine II*, vol. 1, pp. 425–6. It is possible that this description was passed along in conversation between Tooke and Hays during one of their encounters. Also, the phrase is used in a 1778 play, *Percy, a Tragedy*, written by Hannah More, a contemporary and political opponent of Hays. See H. More, *Percy A Tragedy, as it is Acted at the Theatre-Royal in Covent Garden* (London: T. Cadell, 1778), p. 77.

p. 26, l. 6: *Galitzin*: Most likely Prince Alexander Mikhailovich Golitsyn (1718–83), general field marshal, governor to St Petersburg.

p. 27, l. 19: *Veymar*: Possibly Ivan Ivanovich Veymarny (1722–92), who investigated General Apraksin and later ambassador to Poland.

p. 29, l. 14–p. 30, l. 6: *'The volumes ... employ it'*: Castéra and Tooke, *The Life of Catherine II*, vol. 2, pp. 2–3.

p. 29, ll. 24–5: *Sketch of...Europe*: Or *Sketch of the History of the different States of Europe*, published in 1793.

p. 31, l. 23: *Vissensky*: Older sources list him as a possible favourite.

p. 33, l. 9: *Diderot*: Denis Diderot (1713–84), Enlightenment thinker who sold his library to Catherine (1765) and visited Russia (1873–74).

p. 33, l. 14: *Morard*: Sauveni François Morard.

p. 34, l. 23–p. 35, l. 4: *'That were his ... devil'*: Castéra and Tooke, *The Life of Catherine II*, vol. 2, p. 22, note.

p. 36, l. 16: *Repnin*: Prince Nikolai Vasilyevich Repnin (1734–1801), minister to Warsaw (1763–72).

p. 37, l. 5: *de Choiseul*: Étienne-François, comte de Stainville, duc de Choiseul (1719–85), foreign minister of France (1757–70).

p. 37, l. 11: *Vergennes*: Charles Gravier, comte de Vergennes (1719–87), French ambassador to the Ottoman empire (1754–68), foreign minister (1774–81).

p. 40, l. 11: *Bourthurlin*: Countess Maria Romanovna Buturlina, née Vorontsova (b. 1737), maid of honour.

p. 41, ll. 15–19: *'Indigence ... been venial'*: Castéra and Tooke, *The Life of Catherine II*, vol. 2, p. 42.

p. 43, ll. 9–13: *'We are ... depredations'*: Castéra and Tooke, *The Life of Catherine II*, vol. 2, pp. 45–6.

p. 43, l. 24: *Scheremetoff*: Peter Borisovich Sheremetov (1713–88), chamberlain, senator, marshal of the nobility.

p. 44, ll. 10–19: *great* ... mother of her country: Hays adds emphasis. See Castéra and Tooke, *The Life of Catherine II*, vol. 2, p. 42.

p. 44, ll. 14–24: *'That if ... she loved'*: Castéra and Tooke, *The Life of Catherine II*, vol. 2, p. 47.

p. 45, ll. 5–9: *'Semiramis ... deserves it'*: Castéra and Tooke, *The Life of Catherine II*, vol. 2, p. 49.

p. 46, l. 25–p. 47, l. 4: *'If ... of the people'*: Castéra and Tooke, *The Life of Catherine II*, vol. 2, p. 55.

p. 48, ll. 1–3: *not free ... anxiety*: Hays's observation of Catherine's 'weaknesses', in this matter, are her own: see Castéra and Tooke, *The Life of Catherine II*, vol. 2, p. 61.

p. 48, ll. 4–5: Imperial majesty: Hays's emphasis. Castéra and Tooke, *The Life of Catherine II*, vol. 2, p. 61.

p. 48, l. 24: *Tschoglokoff*: Choglokov, not further identified.

p. 50, l. 14: *Euler*: Leonard Euler (1707–83), Swiss, great eighteenth-century mathematician, worked in Russia (1727–41, 1766–83).

p. 52, ll. 5–6: *Thomas Dimsdale*: Baron Thomas Dimsdale (1712–1800), after 1766 publication of his treatise on smallpox inoculation, Catherine invited him to Russia to inoculate her and her grandsons (1768, 1781).

p. 52, ll. 19–26: *'But what...their sovereign'*: Hays omits the word 'honour' from this quote; in Castéra and Tooke it reads 'the honour of their sovereign's company' (p. 80).

p. 53, ll. 7–25: *'My life ... any delays?'*: Castéra and Tooke, *The Life of Catherine II*, vol. 2, pp. 80–2.

p. 54, ll. 8–11: *'Though I wish ... others'*: Castéra and Tooke, *The Life of Catherine II*, vol. 2, p. 82.

p. 57, l. 12: *Henry*: Prince Henry of Prussia (1726–1802), younger brother of Frederick the Great, successful general in Seven Years' War (1756–63), arranged second marriage for Paul to great niece Sophia Dorothea von Württemburg.

p. 61, l. 6: *Charles James Fox*: (1749–1806), supported American and French revolutions, and Russian occupation of Ochakov (1788).

p. 63, l. 6: *Joseph II*: Holy Roman Emperor Joseph II (1741–90), met with Catherine (1780).

p. 63, ll. 9–12: *'I ... amuse France'*: Castéra and Tooke, *The Life of Catherine II*, vol. 2 p. 116.

p. 66, l. 23: *Elphinston*: Captain John Elphinstone (1722–85), under Grigory Orlov aided Russia in victory at Battle of Chesme (1770).

p. 66, l. 23: *Greig*: Admiral Samuel Greig (Samuel Karlovich Grieg in Russia) (1736–88), led Russian navy in Battle of Chesme (1770) and the Russo-Swedish War (1788–90).

p. 66, l. 23 *Dugdale*: Captain-Lieutenant Robert Dugdale (d. 1791), lost the battleship Svyatoslav in the Battle of Chesme (1770) and left Russian service (1771).

p. 68, ll. 3–8: *'It was not ... a fleet?'*: Castéra and Tooke, *The Life of Catherine II*, vol. 2, p. 139.

p. 68, ll. 25–7: *'I grant ... for nothing'*: Castéra and Tooke, *The Life of Catherine II*, vol. 2, p. 140.

p. 69, ll. 21–3: *'It was... such an action'*: Castéra and Tooke, *The Life of Catherine II*, vol. 2, p. 146.

p. 70, l. 9: *Hackert*: Jacob Philipp Hackert (1737–1807), Prussian landscape painter in Italy.

p. 72, ll. 22–5: *'Oh, Mohammed! ... pestilence'*: Castéra and Tooke, *The Life of Catherine II*, vol. 2, p. 164.

p. 74, l. 1: *Yerapkin*: Lieutenant General Peter Dmitrievich Yeropkin (1724–1805), commander-in-chief of Moscow during the plague (1770–2).

p. 80, l. 13: *Radzivil*: Prince Karol Stanislaw Radziwiłł's (1734–90) library in Nieśwież was taken as war booty by Catherine (1772) and given to the Russian Academy of Sciences.

p. 80, l. 25: *Pulaufsky*: General Casimir Pulaski (Kazimierz Pułaski) (1745–79), after failed coup (1771), immigrated to the United States and fought as a cavalry commander.

p. 83, ll. 13–17: *His adversaries ... the empire*: After twelve years together, Catherine discovered that Orlov was cheating on her. Orlov had tried to force a marriage when Catherine first was on the throne, using their son, Bobrinsky, born months before the coup in 1762, as leverage; he was not named Bobrinsky until Catherine rejected the idea.

p. 83, l. 20: *Vassiltschikoff*: Alexander Semenovich Vasil'chikov (1744–1813), favourite of Catherine (1772–4).

p. 84, ll. 15–18: *Possessed with ... gates of Petursburg*: In fact, politics were uppermost in Catherine's mind when she recalled Orlov, whom she stripped of his orders and titles to placate Panin and her son Paul into signing away Holstein, which he had inherited from his father upon coming into his majority in 1772, and to counter Panin's last attempt to place Paul on the throne. Once the danger was past, Catherine returned his orders and titles to Orlov.

p. 85, l. 27: *Osman Effendi*: Yenişehirli Osman Efendi, Ottoman statesman.

p. 85, l. 27–p. 86, l. 2: *'That the grand-seignior ... peace'*: Castéra and Tooke, *The Life of Catherine II*, vol. 2, p. 191.

p. 90, l. 4: *Lewis XIV*: Louis XIV, King of France (1638–1715, r. 1643–1715).

p. 90, l. 19: *Romantzoff*: Count Peter Alexandrovich Rumyantsev-Zadunaisky (1725–96), field marshal general in the first Russo-Turkish War (1768–74), governor of Ukraine (1764–96).

p. 90, ll. 20–6: *'Because ... engage them'*: Castéra and Tooke, *The Life of Catherine II*, vol. 2, p. 226.

p. 91, ll. 11–14: *She dreaded ... formidable*: Elizabeth first used this strategy when she brought Catherine to Russia to marry her nephew Peter in 1744. Previous to Peter the Great heirs married members of the most important Russian families (see note to vol. 6, p 283, ll. 21–4).

p. 91, l. 15: *Hesse Darmstadt*: Louis IX of Hesse-Darmstadt (1719–90), wife Countess Palatine Caroline of Zweibrücken (1721–74), and the three of their five daughters, Princesses Amalie (1754–1832), Wilhelmina Louisa (Grand Duchess Natalya Alekseyevna) (1755–76) and Louise Auguste (1757–1830), went to Russia.

p. 93, ll. 15–17: '*Monsieur Diderot ... ten*': Castéra and Tooke, *The Life of Catherine II*, vol. 2, p. 237.

p. 93, l. 25–p. 95, l. 18: '*Now we ... amply revenged*': The letter quoted is dated from 22 July to 2 August 1771. See Castéra and Tooke, *The Life of Catherine II*, vol. 2, pp. 238–42.

p. 94, l. 22: *Descartes*: René Descartes (1596–1650), philosopher and mathematician.

p. 99, ll. 4–7: '*Why should ... compassion?*': Castéra and Tooke, *The Life of Catherine II*, vol. 2, pp. 269–70.

p. 107, l. 10: *Ikhelman Pugatcheff*: Yemelyan Pugachev (1742–75), pretender as Peter III, led the Pugachev Rebellion (1773–4) for which he was hanged.

p. 107, ll. 20–6: '*If the emperor ... Peter III*': Castéra and Tooke, *The Life of Catherine II*, vol. 2, p. 289.

p. 111, l. 15: *Bibikoff*: General Alexander Il'ich Bibikov (1729–74) died of cholera while leading the attack on Pugachev.

p. 111, l. 27–p. 112, l. 2: '*Peter III ... Ultor*': Castéra and Tooke, *The Life of Catherine II*, vol. 2, p. 308.

p. 112, l. 2: '*Redivivus et Ulto*': 'Renew and Avenge' (Latin).

p. 112, l. 16: *Lovitch*: Georg-Morits Lowitz (1722–74), astronomer, member of the St Petersburg Academy of Sciences.

p. 113, l. 3: *Panin*: General Count Peter Ivanovich Panin (1721–89).

p. 113, l. 22: *Antizoff*: Cossack ataman.

p. 113, l. 27: *Mikelson*: General Ivan Ivanovich Mikhelson (Johann von Michelsohnen) (1740–1807).

p. 114, ll. 19–20: '*Though hast ... emperor!*': Castéra and Tooke, *The Life of Catherine II*, vol. 2, p. 319.

p. 116, l. 27–p. 117, l. 2: '*What I ... root up*': Castéra and Tooke, *The Life of Catherine II*, vol. 2, p. 324.

p. 125, ll. 8–9: '*Your imperial ... would*': Castéra and Tooke, *The Life of Catherine II*, vol. 2, p. 387.

p. 131, l. 13: *Zavadoffsky*: Count Peter Zavadovsky (1739–1812), favourite of Catherine (1776–7).

p. 135, ll. 12–19: '*Madam, there ... partitioned*': Castéra and Tooke, *The Life of Catherine II*, vol. 2, p. 423.

p. 136, ll. 24–7: '*It is only ... son*': Castéra and Tooke, *The Life of Catherine II*, vol. 2, p. 426.

p. 137, ll. 11–21: '*the greatest ... Ottoman's*': Castéra and Tooke, *The Life of Catherine II*, vol. 2, p. 430.

p. 138, ll. 20–1: *Maria Feodorovna*: Princess Sophia Marie Dorothea Augusta Luisa von Württemberg (1759–1828), second wife of Paul.

p. 140, l. 26: *Zoritch*: Semyon Zorich (1745–99), favourite of Catherine (1777–8).

p. 141, l. 5: *Phaeton*: Son of the god Helios, in Ovid's *Metamorphoses*, Phaeton dares and fails to drive the sun chariot.

p. 141, l. 19: *Bernstoff*: Andreas Peter Bernstorff (1735–97), Danish foreign minister (1784–97).

p. 142, l. 1: *Gustavus*: Gustavus III, King of Sweden (1746–92, r. 1771–92), nephew of Frederick the Great.

p. 144, l. 2: manner: Hays's emphasis: Castéra and Tooke, *The Life of Catherine II*, vol. 2, p. 471.

p. 147, l. 2: *Sir James Harris*: first Earl of Malmesbury (1746–1820), Envoy-Extraordinary to St Petersburg (1777–83).

p. 147, ll. 6–11: '*in the name … knighthood*': Castéra and Tooke, *The Life of Catherine II*, vol. 2, p. 484, note.

p. 149, l. 4: 'Amore et fidelitate': 'Love and fidelity' (Latin). Castéra and Tooke, *The Life of Catherine II*, vol. 2, p. 490.

p. 149, l. 19: '*Utility, Honour, and Fame*': Castéra and Tooke, *The Life of Catherine II*, vol. 2, p. 491.

p. 152, ll. 11–17: '*I loved … tongues*': Castéra and Tooke, *The Life of Catherine II*, vol. 2, p. 497.

p. 152, l. 25: *Ivan Rimsky Korzakoff*: Ivan Nikolaevich Rimsky-Korsakov (1754–1831), favourite of Catherine (1778–9).

p. 153, l. 13–p. 154, l. 7: '*What books … within*': Castéra and Tooke, *The Life of Catherine II*, vol. 2, p. 499, note.

p. 157, l. 21: *Bruce*: Countess Praskovya Alexandrovna Bruce (1729–85), Catherine's long-time friend until 1779, when she learned that Bruce was having an affair with Rimsky Korsakov.

p. 158, l. 11: *Lanskoï*: Alexander Lanskoy (1758–84), favourite of Catherine (1778–84).

p. 158, l. 25: *Ivan Osterman*: Count Ivan Andreyevich Osterman (1725–1811), foreign minister (1783–87), chancellor (1796–97).

p. 161, l. 3: '*the Falkenstein arm's*': Omitted from 1798 edition. See Castéra and Tooke, *The Life of Catherine II*, vol. 2, p. 452.

p. 161, l. 17: *Muller*: Gerhard Friedrich Muller (1705–83), ethnographer, co-founder of Academy of Sciences (1725).

p. 162, ll. 8–9: *Multorum providus urbes Et mores hominum inspexit*: 'Who has carefully viewed the cities And investigated the manners of various nations.' (Latin).

p. 162, l. 27–p. 163, l. 1: '*Miscellaneous Pieces, or the Library of the Grand-dukes*': Castéra and Tooke, *The Life of Catherine II*, vol. 3, p. 8.

p. 165, ll. 9–10: '*Tale of Tzarrevitch Chlor*': Castéra and Tooke, *The Life of Catherine II*, vol. 3, p. 9.

p. 165, ll. 26–8: 'Monsieur l'Harpe … beaucoup': 'Mr. Harpe, continue your lessons of this kind; your sentiments please me very much.' (French): Castéra and Tooke, *The Life of Catherine II*, vol. 3, p. 10.

p. 167, l. 19: *Carburg*: Marin Carburi (1729–82), Greek military engineer who sought asylum in Russia.

p. 168, l. 10: *Constantin the Great*: Constantine I (272–337).

p. 168, l. 10: Constantius: Constantius II (317–61).

p. 169, l. 9: *Collot*: Marie-Anne Collot (1748–1821), sculptor and portraitist, in Russia (1766–78).

p. 169, l. 10: *Peter Falconnet*: Peter-Etienne Falconet (1741–91), painter, son of Etienne Maurice Falconet, sculptor (1716–91).

p. 169, l. 14: *PETRV PERVOMU EKATERINA VTORAIA*: 'To Peter the First from Catherine the Second' (Russian).

p. 169, l. 15–16: PETRO PRIMO CATHERINA SECVNDA: 'To Peter the First from Catherine the Second' (Latin).

p. 178, ll. 4–5: 'Voilà … ma vie': 'There is the man who provided the greatest service in the most critical moment of my life.' (French): Castéra and Tooke, *The Life of Catherine II*, vol. 3, pp. 53–4.

p. 179, ll. 9–14: *This anecdote ... equivocal*: This anecdote was taken out of the 1800 edition; the footnote to Paul's burial of Peter and Catherine together, with his murderers Alexei Orlov and Prince Baratinsky as mourners, was moved in the 1800 edition to its chronological place after Catherine's death. These changes are evidence that Hays used the 1798 or 1799 rather than 1800 edition as the basis for her translation.

p. 182, ll. 11–18: *'What an ... acquire?'*: Castéra and Tooke, *The Life of Catherine II*, vol. 3, pp. 78–9.

p. 184, l. 3: *Bezborodko*: Prince Alexander Andreyevich Bezborodko (1747–99), diplomat, chancellor (1797–9).

p. 186, l. 7: *Dashkoff*: Prince Pavel Mikhailovich Dashkov (1763–1807), engineer, on Potemkin's staff, elected Fellow of the Royal Society (1781).

p. 186, l. 13: *Yermoloff*: Alexander Yermolov (1754–1835), favourite of Catherine (1785–86).

p. 186, l. 14: *Momonoff*: Count Alexander Dmitriyev-Mamonov (1758–1803), favourite of Catherine (1786–9).

p. 187, l. 1: *Butterlin*: Count Peter Alexandrovitch Buturlin (1734–87), privy councillor.

p. 188, l. 6: *de Segur*: Louis Philippe, Count de Ségur (1753–1830), ambassador to St Petersburg (1784–9), memoirist.

p. 189, l. 6: *Cobentzel*: Count Ludwig von Cobenzl (1753–1809), Habsburg ambassador to St Petersburg (1779).

p. 189, l. 6: *FitzHerbert*: Alleyne FitzHerbert, the Lord St Helens (1753–1839), diplomat, English ambassador to Russia (1783–8).

p. 190, l. 26: *Paliansky*: Colonel Alexander Ivanovich Polyansky (1721–1818), state counsellor.

p. 192, ll. 3–4: *'dinner of toleration'*: Castéra and Tooke, *The Life of Catherine II*, vol. 3, p. 125.

p. 194, ll. 20–4: *'Madam ... the palace'*: Castéra and Tooke, *The Life of Catherine II*, vol. 3, p. 136.

p. 195, l. 6: *Pallas*: Peter Simon Pallas (1741–1811), professor of natural history at St Petersburg Academy of Sciences (1768–74); among the world's greatest naturalists, he led major expeditions to chart the Russian empire.

p. 198, l. 12: *Constantine*: Grand Duke Constantine Pavlovich (1779–1831).

p. 202, l. 5: *Suvaroff*: Generalissimo Alexander Vasilyevich Suvorov (1730–1800), Russia's greatest general.

p. 202, ll. 5–7: *'And you ... madam'*: Castéra and Tooke, *The Life of Catherine II*, vol. 3, pp. 163, note–164, note.

p. 202, ll. 23–4: *BY THIS...BYZANTIUM*: Castéra and Tooke, *The Life of Catherine II*, vol. 3, p. 165.

p. 203, ll. 3–4: *Miranda*: Francisco de Miranda (1750–1816), Venezuelan revolutionary in Russia to persuade Catherine to intervene in Spain's influence over American colonies.

p. 203, ll. 19–20: *'Do you...Tschesmé'*: Castéra and Tooke, *The Life of Catherine II*, vol. 3, p. 167.

p. 207, l. 18–p. 208, l. 9: *'I am going ... to-morrow'*: Castéra and Tooke, *The Life of Catherine II*, vol. 3, pp. 185–6.

p. 209, l. 18–p. 210, l. 4: *'Perfectly innocent ... Russian empire'*: Castéra and Tooke, *The Life of Catherine II*, vol. 3, pp. 189–90.

p. 210, l. 12: *Sheik Mansour*: Sheikh Mansur (1732–94), Chechen national hero, imam, spread Sufism, fought against Russian expansion, died in Russian prison.

p. 210, ll. 22–3: Pro Deo et Patria ... Pro Deo: 'For God and Country ... For God' (Latin).

p. 213, l. 25–p. 214, l. 2: *'That you ... cannon'*: Castéra and Tooke, *The Life of Catherine II*, vol. 3, p. 212.

p. 219, ll. 6–11: *'What language! ... to do'*: Castéra and Tooke, *The Life of Catherine II*, vol. 3, p. 235.

p. 220, l. 24: *Charles of Hesse*: Prince Charles of Hesse (1744–1836), came to Russia's defense in the Russo-Swedish War (1788–90) as commander-in-chief of the Norwegian army (1772–1814).

p. 223, l. 18: *'What do you cry for?'*: Castéra and Tooke, *The Life of Catherine II*, vol. 3, p. 260, note.

p. 225, l. 4: *O'Brien*: not further identified.

p. 226, ll. 5–13: *'Madam, I ... Catherine'*: Castéra and Tooke, *The Life of Catherine I'*, vol. 3, pp. 271–2.

p. 227, l. 27: Radischeff: In *A Journey from Petersburg to Moscow* (1790), Alexander Radish-chev (1749–1802) attacks serfdom as slavery.

p. 228, l. 12: imprimatur: 'Let it be printed' (Latin), a declaration permitting the publication of a text.

p. 230, l. 1: *Abdul Achmed IV*: Abdul Hamid I (1725–89, r. 1774–89), Sultan of the Ottoman Empire.

p. 230, l. 4: *Selim III*: (1761–1808, r. 1789–1807), Sultan of the Ottoman Empire, reformer.

p. 231, ll. 17–21: *'My friends ... bayonets'*: Castéra and Tooke, *The Life of Catherine II*, vol. 3, p. 287.

p. 232, ll. 5–6: *'Glory to ... in it!'*: Castéra and Tooke, *The Life of Catherine II*, vol. 3, p. 288.

p. 232, l. 14: *One of his mistresses*: Sophie de Witt (1760–1822) married to Józef Witt (*c.* 1779) and Felix Potocki (1798).

p. 233, ll. 7–8: *Roger Damus Langeron*: Count Roger de Damas (1765–1823), colonel, French monarchist, governor of Lyon.

p. 232, l. 22–p. 233, l. 5: *'My brothers ... your feet!'*: Castéra and Tooke, *The Life of Catherine II*, vol. 3, pp. 292–3.

p. 233, ll. 13–19: *'Your countrymen ... your army'*: Castéra and Tooke, *The Life of Catherine II*, vol. 3, pp. 293–4.

p. 233, l. 26: *Sir Charles Whitworth*: Viscount Charles Whitworth (1752–1825), ambassador to St Petersburg (1788–1800).

p. 234, ll. 1–4: *'Sir ... to Constantinople'*: Castéra and Tooke, *The Life of Catherine II*, vol. 3, p. 294.

p. 238, l. 23: *Alexander*: Grand Duke Alexander Pavlovich (1777–1825, r. 1801–25), Alexander I.

p. 242, l. 11: *Plutarch*: Plutarch (46–120), Greek historian, author of *Lives of the Noble Greeks and Romans*, or *Parallel Lives*, which Catherine read.

p. 242, ll. 13–22: *'Think you ... head'*: Hays adds emphasis. Castéra and Tooke, *The Life of Catherine II*, vol. 3, pp. 308–9.

p. 243, l. 19: *Plato Zuboff*: Prince Platon Zubov (1767–1822), last favourite of Catherine (1789–96).

p. 245, ll. 15–17: *'This ... the delinquent'*: Castéra and Tooke, *The Life of Catherine II*, vol. 3, p. 313.

p. 246, l. 17: *Fawkener*: William Fawkener (1750–1811), diplomat, envoy to St Petersburg (1791).

p. 248, l. 26: *Branika*: Alexandra Vasilyevna Branitskaya (Branicka), née Engel'gardt (1754–1838), married (1781), Potemkin's mistress.

p. 251, l. 13–p. 252, l. 4: *'His life ... a character'*: Castéra and Tooke, *The Life of Catherine II*, vol. 3, pp. 333–4.

p. 252, l. 16: *Markoff*: Lieutenant General Evgeny Ivanovich Markov (1769–1828), fought against Poles and Turks.

p. 253, l. 4: *Bulgakoff*: Yakov Ivanovich Bulgakov (1743–1809), diplomat, negotiated treaties to annex Crimea, ambassador to Warsaw (1789–93) during War of the Second Partition (1792).

p. 253, l. 15: *Kosciusko*: Brigadier General Andrzej Tadeusz Bonawentura Kościuszko (1746–1817), fought in American Revolution (1783) and Polish uprising against Prussia and Russia (1794).

p. 253, ll. 20–1: *Frederic William*: Friedrich Wilhelm II, King of Prussia (1744–97, r. 1786–97).

p. 257, l. 6: *Niemchevitch*: Julian Ursyn Niemcewicz (1757–1841), poet, statesman, alternating between participating in Polish rebellions and exile, in Germany, the United States and France.

p. 258, l. 7: *Leopold II*: Archduke of Austria and Grand Duke of Tuscany (1765), then King of Hungary, Croatia, and Bohemia, and Holy Roman Emperor (1747–92, r. 1790–2).

p. 258, ll. 15–16: *'I am … my business'*: Hays adds emphasis. Castéra and Tooke, *The Life of Catherine II*, vol. 3, p. 349.

p. 258, l. 20: *l'Harpe*: César Frédéric de La Harpe (1754–1838), Swiss revolutionary leader, tutor to Grand Dukes Alexander and Constantine (1774–94).

p. 259, l. 3: *Esterhazy*: Count Valentin Ladislas Esterházy de Galántha (1740–1808), author of memoirs.

p. 259, l. 6: Carmagnol *and* Ca Ira: French songs made popular during the French Revolution. Carmagnol, after the Italian town Carmagnola; ça ira, meaning 'it'll be fine'.

p. 260, l. 12: *Gustavus*: Gustav IV Adolf, King of Sweden (1778–1837, r. 1792–1809), refused to marry Alexandra Pavlovna if she did not convert to Lutheranism (1796). He was forced to abdicate in a coup that restored a constitutional monarchy.

p. 260, l. 13: *Mecklenburg*: Louisa Charlotta of Meckenburg-Schwerin (1779–1801), engaged to Gustav IV (1795), married (1797) Augustus, Duke of Saxe-Gotha-Altenburg (1772–1822) and died in childbirth.

p. 261, ll. 14–19: *'No … and admiration'*: See C. F. P. Masson, *Secret Memoirs of the Court of Petersburg: Particularly towards the end of the reign of Catharine II. … Translated from the French*, 1st edn, 2 vols (London: T. N. Longman and O. Rees, 1800), vol. 1, p. 18.

p. 261, l. 23: *Alexandra Paulina*: Grand Duchess Alexandra Pavlovna (1783–1801) married Archduke Joseph of Austria (1799) and died after giving birth in the same week her father was assassinated.

p. 262, ll. 11–12: *'Your majesty is all-powerful'*: Masson, *Secret Memoirs*, vol. 1, p. 25.

p. 263, ll. 12–13: *'No, no … them'*: Masson, *Secret Memoirs*, vol. 1, p. 30.

p. 265, ll. 16–17: *Louisa of Baden Durlach*: Princess Louise Maria of Baden (1779–1826), married Alexander I (1793) and became Empress Elizaveta Alekseyevna.

p. 265, l. 19: *Saxe-Coburg*: Princess Juliane Henriette Ulrike of Sachsen-Koburg-Saalfeld (1781–1860) married Grand Duke Constantine Pavlovich (1796); she travelled to Russia with two sisters, Sophie Fredericka Caroline Louise (1778–1835) and Antoinette Ernestine Amalie (1779–1824).

p. 266, ll. 10–20: *The hope … not immortal*: These two sentences added. The story of her death, which follows, is from Masson, *Secret Memoirs*, 1st edn, vol. 1, pp. 62–70.

p. 266, l. 25: *Moreau*: In the Napoleonic Wars, General Jean Victor Marie Moreau (1763–1813) led the French army of the Rhine and Mosel in both successful attacks and, before the Austrians, a retreat (1795).

p. 267, ll. 1–4: *'I hasten … drubbing'*: Masson, *Secret Memoirs*, 1st edn, vol. 1, p. 62, note.

p. 270, l. 14–p. 271, l. 10: *She still retained ... no supper*: This paragraph interpolates some phrases from Masson, who is negative about Catherine's appearance, with the more positive assessments of Castéra-Tooke.

p. 270, l. 28–p. 271, l. 1: 'the Semiramis of the North': Masson, *Secret Memoirs*, 1st edn, vol. 1, p. 77. Title designated to an especially skillful female ruler, after the legendary Princess Semiramis of Assyria.

p. 273, l. 12: Locke: John Locke (1632–1704), philosopher who argued for the mind as a *tabula rasa* in *An Essay Concerning Human Understanding* (1690).

p. 273, l. 13: Rousseau: Jean-Jacques Rousseau (1712–78), philosopher who argued for education in nature and activity in *Emile, or on Education* (1762).

p. 274, l. 1: *LADY ELIZABETH CAREW*: Lady Elizabeth Cary (not commonly used alternative is Carew) (*née* Tanfield), Viscountess Falkland (*c.* 1585–1639) was the daughter of Lawrence Tanfield (*c.* 1551–1625), lawyer, and his wife Elizabeth Symonds (d. 1629), born at Burford Priory, Oxfordshire. Hays most likely took 'Carew' from G. Langbaine, *An Account of the English Dramatick Poets.* (Oxford: L. L. for G. West and H. Clements, 1691), p. 43. Not to be confused with literary patron Elizabeth Carey [Carew], Baroness Hunsdon (*née* Spencer), whose second married name was Lady Eure (1552–1618).

p. 274, ll. 2–3: *a dramatic piece ... Jewry*: *The Tragedy of Mariam, the Fair Queen of Jewry* (*c.* 1604), the first English play by a woman published under her own name. She was also the first woman writer of an English history, *The History of the Life, Reign and Death of Edward II* (1680); and the first to translate and publish a Catholic polemic, J. D. du Perron (Cardinal of Evreux), *Reply to His Highness the King of Great Britain* (1620).

p. 274, l. 3: *Mariam*: A member of the Jewish Hasmonean dynasty, wife of King Herod.

p. 274, l. 5: *Oldys ... Langbaine*: William Oldys (1696–1761), antiquarian, annotated his copy of Langbaine's *An Account of the English Dramatic Poets.*

p. 274, l. 6: *Henry Carew*: Henry Cary, Viscount Falkland (*c.* 1575–1633). There were eleven children from the marriage, which became acrimonious over education of the children and their religious differences; he was Protestant, she Catholic. They separated 1625–30.

p. 274, ll. 7–8: *dedicated to Lady Carew*: See J. Davies, *The Muses Sacrifice, or Divine Meditations* (London: T. S., 1612) and W. Sheares, *The Works of John Marston, Being Tragedies and Comedies, Collected into One Volume* (London: 1633). Henry John Todd's *The Works of Edmund Spenser* (London: F. C. and J. Rivington, T. Payne, Cadell and Davies, and R. H. Evans, 1805), vol. 1, p. clxxiii says several works were 'dedicated to Lady Carey' including Spenser's *The Faerie Queene* (1590) and Thomas Nash's *Christ's Tears over Jerusalem* (1593), but these refer to Lady Elizabeth Carey, Baroness Hunsdon.

p. 274, l. 9: *Susannah Centlivre*: Susanna Centlivre [née Freeman; other alleged married names Rawkins, Carrol or Carroll and Fox]; also spelled *'Cent Livre'* ('hundred-book' or 'hundred-coin' in French).

p. 274, l. 10: *daughter of Mr. Freeman*: This and most details of her parentage and early life of Centlivre as reported by Hays are considered highly dubious by modern scholars.

p. 274, l. 16: *her mother*: not further identified.

p. 274, l. 16: *Mr. Markham*: not further identified.

p. 274, ll. 11–12: *born in 1667*: Her birthdate is unknown.

p. 275, ll. 12–13: *an air of romance*: Many of the details of her life appear to be fictitious.

p. 275, l. 17: *Anthony Hammond*: The poet, pamphleteer and editor Anthony Hammond (1668–1738) also published in his *Miscellany* poems by Mary Wortley Montagu. See C. Gerrard, 'Eighteenth Century Women Poets', in M. O'Neill (ed.), *The Cambridge History of English Poetry* (Cambridge: Cambridge University Press, 2010), pp. 358–78, on p. 371.

Centlivre contributed poems to Hammond's *New Miscellany* (1720). See Roger Lonsdale (ed.), *Eighteenth-Century Women Poets* (Oxford: Oxford University Press, 1898), p. 74.

p. 275, l. 18: *celebrated author ... elegies*: James Hammond's *Love Elegies* were published posthumously. See J. Hammond, *Love Elegies, Written in 1732* (London: G. Hawkins, 1772), p. iii.

p. 276, l. 13: *a nephew of sir Stephen Fox*: Sir Stephen Fox (1627–1716). His nephew is not further identified.

p. 276, ll. 16–17: *an officer of the name of Carrol*: Little is known of Centlivre's second 'husband', and no record of either marriage exists. She did write under the name Carrol early in her career, as Hays reports.

p. 277, l. 4: *Moliere*: Jean-Baptiste Poquelin (*c.* 1622–73), known by his stage name Molière, French playwright.

p. 277, l. 11: *Le Dissipateur*: by Philippe Néricault Destouches (1680–1754).

p. 277, l. 12: *Mr. Rowe*: Nicholas Rowe (1674–1718), poet and playwright.

p. 277, l. 20: *Lee's 'Rival Queens'*: *The Rival Queens* (1677), a tragedy by Nathaniel Lee (1645–92).

p. 277, l. 21: *Joseph Centlivre*: the royal chef for Queen Anne.

p. 277, l. 28: *duke of Grafton*: In 1706, this title was held by Charles FitzRoy, second Duke of Grafton (1683–1757): see *ODNB*.

p. 278, ll. 5–6: *Mr. Wilkes*: Apparently Thomas Wilkes, author of *A General View of the Stage* (1759).

p. 278, l. 16: *duke of Portland*: William Bentinck (1649–1709), Earl of Portland.

p. 278, l. 21: *Mr. Mottley*: John Mottley (1692–1750), author of *A Complete List of All the English Dramatic Poets* (1747).

p. 279, l. 4: *Mr. Farquhar*: George Farquhar (1676–1707), playwright.

p. 279, l. 9: *Mr. Garrick*: David Garrick (1717–79), preeminent British actor of his time and manager of Drury Lane Theatre (1747–76).

p. 279, ll. 19–20: *Secretary Craggs*: James Cragg the younger (1657–1721), Secretary of State.

p. 280, l. 8: *Mrs. Behn*: see M. Hays, *Female Biography*, 1st edn, 6 vols (London: R. Phillips, 1803), vol. 1, pp. 273–90.

p. 280, l. 11: *Richard Steele*: Sir Richard Steele (1672–1729), publisher of the *Spectator* and the *Tatler*.

p. 280, l. 12: *Dr. Sewell*: George Sewell (1687–1726), author and physician.

p. 280, ll. 12–13: *Eustace and Budgel*: Evidently a typographical error, this suggests the Irish MP and *Spectator* contributor Eustace Budgell (1686–1737). Centlivre received a diamond ring from Budgell after dedicating her play *The Cruel Gift* to him. See S. Staves, *A Literary History of Women's Writing in Britain, 1660–1789* (Cambridge: Cambridge University Press, 2006), p. 163.

p. 280, l. 15: *Mr. Pope*: Alexander Pope (1688–1744), poet and political enemy of Centlivre.

p. 280, l. 16: *Homer*: epic poet of ancient Greece.

p. 280, ll. 26–7: *zeal for ... Hanover*: Politically advantageous in 1790, especially as Centlivre is, at least in Hays's depiction, the daughter of a Dissenter. Hays was a radical Dissenter herself.

p. 281, l. 12: *Boyer*: Abel Boyer (1667–1729), lexicographer and journalist; published Centlivre's early writings in *Letters of Wit, Politicks and Morality* (1701).

p. 281, l. 16: *Dr. Thomas Augustus Arne*: (1710–78), leading British composer, notably of incidental theatre music, masques and operas.

p. 281, ll. 16–17: *the daughter of an upholsterer*: Thomas Arne (b. *c.* 1682, d. 1736) and his wife Anne Wheeler (d. 1757), a midwife. Susannah was born 14 February 1714.

p. 281, ll. 17–18: *first appeared on the stage*: 13 March 1732 in the title role in *Amelia*, an opera by Henry Carey and J. F. Lampe.

p. 281, l. 23: *Mr. Hill ... Drury Lane*: Aaron Hill (1685–1750), playwright, acting theorist.

p. 281, l. 23: *first representation*: *Zara* was first performed 12 January 1736.

p. 282, ll. 16–17: *Theophilus Cibber*: (1703–58), actor, playwright, theatre manager.

p. 282, l. 18–p. 283, l. 8: *The indiscretion ... prison*: Based on *Biographia Dramatica* entry for Theophilus Cibber (new edn 1782, 1:87).

p. 282, ll. 20–1: *they ... continent*: Theophilus fled to France alone to escape his creditors.

p. 282, ll. 22–3: *a young man of fortune*: William Sloper (*c.*1707–89), a wealthy country gentleman, whose relationship with Susannah lasted until her death.

p. 282, l. 24: *connived at his own dishonor*: This love triangle resulted in a notorious and well-publicized trial for criminal conversation in which Theophilus was alleged to have encouraged the affair for his financial benefit and then prosecuted Sloper for damages. An account of the trial was published in 1739.

p. 283, ll. 19–20: *'The Provoked Wife'*: 1697, by Sir John Vanbrugh (1664–1726). Susannah first played Lady Brute on 3 November 1742. Her life resembled that of her character.

p. 284, l. 3: *'stomach worms'*: Her modern biographer speculates that she may have 'suffered from gall-bladder disease, ulcers, or colitis': see M. Nash, *The Provoked Wife: The Life and Times of Susannah Cibber* (London: Hutchinson, 1977), p. 319.

p. 284, l. 6: *Garrick*: David Garrick (1717–79), preeminent British actor of his time who frequently performed with Susannah; co-patentee and manager of Drury Lane Theatre (1747–76).

p. 284, ll. 8–9: *'The Oracle'*: pastoral afterpiece translated and adapted by Susannah from *L'Oracle* (1740) by Germain-François Poullain de Saint-Foix (1698–1776) for her benefit performance on 17 March 1752 at Covent Garden Theatre; she also played the central female character.

p. 284, l. 13: *her father*: Henry Chandler (d. 1717), a dissenting minister.

p. 285, l. 1: *Herbert's Poems*: Hays stresses Chandler's reading of George Herbert (1593–1633), Church of England clergyman and poet, rather than her preference for the Roman poet Horace (Quintus Horatius Flaccus, 65 BC–8 BC). Chandler was however greatly influenced by the Horatian models offered by her contemporary Alexander Pope (1688–1744).

p. 285, l. 5: *Virgil*: Virgil (Publius Vergilius Maro, 70 BC–19 BC), Roman poet.

p. 285, l. 5: *Homer*: the epic poet of ancient Greece.

p. 285, l. 7: *Her poem upon the* Bath: Chandler's poem, *A Description of Bath: a Poem. In a Letter to a Friend* (London: J. Roberts, J. Jackson, J. Gray, and J. Leake and S. Lobb, 1733), was published anonymously in the first edition and went through eight editions by 1767.

p. 285, l. 11: *Her figure was deformed*: Samuel Chandler (1693–1745), her brother, writes in his brief biography of Mary that she was 'grown, by an accident in her childhood, very irregular in her body': see R. Shiells, 'Mrs Mary Chandler', in T. Cibber (ed.), *The Lives of the Poets of Great Britain and Ireland*, 5 vols (London: R. Griffiths, 1753), vol. 5, pp. 345–54.

p. 285, l. 19–p. 286, l. 5: *'Sweet solitude ... voice of God'*: published posthumously in Samuel Chandler, 'Mrs Mary Chandler', in *Lives of the Poets*, vol. 5, p. 347. The poem was reprinted in *Biographium Faemineum*, vol. 1, pp. 127–8.

p. 286, l. 8: *Mrs. Chapone*: Hester Chapone [née Mulso] (1727–1801), daughter of Thomas Mulso (1695–1763), gentleman farmer.

p. 286, ll. 10–11: *married life ... not to have been happy*: Hester Mulso married John Chapone (*c.* 1728–61), law student, in 1760. This assertion follows Anna Letitia Barbauld's 'Memoirs of Mrs Chapone', *Monthly Magazine*, 13:83 (February 1802), pp. 39–40; Barbauld's evidence for it is unknown.

p. 287, ll. 1–2: *her friend Mrs. Carter*: Elizabeth Carter (1717–1806), poet, translator, writer and member of the Bluestocking circle. Hays curiously omits Barbauld's tribute to Chapone, Elizabeth Montagu (*née* Robinson, 1718–1800) and 'another lady' (possibly Elizabeth Carter): neither Carter nor Montagu, author and wealthy patron and hostess of the Bluestockings, appear in *Female Biography*.

p. 287, ll. 2–3: *'Letters on the Improvement of the Mind'*: *Letters on the Improvement of the Mind* (London: J. Walter, 1773) was reprinted fifty-seven times between 1773 and 1851.

p. 287, ll. 7–26: *'It is distinguished ... the preacher'*: see Barbauld, 'Memoirs of Mrs Chapone', p. 39.

p. 287, ll. 21–2: *another widely circulated publication*: J. Fordyce, *Sermons to Young Women*, 2 vols (London: A. Millar and T. Cadell, 1765) went through thirteen editions by 1802.

p. 287, l. 27: *Mrs. Barbauld*: Anna Letitia (Laetitia) Barbauld (*née* Aikin, 1743–1825), leading dissenting writer, poet, essayist and educationalist: see note to p. 286, ll. 10–11, above.

p. 288, ll. 5–6: *the loss of a beloved niece*: Chapone addressed her *Letters* to Jane Mulso (1758–99), the daughter of her brother John Mulso (1721–91), Anglican clergyman and prebendary of Winchester and Salisbury Cathedrals.

p. 288, l. 15: *learned Greek lady*: Hays uses the term 'lady' to describe Charixena twice, the second time being one of the few variations in wording from Charixena's entry in *Biographium Faemineum*. This alteration gives Charixena a status and respect she was not accorded in antiquity. The tenth-century encyclopedia *Suda* (s.v.) describes her as a courtesan, and as simple and stupid: see A. Adler, *Suidae Lexicon*, 4 vols (Leipzig: Teubner, 1967–71). The *Etymologicum Magnum*, a Greek lexical encyclopedia dated to about AD 1150, states that she was remembered as a flute player, composer and lyric poet.

p. 288, ll. 15–16: *author of several compositions*: None of her work has survived. Her music was known enough to be mocked in comic plays of the fifth century BC; it was described as rotten and old-fashioned by the comic writer Theopompus (see fragment 50, T. Kock, *Comicorum Atticorum fragmenta* (Leipzig: Teubner, 1880), vol. 1). Hesychius notes that some sources recorded that she wrote love songs (Hesychius, *Lexicon*, E 5413 on *Charixenes*).

p. 288, l. 17: *'Crumata'*: We do not have the title of any work by Charixena; 'Crumata,' a transliteration of the Greek word 'Kroumata', meaning melodies, is used to describe her work by Eustathius, who calls her 'a composer of melodies' (*On the Iliad*, 2.711).

p. 288, l. 18: *mentioned by Aristophanes*: Aristophanes (*Ecclesiazusae*, 943) and his fellow comic poet Cratinus (see fragment 135, Kock), both suggested that 'things of Charixena's day' had already become a proverbial expression for old-fashioned music.

p. 288, l. 19: Plutarch: Charixena is not mentioned by Plutarch.

p. 288, l. 22: *Lacedemon*: In antiquity the land around the city of Sparta was called Laconia; hence Sparta was commonly called Lacedaemon or Lacedaemonia.

p. 288, l. 22: *Leonidas her father*: Leonidas II was guardian to the child-king, Areus II, after whose death he took the throne. He reigned from *c.* 251–242 BC to *c.* 241–235 BC. Leonidas's wife, Cratisleia, may have been Chelonis's mother, but this is not explicitly stated by Plutarch.

p. 289, l. 1: *deposed by a faction*: *Biographium Faemineum* (and therefore Hays's) account simplifies the political events that underpin this story. Leonidas opposed controversial economic reforms of his fellow king, Agis IV, designed to redistribute wealth in Sparta. Leonidas was charged under an archaic law that forbid a king from having a child by a foreign woman and emigrating from Sparta (*Life of Agis*, 11). It was unusual to depose a king.

p. 289, l. 2: *Cleombrotus her husband*: Cleombrotus's marriage to the daughter of a king indicates he was of high status. Plutarch tells us he was of royal birth (*Life of Agis*, 11).

p. 289, ll. 4–5: *a temple in which he had taken sanctuary*: Leonidas took refuge in the small temple of Athena Chalcioecus, 'Athena of the Bronze House', on the Spartan acropolis.

p. 289, ll. 5–6: *In this retreat ... suppliants*: The story in Plutarch suggests that Chelonis was reacting against the wrong done to her father. She resented the actions of her husband who had usurped the throne (Plutarch, *Life of Agis*, 17). The *Biographium Faemineum* embellishes the story at this point (Bayle's account in his *Historical and Critical Dictionary*, is similar). Hays follows this lead.

p. 289, l. 8: *Tagea*: Tegea was a Greek polis in Arcadia, north of Laconia.

p. 289, l. 9: *Chelonis accompanied him*: The *Biographium Faemineum* (and so Hays) errs in stating that Chelonis accompanied her father into exile. Plutarch states explicitly that she mourned for him when he was in exile, not that she went with him.

p. 289, l. 14: *refuge in the sanctuary*: the shrine of Poseidon, known as a sanctuary for runaway helots; located at Taenarum on the south-west coast of Laconia.

p. 289, l. 28: *resolute refusal*: While Hays and the *Biographium Faemineum* report Chelonis's speech to her father, Bayle reproduces it from Plutarch (*Life of Agis*, 17).

p. 290, ll. 7–8: *Gustavus Adolphus*: Gustavus II Adolphus Wasa (1594–1632), King of Sweden and Protestant commander during the Thirty Years' War; killed at the battle of Lützen.

p. 290, ll. 8–9: *Maria Eleonora of Brandenburg*: German princess and Queen of Sweden (1599–1655).

p. 290, l. 19: *Catherine his sister*: Catharina of Pfalz-Zweibrücken (1615–51), was not King Gustavus Adolphus' sister, but his first cousin.

p. 291, l. 4: *Calmar*: town in south-east Sweden.

p. 292, l. 17: *Larfsen*: probably Larsson, not further identified.

p. 293, ll. 17–18: *Thucydides, Polybius, and Tacitus*: Historians of the Roman empire, models of history writing. Christina also studied Latin, Hebrew and Greek and her Greek readings were advanced, including neo-Platonic texts by Proclus, Hermias and Olympiodorus. She read the Church fathers, but also sought out clandestine manuscripts such as the French philosopher of State Jean Bodin's 'Colloquium of the Seven on the Secrets of the Sublime' (1583).

p. 293, l. 21: *Neymar, Manier, Wrangel, and Torstenson*: Neymar, probably a German general, not further identified; 'Manier' ought to be Johan Banér; Carl Gustaf Wrangel and Lennart Torstensson, Swedish generals in the Thirty Years' War.

p. 294, ll. 1–2: *the kings of Portugal, of Spain, and of the Romans*: Joao IV (1603–56), King of Portugal; Philip IV (1605–65), King of Spain and the Romans.

p. 294, ll. 2–3: *don John of Austria*: don John of Austria the younger (1629–79), Spanish general and political figure.

p. 294, l. 3: *Sigismond of Rakocci*: Sigismund Rakoczi, Prince of Siebenbürgen, younger brother to Georg II Rakoszy (1621–65), King of Hungary.

p. 294, l. 4: *Stanislaus, king of Poland*: most likely Stanislaus's son, Wladislaw IV Wasa (1632–48).

p. 294, ll. 4–5: *John Cassimir*: Johan II Cassimir (1609–72), King of Poland and Lithuania.

p. 294, l. 5: *the prince of Denmark*: Fredrik III (1609–70).

p. 294, ll. 5–6: *the elector Palatine*: Charles II Louis (1617–80).

p. 294, l. 6: *the elector of Brandenburg*: Fredrik Willhelm (1620–88).

p. 294, l. 7: *Charles Gustavus*: of the Palatinate-Zweibrücken. Swedish King (1654–60) and Christina's cousin and successor

p. 294, l. 22: *Nero*: Roman emperor known for his cruelty and insanity, *Augustus*, Roman emperor known for establishing peace throughout the Empire.

p. 295, l. 11: *Baron Brahi*: Per Brahe the younger, governor of Finland, then the eastern realm of Sweden.

p. 296, ll. 4–5: *Oxenstiern*: Gustaf Oxenstierna, peace negotiator in the Thirty Years' War, son of Axel Oxenstierna, chancellor of the realm.

p. 296, l. 9: *Salvius*: Johan Adler Salvius, peace negotiator in the Thirty Years' War.

p. 297, ll. 11–15: *Grotius, Paschal, Bochart, Descartes, Cassendi, Saumaise, Nande, Vossius, Heinsius, Meiborn, Sauvery, Menage, Lucas, Holstenius, Lambecius, Bayle, Fillicaca, and madame Dacier*: Hugo Grotius, Dutch scholar of international jurisprudence; Blaise Pascal, French philosopher, author of *Pensées*, sent Christina his computing machine; Samuel Bochart, French Hebrew scholar; René Descartes, rationalist philosopher, author of *Meditationes de prima philosophia*; Pierre Gassendi, French atomist philosopher; Claude Saumaise, French polymath and Hebrew scholar; Gabriel Naudé, French historian; Isaac Vossius, Dutch Greek scholar; Nicholas Heinsius, Dutch Greek scholar; Marcus Meibom, German humanist and historian of music; Sauvery, not further identified; Gilles Ménage, French humanist; Lucas Holstenius (one person, not two), German humanist; Petrus Lambecius, German Greek scholar; Pierre Bayle, French sceptic and author of *Dictionnaire historique et critique*; Vinzenso da Filicaia, Italian poet; Anne Dacier, Greek scholar (1654–1720), translator of *Florus*, Eutropius, Aristofanes, Terentius and later the *Illiad* and the *Odyssé*.

p. 297, ll. 18–19: *queen[] ... of Sheba*: Queen of Ethiopia or Jemen of the tenth century BC, travelled to King Solomon's court in Jerusalem: see First Kings 10:1–13.

p. 297, ll. 20–1: *Illa docenda ... doceanteur, eunt*: 'She sought knowledge of Solomon's tree, everywhere those who counted as learned walked' (Latin).

p. 298, l. 9: *Michon*: Pierre Michon Bourdelot, French physician and courtier, known for his freethinking.

p. 299, ll. 5–6: *Magnus de la Gardie*: Magnus Gabriel de la Gardie, courtier on Embassy to Paris, later rose to be Swedish chancellor of the realm.

p. 299, l. 8: *Madame de Motteville*: Madame Francoise de Motteville, author of *Memoires de la Fronde*, on the French uprising against Mazarin in the 1650s.

p. 299, l. 23: *Scudery*: Paul Scudery, French poet whose poem *Alaric*, alluded to the Ostrogothic king of the fifth century who conquered Rome; Swedes were falsely regarded as descendants of the Ostrogoths.

p. 300, l. 10: *admiral Herring*: Claes Flemming, Swedish admiral.

p. 300, ll. 12–13: *Anthony Steinberg*: Anton von Steinberg, courtier.

p. 301, l. 10: *M. Canut*: Pierre Chanut, French ambassador to Sweden (1645–54).

p. 302, ll. 1–2: *prince of Condé*: Louis II de Condé, Prince and cousin to the French king, Louis XIV. He was a general and leader of the 1652 Fronde uprising in Paris who subsequently fled to the Spanish Netherlands.

p. 302, ll. 9–10: *abdication ... subject of speculation*: Christina invited several scholars and famously Descartes gave her lessons in 1650. It is debated to what degree their conversations influenced her turn to Catholicism, considering that Christina, rather than becoming Cartesian, developed Neoplatonic and classicist leanings.

p. 302, l. 13: *brook which separates the countries*: Scania in modern southern Sweden was first taken from the Danes in 1658.

p. 303, l. 9: *Anthony Macedo*: Antonio Macedo, Portuguese Jesuit.

p. 303, ll. 9–10: *John IV*: Joao IV, King of Portugal.

p. 303, l. 21: *Francis Maline*: Francesco Malines, Italian Jesuit.

p. 303, l. 22: *Paul Causatus*: Paolo Casati, Italian Jesuit at the Collegio Romano.

p. 304, l. 16: *arch-duke Leopold*: Leopold Wilhelm of Austria, governor of the Spanish Netherlands.

p. 305, l. 13: *St. Bridget*: Birgitta, thirteenth- century Swedish mystic and author of *Revelaciones*; founder of the Birgittine monastic order.

p. 305, l. 27: *Cromwell*: Oliver Cromwell, Lord Protector of England, leader of the Republican uprising in the Civil War.

p. 306, l. 26: *Fronde*: uprising against the rule of Cardinal Mazarin in Paris and other parts of France in the 1650s.

p. 307, l. 7: *Lewis XIV*: Louis XIV (1638–1715), French king known as Louis the Great or the Sun King.

p. 307, ll. 8–9: *madamoiselle de Mancini*: Marie Mancini (1639–1715), author of *Memoires*, (1677), niece of Cardinal Mazarin, the de facto regent of France.

p. 307, l. 13: *Monaldeschi*: Giavanni Rinaldo Monaldeschi. Christina executed this Italian marquise in 1657 because he had betrayed her plan with the Dukes of Modena and Sienna, in a French supported manoeuvre, to attack Naples and be made vice regent, replacing the Spanish government there. The idea of settling in southern Italy was already on her mind at the abdication: see C. Weibull, *Drottning Christina and Monaldescho* (Stockholm, 1936).

p. 307, l. 16: *Père Bell*: Father le Bel, French priest.

p. 307, ll. 17–18: *Fontainebleau*: summer palace of the King of France.

p. 308, l. 2: *Cerfs*: Deer gallery, a hall decorated with deer horns.

p. 311, ll. 7–8: *chief of the three men*: Ludovico Santinelli, Christina's chief courtier, after the execution he was forced to leave her court.

p. 314, l. 12: *musician*: not further identified.

p. 314, l. 13: *duke of Savoy*: Charles Emanuel II of Savoy (1638–75).

p. 314, ll. 19–20: *the revocation of the edict of Nantes*: The Revocation of 1685 forced huge numbers of French Huguenot Protestants to leave France.

p. 315, l. 6: *chemistry*: Christina practised alchemy, had her own laboratory and a library of over 300 alchemy books and some 30 alchemical manuscripts.

p. 316, ll. 11–12: *that of Poland*: Christina was a candidate in the Polish election of 1669. In spite of her campaign, however, a Polish nobleman was chosen to be king and ruler.

p. 316, l. 16: *king of Prussia*: Fredrik Wilhelm (1620–88).

p. 316, l. 21: *LADY MARY CHUDLEIGH*: Mary, Lady Chudleigh is the correct style.

p. 316, ll. 22–3: *daughter of Richard Lee ... August, 1656*: The eldest child of Richard Lee (1625–1704) of Winslade, Devon, and Mary Sydenham (1632–1701).

p. 316, ll. 24–5: *education ... but a passion for books*: Although unnamed, Hays's source was George Ballard whose papers in the Bodleian Library, Oxford, include notes stating that Chudleigh was 'ever from her infancy addicted to reading and [had] a natural genius for poetry': see Ballard MS 74 Bodleian Library, f. 301r.

p. 317, ll. 5–6: *Sir George Chudleigh*: She married Sir George Chudleigh, second Baronet (1612–91), in 1674. They had six children but only two, George and Thomas, survived into adulthood.

p. 317, ll. 8–10: *daughter ... Lucinia and Marissa*: Daughter Eliza died in 1701/2 and her illness was described in this poem (properly titled 'On the Death of my dear Daughter Eliza Maria Chudleigh: A Dialogue between Lucinda and Marissa') and another, 'To the Learn'd and Ingenious Dr. Musgrave of Exeter', both published in *Poems on Several Occasions* (London: Bernard Lintott, 1703), pp. 77–81, pp. 94–9. It was republished 1709, 1713 and 1722.

p. 317, ll. 11–17: '*The Ladies ...* ' ... *several times republished*: *The Ladies Defence or, The Bride-Woman's Counsellor Answer'd* (London: J. Deeve, 1701; republished 1709) was a response to a 1699 wedding sermon by Minister John Sprint of Sherborne that advocated total submission of wives.

p. 317, ll. 22–3: *princess Sophia ... of Brunswic*: Chudleigh dedicated *Essays upon Several Subjects in Prose and Verse* (London: R. Bonwicke, 1710) to Sophia, Electress of Hanover (1630–1714), widow of Ernest Augustus, Elector of Brunswick-Lüneburg, and mother of George I of Great Britain. The brief correspondence between Princess Sophia and Chudleigh is preserved in Stowe 223 British Library MS f. 398 and Stowe f. 224 British Library MS, f. 1 (M. Ezell, *ODNB*).

p. 318, ll. 5–6: '*The Song of The Three Children, paraphrased*': an apocryphal addition to Daniel 3:23–34, a song praising the Lord by one of the young men cast into the fiery furnace for refusing to worship idols.

p. 318, l. 14: *left in manuscript*: see Ballard, family memoir in Ballard 74, MS Oxford, Bodleian Library.

p. 318, ll. 19–21: *Wharton's poems ... Mr. Norris*: some of Chudleigh's correspondence was published in *The Poetical Works of Philip Late Duke of Wharton*, 2nd edn, 2 vols (London: William Warner, 1731), vol. 2, p. 144. Corinna was the pen-name of poet and novelist Elizabeth Thomas (1675–1731) who published their correspondence in *Pylades and Corinna* (1731/2). John Norris (1657–1712) was an Anglican minister and philosopher closely associated with Mary Astell.

p. 319, ll. 5–6: '*Defence of the Ladies*': *The Ladies Defence*.

p. 319, ll. 11–22: '*Yours be the fame ... effects partake,*' *&c.*: from *The Ladies Defence*, p. 18.

p. 320, l. 2: *MARGARET CLEMENT*: alternative is Clements, née Gigs or Giggs (1508–70).

p. 320, l. 2: *niece*: Hays's source is not identified; contemporary sources refer to Clement only as More's kinswoman.

p. 320, ll. 2–3: *sir Thomas More*: (1478–1535), Lord Chancellor of England (1529–32). An opponent of the Protestant Reformation, he was tried for treason and beheaded.

p. 320, l. 4: *his daughters*: Margaret More Roper (1505–44; see Hays, *Female Biography*, vol. 6, pp. 90–102), Elizabeth Dancy (b. *c.* 1498; see Hays, *Female Biography*, vol. 4, pp. 23–4) and Cicely (b. *c.* 1501; see Cecilia Heron, Hays, *Female Biography*, vol. 4, p. 434).

p. 320, l. 6: *Erasmus*: Desiderius Erasmus (1466–1536), Dutch humanist theologian.

p. 320, ll. 8–9: *Mr. More ... Thomas*: biography of Sir Thomas More written by his great grandson Cresacre More (1572–1649), C. More, *The Life and Death of Sir Thomas More, Lord High Chancellour of England* (Douai: B. Belliere, *c.* 1631).

p. 320, ll. 19–20: *John Clement*: (d. 1572), tutor to More's children in Latin and Greek; married Margaret Clement *c.* 1530.

p. 320, l. 21: *John Leland*: (*c.* 1506–52), Henry VIII's chaplain and librarian.

p. 320, ll. 21–2: *Latin epithalamium*: not identified.

p. 320, l. 22: *Winefrid Clement*: Winifred Clement (1526–53). Married William Rastell (1508–65), Sir Thomas More's nephew.

p. 320, l. 23: *the fruit of this union*: she bore eleven children including Thomas; Dorothy who became a Poor Claire; and Margaret, who became Prioress of St Ursula and St Monica's in Louvain, Belgium. See A. W. Reed, 'John Clement and His Books', *The Library*, VI (1926), 4th series, pp. 329–39, on p. 332 and Sr E. Shirley, 'The Life of our Rev. Old Mother Margaret Clement' in J. Morris (ed.), *The Troubles of our Catholic Forefathers: Related by Themselves* (London: Burns and Oates, 1872), pp. 27–56, on p. 27.

p. 321, ll. 4–5: *Mechlin, in Brabant*: Mechelen, a city in Flanders.

p. 321, l. 11: *Cleobule*: Plutarch tells us that her father called her Eumetis ('Clever') (*Dinner of the Seven Wise Men*, 148D). Despite her fame, there is little secure biography for her. Anecdotes about her mixing with other famous sages are later inventions, and contradictions in the essential details lead to some doubt that she actually existed.

p. 321, l. 12: *prince of Lindus*: He was considered one of the seven wise men of antiquity: Plutarch calls him the tyrant of Lindos (*On the E at Delphi*, 3), while Clement of Alexandria (*Stromata*, iv. 19) calls him a monarch. Clobulina was thought to have been a younger contemporary of Thales (Plutarch, *Dinner of the Seven Wise Men*, 3), or the mother of Thales (Diogenes Laertius, *Life of Thales*, 1.22). The link to Thales dates her to his lifetime (*c.* 625–545 BC).

p. 321, l. 12: *Lindus*: a Greek city on Rhodes considered Cleobule's hometown: see Athenaeus, 10.448b and Diogenes Laertius, 1.89.

p. 321, ll. 12–13: *celebrated among the ancients*: Cleobulina was well known enough in the fifth and fourth centuries BC to appear as a character in popular comedies. We know of plays by two comedians (Cratinus and Alexis) called *The Cleobulinas* (Cleobulina in the plural), suggesting the choruses were women portraying 'Cleobulina'.

p. 321, l. 14: *riddles*: Riddles were popular after-dinner entertainments in ancient Greece and received scholarly attention (Aristotle, *Poetics*, 1458 A.22). A corpus of riddles attributed to Cleobulina existed in antiquity (Athenaeus, 10.448b), although how much of this consisted of pseudonymous work we do not know. Three riddles attributed to her remain: for translations see I. M. Plant, *Women Writers of Ancient Greece and Rome* (London: Equinox, & Norman: University of Oklahoma Press, 2004), p. 31. Plutarch suggests that writings attributed to Cleobulina should be classed amongst those of the wise and good, suitable for a woman to learn. After learning them, any woman would give joy to her family and be admired by other women (Plutarch, *Conjugal Praecepts*, 48).

p. 321, l. 17: *Ptolemy Auletes*: Ptolemy XII Neos Dionysus (Auletes: 'Fluteplayer'), Cleopatra's father, became ruler of Egypt in 80 BC. He was part of a Macedonian dynasty that had ruled the country after Alexander the Great's death in 323 BC. Cleopatra succeeded her father after his death in 51 BC.

p. 321, ll. 17–18: *who reigned in Egypt fifty-one years before the Christian æra*: While a close gloss of the *Biographium Fæmineum*, vol. 1, p. 138, Hays here introduces an obscurity: Auletes died in 51 BC.

p. 321, ll. 19–20: *his eldest son and daughter*: A reference to Ptolemy XIII and Cleopatra. Hays's sources seem unaware of her eldest half-sister, Berenice, who was executed by their father in 55 BC.

p. 322, ll. 2–3: *seventeen years of age*: Hays here follows the *Biographium Fæmineum*; in fact, she was probably eighteen or nineteen.

p. 322, l. 3: *her brother*: Ptolemy XIII (b. 61 BC). Contemporary documents indicate that, for a time, Cleopatra expelled him and ruled alone.

p. 322, l. 4: *by the will of her father*: The earliest source for this will is Caesar's *Civil Wars*, 3.108.

p. 322, l. 6: *Posthinus, the eunuch*: Poth(e)inus was a guardian of Ptolemy XIII and the regent of the Ptolemaic kingdom.

p. 322, ll. 6–7: *Achillas*: Ptolemy XIII's 'prefect' who commanded the Egyptian army against Caesar.

p. 322, ll. 7–8: *Theodotus*: a rhetorician of Samos or Chios.

p. 322, ll. 11–12: *raised a force ... Pompey*: Gnaeus Pompeius Magnus ('Pompey the Great') was born in 106 BC. Aid was delivered by Cleopatra and Ptolemy.

p. 322, ll. 12–13: *disputes ... Caesar*: Pompey led the Republic's forces in the civil war which began with Caesar's crossing of the Rubicon in 49 BC.

p. 322, l. 14: *procured a decree*: Pompey's action against the young Cleopatra is known only from the Roman poet Lucan (*The Civil War*, 5. 58–64; 8.448).

p. 322, ll. 16–17: *battle of Pharsalia*: Pompey's defeat at the battle of Pharsalus, Greece, on 9 August 48 BC is regarded as the turning point of Rome's civil war.

p. 322, l. 21: *Arsinoe*: Arsinoe IV (date of birth uncertain), Cleopatra's younger sister. This joint action of the sisters, a little-remarked datum, is derived from Sarah Fielding's historical novel ([The Author of David Simple], *The Lives of Cleopatra and Octavia*, 2nd edn, corrected (London: Andrew Millar et al., 1758), p. 13.

p. 322, l. 28: *confiding in her personal charms*: The picture of Cleopatra selling her favours follows, in abbreviated form, the *Biographium Fæmineum*'s conformity to the traditional picture of Cleopatra utilizing her sexual favours to manipulate men in power.

p. 323, l. 3: *younger brother*: Ptolemy XIII.

p. 323, ll. 12–13: *Apollodorus the Sicilian*: This story is told by Plutarch, *Life of Caesar*, 49, and will have been derived from Fielding, *Lives*, p. 14.

p. 324, l. 6: *terminated in a war*: The so-called 'Alexandrian War', fought in 48 and 47 BC, resulted from Egypt's resistance to Roman interference in its internal affairs.

p. 324, ll. 11–12: *a younger brother of Cleopatra*: Ptolemy XIV.

p. 324, l. 14: *Caesar, plunged in voluptuousness*: The scenario is ultimately based upon an observation of Suetonius (*The Divine Julius*, 52.1) as cited in the *Biographium Fæmineum*, p. 140. Much of Caesar's time in Egypt was taken up with military operations.

p. 324, ll. 17–19: *delivered of a son ... Caesarion*: The reputed son of Caesar. Suetonius is also the source for Caesar's formal recognition of Caesarion.

p. 324, l. 20: *the emperor*: Here and elsewhere, Caesar is anachronistically labelled an emperor, a premature indication of the imperial period to follow.

p. 324, ll. 22–3: *Venus*: A temple of Venus, Goddess of Love, stood at one end of Caesar's new forum. The golden statue of Cleopatra was recorded by the Greek historians Appian (*Civil Wars*, 2.102) and Dio (*Roman History*, 51.22.3).

p. 324, ll. 25–6: *lodged in an apartment*: Cleopatra was housed in Caesar's suburban villa on the right bank of the Tiber (i.e. outside the city proper). There was, as yet, no palace. This image is in accord with the erroneous notion of Hays's sources that Caesar was an emperor.

p. 325, l. 2: *to return*: Cleopatra may have left Rome in 46 BC, but she had returned in 44 BC, as she was present at the time of Caesar's assassination and was still there three months later (Cicero, *Letters to Atticus*, 15.15.2). Hays has here abandoned the *Biographium Fæmineum*, p. 140, following Fielding, *Lives*, p. 18.

p. 325, l. 7: *dispatched by poison*: Her brother Ptolemy XIV died in Egypt.

p. 325, ll. 13–14: *assassination of Caesar in the senate*: on 15 March 44 BC.

p. 325, ll. 16–17: *eldest son of Pompey*: Gnaeus Pompeius had been executed by Caesar in 45 BC.

p. 325, l. 24: *Dollabella in Syria*: Publius Cornelius Dolabella, the governor of Syria in 43 BC and a 'Caesarian'.

p. 325, ll. 24–5: *Serapion, her lieutenant in Cyprus*: Serapion governed Cyprus in Cleopatra's name. No evidence confirms that he acted under orders from Cleopatra, though suspicion is understandable.

p. 325, l. 26: *Cassius*: Gaius Cassius Longinus, one of the leading assassins of Caesar.

p. 325, l. 27: *battle of Philippi*: There were two battles fought at Philippi in eastern Macedonia in October 42 BC between the 'Caesarians' and 'Republicans'.

p. 325, l. 27: *Augustus*: Gaius Julius Caesar (Octavianus), Caesar's adopted son and heir. Hays here calls him Augustus, the name he assumed in 27 BC. From p. 335, ll. 3–4 Hays calls him Octavius (his family name before adoption). These notes will refer to him as Octavian, the name by which he is most recognized in modern works.

p. 326, l. 1: *Mark Antony*: Marcus Antonius served under Caesar in his successful Gallic campaigns and then as deputy ('master of the horse') to Caesar in 48 BC and 47 BC when the latter was dictator. He was consul in 44 BC, and the executor of Caesar's will. In 43 BC, he formed a triumvirate (a board of three with dictatorial powers) with Octavian to combat the 'Republicans'.

p. 326, l. 3: *Delius*: Quintus Dellius wrote a history of the period that served as a source for Plutarch.

p. 326, ll. 19–20: *embarked in regal pomp*: The famous description of Cleopatra's barge upon the river Cydnus derives ultimately from Plutarch (*Antony*, 26).

p. 326, l. 24: *Venus*: the Roman name for Aphrodite, goddess of Love.

p. 326, l. 26: *representing Cupids*: Cupid, son of Venus, embodied lustful desire. The plural used here translates Plutarch's reference to *Erotes* ('Loves') who in antiquity were depicted as accompanying Eros/Cupid.

p. 327, l. 1: *Graces*: According to the Greek poet Hesiod, the three daughters of Zeus and Eurynome, goddesses embodying grace, charm and beauty.

p. 327, l. 8: *Bacchus*: the Roman god of wine.

p. 329, l. 15: *induced Antony*: Arsinoe had been living in exile in Asia Minor.

p. 330, l. 2: *Fulvia*: Antony's Roman wife (see Hays, *Female Biography*, vol. 4, pp. 335–6), who, in concert with his brother Lucius Antonius, supported Antony's interests in Italy during his absence, confronting Octavian. This eventually led to the Perusine War in 41 BC.

p. 330, ll. 2–3: *Augustus*: Octavian: see note to p. 325, l. 27, above.

p. 330, l. 3: *Parthian troops*: The originally nomadic Parthians, in effect, claimed the legacy of the Persian Empire. The Euphrates customarily stood as the frontier between Roman and Parthian interests.

p. 330, l. 5: *Labienus*: Quintus Labienus, a Roman commander who had gone over to the Parthians.

p. 330, l. 8: *Armida*: Saracen sorceress who tempted the knight Rinaldo in Torquato Tasso's sixteenth-century *La Gerusalemme liberata* (Jerusalem Delivered), and known through a number of operatic treatments in the eighteenth century; the allusion was seemingly Hays's own.

p. 330, l. 23: *Inimitable Livers*: This 'Guild, or synod, of Unique Livers' (Plutarch, *Antony*, 28) possibly had some religious significance in connection with the worship of Dionysus.

p. 331, l. 1: *related by historians*: Amongst the ancient sources, the following item is related only by the biographer Plutarch (see note to p. 331, l. 1, below).

p. 331, l. 1: *young Greek*: Philotas, a physician of Amphissa, Greece. He personally retailed these stories to Lamprias, the grandfather of Plutarch (Plutarch, *Antony*, 28).

p. 331, l. 28: *her Hercules*: The Roman name for Heracles, the greatest of the Greek heroes.

p. 331, l. 28: *her Hector*: Prince of Troy, son of King Priam and Hecuba, greatest of the Trojan heroes.

p. 331, l. 28: *her Alexander*: Paris, a Trojan prince, son of King Priam and Hecuba, usually called *Alexandros* in Homer's epic. Famous for his seduction of Helen.

p. 333, l. 28: *to cultivate the sciences*: Cleopatra's cultural achievements are taken from Plutarch's *Antony*, 27.

p. 334, l. 5: *Pergamus*: Pergamum, a city in Mysia, Asia Minor, once the seat of the Attalid dynasty and at this time in the Roman province of Asia. For the veritable destruction of its once-great library, see Plutarch, *Antony*, 58.

p. 334, l. 11: *Troglodytae*: the language spoken by the *Trogodytai*, an Ethiopian tribe living on Egypt's Red Sea coast. Classical accounts depict them as virtually without language.

p. 334, l. 28: *Pacorus*: the son of the Parthian king (Orodes II).

p. 335, l. 1: *Barzapharnes*: This Parthian satrap is known from Josephus' *Antiquities of the Jews* (14.331) and *Jewish War* (1.248–49), with several spelling variations. The Iranian original was *Barzafarna* ('exalted in glory').

p. 335, l. 4: *Hyrcanus, the high-priest*: Hyrcanus II, the *ethnarch* (ruler) of Judaea from 63 BC, though Rome effectively administered the former Hasmonean kingdom.

p. 335, ll. 4–5: *Phazael the brother of Herod*: Phasael and Herod (the infamous Herod 'the Great'), sons of the wealthy Idumaean Antipater, made *procurator* (governor) of Judaea by Caesar, governed Jerusalem and Galilee, respectively. Phasael committed suicide in Parthian captivity to escape execution.

p. 335, l. 7: *filled with consternation*: The counter-move against the Parthians was in Cleopatra's interests.

p. 335, l. 27: *joined by Fulvia*: When Perugia fell in 40 BC Lucius Antonius surrendered to Octavian and Fulvia fled Italy, dying either en route or in Athens.

p. 336, ll. 16–17: *addressed to him an epistle*: Cleopatra's letter to Antony is entirely the invention of Fielding, *Lives*, pp. 76–80.

p. 337, ll. 3–4: *the nuptials of Octavius with Scribonia*: Octavian married Scribonia in 40 BC. He divorced her upon the birth of their daughter Julia the following year.

p. 337, l. 5: *Scyon*: Sicyon. A city in the Greek Peloponnese, close to Corinth. The misspelling of the Greek town follows that of Fielding, *Lives*, p. 83.

p. 337, l. 14: *Pompey*: Sextus Pompey, the younger son of Pompey the Great.

p. 337, l. 17: *Ventidius, his lieutenant*: Publius Ventidius Bassus, who had commanded troops in favour of Lucius Antonius in Italy, was despatched to Syria as proconsul, after the Pact of Brundisium.

p. 337, ll. 25–6: *an event took place*: the famous Pact of Brundisium (40 BC) was so significant that it was celebrated on contemporary coinage.

p. 337, l. 28: *Julia, the mother of Antony*: Julia, sister of Lucius Julius Caesar, consul in 90 BC, had, as the widow of M. Antonius, consul of 99 BC, raised Antony.

p. 338, ll. 2–3: *the hand of his sister Octavia*: Octavian's sister, widow to M. Claudius Marcellus, consul in 50 BC.

p. 338, l. 9: *Codropolis*: The dividing point between East and West is given by the historian Appian (*Civil Wars*, 5.65) as Scodra (in Illyria).

p. 338, ll. 12–13: *Lepidus*: M. Aemilius Lepidus, the third, oft overlooked, member of the triumvirate.

p. 338, ll. 15–16: *Antony accepted the priesthood*: Antony's priesthood followed the Treaty of Misenum in 39 BC (Plutarch, *Antony*, 33).

p. 339, l. 16: *Marsius*: The anecdote about Marsius stems ultimately from Appian's account of the shadowy Manius, a leading agent of Antony in Italy (*Civil Wars*, 5.19; 66).

p. 340, ll. 8–9: *repaired with his wife to Athens*: Antony sailed with Octavia to Athens in 39 BC; she had already borne him a daughter.

p. 340, ll. 15–16: *Antony ... Bacchus*: Inscriptional evidence shows that Antony was indeed hailed as the New Dionysus (whom the Romans called Bacchus).

p. 340, l. 25: *Pallas*: Athena.

p. 341, ll. 3–5: *his father Jupiter ... his mother Semele*: Zeus (Jupiter in Latin) fathered Dionysus (Bacchus in Latin) with Semele, a daughter of Cadmus who founded Thebes in Greece.

p. 341, ll. 17–18: *irritated by some reports concerning Octavius*: This refers to hostilities between Octavian and Sextus Pompey.

p. 341, l. 19: *with a fleet of an hundred sail*: Plutarch reports that Antony sailed west in 37 BC with 300 ships (the figure of 100 is taken from Fielding, *Lives*, p. 101) – whether against or to assist Octavian is debated.

p. 341, l. 20: *Brundusium*: modern Brindisi, the chief port on the Adriatic coast of Italy's heel.

p. 341, l. 21: *Tarentum*: Modern Taranto, the chief port on Italy's instep.

p. 342, l. 2: *in this interview*: This paragraph deals with the Treaty of Tarentum in 37 BC.

p. 342, l. 16: *this letter*: The letter, of which Hays purports to convey the gist and tenor, is again the creation of Fielding, *Lives*, pp. 104–6.

p. 343, ll. 12–13: *Antony advanced to receive his mistress*: This event took place in 36 BC.

p. 344, ll. 4–5: *Lysanius ... king of Chalcis*: Lysanias, king of the Itur(a)eans, may well be identified with Lysimachos, King of Chalcis (in the modern Lebanon).

p. 344, l. 7: *Cyrene, Cyprus*: This catalogue of kingdoms given by Antony is offered by Plutarch (*Antony*, 36), though Plutarch makes no reference to Itur(a)ea. Hays follows the order and the spellings of Fielding, *Lives*, pp. 117–18.

p. 344, l. 7: *Cælo-Syria*: Coele-Syria, perhaps an independent kingdom of Chalcis (ruled over by a Lysimachos or Lysanias), and Ituraea should be thought of as roughly contiguous. Lysimachos and Lysanias may be the same person (see note to p. 344, ll. 4–5, above).

p. 344, ll. 9–10: *kingdoms of Judea and Arabia*: The situations of Jud(a)ea and Arabia were ambiguous; both Herod and Malchus lost a part of their kingdoms, with Herod 'leasing back' the valuable land he had lost around Jericho *c.* 36 BC. Antony's policy was one of conferring power on loyal client-kings.

p. 344, l. 10: *Malchus*: King of the Nabataeans (*c.* 57–30 BC).

p. 345, l. 9: *Arabia Nabath*: In spelling Arabia Nabataea in this fashion, Hays follows Fielding, *Lives*, p. 121.

p. 345, l. 22: *received by Herod*: This interplay of Cleopatra and Herod is told by Josephus in his *Antiquities of the Jews* (15.96–103). Following Fielding, *Lives* (pp. 124–7), Hays is probably unaware of Josephus' assertion that Herod contemplated the murder of Cleopatra.

p. 345, l. 26: *Mariamne*: A princess of the royal Hasmonean family, granddaughter of Hyrcanus II who married Herod in 37 BC. Famously enamoured of her, but suspicious of her disaffection, Herod had her executed in late 29 BC.

p. 346, l. 17: *Lepidas*: Lepidus.

p. 347, l. 3: *Leucone*: Leukè Kóme ('White Village'), between Berytus (modern Beirut) and Sidon (Plutarch, *Antony*, 51). Hays incorrectly retails Fielding's *Leucocome* (*Lives*, p. 130).

p. 348, ll. 27–8: *Nieger, a friend of Antony's*: Correctly spelt Niger.

p. 349, l. 8: *the king of Media*: Artavasdes.

p. 350, ll. 26–7: *Sextus Pompeius ... driven from Sicily*: Sextus lost his army and his fleet to Octavian at the battle of Naulochus in September 36 BC.

p. 351, l. 9: *Titius*: In 35 BC, Sextus Pompeius was killed on the order of M. Titius, Antony's chief officer in Asia, but not certainly at Antony's command.

p. 351, l. 14: *Artabazes*: Artavasdes, king in Armenia from 55 to 30 BC. Not to be confused with Artavasdes of Media. Hays follows the spelling of Fielding, *Lives*, p. 147.

p. 351, ll. 21–2: *the fortune of Octavius in Illyria*: Octavian's campaigns in Illyria took place between 35 and 33 BC.

p. 351, ll. 26–7: *a magnificent portico*: This item is drawn from Fielding, *Lives*, pp. 148–9. The Portico of Octavia was built after Cleopatra's death. The confusion arises from reports in Appian (*Illyrian Wars*, 28) and Dio (*Roman History*, 49.43.8).

p. 354, ll. 10–14: *Antony gave a festival to the Alexandrians ... he declared*: the so-called Donations of Alexandria in 34 BC.

p. 354, l. 14: *Caesario*: Caesarion (see note to p. 324, ll. 17–19, above). Hays follows here the spelling found in Ch. Rollin's *The Ancient History of the Egyptians, Carthaginians, Assyrians, Babylonians, Medes and Persians, Macedonians and Graecians*, translated from the French in ten volumes, 8th edn (London: J. Rivington and Sons et al., 1788), vol. 10.

p. 354, l. 16: *Lybia and Coelo-Syria*: For Latin writers, Libya was the north coast of Africa from Syrtis Major to Egypt, and extending inland to the desert. Coele ('Hollow') Syria was the country behind the Lebanese coastal plain. Both Libya and Coele-Syria are omitted by Fielding. Hays follows Rollin, *Ancient History*, p. 202.

p. 354, l. 19: *to Alexander, the eldest*: Alexander Helios, one of the twins born to Cleopatra in 40 BC. After his parents' deaths, he was raised by Octavia.

p. 354, ll. 19–22: *he gave Armenia, Media, Parthia ... to India*: These lands were not Antony's to assign. The Donations were programmatic rather than actual. Hays here follows Fielding, *Lives*, p. 155, who in the reference to India follows Dio (*Roman History*, 49.41.44) rather than Plutarch (*Antony*, 54).

p. 354, l. 22: *Cleopatra, his twin sister*: Cleopatra Selene.

p. 354, l. 23: *Philadelphus, the younger*: Antony's third child born to Cleopatra. After the death of Cleopatra and Antony, he was spared by Octavian and raised by Octavia.

p. 355, ll. 8–10: *the name of Isis ... that of Osiris, the tutelar deities of the Egyptians*: Egyptian queens had for centuries been associating themselves with Isis, an Egyptian deity connected with creativity and nurturing. Osiris was celebrated for his death and resurrection, and was thus a model for Egyptian kings. As Cleopatra's consort, Antony naturally filled the role of Osiris, which matched the association with Dionysus that he had been pursuing in the Greek East.

p. 355, ll. 15–16: *eldest son of Antony and Fulvia*: Marcus Antonius Antyllus.

p. 355, l. 25: *Caesarian*: Caesarion.

p. 356, l. 3: *splendid feast*: For this famous anecdote Hays footnotes her debt to Rollin, *Ancient History*, pp. 195–6. The story was found in Pliny the Elder's *Natural History*, 9.119–121 and Macrobius's *Saturnalia*, 3.17.14–17 (both of which are cited by Rollin).

p. 356, l. 7: *more than a million of sesterces*: The Latin (derived by Rollin from Pliny) provides one hundred times one hundred thousand sesterces (=10,000,000). Fielding has the dinner cost 'more than the value of Six Million Sesterces' (*Lives*, p. 160). The *Biographium Fœmineum* (p. 142) gives 52,000£.

p. 356, ll. 18–19: *Lucius Blancus*: Misspelling of the name of Lucius Munatius Plancus, one of Antony's closest advisers before he defected to Octavian. Hays follows Fielding, *Lives*, p. 161; the *Biographium Fœmineum* (p. 142) spells the name correctly.

p. 357, l. 13: *Ephesus*: a Greek city on the west coast of Asia Minor.

p. 357, l. 24: *Canidious*: Publius Canidius Crassus.

p. 358, l. 23: *Circe*: a mythological sorceress, a daughter of the sun-god Helios.

p. 360, l. 22: *Octavia from the house of her husband*: The divorce of Octavia may be dated to May/June, 32 BC.

p. 361, l. 19: *this testament*: The notorious will of Antony, the authenticity of which has been the subject of debate in modern scholarship.

p. 361, ll. 19–20: *witnessed by Minucius Plancus*: L. Munatius Plancus is the individual called Blancus: see note to p. 356, ll. 18–19.

p. 361, l. 20: *his nephew*: Marcus Titius.

p. 361, l. 21: *vestal virgins*: Six Roman priestesses charged with tending the goddess Vesta's sacred fire. Octavian's seizure of the will from their custody was a violation of Roman religious and legal custom.

p. 361, ll. 26–7: *a dependent of Octavius*: Gaius Calvisius Sabinus.

p. 362, l. 13: *Turnius, a Roman of distinction*: Gaius Furnius – 'a man of great worth and the ablest orator in Rome' (Plutarch, *Antony*, 58). Hays follows Fielding's misspelling.

p. 363, l. 1: *Germinius*: Probably Gaius Geminius, mentioned on an inscription as a senator in 39 BC.

p. 364, ll. 16–17: *Mardion the eunuch, Photinus, Iras, and Charmion*: These four individuals, Mardion, Potheinos, Iras and Charmion, are mentioned only by Plutarch (*Antony* 60; see Plutarch, *Antony*, 85 for the two women). Hays follows Fielding's misspelling of Potheinos, but offers Plutarch's spelling for Charmion.

p. 364, l. 19–p. 365, l. 2: *two hundred and fifty galleys … twelve thousand horse*: The catalogue of forces on either side basically replicates that of Plutarch (*Antony*, 61), but a divergence shows that Hays follows Rollin, *Ancient History*, pp. 207–8, and has abandoned Fielding, *Lives*, p. 174.

p. 365, l. 6: *Eleven kings*: Plutarch (*Antony*, 61) identifies them as Bocchus of Libya, Tarcondemus of Upper Cilicia, Archelaus of Cappadocia, Philadelphus of Paphlagonia, Mithridates of Commagene, Sadalas of Thrace, Polemon of Pontus, Amyntas of Lycaonia and Galatia, (Artavasdes) of Media, Malchus (see note to p. 344, l. 10, above) and Herod (see note to p. 335, l. 5; p. 344, ll. 9–10 and p. 345, l. 22, above).

p. 365, l. 21: *Cyrea*: Hays follows Fielding's spelling of Cyrene.

p. 365, l. 26: *celebrated battle of Actium*: Actium stands at the entry of the Ambracian gulf in western Greece. The battle was fought on 2 September 31 BC.

p. 366, l. 12: *Agrippa*: Marcus Vipsanius Agrippa (d. 12 BC). A lifelong friend of Octavian/Augustus, whose daughter Julia he married in 21 BC and under whose regime he was awarded substantial powers and recognition.

p. 366, l. 14: *Publicola*: L. Gellius Publicola.

p. 366, l. 20: *Arruntius*: Lucius Arruntius.

p. 366, ll. 23–4: *intent only on escaping*: The picture of Cleopatra's treachery is a traditional one. An alternative modern interpretation suggests that Antony and Cleopatra were committed from the outset to a 'break out', aimed at securing the safety of as many ships and troops as possible and of Cleopatra's treasury.

p. 367, ll. 4–5: *Scellius and Alexander of Syria*: Scellius (Plutarch, *Antony*, 66) is otherwise unknown; Alexas of Laodicea in Syria (Hays follows here the misnomer in Fielding) is later reported by Plutarch (*Antony*, 72) as a trusted friend of Antony who betrayed him but who was put to death by Octavian.

p. 367, l. 22: *Tenarus*: Tainaron, either a promontory in Laconia, southern Greece, at the western entrance to the Laconic gulf, or the nearby town.

p. 369, ll. 4–5: *eighteen legions, and two-and-twenty thousand horse*: Plutarch (*Antony*, 68) says 19 legions and 12,000 horsemen. Hays follows Rollin, *Ancient History*, p. 210.

p. 369, l. 11: *two friends*: Plutarch (*Antony*, 69) names them – the Greek rhetorician Aristocrates and the Roman Lucilius.

p. 369, l. 23: *the commander whom he had appointed in Lybia*: Four legions were left in Cyrene under Lucius Pinarius Scarpus (Dio, *Roman History*, 51.5.6).

p. 370, l. 17: *the Arabians of Petra*: These are the people of Arabia Petraea whose king, Malchus, was no friend of Cleopatra.

p. 370, l. 23: *the isle of Pharos*: Pharos was the island on which stood the famous lighthouse, one of the Seven Wonders of the Ancient World.

p. 370, l. 26: *Athenian Timon*: Timon, according to Plutarch (*Antony*, 69–70), lived in Athens during the fifth century BC and was proverbial – in his lifetime (and subsequently) – for misanthropy.

p. 372, ll. 27–8: *a golden sceptre, crown and chair*: The ultimate source for Cleopatra's secret overtures to Octavian is Dio, *Roman History*, 51.6.5–6. Hays's source is Fielding, *Lives*, p. 189.

p. 373, l. 28–p. 374, l. 1: *Thyreus, a man of address and insinuation*: Plutarch (*Antony*, 73) introduces Thyrsus, 'a man of no mean parts', as a freedman (ex-slave) of Octavian. Hays follows the spelling of Fielding, *Lives*, p. 191.

p. 375, l. 13: *an officer*: The story is told by Plutarch (*Antony*, 74), without reference to Cleopatra's 'ensnaring' of the trooper. Hays's understanding of the episode stems from Fielding's elaborately embroidered presentation (*Lives*, pp. 196–7).

p. 377, l. 11: *Cornelius Dolabella (a favourite of the conqueror)*: Plutarch (*Antony*, 84) calls him a *hetairos* ('companion') of Octavian. Possibly Publius Cornelius Dolabella who later became consul in AD 10.

p. 378, ll. 5–6: *he commanded Eros, a faithful servant*: In Plutarch (*Antony*, 76), Eros, whose name suggests servile status, is as here a slave (*oiketes*). In Dio's account (*Roman History*, 51.10.7), the unnamed man is a bystander.

p. 379, ll. 8–9: *Proculeius*: Gaius Proculeius was to become a prominent member of the equestrian order (i.e. a gentleman outside the senatorial rank).

p. 380, l. 2: *A second officer arrived*: Gaius Cornelius Gallus, another member of the equestrian order, trusted by Octavian.

p. 380, l. 15: *Epaphroditus*: Plutarch (*Antony*, 79) and Dio (*Roman History*, 51.11.4, and 13.4–5) say that the man was one of Octavian's freedmen. Fielding (*Lives*, p. 206) notes him as 'one of [Octavian's] Servants'.

p. 380, l. 22: *the philosopher Ariæus*: The Stoic teacher of Octavian, Areius Didymus, was famous for his influence over him. Hays draws this episode, told by Plutarch (*Antony*, 80) and Dio (*Roman History*, 51.16.4), from Rollin, *Ancient History*, p. 218.

p. 382, ll. 8–9: *one of her treasurers*: In recounting this episode, Plutarch (*Antony*, 83) names the man as Seleucus (otherwise unknown).

p. 383, l. 26: *perished in her fortieth year*: Plutarch (*Antony*, 86) says 'forty years save one'. Rollin, *Ancient History*, p. 222, and the *Biographium Fæmineum*, p. 147, whom Hays is following closely here, say she 'died at thirty-nine years of age' and 'lived thirty-nine', respectively.

p. 384, ll. 5–6: *Archibius, who had been long in her service*: Plutarch (*Antony*, 86) names Archibius (otherwise unknown) as one of Cleopatra's friends.

p. 384, ll. 6–7: *a thousand talents*: Plutarch says that he gave 2,000 talents. Hays follows Rollin, *Ancient History*, p. 222.

p. 384, ll. 9–10: *governed by a praefect*: Octavian preferred to keep Egypt under his personal control. Hence it was governed by prefects to whom he delegated authority. The closing sentence follows Rollin, *Ancient History*, p. 223, almost verbatim.

p. 384, l. 14: *ANN CLIFFORD*: alternative spelling, Anne.

p. 384, l. 17: *George Clifford*: (1558–1605) from Westmorland.

p. 384, l. 19: *Craven*: Craven is in the West Riding of Yorkshire.

p. 384, l. 20: *Elizabeth*: Elizabeth I (r. 1558–1603) (see Hays, *Female Biography*, vol. 4, pp. 70–295); George Clifford was a courtier and her champion from 1590, important at ceremonies such as Accession Day tilts.

p. 385, l. 3: *mother*: Lady Margaret Russell, Countess of Cumberland (1560–1616).

p. 385, ll. 3–4: *earl of Bedford*: William, third Baron Dacre and seventh Baron Greystoke (1500–63).

p. 385, l. 4: *aunt*: Anne Dudley *née* Seymour, Countess of Warwick (1538–87). See Hays, *Female Biography*, vol. 6, pp. 405–8).

p. 385, l. 6: *Samuel Daniel*: (*c.* 1562/3–1619), poet who wrote *Musophilus* (1599), though his more important works were historical, notably *The Civil Wars* (1595) and *The Collection of the History of England* (1612 and 1618).

p. 385, l. 7: *preceptor*: tutor.

p. 385, ll. 10–11: *married lord Buckhurst*: Richard Sackville (1589–1624), third Earl of Dorset, married 25 February 1609. Sackville increasingly pressured her to give up claim to her father's estates.

p. 385, l. 15: *Margaret and Isabel*: Lady Margaret Sackville (1614–76) and Lady Isabelle Sackville (1622–61).

p. 385, ll. 16–17: *earls of Northampton and Thanet*: Margaret married John Lord Tufton, second Earl of Thanet (1609–64) and Isabella married James Compton, third Earl of Northampton (1622–81).

p. 385, l. 18: *Philip Herbert*: Clifford married Philip Herbert (1584–1650) on 3 June 1630.

p. 385, l. 20: *James*: James VI of Scotland and I of England (1566–1625).

p. 386, l. 15: *uncle*: Francis Clifford (1559–1641).

p. 386, l. 20: *jointures*: property settled on a woman at the time of her marriage.

p. 387, l. 2: *civil war*: civil war in England lasted 1642–9.

p. 387, ll. 5–7: *repairing and furnishing … 1657 and 1658*: included her five castles, the Barden Tower and the churches of St Ninian's, Brougham and Holy Trinity, Skipton.

p. 387, l. 16: *Oliver Cromwell*: Oliver Cromwell (1599–1658), Lord Protector of England, Scotland and Ireland from 1653.

p. 387, ll. 9–15: *'This castle … DEO'*: see W. Gilpin, *Observations, Relative Chiefly to Picturesque Beauty, Made in the Year 1772: On Several Parts of England; Particularly the Mountains, and Lakes of Cumberland, and Westmoreland*, 2 vols (London: R. Blamire, 1786), vol. 2, p. 159.

p. 387, l. 24–p. 388, l. 1: *'Let him … my pocket'*: see Gilpin, *Observations*, vol. 2, p. 155.

p. 388, ll. 8–10: *'What … to him?'*: see Gilpin, *Observations*, vol. 2, p. 156.

p. 388, ll. 19–21: *'By no … wear blinkers'* see Gilpin, *Observations*, vol. 2, p. 156.

p. 388, ll. 23–4: *Joseph Williamson*: Sir Joseph Williamson (1633–1701), Cumberland-born government bureaucrat.

p. 388, l. 24: *Charles II*: Charles Stuart (1630–85).

p. 388, l. 28–p. 389, l. 4: *'I have … Montgomery'*: see 1 B.M., 629 i, 4, xiv, 84.

p. 389, ll. 8–9: *forty thousand pounds*: over £3 million spending equivalent today.

p. 389, l. 26: Countess Pillar: built in 1654 in memory of her mother, at Brougham. Hays followed Ballard's *British Ladies* on the topic of her building projects, but she deviated from her source by revealing Clifford's disputes with her two husbands over property; Ballard chose instead to emphasize domesticity and piety.

p. 390, ll. 3–12: *'This pillar ... DEO!'*: see Gilpin, *Observations*, vol. 2, p. 159.

p. 390, l. 17: *portions*: capital brought to a marriage.

p. 390, l. 23: *Spenser*: Edmund Spenser (*c.* 1552–99), poet.

p. 390, ll. 25–6: *King, afterwards bishop of Chichester*: Henry King (1592–1669), poet.

p. 390, l. 26: *Duppa and Morley*: Brian Duppa (1588–1662); George Morley (*c.* 1598–1684).

p. 391, ll. 1–4: *four pounds per annum ... a thousand pounds*: equivalent of a £300 annuity in today's value, which Clifford converted to a lump sum (*c.* £77,000 today).

p. 391, l. 6: *Bearmky*: Beamsley Almshouses, near Skipton.

p. 392, l. 6: *bishop Rainbow*: Edward Rainbow, Bishop of Carlisle (1608–84).

p. 393, l. 4: *Murgatroyd*: this could be Jacob Murgatroyd mentioned in her diary on 25 January 1676.

p. 393, ll. 12–16: *'Come ... between us'*: see Gilpin, *Observations*, vol. 2, pp. 162–3.

p. 393, l. 19: *Dr. Donn*: John Donne (1572–1631), clergyman best known for his metaphysical poetry and sermons.

p. 393, ll. 19–21: *'that she ... slea silk'*: see Gilpin, *Observations*, vol. 2, p. 163.

p. 393, ll. 20–1: *predestination to slea-silk*: the Calvinist doctrine of predestination states that God predestines all humans either to eternal salvation or damnation; 'slea-silk' is sleave-silk, silk thread that can be separated into fine fibre filaments suitable for embroidery work.

p. 393, ll. 24–5: *Veteriponts*: Veteripont family of Skipton.

p. 394, l. 5: *three large volumes*: A. Clifford (ed.), *Collectanea Cliffordiana* (Paris: M. Nouzou, 1817; rep. 1980).

p. 394, l. 15: *earl of Thanet*: at the time of writing this was Sackville Tufton, ninth Earl of Thanet (1769–1825).

p. 395, l. 2: *plain black serge*: either wool or worsted, durable and twilled cloth that is woven diagonally for strength.

p. 395, ll. 4–5: *Two ladies ... resided with her*: Mrs Frances Pate and Mrs Susan Machell: see D. J. H. Clifford (ed.), *The Diaries of Anne Clifford* (Wolfeboro Falls, NH: Alan Sutton Publishing, 1990), p. 242.

p. 395, ll. 20–1: *'Every wise ... her house'*: see E. Rainbow, *A Sermon Preached at the Funeral of the Right Honorable Anne Countess of Pembroke, Dorset, and Montgomery* (London: R. Roysten, 1677), p. 4.

p. 395, l. 24: *the family of Tufton*: the family of the earls of Thanet, Kent.

p. 395, l. 25: *Mr. Pennant*: Thomas Pennant (1726–98), writer of *A Tour of Scotland, 1769* (London: B. White, 1771).

p. 396, ll. 3–4: *two portraits*: *The Great Picture*, attributed to Jan van Belcamp (1646).

p. 396, ll. 10–16: *Eusebius ... second picture*: all of the books in *The Great Picture* are labelled and include the works of Eusebius of Caesarea (AD 263–339) and William Camden (1551–1623).

p. 396, l. 15: *Mrs. Ann Taylor*: alternative name Anne Taylour.

p. 396, l. 21: *narrative ... of her own life*: Clifford's diaries are in four manuscripts – Harleian MS 6177, British Library; WD/HOTH, Cumbria Record Office; Hassell McCosh MS, Dalemain Collection; Sackville Collection, U269 F48/1–3, Kent Record Office.

p. 396, l. 27–p. 397, l. 26: *'I was ... of fortune.'*: Hays varies Clifford's original language in this
   passage: see Clifford's diaries – Harleian MS 6177, British Library; WD/HOTH, Cumbria Record Office; Hassell McCosh MS, Dalemain Collection; Sackville Collection,
   U269 F48/1–3, Kent Record Office.
p. 397, l. 18: *John Denham*: not identified.
p. 397, l. 21: *Pleiades ... Orion*: star constellations.
p. 398, l. 2–p. 399, l. 18: *'In my infancy ... helping me therein'*: see Clifford's diary for 1623,
   which survives in transcript in British Library, Harleian MS 6177.
p. 398, l. 26: *Elizabeth Sackville*: Clifford's daughter's alternative name; Lady Isabelle Sackville
   (1622–61).
p. 399, ll. 5–6: *Knowle in Kent, and Wilton in Wiltshire*: Knole house in Sevenoaks, Kent
   came into the Sackville family in 1603, and Wilton House, three miles west of Salisbury,
   has been in the Herbert family, earls of Pembroke, since 1544.
p. 400, ll. 4–25: *'The first ... well beloved'*: see Clifford's diaries, British Library, Harleian MS
   6177.
p. 400, l. 8: *Thomas Sackville*: Thomas Sackville, first Earl of Buckhurst and first Earl of Dorset
   (*c.* 1536–1608).
p. 400, l. 24: *prince Henry*: Henry Stuart (1594–1612), Prince of Wales, son of James VI and
   I and Anne of Denmark.
p. 400, l. 27–p. 401, l. 14: *'He was ... the realm'*: see Clifford's Kendal Diary for 1650.
p. 401, l. 11: *queen Mary*: Henrietta Maria, of France (1609–69), married Charles I in 1625.
p. 401, l. 18: *CATHERINE CLIVE*: Catherine [Kitty] Clive [née Raftor].
p. 401, l. 19: *William Rafton*: William Raftor, Clive's father.
p. 401, l. 22: *James II*: James II (1633–1701), King of England.
p. 402, l. 2: *Lewis XIV*: Louis XIV (1638–1715), King of France.
p. 402, ll. 5–6: *Several children were the fruit of this union*: Clive's early biographers refer to her
   'numerous' siblings, although records for only two Raftor children are extant.
p. 402, l. 11: *Colley Cibber*: (1671–1757), actor, writer, theatre manager.
p. 402, ll. 15–16: *tragedy of Mithridates*: *Mithridates: King of Pontus* (1678), a tragedy by
   Nathaniel Lee (c. 1653–92). A 1736 edition of *Mithradates* includes an additional song
   in Act IV, scene 1, performed by the page, Immenea.
p. 402, ll. 21–2: *A popular prejudice against the author*: In his autobiography, Cibber blamed
   a cabal for audience rejection of this work. *An Apology for the Life of Colley Cibber ...
   Written by Himself*, ed. B. R. S. Fone (Mineola, NY: Dover, 2000). Other contemporary
   reports blamed the work's weakness and Cibber's execrable singing.
p. 402, ll. 26–7: *whenever she appeared on stage*: Clive's singing reportedly quelled audience
   calls for the performance to cease: see T. Whincop, *Scanderbeg: or, Love and Liberty*
   (London: W. Reeve, 1747).
p. 403, ll. 3–4: *'The Devil to pay ... by Colley Cibber'*: Based on *The Comical Transformation, or
   The Devil of a Wife* (1686) by Thomas Jevon (*c.* 1651–88). *The Devil to Pay* was adapted
   into a ballad opera by Charles Coffey (d. 1745) and John Mottley (1692–1750) and not
   by Cibber, as Hays suggests.
p. 403, l. 5: *her salary to be doubled*: This was first asserted by Thomas Whincop, but financial
   records do not survive to corroborate his report.
p. 403, ll. 9–10: *G. Clive, esq*: Born into one of Shropshire's most established families, George
   Clive (1705–80) was second cousin, not brother, as Hays suggests, to Major-General Robert Clive, first Baron Clive (1725–74), also known as 'Clive of India'. There is no evidence
   to back the claim, standard in all biographical entries on George Clive, that he studied law.

p. 403, ll. 10–11: *These nuptials ... proved fortunate*: No records survive to prove that this union took place. George Clive's obituary of 1780 in the *Gentleman's Magazine and Historical Chronicle* (p. 589) does not mention that he was married. The earliest testimony that the couple had separated is in the biographical entry on Kitty Clive in W. Chetwood's *A General History of the Stage* (London: W. Owen, 1749).

p. 403, l. 20: *Horace Walpole*: Horatio [Horace] Walpole, fourth Earl of Orford (1717–97) author, politician and patron of the arts. When not on the stage, Clive withdrew to a house on Walpole's Strawberry-Hill estate. After 1769 she resided permanently at a villa that Walpole placed at her disposal, 'Little Strawberry Hill'.

p. 404, l. 3: *Marivaux*: Pierre de Marivaux (1688–1763), novelist and dramatist.

p. 404, ll. 8–9: *David Trotter*: Captain John Trotter (d. 1684).

p. 404, ll. 10–11: *August 16th, 1679*: she was in fact born 16 August 1674.

p. 404, ll. 13–14: *the king and his brother*: Charles II (1630–85) and James Duke of York, later James II and VII (1633–1701).

p. 404, ll. 16–17: *James, earl of Perth*: James Drummond, fourth Earl of Perth and Jacobite first Duke of Perth (1648–1716), politician.

p. 404, ll. 17–18: '*an ornament to his country*': See A. Kippis, *Biographia Britannica: or, the lives of the most eminent persons who have flourished in Great Britain and Ireland, from the earliest ages, To The Present Times: collected from the best authorities, Printed And Manuscript, and digested in the manner of Mr. Bayle's Historical and critical dictionary*, 2nd edn, 5 vols (London: W. and A. Strahan, 1778), vol. 3, p. 669, n. 1.

p. 404, l. 22: *Scandaroon*: İskenderon, southern Turkey.

p. 405, l. 10: *queen Ann*: (1665–1714), to whom Catherine Trotter's mother presented a petition (undated) seeking the reinstatement of her husband's pension.

p. 405, ll. 13–14: *Dr. Burnet*: Gilbert Burnet, Bishop of Salisbury (1643–1715).

p. 405, ll. 17–18: *Dr. Inglis*: an Alexander Inglis is listed as Chyrurgeon-General to the Army in 1714–15, with an annual income of £182/10/0; not further identified.

p. 405, l. 20: *the nobleman of that name*: Sir William Ballenden (d. 1670) was raised to the peerage as Lord Ballenden of Broughton by Charles II in 1661.

p. 405, l. 21: *Maitland duke of Lauderdale*: John Maitland, first Duke and second Earl of Lauderdale (1616–82).

p. 406, ll. 24–5: *she addressed some lines to Mr. Bevil Higgons*: (1670–1736), historian and poet. Hays does not mention Cockburn's earliest published work, also in 1693, the novella *Olinda's Adventures ...* , in *Letters of Love and Gallantry ...* , 2 vols (London: S. Briscoe, 1693–4), vol. 1.

p. 407, l. 3: *earl of Dorset and Middlesex*: Charles Sackville (1643–1706), sixth Earl of Dorset and first Earl of Middlesex (1643–1706), poet and politician.

p. 407, l. 8: *Mrs. Behn*: Aphra Behn (*c.* 1640-1689), writer (see Hays, *Female Biography*, vol. 1, pp. 273–90).

p. 407, l. 10: *Mr. Congreve*: William [?] Congreve (1670–1729), playwright and poet.

p. 407, ll. 15–23: '*All the satisfaction ... preferring yours*': Kippis, *Biographia Britannica*, vol. 3, p. 664, n. 4.

p. 408, l. 3: *princess Anne of Denmark*: later Queen Anne.

p. 408, ll. 8–9: *John Hughes*: (*c.* 1678–1720), writer and librettist.

p. 408, l. 10: *George Farquhar*: (1676/7–1707), playwright.

p. 408, l. 15: *Mr Dryden*: John Dryden (1631–1700), poet, playwright and critic.

p. 408, ll. 23–4: *lady Piers, wife to Sir George Piers*: Sarah, Lady Piers, *née* Roydon (d. 1719), poet and literary patron; married *c.* 1694 Sir George Piers (1670-1720), baronet, army officer and Clerk to the Privy Seal from 1696.

p. 409, ll. 12–13: *Charles lord Halifax*: Charles Montagu, first Earl of Halifax (1661–1715), English poet and statesman.

p. 409, ll. 19–20: *love ... heroic sentiment*: Hays's defence of love's potential to be an elevated passion in this sentence is her own.

p. 409, l. 27: *Mr. Locke*: John Locke (1632–1704), philosopher.

p. 410, l. 12: *'a bold unlicensed undertaking'*: Kippis, *Biographia Britannica*, vol. 3, p. 665.

p. 410, l. 15: *George Burnet*: Following her sources, Hays identifies this correspondent wrongly. This should be Thomas Burnet (1656–1729), second Laird of Kemnay, landowner and advocate.

p. 410, ll. 17–20: *'I am more ... conceal myself'*: Kippis, *Biographia Britannica*, vol. 3, p. 665.

p. 410, ll. 24–5: *Mr. King ... a present of books*: Peter King, first Baron King (1669–1734), Lord Chancellor (1725–33); Locke was persuaded by Elizabeth Burnet to add to this present a gift of five guineas.

p. 410, l. 26–p. 411, l. 9: *'Give me ... I am, &c.'*: Kippis, *Biographia Britannica*, vol. 3, p. 665, n. 6.

p. 410, l. 27: *Thomas Burnet*: Thomas Burnet (*c.* 1635–1715), natural philosopher, Master of the Charterhouse, and author of the anonymously published *Remarks upon An Essay concerning Humane Understanding in a Letter address'd to the Author* (London: M. Wotton, 1697), *Second Remarks upon ...* (London: M. Wotton, 1697), *Third Remarks upon ...* (London: M. Wotton, 1699).

p. 411, l. 16: *Mrs. Burnet*: Elizabeth Burnet (1661–1709; see Hays, *Female Biography*, vol. 2, pp. 59–67). Though initially critical of Cockburn's religion and reputation, Burnet was persuaded by Locke to encourage Cockburn's work, and both she and her husband became Cockburn's close friends.

p. 411, ll. 19–20: *Mr. Norris*: John Norris (1657–1711), Rector of Bemerton, Wiltshire, a member of the Cambridge Platonist circle and critic of Locke's empirical philosophy.

p. 411, ll. 20–4: *'It is not...reasoning'*: Kippis, *Biographia Britannica*, vol. 3, p. 666, n. 7.

p. 412, ll. 1–24: *'The bishop...hearing him'*: Kippis, *Biographia Britannica*, vol. 3, p. 666.

p. 412, l. 19: *Abel*: John Abell (1653-*c.* 1716), singer and composer.

p. 412, l. 22: *lord Arundel's*: Thomas Arundell, fourth Baron Arundell of Wardour, (1633–1711/12) was the head of one of the most prominent Catholic families in England, whose family home, Wardour Castle, was in Tisbury, Wiltshire.

p. 412, l. 28: *Denton Nicholas*: Denton Nicholas, MD of Trinity College, Oxford, 1685, Fellow of the Royal College of Physicians, 1696.

p. 413, ll. 10–17: *'That she...church, &c.'*: Kippis, *Biographia Britannica*, vol. 3, p. 666, n. 8.

p. 413, l. 13: *Grotius*: Hugo Grotius (1583–1645), Dutch natural lawyer, author of *De veritate religionis Christianae* (On the Truth of the Christian Religion) (1627; editio novissima, Oxoniae: e Theatro Sheldoniano, 1700) and many other works.

p. 413, l. 19: *a letter to Mr. Burnet*: see note to p. 410, l. 15, above, and *The Works of Mrs Catharine Cockburn: Theological, Moral, Dramatic, and Poetical* (London: J. and P. Knapton, 1751), vol. 2, p. 166.

p. 413, l. 26–p. 414, l. 21: *'I am sorry ... own communion'*: Kippis, *Biographia Britannica*, vol. 3, pp. 666–7.

p. 414, ll. 26: *Sophia Charlotte*: Sophia Charlotte of Hanover (1668–1705), Queen consort of Frederick I of Prussia, was the daughter of Sophia, Electress of Hanover (1630–1714).

p. 415, ll. 3–6: *'charmed with...on her'*: Kippis, *Biographia Britannica*, vol. 3, p. 667.

p. 415, ll. 7–8: *the duke of Marlborough*: John Churchill, first Duke of Marlborough (1650–1722), army officer and politician, husband of Sarah Churchill (see note to p. 405, l. 10, above).

p. 415, ll. 11–12: *Godolphin*: Francis Godolphin, second Earl of Godolphin (1678–1766), politician, officer of the royal household and son-in-law of the Duke and Duchess of Marlborough.

p. 415, l. 17: *Harriet Godolphin*: Henrietta (Harriet) Godolphin, *née* Churchill (1681–1733), daughter of the Duke and Duchess of Marlborough and patron of the arts.

p. 415, ll. 24–5: *'to incite ... public good'*: Kippis, *Biographia Britannica*, vol. 3, p. 667, n. 9.

p. 416, l. 3: *Dr. Birch*: Thomas Birch (1705–66), Anglican minister, compiler of histories and biographer.

p. 416, l. 5: *Gustavus Erickson*: Gustav I of Sweden, born Gustav Eriksson, later known as Gustav Vasa, King of Sweden from 1523 until his death.

p. 416, l. 13: *a return into the bosom of the other*: after Cockburn's reconversion, possibly influenced by her friendship with the Burnets, she largely identified with the Latitudinarian wing of Anglicanism, which advocated religious toleration and a rational morality in everyday Christian life.

p. 416, l. 19: *'a guide in controversies'*: Kippis, *Biographia Britannica*, vol. 3, p. 667.

p. 417, l. 3: *Mr. Fenn*: not further identified.

p. 417, l. 8: *Mr. Cockburn*: Patrick Cockburn (1678–1749), graduated University of Edinburgh 1705, clergyman in the Scottish Episcopal Church and the Church of England.

p. 417, ll. 21–5: *'As piety...moral excellence'*: Kippis, *Biographia Britannica*, vol. 3, p. 668, n. 11.

p. 417, l. 26: *Dr. Cockburn*: John Cockburn (1652–1729), Church of Scotland minister and Church of England clergyman; refused to take the oath of allegiance to William and Mary after 1689, though he finally did so to secure the rectory of Beercrocombe in Somerset in 1709.

p. 418, l. 6: *Dr. Robinson*: John Robinson (1650–1723), diplomat and Bishop of London.

p. 418, l. 22–p. 419, l. 6: *'Our affairs...a fortnight.'*: Kippis, *Biographia Britannica*, vol. 3, p. 668, n. 14.

p. 419, l. 10: *George I*: (1660–1727), King of Great Britain and Ireland and Elector of Hanover from 1714 until his death.

p. 420, l. 2: *George II*: (1683–1760), King of Great Britain and Ireland and Elector of Hanover.

p. 420, l. 16: *Dr. Chandler*: Edward Chandler (*c.* 1668–1750), Bishop of Durham.

p. 420, l. 26–p. 421, l. 4: *'Sundays being...pens and heads.'*: Kippis, *Biographia Britannica*, vol. 3, p. 668, n. 15.

p. 421, l. 2: *Dr. Burnet*: Thomas Burnet (Burnett) (d. 1750), theologian and clergyman of the Church of England and author of three pamphlets responding to *Christianity as Old as the Creation* (London, 1730), by the deist Matthew Tindal (*c.* 1657–1733): *The Argument Set Forth in a Late Book, Entitled Christianity as Old as the Creation, Reviewed and Confuted: In Several Conferences*, 3 parts (London: A. Bettesworth and C. Hitch ... , 1730–2).

p. 421, ll. 9–11: *'In the summer...write less'*: Kippis, *Biographia Britannica*, vol. 3, p. 668, n. 16.

p. 421, l. 12: *Mr. Pope*: Alexander Pope (1688–1744), poet.

p. 421, ll. 12–28: *'You had but...Homer, &c.'*: Kippis, *Biographia Britannica*, vol. 3, p. 668, n. 17.

p. 422, l. 2: *'A letter to Dr Holdsworth'*: Cockburn's pamphlet was directed against *A Sermon Preached Before the University of Oxford at St Mary's on Easter-Monday, 1719. In which the Cavils, False Reasonings, and False Interpretations of Scripture of Mr Lock and Oth-*

ers against the Resurrection of the Same Body are Examin'd and Answered (Oxford: R. Wilkins ... , 1726), by Winch Holdsworth (*c.* 1677–1762), clergyman of the Church of England; he responded in *A Defence of the Doctrine of the Resurrection of the Same Body* (London: C. Rivington, 1727).

p. 422, ll. 18–21: *'the cavils ... same body'*: Kippis, *Biographia Britannica,* vol. 3, p. 669.

p. 423, ll. 17–27: *'Learning denied us ... the sex's cause'*: Kippis, *Biographia Britannica,* vol. 3, p. 669, n, 20.

p. 423, l. 27: *the sex's cause*: Hays here selects lines emphasizing the barriers faced by intellectually ambitious women.

p. 424, ll. 4–5: *'But I, ... shall behold'*: Kippis, *Biographia Britannica,* vol. 3, p. 669, n. 20.

p. 424, l. 8: *the duchess of Hamilton*: Elizabeth Hamilton, née Gerard (*c.* 1680–*c.* 1743/4), widow of James [Hamilton], fourth Duke of Hamilton (1658–1712).

p. 424, l. 16: *'Remarks upon Some Writers'*: In this publication Cockburn considers the following works: W. King, *An Essay on the Origin of Evil ...* , trans. E. Law, 2nd edn (Cambridge: W. Thurlbourn, 1732); [T. Johnson], *An Essay on Moral Obligation ...* (Cambridge: W. Thurlbourn, 1731); 'Phil-Orthos' [G. Johnston], *The Eternal Obligation of Natural Religion ...* (London: T. Cox, 1732); W. Warburton, *Divine Legation of Moses Demonstrated ...* , 2 vols (London: F. Gyles, 1738–41); I. Watts, *Philosophical Essays on Various Subjects ...* (London: R. Ford and R. Hett, 1733).

p. 425, ll. 1–3: *'inscribed, ... moral character'*: Kippis, *Biographia Britannica,* vol. 3, p. 670, n, 21.

p. 425, ll. 8–9: *Samuel Clarke*: (1675–1729), leading Anglican theologian and philosopher whose commitment to an optimistic and rational religion in harmony with natural law was shared by Cockburn and defended in her 'Remarks'.

p. 425, ll. 15–16: *a daughter*: This letter on the death of her daughter Catherine, or Kitty, is quoted in *Biographica Britannica,* p. 670.

p. 425, l. 17–p. 426, l. 16: *'The loss of my ... to preserve them'*: Kippis, *Biographia Britannica,* vol. 3, p. 670, n. 23.

p. 426, l. 22: *Dr. Rutherforth*: Thomas Rutherforth (1712–71), moral philosopher and Church of England clergyman.

p. 426, l. 28: *Mr. Warburton*: William Warburton (1698–1779), Bishop of Gloucester and religious controversialist.

p. 427, ll. 4–9: *'I have had ... ever was written'*: Kippis, *Biographia Britannica,* vol. 3, p. 670, n. 27.

p. 427, ll. 12–18: *'I have very ... great weakness'*: Kippis, *Biographia Britannica,* vol. 3, p. 670, n. 24.

p. 427, ll. 19–22: *'There are about ... abstruse speculations'*: Kippis, *Biographia Britannica,* vol. 3, p. 669, n. 25.

p. 427, l. 23: *a clergyman (dated March, 1748)*: the letter, to an unknown clergyman addressed as 'Rev. Sir', against whom she defends the opinions of Samuel Clarke, is dated March 1747; see *The Works of Mrs Catharine Cockburn,* vol. 2, pp. 347–9.

p. 427, l. 26–p. 428, l. 8: *'Whenever your ... old to learn'*: Kippis, *Biographia Britannica,* vol. 3, p. 670, n. 26.

p. 428, ll. 14–15: *The opinion of Dr. Rutherforth*: Hays's comparison of Rutherforth to 'modern philosophical writers' is her own, possibly arising from her interest in the utilitarian ideas of, for instance, the French writer d'Helvétius.

p. 429, ll. 2–6: *'that it contains ... and religion'*: Kippis, *Biographia Britannica,* vol. 3, p. 671.

p. 431, l. 3: *Mrs. Manley*: Delarivier Manley (*c.* 1670–1724), writer and Tory; worked with Cockburn in the production of *Nine Muses* in honour of John Dryden, but accused her in 1709-10 of prudery and hypocrisy, as well as hinted at lesbian and heterosexual affairs.

p. 431, l. 20: *Dr. Sharp*: Thomas Sharp (1693–1758), Church of England clergyman and theological writer.

p. 432, ll. 3–4: *devoted to letters*: The daughter of Fabrizio Colonna (1460–1520) and Agnese da Montefeltro (1470–1522), Colonne received the highest education and gave early proof of a love of letters.

p. 432, ll. 4–5: *lost a husband ... martial exploits*: The marriage between Colonna and the Marquis of Pescara, Ferdinando Francesco, was planned from their childhood. In 1511 the wars between France and Spain began; the Marquis was away fighting until his death in 1525.

p. 432, l. 7: *most tender poetry*: Colonne's first poetry collection, *Rime de la Divina Vittoria Colonna Marchesa di Pescara*, was published in 1538. It contained 136 of the lyrics written under an imitation of Petrarch praising her husband and mourning his death, which were later published as *Rime Amorose*. Later editions advertised the inclusion of sixteen *Sonetti spirituali* and included an ever-increasing number of *rime spirituali*, reflecting the shift of Colonna's focus. Other publications included *Pianto sulla passione di Cristo* and the *Orazione sull'Ave*.

p. 432, ll. 10–11: *Alexius Comnenus*: The Byzantine emperor Alexios I Komnenos came to power in 1081 (r. 1081–1118) after having deposed the legal emperor Nicephoros III.

p. 432, ll. 13–14: *a passion for study and letters*: Anna Comnena received an exceptional education by private tutors who taught her philosophy, astronomy, history, geography and rhetoric. In the male-dominated Byzantine society, women's education was usually limited to reading and writing, and ended when they turned twelve.

p. 432, ll. 20–1: 'The Alexiad': *The Alexiad* is a medieval biographical text of the emperor Alexios Komnenos, written by Comnena, important for its historical content. It is believed to be the continuation of the 'History' written by Anna Comnena's late husband Nicephorus Bryennios: see A. Comnena, *The Alexiad*, trans. A. Sideri (Athens: Agra, 1991).

p. 433, l. 2: *accused of partiality*: *The Alexiad* reveals the love and respect that Comnena had for her father, as well as the appreciation and pride that she felt for him and her heritage as a Porphyrogenita (daughter of an emperor born in the purple).

p. 433, ll. 9–24: '*The elegance ... her sex*': see *Biographium Fæmineum*. vol. 1, p. 151.

p. 433, l. 11: *strong and eloquent manner*: The text of *The Alexiad* was written in Greek of the classical era which Comnena learnt and used fluently.

p. 434, l. 1: *ISABELLA DE CORDAUD*: Hays's entry is based on Antoine Léonard's *An Account of the Character, the Manners, and the Understanding, of Women* whose entry reads almost identically to hers: see A. Léonard, *An Account of the Character, the Manners, and the Understanding, of Women, In Different Ages, and Different Parts of the World, Translated from the French of Mons. Thomas, by Mr. Kindersley*, trans. M. Thomas (London: J. Dodsley, 1800), pp. 85–6. The person referred to is in all probability Isabella Losa (1491–1564) de Cardona, who at times is confused with Isabel de Josa (1508–75): compare 'Isabella Roser' in *Gale Eighteenth Century Collections Online*. Isabella Losa was born in Cardona, a town 100 km north of Barcelona, Spain. After the death of her husband in 1539, she became a Clarissan abbess and moved to Vercelli in Piedmont in 1553, where she founded an orphanage (Santa Maria di Loreto) and died, at the age of seventy-four, in 1564: see G. De Gregori, *Istoria Della Vercellese Letteratura Ed Arti* ('Torino:

Chirio e Mina, 1820), vol. 2, p. 155 and C. Ferrari, *Valore e sventura episodio storico della gloriosa difesa di Vercelli contro le armi di Spagna nel 1617* (Vercelli, 1851), p. 318.

p. 434, l. 2: *beautiful, rich*: Hays is possibly confusing her with Isabel de Josa i de Cardona, compare entry for Isabella Roser. Isabella Losa was not known for her riches or beauty.

p. 434, ll. 3–4: *Latin, Greek ... degrees in theology*: Isabella Losa's language skills and doctorate are mentioned by F. Vespoli, *Delle donne* (Napoli: Dalla Tipographia di Partenope, 1825), p. 73. No information of where she obtained her doctorate can be traced.

p. 434, l. 6: *Charlotte Cordey*: Marie-Anne Charlotte de Corday d'Armont (Charlotte Corday) (1768–93). The spelling of Corday as Cordey is from Hays's main source, Anon., *Biographical Anecdotes of the Founders of the French Republic, and of Other Eminent Characters, Who Have Distinguished Themselves During the Progress of the Revolution* (London: R. Phillips, 1797).

p. 434, l. 10: *a man attached ... to the court*: her father, Jacques François de Corday, seigneur d'Armont.

p. 434, ll. 10–11: *Jacques Adrian de Cordey*: Corday's grandfather.

p. 434, ll. 11–12: *Mary Renée Adelaide de Belleau*: Corday's grandmother.

p. 434, ll. 14–15: *James Francis de Cordey*: see note to p. 434, l. 10, above.

p. 434, l. 16: *Mary Carola Gautier des Antiers*: Corday's mother, Charlotte-Marie Gautier des Authieux.

p. 434, l. 24: *Marat*: Jean-Paul Marat (1744–93), physician and intellectual, prominent radical Jacobin journalist, staunch defender of the Revolution in France.

p. 435, ll. 9–10: *she stabbed to the heart*: The assassination on 13 July 1793 made Marat a Republican martyr, and Corday a heroine for the anti-Jacobin cause. Hays's account of the moment of the assassination 'on a sopha' is at odds with contemporary representations of the event, which gave authoritative accounts of Marat being in his bath when he was stabbed in the neck: see Jacques-Louis David's painting *La Mort de Marat* (1793). Hays's main source is silent on the matter. See Anon., *Biographical Anecdotes*.

p. 436, l. 15–p. 437, l. 7: '*From ... Cordey*': Anon., *Biographical Anecdotes*, p. 194.

p. 436, l. 16: *Brissot*: Jean-Pierre, known as Brissot de Warville (1754–93); French Revolutionary leader of the 'Brissotin' party, later the Girondins.

p. 436, l. 25: *Robespierre*: Maximilien Robespierre (1758–94), radical Revolutionary leader and prominent Jacobin. He was crucial in orchestrating the Terror in France (September 1793–July 1794).

p. 437, l. 2: *Barbaroux*: Charles Jean Marie Barbaroux (1767–94) participated in the draft of the Girondin constitution to the French National Convention in 1793.

p. 437, l. 4: *Voltaire*: François-Marie Arouet (1694–1778), writer, historian and philosopher renowned for his wit.

p. 437, ll. 4–5: '*that ... scaffold*': '*Le crime fait la honte et non pas l'échafaud*' is by Thomas Corneille (1625–1709), dramatist, and not by Voltaire as Hays suggests. See T. Corneille, *Le Comte d'Essex* (*The Earl of Essex*) (IV. 3, 1678).

p. 437, l. 15: *CORINNA*: Many of the details of Corinna's life come from the *Suda*, the reference work of the tenth century AD, which has three different entries under the Greek form, *Korinna*. It is likely that all three were actually the same person, although the place of origin is given variously as Thebes, Tanagra, Thespiai and Corinth, all located in Boiotia. The dating of Corinna's life is uncertain; the tradition makes her a contemporary of Pindar (*c.* 518–*c.* 438 BC), but some have seen textual reasons for assigning her to a later period. If she was indeed Pindar's contemporary, the presence of later forms in her work can be ascribed to transmission errors, but it is harder to explain why there are no surviving references to her before the first century BC.

p. 437, ll. 16–17: *Archelodorus and Procratia*: the *Suda* gives the forms Acheloiodoros and Prokratia, the first of which Hays has simplified. They are otherwise unattested.

p. 437, l. 17: *Mirthis*: the *Suda* names this female poet as the teacher of both Corinna and Pindar (*s.v. Pindaros*). She is otherwise unknown.

p. 437, ll. 18–19: *borne away … from Pindar*: The second-century AD author Pausanias describes a mural in Tanagra celebrating one of her victories over Pindar, and says that she has her tomb there (9.22.3). Plutarch (*Moralia*, 347f) relates an anecdote in which she attempts to school Pindar in the correct use of mythology in poetry.

p. 437, l. 22: *Propertius*: Roman elegiac poet of the second half of the first century BC. He describes his mistress, who has a high opinion of her own poetry, and compares her verses to those of Corinna (*Elegies*, 2.3.21).

p. 437, l. 24–p. 438, l. 2: *Corinna, the Thespian … Roman Corinna*: see note to p. 437, l. 15, above.

p. 438, l. 1: *Statius*: Roman poet of the second half of the first century AD who includes Corinna in a list of distinguished ancient poets, all of whom are ultimately subordinated to Homer and the foster son for whom the poem is a lament.

p. 438, l. 3: *Augustus*: adopted son of Julius Caesar, first Roman emperor, who ruled from 27 BC until his death in AD 14.

p. 438, l. 3: *Ovid*: Roman poet (43 BC–AD 17) who used the name Corinna to refer to his mistress. In this he follows the precedent set by Catullus, who called his mistress Lesbia in honour of the poet Sappho from the island of Lesbos. It is unclear whether Ovid's Corinna corresponds to an actual person, or whether she is purely a creation of the poet.

p. 438, l. 7: *Helena Lucretia Cornaro*: also known as Elena Lucrezia Cornaro-Piscopia. Most sources of the time cite the Italian spelling of her name, including the surname Piscopia.

p. 438, ll. 7–8: *Gio Baptisto Cornaro*: Giovanni Battista Cornaro-Piscopia (Cornèr); his name can also be found in an assortment of spellings and combinations of last names. Procurator of St Mark's (second highest office only to the Doge), his dates of birth and death are unknown. Cornaro was his fifth daughter.

p. 438, l. 8: *born at Venice*: her mother's name was Zanetta Giovanna Boni. Nothing other than her humble origins is known.

p. 438, ll. 8–9: *a learned and scientific education*: Cornaro's extraordinary intellect was noticed in her childhood; she began her academic studies at the age of seven. She became proficient in several languages (Latin, Greek, Hebrew, Arabic, Chaldaic, French, Spanish and English), earning her the title *Oraculum Septilingue*, meaning Master (Oracle) of seven languages besides her native one (E. Probst, *Superfrauen. V: Wissenschaft* (Norderstedt: GRIN, 2001), p. 153).

p. 438, l. 10: *a doctor's degree*: awarded on 25 June 1678, Cornaro's doctoral examination attracted much attention. Because of the multitude of spectators, the examination had to be moved from the University Hall to the Cathedral in Padua. During the examination, Cornaro spoke for more than an hour in Latin, explaining difficult passages of Aristotle's work, and left her examiners so stunned that they dispensed with regular procedures and granted her the degree of *doctor* by acclamation. See D. M. Robin, A. R. Larsen, and C. Levin (eds), *Encyclopedia of Women in the Renaissance: Italy, France, and England* (Santa Barbara: ABC-CLIO, 2007), p. 292.

p. 438, l. 14: *Pope*: Pope Alexander VII (1599–1667), Fabio Chigi, was pope from 7 April 1655 until his death.

p. 438, ll. 15–16: *unalterable ... humble*: Hays mistakenly states that Cornaro was given the title of 'unalterable' in Padua and 'humble' in Rome because of her personal qualities, mistranslating names of literary circles of which she was a member (see J. Stevenson, *Women Latin Poets. Language, Gender, and Authority from Antiquity to the Eighteenth Century* (London: Oxford University Press, 2005), p. 306). See p. 439, ll. 15–17.

p. 438, ll. 24–5: *Cardinal Bouillon*: Emmanuel Théodose de La Tour d'Auvergne (1643–1715). French prelate and diplomat, died in self-imposed exile in Rome.

p. 438, l. 25: *Cardinal d'Etrees*: César d'Estrées (1628–1714), French cardinal and diplomat.

p. 439, l. 1: *the king of France*: Louis XIV (1638–1715), with whom Cardinal Bouillon was often in conflict.

p. 439, ll. 5–6: *Greek and Roman languages*: *Dictionnaire Historique* (vol. 1, p. 343) mentions her language skills and that her works are collected in eight volumes, and notes that they are worse than their reputation. Benedetto Croce had the same scarce opinion of Cornaro's literary merit (see B. Croce, *Appunti di letteratura secentesca inedita o rara*, 'La critica', 3:27 (1929), pp. 671–2).

p. 439, l. 7: *constitution failing*: she most likely suffered from tuberculosis: see J. H. Guernsey, *The Lady Cornaro: Pride and Prodigy of Venice* (Clinton Corners: Attic Studio, 1999), p. 70; Stevenson, *Women Latin Poets*, p. 306.

p. 439, ll. 8–9: *she expired ... 1685*: 1684 is the correct year.

p. 439, ll. 9–14: *A twelvemonth ... coffin*: no confirmation of this legend of the cypress tree to be used for her coffin can be found.

p. 439, l. 15: *academicians of Rome*: L'Accademia degli Infecondi (Academy of the Sterile), a literary society active in Rome between 1613 and 1734.

p. 439, ll. 16–17: *eulogies and odes*: The text of the Funerary oration was published in Brescia shortly after its delivery by the editor Rizzardi (in 1685) and a description of the funerary oration and its celebrations was published in Padua in 1686, dedicated to the Republic of Venice: see A. Chalmers, *The General Biographical Dictionary Containing an Historical and Critical Account of the Lives and Writings of the Most Eminent Persons in Every Nation Particularly the British and Irish from the Earliest Accounts to the Present Time the General* (London: J. Nichols, 1816), vol. 25, p. 148.

p. 439, l. 18: *funeral solemnities*: although Hays alludes to a burial in Rome, Cornaro was buried in Padua.

p. 439, l. 27: *Pompey*: Gnaeus Pompeius Magnus (106 BC–48 BC), political and military leader.

p. 440, l. 7: *daughter of ... gentleman*: Betisia, or Bitisia, or Bettina Gozzadini (Bologna, 1236–62), daughter of Amadore. See C. Ghirardacci, *Della Historia di Bologna*, part one, (Bologna: G. Rossi, 1596). His primary sources are unknown.

p. 440, l. 11: *a funeral oration*: Ghirardacci's narrative is full of details, likely imaginary, on Betisia's intellectual achievements. The biography of Betisia Gozzadini was written three centuries after her death. Even her existence is dubious; Ghirardacci was not reputed to be a reliable source for the ancient events of Bologna.

p. 440, ll. 14–15: *the* Institutions of Justinian: A part of the *Corpus Iuris Civilis* used as a textbook by law students since the sixth century.

p. 440, l. 16: *the chair of the professor*: Alessandro Macchiavelli, in his book *Bitisia Gozzadina seu De mulierum doctoratu* (Bologna: Blanchus, 1722), under the pseudonym of his brother Carlo, published a document attesting Betisia's professorship. This was later found to be false. See G. Fantuzzi, *Notizie degli scrittori Bolognesi* (Bologna: S. Tommaso d'Aquino, 1786), vol. 5, p. 102. Gozzadini's professorship remains unproven.

p. 440, ll. 20–2: *The same example ... in the 15th*: Milancia dell'Ospedale, her daughters Bettina and Novella d'Andrea, Giovanna Bianchetti, Dorothea Bocchi and Maddalena Bonsignori, studied and taught law or medicine at the University of Bologna in those centuries: see Ghirardacci, *Della Historia di Bologna*, part two (Bologna: G. Rossi, 1657), N. P. Alidosi, *I dottori Bolognesi ... dall'anno 1000 al 1623* (Bologna: Nicolò Tebaldini, 1623). Their names were recalled in Macchiavelli's book to justify the request of a law degree for an aristocratic girl, Maria Vittoria Delfini Dosi. M. Sarti, *De claris Archigymnasii Bononiensis professoribus*, 2 vols (Bologna, 1769–72), is skeptical about the historical soundness of the tradition of these female doctors and teachers. See also Hays, *Female Biography*, 'Anonymous', vol. 3, p. 438.

p. 440, l. 22: *in more modern times*: Laura Maria Caterina Bassi (1711–78) obtained a chair of philosophy in 1732: see G. Fantuzzi, *Notizie degli scrittori Bolognesi*, vol. 1, pp. 384–91.

p. 441, l. 2: *Scipio Africanus*: an error taken from the *Biographium Fæmineum* (p. 154). Cornelia was married to Tiberius Sempronius Gracchus, a Roman Consul in 177 and 163 BC. She was the daughter of P. Cornelius Scipio Africanus, who defeated Hannibal in 202 BC and Aemilia, the daughter of L. Aemilius Paullus who conquered Macedonia in 168 BC.

p. 441, l. 3: *the Gracchi*: Tiberius (*c.* 163/162–133 BC) and Gaius Gracchus (*c.* 154/153–121 BC) were two of Cornelia's children who, as reformers, died violently at the hands of Roman senators. In antiquity it was a matter of contention whether Cornelia acted as a goad in support of sons, or whether she counselled restraint.

p. 441, l. 3: *public lectures*: Of this (from the *Biographium Fæmineum*, p. 154) there is no evidence.

p. 441, ll. 9–10: *first place among philosophers*: Quintilian (*Institutes of Oratory*, 1.1.6) praised her eloquence, as did Cicero (*Brutus*, 210–11), though the latter says nothing of her philosophy. This observation derives from the *Biographium Fæmineum* (p. 154).

p. 441, l. 13: *well known*: Cornelia is best known for her relationship with two of her sons, Tiberius and Gaius Gracchus (see note to p. 441, l. 3). The anecdote of the jewels to which Hays refers was the subject of a number of paintings (including one by Angelica Kauffman in 1785).

p. 441, l. 13: *statue*: The statue is recorded by Plutarch (*Caius Gracchus*, 4).

p. 441, l. 15: *most learned*: The first sentence of the epitaph (taken from the *Biographium Fæmineum*, p. 154) follows Plutarch's account which does not include the word 'learned'.

p. 441, l. 18: *children*: The epitaph's second sentence is imaginative (and takes up the theme of Cornelia as teacher). A statue base was discovered in 1878; the epitaph reads 'Cornelia, daughter of Africanus, (mother) of the Gracchi'.

p. 441, l. 21: *sir James Bourchier*: (*c.* 1574–1635), merchant and furrier.

p. 441, l. 22: *ancient earls of Essex*: Her family was not related to the ancient earls of Essex; rather they originated in Worcestershire.

p. 441, l. 23: *wife of Oliver Cromwell*: Elizabeth married Oliver Cromwell (1599–1658), the future Lord Protector, on 22 August 1620.

p. 442, ll. 3–4: *wife of the lord protector*: Her promotion to Lady Protectress was a role not found in the constitutions of the 1650s.

p. 442, ll. 5–6: *career of ambition*: Elizabeth was the subject of increasingly vicious Royalist satire which labeled her immodest, proud, stingy and sexually loose, but also as a spendthrift with a 'love of liquor'.

p. 442, l. 6: *her children*: She had nine children, five sons and four daughters, most of them surviving into adulthood.

p. 442, l. 7: *governed her family*: The family lived in Huntingdon until 1631, then St Ives (1631–36), then Ely (1636–46) and lastly in London.

p. 442, l. 9: *retired*: After April 1660 she moved to Northamptonshire.

p. 442, l. 10: *obscurity*: In a petition of 1660 to Charles II she distinctly claimed to have no hand in 'public transactions'.

p. 442, l. 10: *died October 8th, 1672*: She died in November 1665 – she was buried in Northborough Church in Northhamptonshire on 19 November 1665 following a long and painful illness: see British Library, Sloane MS 952, ff. 33, 96, medical prescriptions by Dr Goddard in the 1650s.

p. 442, l. 11: *Letters published by Mr. Duncombe*: John Duncombe, *A Select Collection of Original Letters; Written by the Most Eminent Persons, on Various Entertaining Subjects, and on Many Important Occasions: From the Reign of Henry the Eighth, to the Present Time ...* (1755). There is little about Elizabeth Cromwell in it for Hays to reference; she is more likely to have consulted Mark Noble, *Memoirs of the House of Cromwell* (London: G. G. J. and J. Robinson, 1787), vol. 1, pp. 123–8.

p. 442, ll. 13–14: *November, 1651*: 1651 is the date given by Cruz's first biographer, Father Diego Calleja. Octavio Paz, however, asserts that her birth year is 1648 based on a San Miguel Nepantla, Mexico baptismal record of 2 December 1648 for 'a girl child': 'Inés, daughter of the Church': see D. Calleja, *Fama y obras pósthumas, tomo tercero, del Fenix de Mexico y dezima musa, poetisa de la América Sor Juana Inés de la Cruz religiosa professa en el Convento de San Geronimo, de la Imperial Ciudad de México* (Barcelona: Rafael Figueró, 1701) and O. Paz, *Sor Juana, or, The Traps of Faith*, trans. Margaret Sayers Peden (Cambridge: Harvard University Press, 1988), p. 65.

p. 442, ll. 14–15: *Her father*: Pedro Manual de Asbaje y Vargas, a Basque; not further identified.

p. 442, ll. 16–17: *in America ... a lady of the country*: Sor Juana's mother, Doña Isabel Ramírez de Santillana, was a Creole from Chimalhuacán, Mexico: see Paz, *Sor Juana*, p. 65.

p. 442, ll. 21–2: *an uncle*: Juan de Mata and her maternal aunt Doña María Ramírez in Mexico City.

p. 442, l. 25: *the lady of the viceroy, the marquis de Mancera*: Vicereine Leonora María del Carretto, wife of Antonio Sebastián Álvarez de Toledo Molina y Salazar, second Marquis of Mancera (*c*. 1608–1715), Viceroy of New Spain [Spanish territories in North America and Philippines] (1664–73).

p. 443, l. 1: *a Spanish encomiast*: not further identified.

p. 443, l. 5: *protogée*: one who receives support from an influential patron.

p. 443, l. 22: *She lived forty-four years*: Cruz died at the convent of St Jerome on 17 April 1695 at age forty–seven: see Paz, *Sor Juana*, p. 464.

p. 443, ll. 23–4: *St. Geronimo*: Cruz joined the Hieronymite order at the Convent of San Jerónimo (Santa Paula) in 1669: see Paz, *Sor Juana*, p. 99.

p. 444, l. 15: *three 4to. volumes*: *Poëmas de la unica poetisa americana, musa dezima, Soror Juana Ines de la Cruz, religiosa professa en el monasterio de san Geronimode la imperial Ciudad de Mexico* (Barcelona: Joseph Llopis, 1691), vol. 1; *Segundo volume de las obras de Soror Juana Ines de la Cuz, monja profesa en el monasterio del Señor San Geronimo de la Ciudad de Mexico* (Sevilla: Tomas Lopez de Haro, 1692); and published posthumously *Fama y obras pósthumas, tomo tercero, del Fenix de Mexico y dezima musa, poetisa de la América Sor Juana Ines de la Cruz religiosa professa en el Convento de San Geronimo, de la Imperial Ciudad de México* (Madrid: Manuel de Murga, 1700).

p. 444, l. 19: *father Feyjoo*: Benito Jerónimo Feijoo y Montenegro (1676–1764). See B. J. Feijoo, *Teatro crítico universal ó Discursos varios en todo género de materias, para desengaño de errors comunes* (Madrid: Imprenta Real de la Gaceta, 1773), vol. 1, p. 431.

p. 445, l. 3–p. 446, l. 8: '*Weak men ... happy hour*': See *Sketches of the History, Genius ... By a Friend to the Sex* (Philadelphia, S. Sansom, *c.* 1796), pp. 186–7.

p. 446, l. 11: *AGESILAUS*: Spartan king, 400–360 BC.

p. 446, l. 13: *enter the lists*: In ancient times *hippotrophy* – the breeding of racehorses – was undertaken by those of extensive, even royal, means. Herodotus tells us in *Histories* (6.71) that Cynisca was of royal lineage. Her brother persuaded her 'to rear chariot horses, and thus by her victory showed that to keep a stud of that sort, however much it might be a mark of wealth, was hardly a proof of manly virtue' (Xenophon, *Scripta Minora*, 9.6). Cynisca's wealth and status, along with the Spartans's nurturance of strong women, combined to make her a successful breeder: her victories are dated between 396 and 392 BC, but there is no secure evidence for these dates.

p. 446, ll. 15–16: *first woman who obtained this honour*: Pausanias's *Description of Greece*, III.8, notes that after Cynisca, other women, especially those from Lacedaemon, also won equestrian Olympic victories.

p. 446, l. 19: *Simonides*: Greek lyric poet, 556–468 BC. Sarti

p. 446, ll. 19–20: *epigram in her praise*: The epigram is extant on the base for her dedication in the Museum at Olympia: see *Inschriften von Olympia* 160 (*IG* V 1.1564a). It reads: 'Kings of Sparta were my fathers and brothers, and I, Cynisca, winning the race with my chariot of swift-footed horses, erected this statue. I assert that I am the only woman in all Greece who won this crown' (*Greek Anthology*, 13.16). This account is one of few examples of a woman's voice heard from the ancient world. Simonides, however, died *c.* 468/7 BC (Parian Marble), so he cannot have been the author.

p. 446, l. 20: *Appelles*: Greek sculptor and painter, fourth century BC.

p. 446, l. 20: *Her statue*: In his commentary on Pausanius's *Description of Greece*, IV:6:3 (London: MacMillan, 1913), editor James Frazer notes his discovery of part of this statue.

p. 446, l. 22: *Elis*: Greek city-state in north-west Peloponnesus.

p. 446, l. 23: *erected to her a monument*: Pausanias tells us that the Spartans also honoured her with a hero shrine: Pausanias, *Description of Greece*, III.15.1.

CONTRIBUTORS TO VOLUMES 5–7

VOLUME	SUBJECT	SCHOLAR	RESEARCHER(S) in alphabetical order
5	General Introduction	Gina Luria Walker	
5	Abbassa	Helena Bergmann	
5	Cornelia Adricomia	Carolyn Vellenga Berman	Joseph Kampff
5	Mary de Agreda	Carme Font Paz	Kristen Stevens
5	Agrippina	J. Lea Beness, Tom Hillard	
5	Agrippina the Younger	Peter Keegan	
5	Jane d'Albert	Elena Woodacre	
5	Aldrude, Countess of Bertinoro	Valerie Eads	
5	Amalasenta	Mark Aloisio	
5	Frances d'Amboise, Duchess of Brittany	Helena Bergmann	
5	Laura Battiferri Ammannati	Elizabeth A. Pallitto	
5	Isabella Andreina	Antonella Valoroso	
5	Anne of Austria	Abby E. Zanger	Koren Whipp
5	Anne of Beaujeu	Elena Woodacre	
5	Anne of Bretagne	Elena Woodacre	
5	Antonia	Peter Keegan	
5	Joan d'Arc	Gail Orgelfinger	
5	Aretaphila	Ian Plant	
5	Arete	Ian Plant	
5	Polla Argentaria	Peter Keegan	
5	Lady Mary Armyne	Jackie Eales	
5	Marie Angelique Arnauld	Daniella Kostroun	Lindsay Smith
5	Catherine Agnes Arnauld	Daniella Kostroun	Lindsay Smith
5	Angelique Arnauld	Daniella Kostroun	Lindsay Smith
5	Arria	J. Lea Beness, Tom Hillard	
5	Artemisia [Queen of Caria]	Ian Plant	
5	Artemisia [Wife of Mausolus]	Ian Plant	
5	Mary, Countess of Arundel	Jamie Goodrich	
5	Blanche, Lady Arundel	Kristen Stevens	Lindsay Smith
5	Margaret Ascham	Frances A. Chiu	Koren Whipp

VOLUME	SUBJECT	SCHOLAR	RESEARCHER(S) in alphabetical order
5	Anne Askew	Elaine V. Beilin	Koren Whipp
5	Aspasia	Madeleine M. Henry	
5	Mary Astell	Jane Rendall	
5	Athenais	Ian Plant	
5	Madeleine de l'Aubespine	Edith J. Benkov	
5	Maria Catherina le Jumel de Berneuille, Countess d'Aulnoi	Daphne M. Hoogenboezem	
5	Lady Bacon	Claire McEachern	
5	Mary Anne Barbier	Alicia C. Montoya	
5	Agnes Sorrel	Rachel C. Gibbons	Lindsay Smith
5	Aloysia Sigea of Toledo	Nieves Baranda	
5	Margaret of Anjou	Melissa Ridley Elmes	Koren Whipp
5	Arnaude de Rocas	Ian Plant	
5	Isabella of Aragon	Elizabeth A. Pallitto	
5	Joan of Aragon	Alison Hicks	
5	Tullia of Aragon	Elizabeth A. Pallitto	
5	Artemisia Gentileschi	Laura Auricchio	
5	Aspasia or Milto	Ian Plant	
5	Isabella of Bavaria	Josette A. Wisman	
5	Frances Bertaut, Madame de Motteville	Séverine Genieys-Kirk	
5	Elizabeth Frederica, of Bohemia	Elisabeth Lenckos	
5	Henrietta of Bourbon, Mademoiselle de Montpensier	Rebecca Nesvet	
5	Mary Bruneau des Loges	Helena Bergmann	
5	Leonora Baroni	Janet Pollack	Marie Caruso
5	Basine, or Bazine	Zina Petersen	Koren Whipp
5	Anne Baynard	Helena Bergmann	
5	Mary Beale	Kristen Stevens	
5	Joan Beaufort, Queen of Scotland	Lorna G. Barrow	Lindsay Smith
5	Margaret Beaufort	Philippa Gregory	Melissa Ridley Elmes, Koren Whipp, Alix Korn
5	Claude de Bectoz	Catherine M. Müller	
5	Aphara Behn	Mary Spongberg	Stefanie Bendik
5	Bridget Bendish	Frances A. Chiu	
5	Berenice	Peter Keegan	
5	Catherine Bernard	Alicia C. Montoya	
5	Juliana Berners, or Barnes	Lorna G. Barrow	
5	Blanche of Castile	Elena Woodacre	
6	Elizabeth Bland	Mary Spongberg	
6	Boadicea	Arianne Chernock	

VOLUME	SUBJECT	SCHOLAR	RESEARCHER(S) in alphabetical order
6	Anne Boleyn	Philippa Gregory	Melissa Ridley Elmes, Ashleigh Lay, Koren Whipp, Lindsay Smith
6	Madame Bontems	Peggy Schaller	
6	Catherine Bovey	Jessica Munns, Penny Richards	
6	Clemence de Bourges	Christine Clark-Evans	
6	Antoinette Bourignon	Mirjam P. A. de Baar	
6	Countess de Bregy	Séverine Genieys-Kirk	
6	Marchioness de Chatelet	Judith P. Zinsser	
6	Anne Broadstreet	Carolyn Vellenga Berman	Joseph Kampff
6	Lady Mildred Burleigh	Caroline Bowden	Koren Whipp
6	Elizabeth Burnet	Isobel Grundy	
6	Elizabeth Bury	Phyllis Thompson	Koren Whipp
6	Calphurnia	J. Lea Beness, Tom Hillard	
6	Calpurnia	Diane Johnston	
6	Bianca Capello	Piera Carroli	Lindsay Smith, Koren Whipp
6	Carolina, Wife to George II	Helena Bergmann	
6	Catherine of Aragon	Timothy G. Elston	
6	Catherine of Medicis	Caroline zum Kolk	Lindsay Smith
6	Catherine I, Empress of Russia	Arianne Chernock	Alix Korn, Kristen Stevens
6	Catherine II, Empress of Russia [Part I]	Hilde Hoogenboom	Andrew Beyea, Alix Korn
7	Catherine II, Empress of Russia [Part II]	Hilde Hoogenboom	Andrew Beyea, Alix Korn
7	Lady Elizabeth Carew	Rebecca Nesvet	Lindsay Smith, Koren Whipp
7	Susannah Centlivre	Rebecca Nesvet	
7	Susannah Maria Cibber	Nancy Copeland	
7	Mary Chandler	Jane Rendall	
7	Mrs Chapone	Jane Rendall	
7	Charixena	Ian Plant	
7	Chelonis	Ian Plant	
7	Christina, Queen of Sweden	Susanna Åkerman	
7	Lady Mary Chudleigh	Margaret J. M. Ezell	
7	Margaret Clement	Koren Whipp	
7	Cleobule	Ian Plant	

VOLUME	SUBJECT	SCHOLAR	RESEARCHER(S) in alphabetical order
7	Cleopatra	J. Lea Beness, Tom Hillard	
7	Ann Clifford, Countess of Pembroke, Dorset and Montgomery	Amanda L. Capern	Stefanie Bendik
7	Catherine Clive	Berta Joncus	
7	Catherine Cockburn	Jane Rendall	
7	Victoire Colonne, Marquise de Pescaire	Nadia Verdile	
7	Anna Comnena	Alexandra Karagianni	
7	Isabella de Cordaud	Elgin Kirsten Eckert	
7	Charlotte Cordey	Gillian Dow	Koren Whipp
7	Corinna	Deborah Lyons	
7	Helena Lucretia Cornaro	Elgin Kirsten Eckert	
7	Anonymous	Marta Cavazza	Elena Testi, Koren Whipp
7	Cornelia	J. Lea Beness, Tom Hillard	Deborah Russell
7	Elizabeth Cromwell	Alan Marshall	
7	Juana Inez de la Cruz	Koren Whipp	Joseph Kampff
7	Cynisca	Diane Johnston	